PRISONERS
ONCE
REMOVED

Also of interest from the Urban Institute Press:

Clearing the Way: Deconcentrating the Poor in Urban America,
by Edward G. Goetz

*Choosing a Better Life: Evaluating the Moving to Opportunity Social
Experiment,* edited by John Goering and Judith D. Feins

Welfare Reform: The Next Act,
edited by Alan Weil and Kenneth Finegold

Low-Wage Workers in the New Economy,
edited by Richard Kazis and Marc S. Miller

*Who Speaks for America's Children? The Role of Child Advocates in
Public Policy,* edited by Carol J. De Vita and Rachel Mosher-Williams

PRISONERS ONCE REMOVED

The Impact of Incarceration and Reentry
on Children, Families, and Communities

edited by **Jeremy Travis**
and Michelle Waul

THE URBAN INSTITUTE PRESS
WASHINGTON, D.C.

THE URBAN INSTITUTE PRESS
2100 M Street, N.W.
Washington, D.C. 20037

Library of Congress Cataloging in Publication Data

Prisoners once removed: the impact of incarceration and reentry on children, families, and communities / edited by Jeremy Travis and Michelle Waul.
     p. cm.
Includes biographical references and index.
    ISBN 0-87766-715-2 (pbk. : alk. paper)
    1. Prisoners' families—Effect of imprisonment on—United States. 2. Children of prisoners—Effects of imprisonment on—United States. 3. Prisoners—United States—Family relationships. 4. Prisoners—Rehabilitation—United States. I. Title: Impact of incarceration and reentry on children, families, and communities. II. Travis, Jeremy. III. Waul, Michelle.
    HV8886.U6P75 2003
    362.82′95′0973—dc22

                          2003017077

ISBN: 0-87766-715-2

Printed in the United States of America
10 09 08 07   3 4 5

The initial versions of the papers in this volume were developed for presentation at a conference sponsored by the Office of the Assistant Secretary for Planning and Evaluation and the Substance Abuse and Mental Health Services Administration of the Department of Health and Human Services. The conference, From Prison to Home: The Effect of Incarceration of Children, Families and Communities, was held on January 30-31, 2002, at the National Institutes of Health Natcher Conference Center in Bethesda, Maryland. Any opinions, findings, conclusions, or recommendations expressed in these papers are those of the authors and do not necessarily reflect the view of the agencies that provided support for their development.

THE URBAN INSTITUTE is a nonprofit policy research and educational organization established in Washington, D.C., in 1968. Its staff investigates the social, economic, and governance problems confronting the nation and evaluates the public and private means to alleviate them. The Institute disseminates its research findings through publications, its web site, the media, seminars, and forums.

Through work that ranges from broad conceptual studies to administrative and technical assistance, Institute researchers contribute to the stock of knowledge available to guide decisionmaking in the public interest.

Conclusions or opinions expressed in Institute publications are those of the authors and do not necessarily reflect the views of officers or trustees of the Institute, advisory groups, or any organizations that provide financial support to the Institute.

*To Susan and Ben, for their love,
support, and understanding*

Contents

Preface

As the nation debates the wisdom of a fourfold increase in the rate of incarceration over the past generation, one impact is clear—prisons separate people from their families. Every individual sent to prison leaves behind a network of family relationships. Prisoners are the children, parents, siblings, and kin of untold numbers of individuals who are affected in different ways when family members are arrested, removed, incarcerated, and ultimately returned home from prison.

Little is known about imprisonment's impact on these family networks. Simple descriptive data about the children of incarcerated parents begin to tell the story, however. During the 1990s, as the nation's prison population increased by 50 percent, the number of children who had a parent in prison increased by the same proportion—from 1 million to 1.5 million children. These children represent 2 percent of all minor children in America, and a sobering 7 percent of all African-American children. With little if any public debate, we have extended prison's reach to include hundreds of thousands of young people who were not the prime target of the criminal justice policies that put their parents behind bars.

In the simplest terms, imprisonment places an indescribable burden on the relationships between these parents and their children. Incarcerated fathers and mothers must learn to cope with the loss of normal contact with their children, infrequent visits in inhospitable surroundings, and lost opportunities to contribute to their children's development. Their children must come to terms with the reality of an absent parent, the stigma of parental imprisonment, and an altered support system that may include grandparents, foster care, or a new adult in the home. And in those communities where incarceration rates are high, the experience of parental incarceration is now quite commonplace, with untold consequences for foster care systems, social services delivery, community norms, childhood development, and parenting patterns.

To date, there has been precious little research documenting the ripple effects of incarceration. This book, however, reflects a commitment by the U.S. Department of Health and Human Services (HHS) to develop a deeper understanding of incarceration's consequences. In the fall of 2000, the office of the Assistant HHS Secretary for Planning and Evaluation asked the Urban Institute to organize a conference to document the state of knowledge on the consequences of imprisonment and reentry for individual prisoners, their families, and the communities to which these prisoners return. In preparation for this conference, we commissioned papers from some of the nation's leading researchers in a number of diverse fields.

The conference, held in January 2002 at the Natcher Center of the National Institutes of Health, was more than a traditional meeting of researchers. In collaboration with our colleagues in HHS and other agencies of the federal government, we extended invitations to a wide range of individuals. Attendees included academics from different disciplines, policymakers from several states wrestling with the impact of parental incarceration on corrections and service delivery systems, practitioners running innovative programs that aim to ameliorate the harmful effects of imprisonment on families and children, filmmakers who have documented the personal stories of prisoners and their children, community leaders struggling with the effect of criminal justice policies at the block and neighborhood level, and former prisoners who have experienced firsthand the processes of removal, isolation, and return.

The chapters in this volume are expanded versions of papers presented at that conference (the chapter by Braman and Wood was commissioned after the conference) and are organized to reflect three concentric circles of inquiry into incarceration's impact on familial networks. Preceded by an introductory chapter outlining current data on prisoners and their children and families, Part One examines the impact of prison itself. How does the prison experience change a prisoner's ability to function as a family member? Craig Haney first examines the psychological impact of imprisonment, asking how the prison experience affects the individual's functioning after release from prison. Stephanie Covington views the prison experience from the distinctive perspective of female prisoners. Gerald Gaes and Newton Kendig then provide an overview of recent research on one of the oldest questions in criminological literature: Can prison programs improve prisoners' ability to hold jobs, stay sober, and avoid criminal behavior once they leave prison?

Part Two examines the impact of imprisonment on the relationships between parents and children, recognizing the important developmental differences between young children and adolescents. How does parental removal affect the development of the children left behind? How do prisoners relate to their children during the period of imprisonment? And how does the high level of incarceration in poor communities, aptly labeled by Marc Mauer and Meda Chesney-Lind as the phenomenon of "mass imprisonment," affect community norms regarding parenting roles, marriage rates, intimate partner relationships, and coming of age? Donald Braman and Jenifer Wood document the deep consequences of mass incarceration on familial relationships in one community (Washington, D.C.) while Ross Parke and Alison Clarke-Stewart explore the effects of parental incarceration on child development and the many factors that may help or hinder children's ability to cope with the loss of a parent. Mark Eddy and John Reid then focus on the potential negative consequences of parental incarceration on adolescent children in particular. Finally, Creasie Finney Hairston examines the challenges an entire family faces when a loved one is incarcerated.

Part Three goes on to explore the impact of parental incarceration on the formal and informal service networks that are designed to support families and children, particularly those networks that serve the poor communities most affected by the increase in imprisonment. How does the safety net of public welfare respond to the removal of hundreds of thousands of parents each year? To what extent are social services organized—or could such services be organized—to mitigate some of the harms resulting from these disrupted relationships? And how does the high rate of incarceration affect the ability of informal networks—the reciprocal relationships that sustain neighborhood life and foster individual growth—to sustain healthy communities? Eric Cadora uses spatial analyses to display the overlaps and connections between neighborhoods experiencing high rates of prisoner removal and the distribution of public assistance. Dina Rose and Todd Clear consider the potential harm high levels of incarceration may have on a community's capacity to meet the needs of residents, especially children. Finally, Shelli Rossman examines the potential for—and the obstacles to—the coordination of services that meet the needs of prisoners and their families.

The broad representation of different perspectives at the Natcher Center conference represented a commitment by the Department of Health and Human Services and the Urban Institute to supporting a vibrant and vigorous dialogue on the ripple effects of the removal of prisoners from their family networks. This book reflects the same commitment. It is our hope that these chapters will spur new research, promote new policies, and support a new public debate on the costs and consequences of imprisonment in America.

Acknowledgments

This book was made possible by the generous contributions of many colleagues and institutions. We offer special thanks to the U.S. Department of Health and Human Services (HHS) for the funding that supported the 2002 conference at the Natcher Center, the commissioned papers that provide the foundation for this book, and the Urban Institute background research documenting the impact of incarceration and reentry on children, families, and communities. In particular, we wish to acknowledge the contributions of Linda Mellgren and Evvie Becker, our partners in the HHS Office of the Assistant Secretary for Planning and Evaluation, who conceived this initiative, guided its intellectual development, and served as its advocates within the federal government. Both are remarkable public servants.

The Urban Institute provided a rare environment where a project such as this could move smoothly from incubation through book production, all under one roof. Within the Institute, we were extremely fortunate to work with a talented team of colleagues who provided both constructive criticism and substantive knowledge at critical points in the project's lifespan. First, we thank Amy Solomon, a full partner in this enterprise, who contributed her sharp insights into the world of policymaking and her strong belief that researchers and practitioners can learn from each other. In addition, Adele Harrell helped us design the project, Christy Visher provided significant research expertise, and

Dionne Davis provided superb logistical support for the conference. Furthermore, the team at the Urban Institute Press brought the project from the idea stage to a finished book in record time, with commendable professionalism. In particular, we thank Suellen Wenz for her outstanding editorial contributions.

Finally, we thank the authors who contributed the chapters and the many friends and colleagues who attended the Natcher Center conference. They have brought to this important national conversation their wisdom, experience, and passion. If this book contributes to that discussion, it will be because those individuals, and many more with similar energy and commitment, have shared the lessons learned in its pages.

1

Prisoners Once Removed

The Children and Families of Prisoners

Jeremy Travis and Michelle Waul

Imprisonment casts a long shadow in the United States. Incarceration rates have grown substantially over the past three decades, resulting in a fourfold increase since the early 1970s. Currently, 1.4 million individuals are behind bars in America's state and federal prisons, and more than 600,000 individuals—about 1,600 a day—will be released to return to their communities this year (Beck, Karberg, and Harrison 2002). These prisoners are parents to 1.5 million children—an increase of more than a half-million children in the last decade (Mumola 2000). Furthermore, if we include adults who have recently been released from prisons and jails and those adults on parole, the number of affected children more than doubles—to an estimated 3.2 million in 2001 (Mumola 2002). Now more than ever before, we need to ask whether the intersection of systems— corrections, and health and human services—can better serve the growing population of children, families, and communities affected by the incarceration of a family member.

For policymakers, researchers, professionals, and community leaders who are concerned about child development, foster care placement, family strengthening, and individual postprison adjustment, incarceration's influences on a growing number of children and families are rapidly becoming salient issues. To begin with, families impacted by incarceration are already typically at high risk along several dimensions. A parent's incarceration does not necessarily signal the onset of family and child development needs, but rather in most cases adds to the burdens of a family already struggling to overcome life's obstacles and setbacks. The incarceration of a family member may further exacerbate an environment already characterized by ongoing poverty, stress, or trauma. While the problems and needs of these children and families clearly intersect both the criminal justice and health and human services systems (see chapter 9), these systems do not always recognize that the incarceration and reentry of a parent produce consequences for a larger family unit.

Moreover, an increasing number of prisoners are returning home with less preparation for the challenges they will face on the outside, with less assistance in their reintegration and, at best, with strained connections to their families and communities (Travis, Solomon, and Waul 2001). Many will have difficulty with the most basic requirements of life outside of prison, such as finding a steady job, locating stable and affordable housing, and reestablishing positive relationships with families and friends. Many will remain plagued by substance abuse and health problems. Most will be rearrested and many will be returned to prison for new crimes or parole violations. And this cycle of removal and return of large numbers of individuals—mostly men (although the number of incarcerated women is growing exponentially)—is increasingly concentrated in a small number of communities already facing enormous social and economic disadvantages (see chapter 10).

Prisoners, their children, and their families experience risks and disadvantages experienced by few others in our society. The incarceration of a parent for months or years on end—typically in a prison located many miles away—and the sometimes-abrupt return of that parent to free society, may have deep and unexamined consequences for all involved. Too often, prisoners returning home experience high recidivism rates, frequent relapses to alcohol and drug abuse, and significant family tensions—sometimes erupting in violence. At the same time, the opportunities for a smoother reentry process are substantial and bear the promise of profound and far-reaching benefits for all involved. In short, the stakes are high. To date, however, policymakers and public officials have paid little attention to how the annual removal and return of hundreds of thousands of adults—many of whom are parents—affect the families and communities left behind, and how the needs of these populations can best be met collaboratively by the health and human services and criminal justice systems. This chapter will review what we know about prisoners as parents and how their incarceration and reentry affect their children and families.

Prisoners as Parents

Of the 1.4 million people currently in prison, nearly all of them will return home to their families and communities after completing their sentences (Travis 2000). This population of Americans is at high risk on a number of fronts due to high rates of communicable disease, substance abuse, mental illness, homelessness, and unemployment. And a growing number of these prison inmates are parents. In fact, the total number of parents in prison has increased sharply in the last decade—up 60 percent from 452,500 held in state and federal facilities in 1991 to 721,500 in 1997. Indeed, over half of state and federal inmates report having at least one minor child (Mumola 2000).

The population of returning prisoners is generally at high risk along several critical dimensions. Most have not completed high school, have limited employment skills, and are struggling with substance abuse and various health problems. Many returning offenders also struggle with finding affordable housing, a basic but often overlooked prerequisite for establishing stability upon release. Further, returning prisoners today have generally served longer prison sentences, which means they may be less attached to the job market, their families, and the communities to which they return. The prison experience and its psychological consequences can often also impact an individual's postprison adjustment (see chapter 2).

Taken together, the employment, physical and mental health, substance abuse, education, and housing issues facing returning inmates present formidable challenges for their successful reintegration and tax the strained resources of their families, children, and communities. Although inmate parents struggle with a host of issues that in many ways mirror those of the general inmate population, their needs deserve particular attention due the potential consequences for their children. Therefore, an examination of the impact of incarceration and reentry on children and families necessarily starts with the challenges facing prisoners because those challenges all translate into risks and needs for the family members, caregivers, and children left behind. The following section[1] will highlight the characteristics of returning prisoners, particularly prisoners who are parents, and briefly examine how they are prepared for release back to their families and communities.

Characteristics of Prisoners with Children

Over half (55 percent) of all state prisoners reported having at least one minor child back in the community.[2] Because the overwhelming majority of state prisoners are men, incarcerated parents are predominately fathers (93 percent) (table 1.1). However, the number of incarcerated mothers has grown dramatically in the past decade. Between 1991 and 2000, the number of incarcerated mothers increased by 87 percent, compared with 60 percent for fathers. Incarcerated women are also more likely than male inmates to report having a child (65 percent vs. 55 percent). Nearly half of all parents in state prisons are African American, 29 percent are white, and 19 percent are Hispanic. The median age of inmate parents is 32 years. The majority of parents in state prison (70 percent) do not have a high school diploma, although 31 percent have completed their GED. Less than one-quarter of incarcerated parents reported that they are currently married. (To put this in perspective, inmates without children were less than half as likely to report being married [9 percent]). The majority of inmate parents—three-quarters—reported they never had been or were no longer married (figure 1.1).

Overall, the majority of parents in state prison were either serving time for violent offenses (44 percent) or drug offenses (24 percent). However,

Table 1.1. *Selected Characteristics of Parents in State Prison, 1997*

	Percentage		*Percentage*
Gender		Age (years)	
Male	92.6	24 or younger	15.8
Female	7.4	25–34	44.9
Race/Hispanic origin		35–44	32.1
White non-Hispanic	28.9	45–54	6.6
Black non-Hispanic	49.4	55 or older	0.6
Hispanic	18.9		
Other	2.8	Median	32 years

Source: Mumola (2000).

mothers and fathers were serving time for different types of offenses. For example, inmate fathers were more likely than mothers to be incarcerated for a violent offense (46 percent vs. 26 percent). Inmate mothers, on the other hand, were more likely than fathers to be serving time for a drug crime, such as possession or trafficking (35 percent vs. 23 percent) (figures 1.2 and 1.3).

Parents in state prisons were serving sentences with an average maximum sentence length of 12 years.[3] For mothers, however, the average maximum sentence length was nearly 5 years less than that for fathers. Nearly half of mothers were serving sentences with maximum terms of less than 5 years, compared with 15 percent of fathers. Overall, fathers reported that they expected to serve nearly 7 years, while mothers expected to serve 4 years until their release. Sentence length affects how incarcerated parents and their families maintain connections and produces legal and emotional consequences for the reunification process.

Many incarcerated parents come to prison with a record of prior criminal activity. More than three-quarters of parents in state prison reported a prior conviction and, of those, over half had been previously incarcerated. During the time leading up to their most current arrest and incarceration, nearly half of incarcerated parents were on some type of conditional release, such as probation or parole. Fathers were more likely than mothers to be arrested while on parole from a previous prison term (25 percent vs. 19 percent).

Figure 1.1. *Marital Status of Parents in State Prison, 1997*

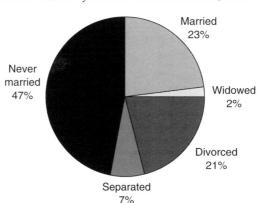

Source: Mumola (2000).

Figure 1.2. *Current Offense of Incarcerated Mothers in State Prison, 1997*

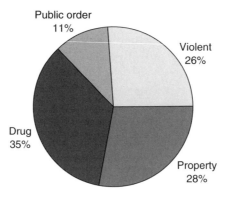

Source: Mumola (2000).

A significant number of incarcerated parents struggle with substance abuse. Most parents in state facilities reported some level of previous drug use (85 percent) and more than half (58 percent) reported using drugs in the month before their current arrest. Further, one-quarter of parents in state prison are believed to be alcohol dependent and more than one-third were under the influence of alcohol at the time of their current offense.

Figure 1.3. *Current Offense of Incarcerated Fathers in State Prison, 1997*

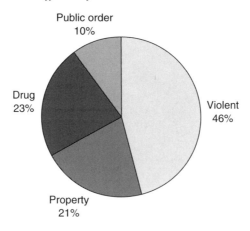

Source: Mumola (2000).

Incarcerated mothers reported more extensive and serious histories of drug use than fathers. Mothers in state prison were more likely than fathers to report drug use in the month before their arrest (65 percent vs. 58 percent). In comparison with fathers, drug use among incarcerated mothers was more likely to involve use of cocaine-based drugs or opiates. Mothers were more likely than fathers to report using cocaine/crack in the month before their arrest (45 percent vs. 25 percent of fathers), while fathers were more likely to report using marijuana (40 percent vs. 28 percent of mothers). Mothers were also more likely to report that drugs were involved in the offense that led to their incarceration. Nearly one-third of mothers reported committing their crime to get drugs or money for drugs, compared with 19 percent of fathers.

Although female prisoners make up only a small portion of the corrections population, they experience a range of risks and challenges that in some ways are more serious and widespread than those facing their male counterparts (see chapter 3). Females accounted for 6 percent of the prison population and 12 percent of the parole population in 1998 (Greenfeld and Snell 1999). However, 65 percent of female inmates have children. Furthermore, women generally have fewer economic resources than men before entering prison. Thirty percent of incarcerated women were receiving welfare assistance before their arrest (Richie 2001), and this proportion may be even higher among the subset of incarcerated mothers. Women in prison also frequently have significant mental health needs. Among parents in state prison, mothers were more likely than fathers to report indications of mental illness (23 percent vs. 13 percent). Within the entire female prisoner population in 1998, nearly one-quarter received medication for emotional disorders and over half (60 percent) reported a history of physical or sexual abuse (Greenfeld and Snell 1999; Richie 2001).

Taken together, the characteristics of parents in prison highlight the profound challenges their families confronted before the parents' incarceration and hint at the challenges these families will continue to face when released parents return home.

In-Prison Preparation for Return to Families and Communities

Given that nearly all prisoners will eventually return to their families and communities, prison can be viewed as an opportunity to improve inmates' skills, treat their addictions, and generally prepare them for life on the outside. As discussed earlier, many prisoners have histories of substance abuse and addiction, mental and physical health problems, and inadequate job skills and education. Importantly, these issues have consequences for the health and well-being of the families and communities to which inmates will return. There is some evidence that in-prison programs are cost-effective and beneficial in preparing inmates for life outside of prison. This is particularly true when in-prison programs are followed by services and treatment in the community. However, recent surveys indicate that relatively few inmates receive treatment or training while in prison, and even fewer receive coordinated services that continue through to their return to the community.

While the quality and the quantity of the available evidence vary widely, it appears that certain interventions—including cognitive skills training, drug treatment, vocational training, educational, and other prison-based programs—can be effective in reducing recidivism (Gaes et al. 1999; Lawrence et al. 2002). These interventions are most effective when programs are matched to prisoner risks and needs, well managed, and supported through postrelease supervision. While current studies cite only modest reductions in recidivism rates for participants, these small reductions can have significant aggregate impacts on criminal behavior in communities with high concentrations of returning prisoners. Lower rates of return to criminal behavior also have clear benefits for families of former inmates.

However, the participation rate in prison programs is low and has dropped over the last decade. In fact, only about one-third of "soon-to-be-released" inmates reported that they participated in vocational programs (27 percent) or educational programs (35 percent) in 1997, down from 31 percent and 43 percent, respectively, in 1991 (Lynch and Sabol 2001). Moreover, very few inmates participate in actual prerelease preparation activities—that is, activities that would presumably prepare inmates for life outside of prison. The number participating in these programs has remained stable over the past decade, hovering at about 13 percent of the state prison population. These decreases in the participation rates are even steeper than they appear because smaller shares of bigger populations are involved—meaning significantly more prisoners are being released without vocational, educational, and prerelease preparation now than in the past.

Furthermore, although the majority of prison inmates enter prison with histories of substance abuse, only 10 percent of state inmates in

1997 reported receiving professional substance abuse treatment while in prison, down from about 25 percent in 1991. An additional 20 percent (up from 16 percent in 1991) participated in other drug abuse programs, such as peer counseling groups and awareness programs. More inmates reported receiving treatment for alcohol abuse compared with drug abuse (Mumola 1999). One-quarter of state inmates reported participating in some type of alcohol treatment or program since admission; participation among those with a history of alcohol abuse was even higher (about one-third). In the absence of treatment, prisoners run a high risk of relapse following release (Harrison 2001). For example, one study found that an estimated two-thirds of untreated heroin abusers resume their heroin/cocaine use and involvement in criminal behavior within three of months of release (Wexler, Lipton, and Johnson 1998).

The rate of communicable disease is much higher among incarcerated populations than among the general population (Hammett, Roberts, and Kennedy 2001). People passing through our nation's prisons and jails account for a significant share of the total population who are infected with HIV or AIDS, hepatitis C, and tuberculosis. In 1997, nearly one-quarter of all people living with HIV or AIDS, nearly one-third of people with hepatitis C, and more than one-third of those with tuberculosis were released from a prison or jail that year. The extent of mental health disorders is also relatively high. Rates of serious mental illness, such as schizophrenia/psychosis, major depression, bipolar disorder, and posttraumatic stress disorder, are at least twice (some estimates range as high as four times) as high among incarcerated individuals as rates among the general population (NCCHC 2002).

With such a high proportion of prisoners experiencing mental and physical illness and engaging in substance abuse, the presence of dual and triple diagnoses is not surprising. These multiple diagnoses pose additional challenges in terms of treatment, both in prison and after release. Though exact numbers are not available, it appears that dual diagnoses of mental health and substance abuse issues are not uncommon among the prisoner population (Hammett et al. 2001).

While most prisoners receive needed health care services while in prison, access to mental health services is more limited. Interestingly, for some prisoners, a period of incarceration may prove beneficial to their physical health—in part because they can receive better health care in prison than what they may have received in the community. A survey of state inmates found that 80 percent reported receiving a medical exam once they were admitted to prison, and of those who reported a medical problem after admission, 91 percent reported visiting a health care professional about it (Maruschak and Beck 2001). In terms of access to mental health services while in prison, more than half (60 percent) of mentally ill state inmates reportedly received some form of mental health treatment during their period of incarceration (Beck and Maruschak 2001). Of these, half said they had taken prescription medication and 44 percent had received counseling services. A key component to successful physical and mental health outcomes for both inmates and the families they return to is linking prison-based services with community-based services (see chapter 10).

Ignoring the health, education, and prerelease preparation needs of reentering prisoners can be very costly. The profile of the prison population reveals significant deficiencies in human capital that can limit prisoners' capacity to function and contribute to the care and well-being of their families and communities. Many of these deficits are also associated with high rates of recidivism. The emerging research knowledge about effective prison programs suggests that targeted investments in the interventions discussed here could produce public safety benefits and increase social functioning overall (see chapter 4)—benefits that are clearly important not only for returning prisoners, but also for their families and communities. The research consensus on this point, however, comes at a time when a smaller share of prisoners than ever before are receiving treatment and training.

Importance of Family Connections

Family is an important component of the reentry process. Families can be natural supports for prisoners during prison terms and upon release (Shapiro and Schwartz 2001). Families provide an important anchor to life in the community while inmates are in prison and offer a source of stability, support, and encouragement during the difficult transition from prison to home. These connections can in fact mean the difference between success and recidivism. Several studies have shown that continued contact with family members during and following incarceration can reduce prisoner recidivism and foster reintegration into the community, a fact that has broad benefits for all involved (see chapter 8; Hairston 1988a; Visher and Travis 2003).

During incarceration, prisoners can maintain connections with a family member in a number of ways: letters, phone calls, in-prison visits, and participation in family furlough and other programs designed to strengthen family ties. A number of studies have compared outcomes of prisoners who maintained family ties during incarceration with those who did not. Each study found that in terms of recidivism, inmates with close ties to family or friends fared better upon release than those who did not have contacts with friends and family (see Visher and Travis 2003).[4] There are a number of barriers, however, to maintaining these relationships. In addition to such challenges as illiteracy, prisoners' families must deal with the high cost of receiving collect calls from prison, long travel times to the correctional facility, inconvenient visiting hours, and uncomfortable or humiliating security procedures at the prison—challenges that can strain even the strongest relationships (see chapter 5). Furthermore, the longer the prison term, the more difficult it becomes for prisoners to maintain these ties and reconnect upon release (McMurray 1993).

Families can also play a powerful role in the lives of returning prisoners upon release. A family member may provide an immediate source of support by offering a place to stay, a meal, a little money, a connection to a job opportunity, and a listening ear. The most critical time for this support is in the hours and days immediately following release when anxiety levels and the risk of recidivism are particularly high (Nelson, Deess, and Allen 1999; Travis et al. 2001).[5] In a study of 49 people released from New York state prisons and city jails, the Vera Institute of Justice found that family support played an important role in the days and weeks after release (Nelson et al. 1999). Former prisoners reported that providing emotional support and an immediate place to stay were the two most critical aspects of family support. Former prisoners who felt that their family was a source of support and acceptance had better success in finding a job and staying off drugs. Those who returned to live with a family member were also less likely to abscond from parole.

Involving the family in the prisoner's transition process has also shown promise for improving postprison outcomes. Not only are families the first people to whom released prisoners return, but many times families are also the first to know whether that person is struggling and on the brink of relapse or return to crime. A program in Manhattan's Lower East Side, La Bodega de la Familia, builds on this concept by providing a range of services and supports to substance-abusing individuals and their families. The idea is that by engaging and strengthening the family unit through a system of family case management, the family system can become better equipped to withstand reentry, addiction, and other challenges. A recent evaluation of La Bodega found that the program participants showed lower levels of drug use, arrests, and convictions for new crimes than did the comparison group (Sullivan et al. 2002). In addition, the reductions in drug use were not the result of greater access to drug treatment, but rather due to pressure and support from family members and La Bodega case managers.

Other research suggests that returning prisoners who assume conventional roles in their families have greater success upon release. Although all of these studies focused exclusively on men, they can be instructive about the role families can play in providing a measure of stability and structure in the transition from prison. Several studies have found that married men experience more successful transitions from prison to home than do single men (Hairston 1988b; Hairston and Lockett 1987; Holt 1986). Another study found that men who returned to live with their wives and children were more successful than those who lived alone or with a parent (Curtis and Schulman 1984). Those who reported having a happy marriage also experienced more successful transitions than those who described their marriages as characterized by conflict (Burstein 1977; Fishman 1986).

Not all families may be in a position to offer help to a returning inmate, however. Families dealing with their own crises, such as poverty, physical or mental health problems, or their own addictions, may not be able to provide financial, emotional, or social support to a family member returning home from prison. Likewise, some individuals may be better served by not returning to a family environment characterized by substance abuse and other negative influences—an environment that could result in a return to criminal behavior. On the other hand, families in a position to help may not want to help. The returning inmate may have significantly strained and alienated relationships with family members. These family members may have experienced a series of broken promises, mistreatment, material losses, or even violence at the hands of the inmate relative.

Although it is clear that families can play a powerful role in assisting a returning prisoner and serve as a "buffering agent" against the many transition challenges newly released prisoners face, there are some caveats. As detailed in the next section, there may be good and complicated reasons why families cannot or will not provide support for a loved one returning from prison.

Children and Families of Prisoners

There is surprisingly little research on the impact of incarceration on the children and families left behind (Johnston 2001). We can hypothesize, however, that the consequences for these families can be substantial, ranging from the loss of financial and emotional support to the social stigma attached to having a family member in prison. This section explores the consequences of parental incarceration on children, looks at family functioning during a period of imprisonment, and examines how families are affected by the return of an incarcerated parent.

Life for families during and following incarceration is complicated by the fact that these are not typically traditional family configurations. Hairston's study of incarcerated fathers (1995, 1998) found that half of her sample had children with multiple women and were therefore not living with all of their children. In fact, many of these children were living with caregivers other than their parents before the incarceration of their mother or father. Several studies have concluded that anywhere from 26 to 44 percent of children of incarcerated mothers were living with a caregiver other than their mother before the mother's incarceration (Johnston 2001). This is particularly true among women who have been incarcerated more than once. According to a report from the U.S. Department of Justice, less than half of parents in state prison reported living with their children before admission (table 1.2). Furthermore, less than one in five of these families had both parents living with their children before incarceration. In general, these are very fragile and fragmented families, a finding with important implications for how these families function both during and following a period of parental incarceration.

Impact of Parental Incarceration on Children

More children are affected by the incarceration of a parent now than at any other time in our nation's history. Two percent of all minor children in the United States and about 7 percent of all African-American children had a parent in state or federal prison in 1997—a total of more than 1.5 million children (Mumola 2000), the majority of whom were under the age of 14 (figure 1.4). These young people are already at high risk along several dimensions and tend to live in conditions characterized by poverty, instability, and diminished access to sources of support. While parental incarceration is generally not the cause of these precarious living conditions

Table 1.2. *Living Arrangements of Minor Children of State Inmates before and during Incarceration, 1997*

	Total (%)	Male (%)	Female (%)
Percentage of prisoners who reported living with children at time of admission	45.3	43.8	64.3
Current caregiver[a]			
Other parent of child	85.0	89.6	28.0
Grandparent of child	16.3	13.3	52.9
Other relatives	6.4	4.9	25.7
Foster home or agency	2.4	1.8	9.6
Friends, others	5.3	4.9	10.4

Source: Mumola (2000).

a. Columns do not add to 100 because some prisoners reported children in different homes.

(although the root causes may be similar, e.g., cycles of poverty and violence), it certainly exacerbates the situation for many children and has been associated with a number of negative outcomes. Yet until recently, the health and human services and juvenile justice systems have paid little attention to the impact of parental incarceration on children's service needs.

Figure 1.4. *Age Distribution of Children with Parents in State or Federal Prison, 1997*

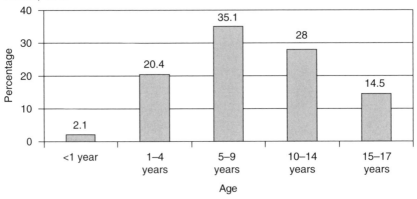

Source: Mumola (2000).
Note: Mean = 8 years.

How does parental incarceration affect these children and what are its long-term consequences? We know that children whose parents have been incarcerated experience a range of negative outcomes. It is difficult, however, to determine whether those consequences are a direct result of a parent being in prison or the nature of family life in that household. For instance, a few studies have found that children of incarcerated parents are more likely to exhibit low self-esteem, depression, emotional withdrawal from friends and family, and inappropriate or disruptive behavior at home and in school (Henriques 1982; Johnston 1995a; Jose-Kampfner 1995; Stanton 1980). In addition, some evidence suggests that children of incarcerated parents are at high risk for future delinquency and/or criminal behavior (Johnston 1995a; see also chapter 7). Understanding the impact of parental incarceration on children is complicated because these outcomes may be related to any number of conditions—parent-child separation, the crime and arrest that preceded incarceration, or general instability, poverty, and inadequate care at home. Furthermore, the degree to which a child is affected by a parent's incarceration may be determined by a number of variables, including the age at which the child is separated from his/her parent, the length of the separation, the level of disruption, the number and result of previous separation experiences, and the availability of family or community support (Seymour 1998; see also chapter 6).

Few studies have directly examined the lives and outcomes for children of incarcerated parents. In fact, most studies have been methodologically limited in that they looked at only a small sample or used inadequate comparison groups, therefore making it difficult to form generalizations (Seymour 1998). There have been no longitudinal studies following children from a parent's incarceration through release. Only a limited number of studies have employed standardized assessment tools and even fewer have relied on direct contact with these children (Johnston 2001). Most of the work to date on children of offenders has relied on self-reporting by an incarcerated parent or a caregiver and has tended to focus on mothers. There have been only a few attempts to document how having a father in prison impacts children (e.g., Brodsky 1975; Carlson and Cervera 1992; Fishman 1990; Hairston 1995; King 1993; Lanier 2003).

A review of the existing literature, however, allows us to hypothesize that parental incarceration has a range of negative effects on children. Some general principles from the literature on child development and trauma as to how children experience the loss of a parent provide an important context for understanding how children experience the incarceration of a parent (Wright and Seymour 2000).

- *Children always experience the loss of a parent as a traumatic event,* regardless of the circumstances surrounding the parent's departure (death, divorce, moving away, or incarceration). Parental absence affects children differently depending on age, but is well documented as an important life event in the child welfare and divorce literature. Reactions include inability to form attachments with others, emotional numbing, anger, depression, regression, and various antisocial behaviors.
- *Trauma diverts children's energy from developmental tasks.* Children in stable environments use their emotional energy to master various age-specific developmental tasks. However, if children's life circumstances overwhelm their capacity to cope, emotional survival begins to take precedence over developmental tasks, resulting in delayed development, regression, or other maladaptive coping strategies.
- *Children find it even more difficult to cope in situations characterized by uncertainty.* Children with a parent in prison often face a great deal of instability and uncertainty as questions about their continued care are being sorted out. Some well-meaning caregivers keep basic information from children to protect them, but this often serves to only heighten the children's feelings of stress and uncertainty.
- *Children's reactions to a situation will vary over time.* Although there have been no longitudinal studies of children of incarcerated parents, we do know that there are differences between a crisis reaction and a long-term response (adaptive or maladaptive) to trauma. Additionally, interventions may be more effective if offered before maladaptive coping behaviors become habitual.
- *Children experience the stigma of having a parent in prison.* For most children, the stigma of losing a parent to prison is felt in their neighborhood, among their peers, and from their teachers and family members—often resulting in feelings of shame and low self-esteem. For other children who come from neighborhoods or families where incarceration is a more common event, the stigma may be less intense but the needs are not (Gaudin and Sutphen 1993). Typically, schools and communities offer no specific programs to help these children cope with the loss of a parent to prison.

The role parents play in their children's development and the potential impact of a parent-child separation due to incarceration also highlight the need for social service agencies to find ways to help families stay in touch during incarceration and reunite upon release, where appropriate. One researcher has concluded that visitation can be beneficial for children trying to cope with the loss of a parent to prison (Johnston 1995b). However, maintaining these relationships—between the parents (or other caregivers) and between the parent and the child(ren)—during a period of incarceration can be difficult.

Finally, it is important to reiterate that many of these children are already at high risk: Their problems did not begin with parental incarceration. Rather, these children typically already live in circumstances that can be considered as posing high risks for unhealthy development, including poverty, diminished access to resources, parental substance abuse, mental illness among parents and/or caregivers, and a family history of involvement in the criminal justice system (Johnston 2001).

Certainly, parental incarceration has a profound impact on the children left behind, but as yet no research studies have parsed out the effects of loss of a parent due to incarceration from the other stressful and traumatic circumstances that also generally characterize the lives of these children. Drawing from the general literature on child development and trauma, we can hypothesize that the effects of parental incarceration on a child's life could depend on a number of factors, including the child's developmental level, emotional characteristics, and available social support network (Rickel and Becker 1997).

Impact of Incarceration on Family Functioning

We turn next to an examination of the impact of incarceration on family functioning, including the loss of financial and emotional support, changed parenting roles, new governmental interventions (e.g., foster care), and shifts in eligibility for public assistance.

STRUCTURAL CHANGES

One of the most immediate changes experienced by the family of an incarcerated parent is a change in family composition and living arrangements. Most children are not present at the time of their parent's arrest, and parents typically do not tell the police that they have minor children (American Bar Association 1993). As a result, many children are informally "placed" with other family members and do not enter the foster care system following the arrest of a parent. However, placement of a child varies depending on whether the father or mother is arrested and incarcerated. Children of incarcerated fathers typically reside with their mothers (90 percent), while children of incarcerated mothers are often placed with other family members (79 percent) (Mumola 2000). Children are more likely to be placed in foster care (10 percent) if their mother is sentenced to prison than if their father is incarcerated (2 percent).

The allocation of child care responsibilities before incarceration influences how much the incarceration affects these arrangements during the prison term. Although incarcerated fathers are less likely to have been living with at least one of their children before imprisonment, these fathers are nevertheless involved in their children's lives to some extent. Hairston (1995) reports that many fathers in her study provided regular financial support and/or regularly visited their children even though they did not live with them. Yet, because a mother is typically the primary caregiver for her child, her imprisonment will likely have a greater effect on family structure and functioning.

Because most incarcerated parents are fathers, most children with an incarcerated parent live with their mothers. In families where the father *was not* present in the home, his incarceration may have no impact on family structure but may, because of the elimination of financial support and other care for the children, create a disruption in the mother's ability to care for the children. In families where the father *was* present in the home, his removal will place an even greater financial and care burden on the remaining parent. In families where the only parent present in the home is subsequently incarcerated, children are most likely to be placed with a related caregiver—a grandparent or other family member. For these families, adjustment to the new caregiving arrangements may be relatively minimal.

However, "family" caregivers who did not have much contact with the children before parental incarceration will have to establish themselves as de facto parents and develop a relationship with the children. This can be even more challenging for unrelated caregivers who do not share a sense of history with the child. Contributing to the trauma of this changing family structure, the children of both male and female prisoners are sometimes separated from their siblings during incarceration because caregivers may not be able to care for the entire sibling group (Hairston 1995).

The caregiver-parent relationship is also important during incarceration and has implications for reunification efforts following release. A lack of participation in decisionmaking about their children contributes to a sense of powerlessness among incarcerated parents. In fact, less than half of incarcerated parents reported regular communication with the caregivers of their children (Bloom and Steinhart 1993; Hairston 1998).

LOSS OF FINANCIAL SUPPORT

Incarceration disproportionately affects families living in poverty, and imprisonment of a parent contributes to the financial strain among the families and caregivers left behind. Most parents either earned income or received public assistance before being incarcerated. Most parents in state prison (71 percent) reported either full-time or part-time employment in the month preceding their current arrest, slightly higher than state prisoners who were not parents (65 percent) (Mumola 2000). Wages or salary was the most common source of income among incarcerated fathers before imprisonment, 60 percent of whom reported having a full-time job. Mothers, on the other hand, were less likely to have a full-time job (39 percent). For them, the most common sources of income were wages (44 percent) or transfer payments (42 percent). Although very few mothers reported receiving formal child support payments (6 percent), they did report receiving other forms of assistance from the fathers of their children, including some level of financial support (Hairston 1998).

When an income-producing parent is incarcerated, the family must adjust to the loss of that income during the prison term. And during imprisonment, most parents are not able to provide financial support to their families. A small minority of all inmates (7 percent) is employed in prison industries that pay a nominal wage, but it is typically not enough to provide meaningful financial support (Travis et al. 2001). Inmates typically receive money from their families, not the other way around.

Caregivers often struggle to make ends meet during the period of incarceration. Many caregivers rely on child support payments, their own income, and public assistance for support. Two studies found a similar level of reliance on Aid to Families with Dependent Children (AFDC) payments (now Temporary Assistance to Needy Families, or TANF) to meet basic needs: 44 percent of families caring for children of an incarcerated parent reported receiving AFDC (Bloom and Steinhart 1993). However, recent welfare reform legislation may severely limit public assistance (i.e., TANF) as a form of support for families both during and following incarceration by capping lifetime eligibility at 60 months, instituting work requirements, and placing restrictions on those who have violated probation or parole and those who have been convicted of certain drug crimes (Phillips and Bloom 1998). Regardless of the source, most caregivers reported that they did not have sufficient resources to meet basic needs (Bloom and Steinhart 1993).

The formal kinship foster care system represents another potential source of support for caregivers. Although the average monthly foster care payment is greater than the average TANF child-only payment in nearly all states, very few families of an incarcerated parent access the foster care system (Bloom and Steinhart 1993). Only 10 percent of incarcerated mothers and less than 2 percent of incarcerated fathers reported having a child in foster care (Mumola 2000).

Maintaining Ties with Family

Maintaining ties with family members—between the parents (or other caregivers) and between the parent and child—during the prison term can be difficult. Obstacles identified by the Women's Prison Association include inadequate information on visiting procedures, little help from correctional facilities about visiting arrangements, the time involved in traveling great distances to get to the correctional facility, visiting procedures that are uncomfortable or humiliating, and concerns about children's reactions to in-prison visits (Women's Prison Association 1996). These circumstances can easily strain family relationships and continued connections with children. Furthermore, inmates' communications with their families—via phone, mail, or personal visits—are highly regulated by correctional facilities, with the primary concern focused on security issues. This concern translates into policies that do not necessarily promote or facilitate prisoner-family connections.

Mothers in prison tend to stay in closer contact with their children than do fathers (Mumola 2000). Nearly 80 percent of mothers reported monthly contact and 60 percent reported at least weekly contact. However, as with fathers, more than half of all mothers reported never receiving a personal visit from their children. Visits can be even more difficult for incarcerated mothers who, because of the scarcity of female prison facilities, tend to be an average of 160 miles farther away from their children than are incarcerated fathers. Despite this separation, most mothers expected to be reunited with their children upon release (Hagan and Coleman 2001).

Forty percent of incarcerated fathers reported having weekly contact with their children, mostly by mail or phone (Mumola 2000). The frequency of contact decreases, however, as the length of time served in prison increases (Lynch and Sabol 2001). Given that the majority of state prisoners (60 percent) are held in facilities more than 100 miles from their homes, it is not surprising that most fathers (57 percent) also reported never receiving a personal visit from their children after admission to prison. A primary source of depression among both incarcerated mothers and fathers is the lost connections with family—particularly their children (Adams 1992).

Prison also creates enormous strain on intimate relationships—whether or not children are involved. It is not uncommon for marital relationships to end in divorce during a prison term. Only half of married male inmates in Hairston's study (1995) reported that their primary source of emotional support was their wife. Hairston reported that for many male prisoners, family stability and connections were maintained by their mothers.

Prisoners' success in maintaining ties with their children also often depends on the quality of their relationship with their children's caregiver. In her review of the research, Anne Nurse (2001) suggests that the quality of parent-child interaction among juvenile and adult fathers depends a great deal on their relationship with their children's mother. Frank Furstenberg's (1995) work with young fragile families suggests that fathers typically do not view the relationship with their children as separate from their relationship with the mother—they see it as a "package deal." As a result, when the bond between the couple begins to falter, the father-child relationship becomes more tenuous. This is also true for kinship caregivers who may harbor negative feelings toward the incarcerated parent and may believe that allowing a child to visit his/her parent in prison will negatively affect the child. In addition, caregivers also may not have the necessary resources—time, money, and transportation—to make the often long and expensive trips to a prison facility for a visit.

Although removing specific family members can clearly be beneficial for some families—resulting in more attention to the children, more available resources, fewer distractions, and less fear or actual violence in the home—there is considerable evidence that most children and families suffer when a parent is removed from the home or community. Likewise, there are many indications that maintaining family ties benefits both incarcerated parents and their children, and that these ties may aid adjustment to the loss of a parent and ease the process of return.

Reentry Challenges for Families

Returning prisoners face a host of challenges upon release from prison, challenges that translate into important issues for the well-being of their children and families. Many returning prisoners with substance abuse problems before incarceration may still need treatment. Others face the prospect of homelessness without help from family members and the challenge of finding a stable job to support themselves and their children. In addition, a criminal record will limit many returning prisoners' access to public assistance and governmental benefits. In most cases, the criminal justice system does not help families plan for and negotiate the process of returning home. Moreover, the child welfare system becomes involved only in those situations where caseworkers have formally been involved in the placement and ongoing care of children of incarcerated parents. Therefore, families of prisoners typically are on their own in navigating the challenges of having a family member return home from prison.

REESTABLISHING RELATIONSHIPS

The months leading up to release are a particularly stressful time for inmates and their families. Each has developed expectations for what life will be like after the prison term ends. Male inmates reported returning to their partners with the expectation that nothing would have changed between them. The literature on inmates' spouses indicates that the most significant change is that the partner left behind becomes more independent and self-sufficient (Furstenberg 1995). Inmates' families change in their absence, and returning prisoners are often unable to resume their former roles, which in turn causes stress and tension.

Inmates must also confront the challenge of reestablishing bonds with and authority over children with whom they had little contact while in prison. In many cases, other adults have stepped in to fill the role of the absent inmate parent. Family members may subsequently limit or discourage children's contact with the former inmate. Research on the African-American community, for example, has found that maternal grandmothers and other female family members will sometimes try to limit an unemployed father's access to his children (Sullivan 1993).

New relationships that developed during the period of incarceration may also contribute to stress and strained connections upon release, and may result in diminished involvement between returning inmates and their children. Some studies indicate that inmates will start to withdraw from active involvement in their children's lives when they discover their former partner has started a new relationship (Furstenberg 1995; Nurse 2001).

All of these issues relating to reunification of families are further complicated when a former prisoner's home life involves a history of domestic violence. Although most inmates in state prison have been convicted of a violent crime (44 percent of parents and 51 percent of nonparents), we do not know the extent to which these were crimes against an intimate partner or a family member. However, given that certain violent crimes—such as assault or rape—are most frequently committed by an intimate partner, relative, friend, or acquaintance, there is reason to assume that a high portion of inmates convicted of violent crimes committed those crimes against partners or family members (Herman and Wasserman 2001). Families with a history of domestic violence need extra care and consideration to help them heal during the prison term and to plan for the release of a family member implicated in past violent behavior. To date, little research exists on these families' experiences during the incarceration of a violent family member or the consequences of that individual's return.

HOUSING AND EMPLOYMENT

Stable and adequate income and housing are important factors in an individual's transition back to family and the community. One of the first tasks a returning prisoner must tackle following release from prison is finding a place to stay. The challenge of finding stable and affordable housing for one's family is only compounded by time spent in prison. Returning prisoners rarely have the financial resources or personal references needed to secure housing in the private market. Most individuals leave prison without enough money for a security deposit on an apartment. Furthermore, landlords typically require potential tenants to list employment and housing references and to disclose financial and criminal history information, a likely obstacle for returning prisoners.

Public housing also may not be an option for returning prisoners. Federal housing policies permit—and in some cases require—public housing authorities, Section 8 providers, and other federally assisted housing programs to deny housing to individuals who have engaged in certain criminal activities (Legal Action Center 2000a). The guidelines for denying housing are fairly broad and may encompass those who have, at any point in the past, engaged in drug-related activity, violent criminal activity, or other criminal activity that could negatively affect the health and safety of other residents. However, housing providers can make exceptions for individuals who demonstrate that they are receiving help by participating in a treatment or rehabilitation program.

A parent in prison means lost financial support that can place a child—in many cases already living in poverty—in even more dire circumstances. Therefore, another important aspect of returning prisoners' successful transition back into the community, and to the loved ones left behind, is finding a job. Unemployment rates before admission to prison are high among incarcerated parents. In the month before the arrest that led to their admission to prison, nearly 30 percent of fathers and 50 percent of mothers were unemployed (Mumola 2000). Legitimate employment not only lowers the likelihood that a former prisoner will reoffend, but also provides an important means of stable family support.

Finding a job is particularly important for parents who were subject to a formal child support agreement during their prison term. In some cases, if inmates are not able to amend court-ordered child support arrangements during their prison terms, child support obligations continue to accumulate. These unpaid child support obligations may have legal and financial implications for inmates once they are released.

ACCESS TO PUBLIC ASSISTANCE

Recent changes to welfare legislation could also make it very difficult for parents to rebuild a life with their children. As just described, for a variety of reasons, former inmates are often at a disadvantage when seeking a job. Therefore, access to public benefits that could provide a safety net to help these families find stable footing following parental incarceration is critical. Yet, in many circumstances, this safety net has been severely limited for returning prisoners and their families. Individuals in violation of a condition of their parole or probation can be barred from receiving federal welfare benefits (TANF), food stamps, Supplemental Security Income, and access to public housing (Legal Action Center 2000b). In fact, individuals convicted of a drug felony can be permanently banned from receiving TANF or food stamps. (States can, however, opt out of this ban and about half have instituted some type of exception to this rule.) These federal regulations can have an unanticipated impact: Indeed, in 1997, 35 percent of incarcerated mothers and 23 percent of incarcerated fathers were serving time for some type of drug offense (Mumola 2000).

NAVIGATING THE CORRECTIONS AND CHILD WELFARE SYSTEMS
Inmates with children who have been formally placed in foster care or some other out-of-home care may confront several additional barriers to reunification. First, while incarcerated, prisoners have difficulty accessing the services that the child welfare system requires for reunification. Additionally, communication between inmates and caseworkers regarding permanency planning and other important issues for reunification is hampered by the fact that prisoners are typically housed in facilities many miles from their community. Finally, inmates have problems remaining in touch with their children while in prison, which is the most basic requirement for reunification. Most correctional facilities impose significant restrictions on any form of contact between inmates and family members. In fact, most correctional facility policies are focused on inmate management and security concerns, policies that often create obstacles for prisoners and their families as they try to stay connected (Hairston 1998).

Though children may be better off without a neglectful and abusive parent in their lives, there are many caring and committed incarcerated mothers and fathers who expect to resume their parenting roles upon release. Recent legislative initiatives, however, have made it more difficult for incarcerated parents—particularly mothers—to reunite with their children upon release. For example, the 1997 Adoption and Safe Families Act, replacing the 1980 Adoption Assistance and Child Welfare Act, authorizes termination of parental rights once a child has been in foster care for 15 or more months of a 22-month period. Incarcerated women serve an average of 18 months in prison (Hagan and Coleman 2001). Therefore, the average female prisoner whose children are placed in foster care could lose the right to reunite with her children upon release.

Conclusion

Families of prisoners generally struggle with a range of challenges that are often exacerbated by the imprisonment of a family member. Broadening our perspective to include incarceration's impact on prisoner families—from the arrest, to imprisonment, and on through release—

raises a number of important questions. How can family bonds be strengthened during the prison term? Are there ways to help families cope with the period of incarceration? How should a parent and child be reunited? Is there a risk that the stresses of incarceration will limit inmates' ability to be effective parents upon release? Is there a heightened risk of domestic violence and child abuse as prisoners adjust to their new reality? Can the process of reentry be viewed as an opportunity for intervention with these families?

Developing innovative answers to these questions would require new policy collaborations and partnerships between corrections departments and child and family welfare agencies. These new alliances could help smooth the transition by helping prisoners and their families stay in touch and work through the difficult dynamics of reunification. Working together, corrections professionals and local service providers could develop policies and programs that significantly improve the likelihood of a successful transition from prison to home—an outcome that has far-reaching benefits for all involved.

NOTES

1. Unless otherwise noted, most of the information in this section comes from a comprehensive report by the Bureau of Justice Statistics on the characteristics of incarcerated parents and their children (Mumola 2000). The data were gathered through personal interviews with inmates in state and federal facilities in 1997.

2. The majority of all inmates are housed in state prison facilities. In fact, nearly 90 percent of all incarcerated parents are in state prisons, and therefore this chapter will focus on these inmates.

3. "Sentence length" is the amount of time imposed by the sentencing court. The actual length of the sentence served will depend upon state sentencing laws, parole board decisions, and good time credits earned while in prison.

4. Most research to date looking at the role of families has only focused on a narrow definition of postprison success—recidivism rates—rather than considering a range of outcomes, such as finding stable housing, finding and maintaining employment, providing financial support for his/her children, and remaining in a drug treatment program (see Visher and Travis 2003).

5. Most prisoners are released with little more than a bus ticket and a nominal amount of spending money. Prisoners are often released and returned to their home community at odd hours of the night, making it difficult to connect with family members and services providers. They may be immediately exposed to high-risk places, people, and situations, and few have developed the relapse prevention skills in prison to deal with these risks on the outside.

REFERENCES

Adams, Kenneth. 1992. "Adjusting to Prison Life." In *Crime and Justice: A Review of Research*, edited by Michael Tonry (275–359). Chicago: University of Chicago Press.

American Bar Association. 1993. *Children on Hold: What Happens When Their Primary Caregiver Is Arrested?* Washington, D.C.: Author.

Beck, Allen J., and Laura M. Maruschak. 2001. *Mental Health Treatment in State Prisons, 2000.* Bureau of Justice Statistics Special Report. Washington, D.C.: U.S. Department of Justice.

Beck, Allen J., Jennifer C. Karberg, and Paige M. Harrison. 2002. *Prison and Jail Inmates at Midyear 2001.* Bureau of Justice Statistics Bulletin. Washington, D.C.: U.S. Department of Justice.

Bloom, Barbara, and David Steinhart. 1993. "Why Punish the Children? A Reappraisal of the Children of Incarcerated Mothers in America." San Francisco, Calif.: National Council on Crime and Delinquency.

Brodsky, Stanley L. 1975. *Families and Friends of Men in Prison.* Lexington, Mass.: Lexington Books.

Burstein, Jules. 1977. *Conjugal Visits in Prison.* Lexington, Mass.: Lexington Books.

Carlson, Bonnie E., and Neil Cervera. 1992. *Inmates and Their Wives.* Westport, Conn.: Greenwood Press.

Curtis, Russell L., Jr., and Sam Schulman. 1984. "Ex-offender's Family Relations and Economic Supports: The Significant Women Study of the TARP Project." *Crime and Delinquency* 30 (4): 507–28.

Fishman, Laura T. 1986. "Repeating the Cycle of Hard Living and Crime: Wives' Accommodations to Husbands' Parole Performance." *Federal Probation* 50: 44–54.

———. 1990. *Women at the Wall.* Albany: State University of New York Press.

Furstenberg, Frank F., Jr. 1995. "Fathering in the Inner-City: Paternal Participation and Public Policy." In *Fatherhood: Contemporary Theory, Research, and Social Policy*, edited by William Marsiglio (119–47). Thousand Oaks, Calif.: Sage Publications.

Gaes, Gerald G., Timothy J. Flanagan, Laurence L. Motiuk, and Lynn Stewart. 1999. "Adult Correctional Treatment." In *Prisons: Crime and Justice: A Review of Research*, edited by Joan Petersilia (321–426). Chicago: University of Chicago Press.

Gaudin, James M., Jr., and Richard Sutphen. 1993. "Foster Care vs. Extended Family Care for Children of Incarcerated Mothers." *Journal of Offender Rehabilitation* 19 (3/4): 129–47.

Greenfeld, Lawrence A., and Tracy L. Snell. 1999. *Bureau of Justice Statistics Special Report, Women Offenders.* Washington, D.C.: U.S. Department of Justice.

Hagan, John, and Juleigh Petty Coleman. 2001. "Returning Captives of the American War on Drugs: Issues of Community and Family Reentry." *Crime and Delinquency* 47 (3): 352–67.

Hairston, Creasie Finney. 1988a. "Family Ties during Imprisonment: Do They Influence Future Criminal Activity?" *Federal Probation* 52 (1): 48–52.

———. 1988b. "Men in Prison: Family Characteristics and Family Views." *Journal of Offender Counseling, Services and Rehabilitation* 14 (1): 23–30.

———. 1995. "Fathers in Prison." In *Children of Incarcerated Parents*, edited by Katherine Gabel and Denise Johnston (31–40). New York: Lexington Books.

———. 1998. "The Forgotten Parent: Understanding the Forces That Influence Incarcerated Fathers' Relationships with Their Children." *Child Welfare* 5: 617–39.

Hairston, Creasie Finney, and Patricia Lockett. 1987. "Parents in Prison: New Directions for Social Services." *Social Work* 32 (2): 162–64.

Hammett, Theodore M., Cheryl Roberts, and Sofia Kennedy. 2001. "Health-Related Issues in Prisoner Reentry." *Crime and Delinquency* 47 (3): 390–409.

Harrison, Lana D. 2001. "The Revolving Prison Door for Drug Involved Offenders: Challenges and Opportunities." *Crime and Delinquency* 47 (3): 462–85.

Henriques, Zelma Weston. 1982. *Imprisoned Mothers and Their Children: A Descriptive and Analytical Study.* Washington, D.C.: University Press of America.

Herman, Susan, and Cressida Wasserman. 2001. "A Role for Victims in Offender Reentry." *Crime and Delinquency* 47 (3): 428–45.

Holt, Norman. 1986. "Statistical Tables Describing the Background Characteristics and Recidivism Rates for Released Prisoners from Massachusetts Pre-release Facilities during 1983." Milford: Massachusetts Department of Correction.

Johnston, Denise. 1995a. "Effects of Parental Incarceration." In *Children of Incarcerated Parents,* edited by Katherine Gabel and Denise Johnston (59–88). New York: Lexington Books.

———. 1995b. "Parent-Child Visitation in the Jail or Prison." In *Children of Incarcerated Parents,* edited by Katherine Gabel and Denise Johnston (135–43). New York: Lexington Books.

———. 2001. "Incarceration of Women and Effects on Parenting." Paper prepared for a conference, "Effects of Incarceration on Children and Families," sponsored by Northwestern University, Evanston, Ill., May 5.

Jose-Kampfner, Christina. 1995. "Post-Traumatic Stress Reactions in Children of Imprisoned Mothers." In *Children of Incarcerated Parents,* edited by Katherine Gabel and Denise Johnston (89–100). New York: Lexington Books.

King, Anthony O. 1993. "The Impact of Incarceration on African-American Families: Implications for Practice." *Journal of Contemporary Human Service* 73: 145–53.

Lanier, Charles S. 2003. "Who's Doing the Time Here, Me or My Children? Addressing the Issues Implicated by Mounting Numbers of Fathers in Prison." In *Convict Criminology,* edited by Jeffrey Ian Ross and Stephen C. Richards (170–90). London: Wadsworth.

Lawrence, Sarah, Daniel P. Mears, Glenn Dubin, and Jeremy Travis. 2002. *The Practice and Promise of Prison Programming.* Washington, D.C.: The Urban Institute.

Legal Action Center. 2000a. "Housing Laws Affecting Individuals with Criminal Convictions." Washington, D.C.: Legal Action Center.

———. 2000b. "Public Assistance Laws Affecting Individuals with Criminal Convictions." Washington, D.C.: Legal Action Center.

Lynch, James P., and William J. Sabol. 2001. *Prisoner Reentry in Perspective.* Crime Policy Report No. 3. Washington, D.C.: The Urban Institute.

Maruschak, Laura M., and Allen J. Beck. 2001. *Bureau of Justice Statistics Special Report, Medical Problems of Inmates, 1997.* Washington, D.C.: U.S. Department of Justice.

McMurray, Harvey L. 1993. "High Risk Parolees in Transition from Institution to Community Life." *Journal of Offender Rehabilitation* 19 (1/2): 145–61.

Mumola, Christopher J. 1999. *Substance Abuse and Treatment, State and Federal Prisoners, 1997.* Bureau of Justice Statistics Special Report. Washington, D.C.: U.S. Department of Justice.

————. 2000. *Incarcerated Parents and Their Children.* Bureau of Justice Statistics Special Report. Washington, D.C.: U.S. Department of Justice.

————. 2002. "Incarcerated Parents and Their Children." Presentation to National Center for Children and Families colloquium, "Overcoming the Hidden Costs of Incarceration on Urban Children," Washington, D.C., Oct. 31.

National Commission on Correctional Health Care. 2002. *The Health Status of Soon-to-Be-Released Inmates.* A Report to Congress. Chicago: Author.

NCCHC. See National Commission on Correctional Health Care.

Nelson, Marta, Perry Deess, and Charlotte Allen. 1999. *The First Month Out: Post Incarceration Experiences in New York City.* New York: Vera Institute of Justice.

Nurse, Anne. 2001. "Coming Home to Strangers." Paper prepared for a conference, "Effects of Incarceration on Children and Families," sponsored by Northwestern University, Evanston, Ill., May 5.

Phillips, Susan, and Barbara Bloom. 1998. "In Whose Best Interest? The Impact of Changing Public Policy on Relatives Caring for Children with Incarcerated Parents." *Child Welfare* 77 (5): 531–42.

Richie, Beth E. 2001. "Challenges Women Face as They Return to their Communities: Findings from Life History Interviews." *Crime and Delinquency* 47 (3): 368–89.

Rickel, Annette U., and Evvie Becker. 1997. *Keeping Children from Harm's Way: How National Policy Affects Psychological Development.* Washington, D.C.: American Psychological Association.

Seymour, Cynthia. 1998. "Children with Parents in Prison: Child Welfare Policy, Program, and Practice Issues." *Child Welfare* 77 (5): 469–93.

Shapiro, Carol, and Meryl Schwartz. 2001. "Coming Home: Building on Family Connections." *Corrections Management Quarterly* 5 (3): 52–61.

Stanton, Ann Marie. 1980. *When Mothers Go to Jail.* Lexington, Mass.: Lexington Books.

Sullivan, Eileen, Milton Mino, Katherine Nelson, and Jill Pope. 2002. *Families as a Resource in Recovery from Drug Abuse: An Evaluation of La Bodega de la Familia.* New York: Vera Institute of Justice.

Sullivan, Mercer L. 1993. "Young Fathers and Parenting in Two Inner-City Neighborhoods." In *Young Unwed Fathers: Changing Roles and Emerging Policies,* edited by Robert I. Lerman and Theodora J. Ooms (52–73). Philadelphia: Temple University Press.

Travis, Jeremy. 2000. "But They All Come Back: Rethinking Prisoner Reentry." Sentencing and Corrections—Issues for the 21st Century Brief No 7. Washington, D.C.: National Institute of Justice.

Travis, Jeremy, Amy L. Solomon, and Michelle Waul. 2001. *From Prison to Home: The Dimensions and Consequences of Prisoner Reentry.* Washington, D.C.: The Urban Institute.

Visher, Christy A., and Jeremy Travis. 2003. "Transitions from Prison to Community: Understanding Individual Pathways." *Annual Review of Sociology* 29 (August): 89–113.

Wexler, Harry K., Douglas S. Lipton, and Bruce D. Johnson. 1998. *A Criminal Justice System Strategy for Treating Cocaine-Heroin Abusing Offenders in Custody* (NCJ 113915). Washington, D.C.: National Institute of Justice.

Women's Prison Association. 1996. *When a Mother Is Arrested: How the Criminal Justice and Child Welfare Systems Can Work Together More Effectively.* Baltimore: Maryland Department of Human Resources.

Wright, Lois E., and Cynthia B. Seymour. 2000. *Working with Children and Families Separated by Incarceration.* Washington, D.C.: Child Welfare League of America Press.

PART I
The Impact of Incarceration and Reentry on Individual Prisoners

2

The Psychological Impact of Incarceration

Implications for Postprison Adjustment

Craig Haney

The psychological impact of incarceration and its implications for postprison, freeworld adjustment are substantial. Nearly a half-century ago, Gresham Sykes wrote that "life in the maximum security prison is depriving or frustrating in the extreme," and little has changed to alter that view (Sykes 1958, 63). Indeed, Sykes's observation is perhaps more meaningful now than when he first made it. Moreover, prolonged adaptation to the deprivations and frustrations of life inside prison—the "pains of imprisonment"—carries certain psychological costs. This chapter briefly explores some of those costs and examines their implications for adjustment in the world beyond prison. It concludes with some programmatic and policy-oriented suggestions to minimize disruptions in the transition from prison to home.

My approach to the topic of postprison adjustment requires one important caveat, however. Although much of my discussion is organized around the themes of psychological changes and adaptations, I do *not* mean to suggest that criminal behavior can or should be equated with mental illness, that persons who suffer the acute pains of imprisonment necessarily manifest diagnosable psychological disorders or other forms of personal pathology, that psychotherapy should be the primary tool of prison rehabilitation, or that therapeutic interventions are the most effective ways to optimize the transition from prison to home. I am well aware of the excesses that have been committed in the name of correctional psychology in the past, and it is not my intention to contribute in any way to repeating them.

The chapter is organized around several basic propositions. First, prisons have become in some ways much more difficult places in which to adjust and survive over the past several decades. In light of these changes, adaptation to modern prison life incurs severe psychological costs for many incarcerated persons, some of whom are more vulnerable than others to the pains of imprisonment. Finally, although the psychological costs and pains of imprisonment can and do serve to impede postprison adjustment, there are ways to minimize these impediments, both in and out of prison.

The State of the Prisons

Prisoners in the United States and elsewhere have always confronted a unique set of contingencies and pressures to which they were required to react and adapt in order to survive the prison experience. However, a combination of forces have transformed the nation's criminal justice system and modified the nature of imprisonment over the past three decades (Haney 1998; Haney and Zimbardo 1998). As a result, the challenges prisoners must now overcome in order to both endure incarceration and eventually reintegrate into the freeworld also have changed and intensified.

These changes in the nature of imprisonment have included, among other things, a series of interrelated, negative trends in American corrections. Perhaps the most dramatic changes have resulted from the unprecedented increases in the rate of incarceration, which in turn have added to the U.S. prison population and brought about widespread overcrowding. Over the past 25 years, penologists repeatedly have described U.S. prisons as "in crisis," characterizing each new level of overcrowding as "unprecedented" (Cullen 1995; Zalman 1987). The dramatic increases in the prisoner population have been primarily policy driven and not the result of increases in crime rates or the population in general. In fact, the *rate* of incarceration (which corrects for population increases) in the United States remained remarkably stable for the 50-year period between 1925 and 1975, at just around 125 persons incarcerated in prisons and jails per 100,000 persons in the population. However, between 1975 and 1995, that rate soared approximately fivefold to an unprecedented 600 per 100,000. By 2001, it hovered close to 700 per 100,000 (Haney and Zimbardo 1998; Harrison and Beck 2002).[1]

These dramatic increases were not part of some international trend. By the early 1990s, the United States incarcerated more persons per capita than any other nation in the modern world, and it has retained that dubious distinction nearly every year since. The international disparities are most striking when the U.S. incarceration rate is contrasted to those of other nations with whom the United States is often compared, such as Japan, the Netherlands, Australia, and the United Kingdom. In the 1990s—as Marc Mauer and the Sentencing Project have effectively documented—incarceration rates in the United States were consistently between four and eight times greater than these other nations (Mauer 1992, 1995). For example, in 1995, when the U.S. rate first reached 600 prisoners per 100,000 in the population, Canada was incarcerating a little less than one sixth as many of its citizens per 100,000 (115) and Japan just short of one-twentieth (37) as many people.

The rapidly expanding prisoner population and the resulting high levels of overcrowding in prisons across the country have adversely affected conditions of confinement, jeopardized prisoner safety, compromised prison management, and greatly limited prisoner access to meaningful programming. The two largest prison systems in the nation—those in California and Texas—provide instructive examples. Over the past 30 years, California's total prisoner population has increased *eightfold* (from roughly 20,000 in the early 1970s to its current population of approximately 160,000), and its incarceration rate has grown to match the rapidly increasing national average (Travis and Lawrence 2002). Although the state corrections budget has skyrocketed, no remotely comparable increase in funds for prisoner services or inmate programming has occurred. For example, between 1979 and 1986, the number of California prisoners increased 139 percent and the caseloads of its prison psychiatrists and psychologists doubled. However, the budgeted positions for clinical staff increased by only 29 percent (Specter 1994, 112). In addition, despite an unprecedented surge in new prison construction, the state has been unable to keep pace with the influx of prisoners—the system currently operates at approximately 190 percent of capacity (California Department of Corrections 2002).

Texas's prison system, the nation's second largest, has been plagued by many of the same problems. Although Texas had managed to avoid the kind of rapid expansion of its prison population that plagued California throughout the 1980s, and in spite of research favorably comparing the crime rates in Texas with those in California during the same period (Ekland-Olson, Kelly, and Eisenberg 1992; Petersilia 1992), state politicians finally succumbed to nationwide trends toward overincarceration in the early 1990s. Between 1992 and 1997, the prisoner population more than doubled as the state achieved one of the highest incarceration rates in the nation (Texas Department of Criminal Justice 1997). Nearly 70,000 additional prisoners were added to the state's prison rolls in that brief five-year period alone. Resources that might have been devoted to prisoner programs, mental health and drug treatment services, and the like were spent on creating bed space as the state scrambled to create room for this enormous influx of prisoners. Not surprisingly, California and Texas were among the states that faced major prison lawsuits in the 1990s. Federal courts in both states found substandard, unconstitutional conditions of confinement and ruled that the prison systems had failed to provide adequate treatment services for those prisoners suffering the most extreme psychological effects of being housed in deteriorated and overcrowded facilities.[2]

Paralleling these dramatic increases in incarceration rates and the numbers of persons imprisoned throughout the United States has been an equally dramatic change in the rationale for prison itself. In the mid-1970s, American society moved abruptly from justifying imprisonment on the basis of the belief that incarceration would somehow facilitate productive reentry into the freeworld to using imprisonment merely to inflict pain on wrongdoers ("just desserts"), to disable criminal offenders ("incapacitation"), or to keep them far away from the rest of society ("containment"). Abandoning the once-avowed goal of rehabilitation certainly decreased the perceived need for and availability of meaningful programming for prisoners, as well as social and mental health services provided to them both inside and outside the prison. Indeed, once prisons were no longer conceptualized as places that existed—at least in part—for the benefit of prisoners, general support for overall prisoner well-being declined.

In a number of instances, abandoning the goal of rehabilitation also resulted in the erosion of modestly protective norms against cruelty toward prisoners. Many corrections officials became far less inclined to address prison disturbances, tensions between prisoner groups and factions, and disciplinary infractions in general by using ameliorative techniques aimed at addressing the root causes of conflict and designed to de-escalate discord. Instead, the rapid influx of new prisoners, serious shortages in staffing and other resources, and the embrace of an openly punitive approach to corrections led to the "de-skilling" of many correctional staff members. Corrections personnel, in turn, often resorted to extreme forms of prison discipline (such as punitive isolation or "super-max" confinement) that were especially destructive and designed to repress conflict rather than resolve it (Haney and Lynch 1997). Increased tensions and higher levels of fear and danger resulted.

Stressing the punitive aspects of incarceration made prison more alienating and stigmatizing. This emphasis resulted in the further literal and psychological isolation of prisons from surrounding communities, and compromised prison visitation programs and the already scarce resources that had been used to maintain ties between prisoners and their families and others in the outside world. Support services to facilitate the transition from prison to the freeworld were undermined at precisely the moment they needed to be enhanced. Because of longer sentences and a greatly expanded scope of incarceration, more prisoners experienced the psychological pains of imprisonment for longer periods, more people were incarcerated than ordinarily would have been (e.g., drug offenders), and more minority communities (because of differential enforcement and sentencing policies) suffered the social costs of incarceration in increasing concentrations (Tonry 1995).

Thus, in the first decade of the 21st century, more people have been subjected to the pains of imprisonment for longer periods and under conditions that threaten greater psychological distress and potential long-term dysfunction. They will be returned to communities already disadvantaged by a badly frayed "safety net," and they will sorely need social services and supportive resources that their neighborhoods unfortunately will be too often unable to provide.

The Psychological Effects of Incarceration: On the Nature of Institutionalization

Adjusting to imprisonment is difficult for virtually everyone. It can create habits of thinking and acting that are extremely dysfunctional outside the prison walls. Yet, the psychological effects of incarceration vary from individual to individual and they are often reversible. To be sure then, not everyone who is incarcerated is disabled or psychologically harmed by the experience. However, few people leave prison completely unchanged or unscathed by it. At the very least, prison is painful. Many incarcerated persons suffer the long-term consequences of having been subjected to this pain. In the course of coping with the deprivations of prison life and adapting to its extremely atypical patterns and norms of living and interacting with others, many people are permanently changed.

At the same time, empirical studies of the most negative effects of incarceration are reasonably consistent: Most people who have done time in the best-run prisons return to the freeworld with little or no permanent, clinically diagnosable psychological disorders resulting from their imprisonment (Haney 1997). Prisons do not, in general, make people "crazy." However, even researchers who are openly skeptical about whether the pains of imprisonment generally translate into psychological harm concede that, for at least some people, prison can produce negative, long-lasting change.[3] And experts generally agree that more extreme, harsh, dangerous, or otherwise psychologically taxing confinement results in more people suffering and longer-lasting damage.[4]

Rather than concentrating on the most extreme or clinically diagnosable effects of imprisonment, my focus in this chapter is on the broader and subtler psychological changes that occur in the routine course of adapting to prison life. The term "institutionalization" is used to describe the process by which inmates are shaped and transformed by the institutional environments in which they live. Sometimes called "prisonization" when it occurs in correctional settings, it is the shorthand expression for the broad, negative psychological effects of imprisonment.[5] The process has been studied extensively by sociologists, psychologists, psychiatrists, and others, and involves a unique set of psychological adaptations that typically occur—in varying degrees—in response to the extraordinary demands of prison life (Clemmer 1958; Goffman 1961; Goodstein 1979; McCorkle and Korn 1954; Peat and Winfree 1992; Thomas and Peterson 1981; Tittle 1972). In general terms, the process of prisonization involves the incorporation of the norms of prison life into one's habits of thinking, feeling, and acting.

It is important to emphasize that these changes are the result of natural and normal adaptations made by prisoners in response to the unnatural and abnormal conditions of prison life. The dysfunctionality of these adaptations is not "pathological" in a traditional sense (even though, in practical terms, they may be destructive in effect). Instead, the adaptations themselves are normal reactions to a set of pathological conditions that become problematic when they are taken to extreme lengths, or become chronic and deeply internalized so that, even though surrounding conditions may change, many of the once-functional but ultimately counterproductive patterns remain.

Like most processes of gradual change, of course, prisonization is progressive or cumulative. Thus, all other things being equal, the longer persons are incarcerated, the more significant is the nature of their institutional transformation. This is true despite variations in the ease of their apparent adjustment or adaptation to prison. When most people first enter prison, they naturally find that the experience of being forced to adapt to an often harsh and rigid institutional routine, deprived of privacy and liberty, assigned a diminished, stigmatized status, and living under extremely sparse material conditions is stressful, unpleasant, and difficult. However, in the course of becoming institutionalized, a transformation begins. Prisoners gradually become more accustomed to the wide range of restrictions, deprivations, and indignities that institutional life imposes.

The various psychological mechanisms that must be employed to adjust (and, in some harsh and dangerous correctional environments, to survive) become increasingly natural—second nature in fact—and, to a degree, internalized. To be sure, the process of institutionalization can be subtle and difficult to discern as it occurs. Thus, prisoners do not choose to succumb to it or not, and many people who become institutionalized are unaware that it has happened to them. Few of them consciously decide to allow such a transformation to take place (Irwin 1970).

Institutionalization may have more profound effects on persons who enter institutional settings at an early age—before they have formed the ability to control many of their own life choices. Thus, their institutionalization may proceed more quickly, with deeper and more long-lasting consequences. Some young inmates experience powerful psychological reactions and changes after just brief periods in institutional environments. Typically, however, the longer prisoners remain in an institution, the more likely it is that the process will significantly transform them. Inmates who are "state raised"—housed in one or another institutional setting for most of their young lives—will have passed through key developmental stages at the same time they were accommodating to institutional norms and contingencies. Therefore, the likelihood that much of the institutional structure and routine will be deeply incorporated into their identity during these formative periods is increased

(Bartollas, Miller, and Dinitz 1976; Wright 1991). Because many younger inmates lack mature identities and independent judgment when they are first institutionalized, they have little internal structure to revert to or rely upon when institutional controls are removed. Consequently, they often face more serious postprison adjustment problems.

The process of institutionalization (or prisonization) includes some or all of the following psychological adaptations.

Dependence on Institutional Structure and Contingencies

Among other things, penal institutions require inmates to relinquish the freedom and autonomy to make many of their own choices and decisions. Abandoning such self-sufficiency requires a painful adjustment that some people never fully achieve. Over time, however, many prisoners adapt to their loss of independence by moderating or relinquishing self-initiative and becoming increasingly dependent on the institutional contingencies that they once resisted. Eventually, some prisoners find it more or less natural to be denied significant control over the day-to-day decisions that affect their lives in myriad ways. In the final stages of the process, some inmates come to depend on institutional decisionmakers to make choices for them, relying on the prison's structure and schedule to organize their daily routine. In extreme cases, prisoners' decision-making capacity is significantly impaired and they lose the ability to routinely initiate their own behavior or exercise sound judgment in making their own decisions. Profoundly institutionalized persons may even become extremely uncomfortable and disoriented when and if previously cherished freedoms, autonomy, and choices are finally restored.

A slightly different aspect of this process involves prisoners developing a subtle dependency on the institution to control or limit their behavior. Correctional institutions force inmates to adapt to an elaborate network of typically very clear boundaries and rigid behavioral constraints. The consequences for violating these bright-line rules and prohibitions can be swift and severe. Continuous and increasingly sophisticated surveillance means that prisons are quick to detect and punish even minor infractions. Correctional settings surround inmates so thoroughly with *external* limits, immerse them so deeply in a network of rules and regulations, and accustom them so completely to such highly visible systems of monitoring and restraints that *internal* controls may atrophy or, in the case of especially young inmates, sometimes fail to develop altogether. Thus, institutionalization or prisonization renders some people so dependent on external constraints that they gradually cease to rely on their own self-imposed internal organization to guide their actions or restrain their conduct. If and when this external structure is taken away, severely institutionalized persons may find that they no longer know how to do things on their own, or know how to refrain from doing those things that are ultimately harmful or self-destructive.

Hypervigilance, Interpersonal Distrust, and Suspicion

Because many prisons are clearly dangerous places from which there is no exit or escape, prisoners learn quickly to become hypervigilant, always alert for signs of threat or risks to personal safety. Because the stakes are high, and because there are people nearby who are poised to exploit weakness, carelessness, or inattention, prisoners learn to become interpersonally cautious, even distrustful and suspicious. Some prisoners learn to project a tough "convict" veneer that keeps all others at a distance. Indeed, as one prison researcher put it, many prisoners "believe that unless an inmate can convincingly project an image that conveys the potential for violence, he is likely to be dominated and exploited through-out the duration of his sentence" (McCorkle 1992, 161). For many, these survival strategies develop quickly and soon become reflexive.

McCorkle's (1992) study of a maximum security Tennessee prison attempted to quantify the behavioral strategies prisoners employed to survive dangerous prison environments. He found that "fear appeared to be shaping the life-styles of many of the men," that it had led over 40 percent of prisoners to avoid certain high-risk areas of the prison, and about an equal number of inmates reported spending additional time in their cells as a precaution against victimization. At the same time, almost three-quarters of the prisoners reported that they had been forced to "get tough" with another prisoner to avoid victimization, and more than one-quarter kept a "shank" or other defensive weapon nearby. McCorkle found that age was the best predictor of the type of adaptation a prisoner took, with younger prisoners being more likely than older prisoners to employ aggressive avoidance strategies. Indeed, younger prisoners often seem particularly susceptible to the combative norms of imprisonment; many have not yet learned alternative ways of handling the threats, perceived slights, and potential conflicts that are regular aspects of prison life.

Emotional Overcontrol, Alienation, and Psychological Distancing

Frank admissions of vulnerability to other prisoners or to prison staff are potentially dangerous because they invite exploitation. As one experienced prison administrator wrote: "Prison is a barely controlled jungle where the aggressive and the strong will exploit the weak, and the weak are dreadfully aware of it" (Keve 1974, 54). However, shaping an outward image of tough invulnerability requires carefully measured emotional responses. Many prisoners struggle to control and suppress their own internal reactions to events around them; emotional overcontrol and a generalized lack of spontaneity often result. In addition, many prisoners are forced to become remarkably skilled "self-monitors" who calculate the anticipated effects of every aspect of their behavior on the rest of the prison population. They strive to make such calculations second nature.

Prisoners who labor at both an emotional and behavioral level to develop an unrevealing and impenetrable "prison mask" simultaneously risk alienation from themselves and others. Constantly hiding their feelings from others leads some prisoners to forget that they have any feelings at all. They may develop a chronic emotional flatness that debilitates their social interactions and intimate relationships. Many for whom the mask has become especially thick and effective in prison find that they have created what feels like a permanent and unbridgeable distance between themselves and other people. This alienation and social distancing is primarily a defense against exploitation. In addition, however, it is a functional adaptation to the lack of interpersonal control that characterizes prison environments and makes emotional investments in relationships unpredictable and risky. Unfortunately, the disinclination for engaging in open communication with others that prevails in prison leads some prisoners to withdraw from authentic social interactions altogether, and this extreme adaptation can be especially difficult for former prisoners to reverse once they have returned to the freeworld (Jose-Kampfner 1990; Sapsford 1978).

Social Withdrawal and Isolation

Some prisoners learn to create psychological and physical safe havens through social invisibility; they become as inconspicuous and unobtrusive as possible by disconnecting from the people and events around them. Such self-imposed social withdrawal often means that inmates retreat deeply into themselves, trust virtually no one, and adjust to prison stress by leading isolated lives of quiet desperation. Thus, Levenson (1975) found not surprisingly that prisoners who were incarcerated for longer periods and those who were punished more frequently by being placed in solitary confinement were more likely to believe that their world was controlled by "powerful others." Such beliefs are consistent with an institutional adaptation that undermines autonomy and self-initiative. In extreme cases, especially when combined with apathy and the inability to independently initiate behavior, this pattern closely resembles clinical depression. It is a psychological adaptation to which long-term prisoners especially are vulnerable. Indeed, Taylor wrote that the deteriorated, long-term prisoner "shows a flatness of response which resembles slow, automatic behavior of a very limited kind, and he is humorless and lethargic" (Taylor 1961, 374). In fact, Jose-Kampfner has analogized the plight of long-term women prisoners to that of persons who are terminally ill, whose experience of this "existential death is unfeeling, being cut off from the outside . . ." and who, therefore, "adopt this attitude because it helps them cope" (Jose-Kampfner 1990, 123).

Incorporation of Exploitative Norms of Prison Culture

Prisons are characterized by elaborate informal rules and norms that are part of the unwritten but essential culture and code that prevail inside the walls and among prisoners. Like the formal rules of the institution, these, too, must be abided. Some prisoners, eager to defend themselves against what they perceive as the constant dangers and deprivations surrounding them, embrace as many of these informal norms as possible, including those that are harsh and exploitative. Especially as the avowed goal of rehabilitation has been replaced by the ethic of punishment for punishment's sake, prisoners have been given too few meaningful options or alternative cultures in which to invest themselves. Moreover, the choice to categorically "drop out" or completely refrain or otherwise hide from the informal but dominant and sometimes domineering prisoner culture is not readily available.

Thus, the lack of meaningful programming in many institutions has deprived prisoners of prosocial or positive activities in which to engage while incarcerated. Too few are given access to gainful employment where they can obtain marketable job skills or earn adequate compensation; in many places, those who do work are assigned to menial tasks that they perform for only a few hours a day. With rare exceptions—those very few states that permit highly regulated and infrequent conjugal visits—prisoners are prohibited from sexual contact of any kind. Because many basic human needs and desires that are taken for granted in the freeworld—the need to work, to love, to recreate—are ignored or suppressed in prison, prisoners must find alternative ways of addressing them. As a result, inmates are drawn closer to—some would say compelled to participate in—an illicit culture that appears to offer the only meaningful, tolerable, or survivable way of life under conditions of extreme deprivation.

However, as noted earlier, signs of weakness or vulnerability are disfavored in prison settings, and the expression of candid emotions or intimacy discouraged. Prisoner culture strongly reinforces these norms, helping to turn them into self-fulfilling prophecies as well as survival strategies. Some prisoners embrace these expectations by promoting their own reputation for toughness, reacting quickly to seemingly insignificant insults, affronts, or signs of disrespect, sometimes with decisive (even deadly) force. In some contexts, the failure to exploit weakness is itself taken as a sign of weakness and an invitation for exploitation. In men's prisons, especially, these values and orientations promote a kind of hypermasculinity in which force and domination may be glorified as essential components of personal identity and self-respect. Finally, in an environment characterized by enforced powerlessness and social deprivation, men and women prisoners confront distorted norms of sexuality in which dominance and submission often become entangled with and mistaken for the basis of intimate relations.

Of course, persons who internalize too many of these values may experience serious difficulties in forming meaningful interpersonal relationships in the freeworld. The tough convict veneer that prevents someone from seeking appropriate help for their personal problems, or a generalized reluctance to trust others out of fear of exploitation may be necessary in prison contexts, but inappropriate and dysfunctional in others. This is equally true of the learned tendency to strike out in response to minimal provocation. Particularly in interactions with persons who have not been socialized into the norms of prisoner culture in which the maintenance of interpersonal respect and personal space is inviolate, these "normal" prison responses are seen as impulsive and even dangerous overreactions.

Even though prisoner culture has been described here as "informal," its norms are often very forcefully imposed; its effects on prisoners can be powerful and long lasting. The habits of thinking and acting that are formed as a result of such enculturation may account for as much of the prisonization process as the adaptations to the institution's formal rules, routines, and structure, and they may be at least as difficult to relinquish upon release.

Diminished Sense of Self-Worth and Personal Value

Prisoners are denied basic privacy rights and lose control over the most mundane aspects of their day-to-day existence. They live in small, sometimes extremely cramped and deteriorating spaces; the 60-square-foot cell typical of maximum-security prisons is roughly the size of a king-size bed. Prisoners who are double-celled share this space with another person, one whose identity they typically have little or no control over. Somehow they must negotiate the intimate forms of daily contact these living conditions require. Prisoners generally have no choice in when they get up or have lights out; when, what, or where they eat; whether and for how long they shower or make a phone call; and most of the other countless daily decisions that citizens in the freeworld naturally make and take for granted. Of course, prisoners feel infantalized by this loss of control. The degraded conditions under which they live serve as constant reminders of their compromised social status and their stigmatized social role as prisoners. A diminished sense of self-worth and personal value may result. In extreme cases of institutionalization, prisoners internalize the symbolic meaning of externally imposed substandard treatment and degraded circumstances. Prisoners may come to think of themselves as the kind of people who deserve no more than the degradation and stigma to which they have been subjected while incarcerated and carry this degraded sense of self with them upon release.

Posttraumatic Stress Reactions to the Pains of Imprisonment

For some prisoners, incarceration is so stark and psychologically painful that it represents a form of trauma severe enough to produce posttraumatic stress reactions in the freeworld. Ex-convicts may experience unexplained emotional reactions in response to stimuli that are psychologically reminiscent of painful events that occurred during incarceration.

They may suffer free-floating anxiety, an inability to concentrate, sleep-lessness, emotional numbing, isolation, and depression—all connected to their prison traumas. Some former prisoners may relive especially stress-ful or fear-arousing events that traumatized them during incarceration. In fact, Judith Herman has suggested that a new diagnostic category—what she has termed "complex" posttraumatic stress disorder (PTSD)—be used to describe the trauma-related syndrome that prisoners are likely to suffer in the aftermath of their incarceration because it comes about as a result of "prolonged, repeated trauma or the profound deformations of person-ality that occur in captivity" (Herman 1992, 119; 1995).

Moreover, we now understand that there are certain features common to the lives of many prisoners that may predispose them to these post-traumatic reactions. The literature on these common features has grown vast over the last several decades (e.g., Dutton and Hart 1992; Haney 1995; Huff-Corzine, Corzine, and Moore 1991; McCord 1991; Sampson and Laub 1993; Widom 1989). A "risk factors" model helps to explain the potentially powerful long-term effects of traumatic childhood events (such as poverty, abusive and neglectful mistreatment, and other forms of victimization) in the social histories of many criminal offenders. As Ann Masten and Norman Garmezy (1985) noted in the seminal article outlin-ing this model, the presence of these background risk factors and traumas in childhood increases the probability of a range of other problems later in life, including delinquency and criminality. The fact that a high percentage of persons presently incarcerated have experienced many of these child-hood traumas means, among other things, that the harsh, punitive, and often uncaring nature of prison life may represent a re-traumatization experience for many of them. Some prisoners will find exposure to the rigid and unyielding discipline of prison, the unwanted proximity to vio-lent encounters, the threat or experience of physical or sexual victimiza-tion, the need to negotiate the dominating intentions of others, and the absence of genuine respect and regard for their personal well-being in the environment around them all too familiar. Time spent in prison may rekindle not only bad memories but also the disabling psychological re-actions and consequences of these earlier damaging experiences.

Challenges in Transitioning to Postprison Life

The range of psychological consequences of institutionalization described above are not always immediately obvious once the structural and procedural imperatives that created them have been removed. The relatively few prisoners who are fortunate enough to leave prison and return to moderately structured and especially supportive environments—stable families, work, helpful forms of parole supervision, and supportive communities—may experience relatively unproblematic transitions. Those who return to difficult and stressful circumstances lacking supportive structure and services are at greater risk for postprison adjustment problems. They may be forced by social and economic disadvantage to live at the margins of society and, as a result, are more vulnerable to a host of problems, including reoffending. Often in these cases, the negative aftereffects of institutionalization first appear in the form of *internal* chaos, disorganization, stress, and fear. Because the process of institutionalization has taught most people to cover these internal states, and to mask intimate feelings or reactions that may indicate vulnerability or dysfunction, the outward appearance of normality and adjustment may hide a range of common but serious problems that many ex-convicts encounter in the freeworld.

Ex-convicts who have few close, personal contacts with caring people who know them well enough to sense that something may be wrong are especially vulnerable. Without such supportive contact, resources, or needed services, severely institutionalized persons eventually confront complicated and challenging problems, conflicts, or events that they cannot plan for in advance and for which they often lack the resiliency to navigate or overcome. Life on the streets may feel joyously free and, alternately, frighteningly chaotic and overwhelmingly burdensome. Coping mechanisms learned in prison may make daily problems worse rather than better. Prisoners who were forced to rely on the external structure and constraints of prison for their direction and balance often find their behavioral and emotional stability eroded in the freeworld. Dysfunctional and even destructive behavior may follow.

Of course, there is more to postprison success than simply learning to relinquish now-dysfunctional prison coping mechanisms and managing newfound and unfamiliar freedoms independently. Quite apart from the lasting effects of prisonization, returning prisoners face an extremely complicated transition that is rooted in the difficult life circumstances they often confront in the freeworld. These difficulties include the challenge of reconnecting with family and friends from whom they have been separated (and whose lives also may have significantly changed in their absence), the hard tasks of finding and maintaining work and affordable housing, and the need to grapple with a range of preexisting problems (such as alcohol or drug addiction) that are likely to have gone untreated in prison. Furthermore, all of these otherwise difficult issues are overlaid with the stigma of past incarceration and present ex-convict status (Homant 1984). Thus, institutionalization makes an already difficult transition from prison to home even more challenging.

Special Populations and the Pains of Prison Life

Although everyone who enters prison is subjected to the pressures of institutionalization, and prisoners adapt in various ways that incur different kinds of psychological costs, some prisoners are more vulnerable to the pains of imprisonment than others. Because of their unique problems (e.g., "special needs" prisoners with mental health or other conditions that often are inadequately addressed under current prison policies [Haney and Specter 2001]) or because of the especially harsh conditions of confinement to which they are subjected (e.g., the increasing numbers of supermax or solitary confinement prisoners [Haney 2003; Haney and Lynch 1997]), these especially vulnerable prisoners have a more significant set of obstacles and challenges to overcome as they make the transition from prison to home. The plight of several of these special populations of prisoners is discussed briefly below.

Alcohol- and Drug-Addicted Prisoners

A significant amount of research confirms what prison experts and correctional administrators have long known—a very large percentage of persons entering prison are drug or alcohol addicted (Lo and Stephens 2000). Much of that same research now underscores a major flaw in contemporary prison policy; although the nation has committed itself to addressing substance abuse problems through incarceration, it has failed to ensure that minimally adequate treatment is available to the hundreds of thousands of prisoners who need these services (Inciardi and Martin 1993; Lipton 1995; Morash, Haarr, and Rucker 1994). This policy failure affects minority communities much more significantly than it affects other communities. For example, in the federal prison system—where drug offenders now predominate—the numbers of African Americans incarcerated for drug violations are shockingly high: Fully 64 percent of male and 71 percent of female black prisoners incarcerated in federal institutions in 1995 had been sent there for drug offenses (Bureau of Justice Statistics 1996). Among state prisoners, the number of incarcerated black drug offenders increased by 707 percent between 1985 and 1995, while the number of incarcerated white drug offenders increased by 306 percent (Mumola and Beck 1997).

The pitfalls of institutionalization are especially evident among drug- and alcohol-addicted prisoners. Although it is certainly possible for prisoners to obtain drugs and alcohol in most prisons, the nature of institutional life limits their use. Obviously, nonprisoners are able to bring drugs into prisons. However, drugs are often expensive, especially in an "economy" in which most prisoners have very limited resources. In addition, prisoners are under fairly careful surveillance most of the time, have little real privacy even when they are in their cells, are subjected to unannounced searches (and in some prison systems, random drug testing), are required to be in certain places at certain specified times, and must conform to myriad prison rules and regulations that would be compromised by consistently or flagrantly impaired consciousness. Unlike the freeworld, then, significant drug or alcohol use over a long period in prison is likely to be detected and punished.

Many prisoners with serious drug or alcohol addictions report that prison is the only place where they have been able to remain clean and sober for an extended period. However, they do so by depending heavily on the institution to limit and control their behavior. Of course, in the absence of treatment, little or nothing is done to enable these prisoners to address or manage addictive behavior on their own, or even to recognize the signs or symptoms that indicate they may be at risk of resuming their substance abuse. Indeed, the untold story in recidivism statistics, data that underscore the consistently high likelihood that former prisoners will reoffend, is the frequency with which the resumption of drug and alcohol use and abuse has preceded a return to crime.

Nonetheless, high percentages of persons incarcerated for drug-related offenses are or will be returned to the communities in which their drug and alcohol addictions began and were maintained, never having been given adequate or effective treatment for their original problem. Indeed, despite the increased rate of incarceration of drug offenders, the availability of drug treatment programs has actually declined nationally. In fact, the Bureau of Justice Statistics reported that only 10 percent of state prisoners received formal substance abuse treatment in 1997, a decrease from 25 percent reported in 1991 (Bureau of Justice Statistics 2000). The strains of postprison adjustment and the lack of available community-based

treatment programs and social services for this and other potential problems increase the likelihood that recently released prisoners will turn to
drugs or alcohol as a form of self-medication and, as a result, severely
compromise their successful reintegration into society.

Mentally Ill and Developmentally Disabled Prisoners

Mental illness and developmental disability represent the largest categories of disabilities among prisoners.[6] For example, a national survey of
prison inmates conducted in 1987 indicated that although less than 1 percent suffered from visual, mobility/orthopedic, hearing, or speech
deficits, much higher percentages suffered from cognitive and psychological disabilities (Veneziano, Veneziano, and Tribolet 1987). A more
recent follow-up study obtained similar results: although less than 1 percent of the prison population suffered visual, mobility, speech, or hearing
deficits, 4.2 percent were developmentally disabled, 7.2 percent suffered
psychotic disorders, and 12 percent reported "other psychological disorders" (Veneziano and Veneziano 1996; see also Long and Sapp 1992).

In some instances, however, these estimates are based exclusively on
reports from prison staff. Because such reports may be limited by the poor
quality of the reporting itself or by flaws in the procedures used to
detect special-needs prisoners, the size of the group may be under-
stated. The situation in California provides an instructive example.[7]
Based on internal estimates of the numbers of mentally ill prisoners in
the 1970s and early 1980s, the California Department of Corrections
reassured lawmakers that their needs were being adequately addressed.
However, in the late 1980s, the state commenced one of the most sophisticated and comprehensive studies ever conducted on mental illness in
such a large state prison system. The results were unsettling. By conducting a series of face-to-face diagnostic interviews with a carefully selected
sample of California prisoners, the study determined that approximately
27 percent of California prisoners were suffering from some form of "serious mental disorder" *and* were experiencing some current symptoms
within a month of being interviewed.[8] The study's authors concluded
that "the prevalence of mental problems among California offenders is
little short of staggering" (Cotton and Associates 1989, 34).

In addition, nearly 7 percent of the California prisoner population
displayed current symptoms of one of four "severe" mental disorders
(severe organic brain syndrome, schizophrenia, major depression, or

bipolar disorder) that had gone *undetected* by the prison authorities.[9] By the time these issues were actually brought to light in federal court in the early 1990s, the California prison system had grown so large that this figure translated into an estimated 10,000 prisoners suffering from severe mental disorders that authorities had failed to identify and, presumably, for whom they had neglected to provide meaningful or adequate treatment.[10] In 1992, the outpatient clinical staff still numbered less than 20 percent of the total staff recommended by the statewide mental illness prevalence study. In fact, seven of the state's prisons—including some with as many as 5,000 prisoners—lacked a single staff psychiatrist, six had no mental health professional on staff, and 10 had less than one mental health clinician (i.e., employed only part-time staff). It is clear that there were far more mentally ill prisoners in California than state officials would have estimated or that simple inmate self-report studies were likely to reveal. It is also clear that the needs of these prisoners, many of whom were not even identified by the prison system, were being ignored or otherwise inadequately met (Specter 1994).

The same fate likely befalls developmentally disabled prisoners in many prison systems. A number of states do little or no systematic screening to determine the level of basic cognitive functioning among incoming prison inmates, so it is impossible to estimate with any degree of certainty exactly how many developmentally disabled prisoners there are in the United States. A simple extrapolation from the population at large, where 2 to 3 percent of the population is developmentally disabled, would produce an estimate of tens of thousands of developmentally disabled prisoners. But most empirical studies of the number of developmentally disabled prisoners put the figure higher, at 3 to 10 percent. Most experts agree that many of these prisoners also are undetected in the prison systems in which they are housed, which means that many of them participate in no meaningful or systematic habilitation programs in preparation for postprison life.

Again, California's experience is enlightening. Like a number of states, the California Department of Corrections until recently conducted no systematic screening for cognitive disability as prisoners were being processed into the prison system.[11] Based on the national estimates of percentages cited above, however, one would expect 3 to 10 percent of California prisoners to be developmentally disabled (i.e., between 4,800 and 16,000, based on a total of 160,000 state prisoners).[12] Yet, California corrections officials claimed that there were no more than a *handful* of developmentally disabled prisoners in their entire system. Indeed, they argued that they did not need to use special screening procedures to detect them since their developmental disabilities made them "readily identifiable." In a system where only a handful of such prisoners had been identified and were receiving appropriate habilitation services, literally thousands were being ignored. The system expected them to somehow fend for themselves in the complicated and harsh environment of prison and, presumably, in the freeworld once released.

Based on the various studies and estimates cited above,[13] it is probably safe to assume that up to 20 percent of the current prisoner population nationally suffer from either some sort of significant mental or psychological disorder or a developmental disability. However difficult the task of negotiating prison's complex social environment is for fully functioning persons, it is surely far more difficult for vulnerable mentally ill and developmentally disabled prisoners. Under the best of circumstances, prison can be a confusing and dangerous situation. For mentally ill prisoners whose defining (but often undiagnosed) disability includes difficulty maintaining close contact with reality or problems controlling and conforming their emotional and behavioral reactions, the regimented and rule-bound nature of institutional life may prove impossibly difficult. For developmentally disabled prisoners whose cognitive limitations impede their information processing, comprehension, and learning, the complex, nuanced, and "every man for himself" atmosphere of prison may present insurmountable challenges. Yet, both groups are too often left to their own devices, to somehow survive in prison and eventually leave without having had any of their unique needs addressed.

Combined with the de-emphasis on treatment that now characterizes our nation's correctional facilities, these behavior patterns can significantly impact the institutional history of vulnerable or special-needs inmates. One commentator has described the vicious cycle into which mentally ill and developmentally disabled prisoners can fall:

> The lack of mental health care for the seriously mentally ill who end up in segregation units has worsened the condition of many prisoners incapable of understanding their condition. This is especially true in cases where prisoners are placed in levels of mental health care that are not intense enough, and begin to refuse [to take] their medication. They then enter a vicious cycle in which their mental disease takes over, often causing hostile and aggressive behavior to the point that they break prison rules and end up in segregation units as management problems. Once in punitive housing, this regression can go undetected for considerable periods of time before they again receive more closely monitored mental health care. This cycle can, and often does, repeat (Streeter 1998, 167).

Of course, prison systems that fail to detect or to provide adequate services for these special needs prisoners while they are incarcerated are unlikely to properly prepare them for the transition from prison to home. They are also unlikely to ensure that appropriate community agencies are notified about returning special-needs prisoners so that meaningful treatment plans and social and other services can be provided to facilitate their reintegration and freeworld adjustment.[14]

Prisoners in Supermax or Solitary Confinement

An increasing number of prisoners are subjected to the unique and potentially more destructive experience of punitive isolation in so-called "supermax" facilities where they are kept under conditions of unprecedented social deprivation for unparalleled lengths of time. This kind of confinement creates its own set of psychological pressures that, in some instances, can uniquely disable prisoners for freeworld reintegration (Haney 2003; Haney and Lynch 1997). Indeed, there are few if any forms of imprisonment that produce so many indices of psychological trauma and symptoms of psychopathology. Published studies document a range of negative psychological consequences from long-term, solitary-like confinement, including an impaired sense of identity; hypersensitivity to stimuli; cognitive dysfunction (confusion, memory loss, ruminations); irritability, anger, aggression, and/or rage; other-directed violence, such as stabbings, attacks on staff, property destruction, and collective violence; lethargy, helplessness, and hopelessness; chronic depression; self-mutilation and/or suicidal ideation, impulses, and behavior; anxiety and panic attacks; emotional breakdowns and/or loss of control; hallucinations, psychosis, and/or paranoia; and overall deterioration of mental and physical health (Haney 2003; Haney and Lynch 1997).

Human Rights Watch (2000) has estimated that there are approximately 20,000 prisoners confined to supermax-type units in the United States. Most experts agree that the number of such units is increasing. Although solitary or supermax confinement is not meted out as part of court-ordered sentences in the United States, corrections departments are using it with increasing frequency as a management tool that may result in very long term isolation. In fact, in many states, the majority of prisoners in these units are serving indeterminate solitary confinement terms, which means that their entire prison sentence will be served in isolation (unless they "debrief" by providing incriminating information about other prisoners). Unfortunately, few states provide meaningful or effective "decompression" programs for prisoners who leave these units. In other words, many prisoners who have experienced these extreme conditions of confinement—some for considerable periods—are released directly into the community. Not only do most prisons systems fail to prepare these prisoners for the transition from (supermax) prison to home, but they also fail to arrange for special support services or postrelease programs designed to address and ameliorate the lasting psychological consequences resulting from this traumatic form of incarceration.

Implications for the Transition from Prison to Home

The psychological consequences of incarceration represent significant impediments to postprison adjustment. These effects may interfere with the prisoner's transition from prison to home, impede an ex-convict's successful reintegration into a social network and employment setting, and compromise a formerly incarcerated parent's ability to resume his or her role with family and children. These consequences include the sometimes subtle but nonetheless broad-based and potentially disabling effects of institutionalization or prisonization—dependence on institutional structure and contingencies, hypervigilance, interpersonal distrust and suspicion, emotional overcontrol, alienation, psychological distancing, social withdrawal and isolation, the incorporation of exploitative norms of prisoner culture, and a diminished sense of self-worth and personal value. In addition, some prisoners will suffer posttraumatic stress reactions to the pains of imprisonment, and others will continue to grapple with the persistent effects of untreated or exacerbated mental illness, the long-term legacies of developmental disabilities that were improperly addressed, or the pathological consequences of supermax confinement.

There is little evidence that prison systems across the country have responded in a meaningful way to these psychological issues, either in the course of confinement or at the time of release. Indeed, they do little to provide prisoners with insight into the ways in which the prison experience may change them, to ameliorate the potentially harmful psychological consequences, or to effectively address such consequences once they emerge. Over the next decade, the impact of unprecedented levels of incarceration will be felt in many American communities as unprecedented numbers of ex-convicts complete their sentences and return home.

Among other things, these communities will be expected to absorb and address the high level of psychological trauma and untreated disorders that a number of former prisoners will bring with them.

The implications of the psychological consequences of imprisonment for parenting and family life are significant. Parents who return from periods of incarceration still dependent on institutional structures and routines cannot be expected to easily organize the lives of their children or exercise the initiative and autonomous decisionmaking that parenting requires. Those who still suffer the negative effects of a distrusting and hypervigilant adaptation to prison life may find it difficult to promote trust and authenticity within their children. Those who remain emotionally overcontrolled and alienated from others may experience problems being psychologically available and nurturant. Tendencies to socially withdraw, remain aloof, or seek social invisibility are more dysfunctional in family settings where closeness and interdependency are needed. Ex-convicts who continue to embrace many of the most negative aspects of exploitative prisoner culture or find themselves unable to overcome the diminished sense of self-worth that prison too often instills may find many of their social and intimate relationships significantly compromised.

Clearly, the residual effects of the posttraumatic stress of imprisonment and the re-traumatization experiences that prison life may inflict can jeopardize the mental health of persons attempting to reintegrate into the freeworld communities from which they came. Indeed, there is evidence that not only may incarcerated parents themselves continue to be adversely affected by the traumatizing risk factors to which they have been exposed, but also that the experience of imprisonment has done little or nothing to provide them with the tools to safeguard their children from many of the same potentially destructive experiences (Greene, Haney, and Hurtado 2000).

The excessive *and* racially disproportionate use of imprisonment over the last several decades means that the significant problem of postprison adjustment will be concentrated in certain communities whose residents were selectively targeted for criminal justice system intervention. Thus, our society is about to absorb the consequences not only of the "rage to punish" (Forer 1994) that was so fully indulged in the last quarter of the 20th century, but also of the "malign neglect" (Tonry 1995) that led us to concentrate this rage so heavily on African-American men and women. Remarkably, as the present decade began, the number of young black men (age 20–29) under the control of the nation's criminal justice system (including probation and parole supervision) was greater than the total number in college (Mauer 1992).[15] Indeed, the negative psychological consequences of imprisonment and their adverse effects on prisoner reintegration will be felt in unprecedented ways in African-American communities and families. Not surprisingly, then, one scholar has concluded that "crime control policies are a major contributor to the disruption of the family [and] the prevalence of single parent families" (Chambliss 1994, 183). Like so many burdens in this society, this one, too, has been visited disproportionately on African-American parents and their children (King 1993).

Policy and Programmatic Responses to the Adverse Effects of Incarceration

An intelligent, humane response to the implications of what is known about the adverse psychological effects of imprisonment must occur on at least two levels. We must simultaneously address the prison policies and conditions of confinement that have created or worsened many of these problems, and at the same time make psychological and social services available to ex-convicts and families who are grappling with their problematic consequences. Both things must occur if the successful transition from prison to home is to occur on a consistent and widespread basis. In order to address these two levels of concern, policy interventions must be concentrated in three areas: prison conditions, policies, and procedures; transitional services; and community-based services.

Prison Conditions, Policies, and Procedures

No significant amount of progress can be made in easing the transition from prison to home until and unless significant changes are made in the normative structure of American prisons. Specifically:

- The goal of penal harm must give way to a clear emphasis on prisoner-oriented rehabilitative services.
- The adverse effects of institutionalization must be minimized by structuring the routines of prison life to replicate, as much as security constraints permit, life in the world outside prison.
- Prisons that provide pockets of freedom and give inmates opportunities to exercise real autonomy and personal initiative must be created.

- Safe correctional environments that remove the need for hypervigilance and pervasive distrust, where prisoners can establish authentic selves and learn the norms of interdependence and cooperative trust, must be maintained.
- A clear and consistent emphasis on maximizing visitation and supporting contact with the outside world must be implemented, both to minimize the distinction between prison and freeworld norms and to discourage dysfunctional social withdrawal that is difficult to reverse upon release.
- Program-rich institutions must be established that give prisoners meaningful activities in which to participate and goals in which to invest as genuine alternatives to the most exploitative aspects of the prisoner culture. Such programs also enhance self-esteem, empowering prisoners to transcend the degraded, stigmatized status in which they have been placed. Prisoners must be given opportunities to engage in positive things that allow them to grow as people, including opportunities to work and to love while incarcerated.
- Adequate therapeutic and habilitative resources must be provided to address the needs of the many addicted, mentally ill, and developmentally disabled persons now incarcerated.
- Trends toward increased use of supermax and other forms of extremely harsh and psychologically damaging confinement must be reversed. Strict time limits must be placed on the use of punitive isolation, time limits that approximate the much briefer periods of such confinement that once characterized American corrections. In addition, prisoners must be screened for special vulnerability to isolation, and carefully monitored so that they can be removed upon the first sign of adverse reactions.

Transitional Services to Prepare Prisoners for Community Release

No significant amount of progress can be made in easing the transition from prison to home until and unless significant changes are made in the way prisoners are prepared to leave prison and reenter the freeworld communities from which they came. Specifically:

- Prison systems must begin to take the pains of imprisonment and the nature of institutionalization seriously and provide all prisoners with effective decompression programs in which they are re-acclimated to the nature and norms of the freeworld.

- Prisoners must be given some insight into the changes brought about by their forced adaptation to prison life. They must be given some understanding of the ways in which prison may have changed them and then given the tools to help them respond to the challenge of adjusting to the freeworld.

- The reentry process must begin well in advance of a prisoner's release, and take into account all aspects of the transition he or she will be expected to make. This means, among other things, that all prisoners will need occupational and vocational training and pre-release assistance in finding gainful employment. It also means that prisoners who are expected to resume their roles as parents will need access to prerelease assistance in establishing, strengthening, and/or maintaining ties with their families and children, and whatever other assistance they feel they need to function effectively in this role (such as parenting classes and the like).

- Prisoners who have manifested signs or symptoms of mental illness or developmental disability while incarcerated will need specialized transitional services to facilitate their reintegration into the freeworld. These should include, where appropriate, prerelease outpatient treatment and habilitation plans.

- No prisoner should be released directly out of supermax or solitary confinement back into the freeworld. Supermax prisons must provide long periods of decompression, with adequate time for prisoners to be treated for the adverse effects of long-term isolation and to reacquaint themselves with the social norms of the world to which they will return.

- As with all effective forms of education, counseling, and therapy, these programs should not be implemented as part of a punitive regime in which prisoner participation is compelled or coerced, or structured in such a way that they become a justification for denying freedoms or delaying scheduled releases.

Community-Based Services to Facilitate and Maintain Reintegration

No significant amount of progress can be made in easing the transition from prison to home until and unless significant changes are made in the way ex-convicts are treated in the communities from which they came. Specifically:

- In the wake of decades of overincarceration, with little thought given to long-term consequences, the nation now must clearly recognize that individuals who return home from prison face significant personal, social, and structural challenges for which they have neither the ability nor the resources to overcome entirely on their own. Postrelease success often depends heavily on the nature and quality of services and support available in the community. Yet, this issue typically receives the least amount of societal attention and resources. This tendency must be reversed.
- Gainful employment is perhaps the most critical aspect of post-prison adjustment. Overcoming the stigma of incarceration and the psychological residue of institutionalization requires active and prolonged agency intervention. Job training, employment counseling, and employment placement programs all must be seen as essential parts of an effective reintegration plan.
- A broadly conceived, family systems approach to counseling for ex-convicts and their families and children must be made available to those who need and want it. Rather than traditional models of psychotherapy, this approach would make the long-term problematic consequences of "normal" adaptations to prison life and their implications for postprison adjustment the focus of discussion.
- Parole and probation services and agencies need to return to their original role of assisting with reintegration. Here, too, the complexity of the transition from prison to home needs to be fully appreciated, and parole revocation should only occur after every possible, relevant community-based resource has been tapped and all feasible alternative approaches have been attempted.

An Essential Challenge That Must Be Met

We now face numerous critically important problems that stem from the institutionalization and prisonization of massive numbers of persons who are now or will soon be returning to free society. The pains of imprisonment have always been severe, but they have gotten decidedly more severe for many more people over the past three decades. Although certainly not everyone who goes to prison is damaged by the experience, we know that prison can hurt people in significant ways and that some people are hurt more than others. Very few prison programs even acknowledge the psychological risks of incarceration, and fewer still are designed to address or ameliorate the negative effects of imprisonment and the long-term problems these effects may produce.

Normal adaptations to the atypical and abnormal nature of prison life create many problematic ways of thinking, feeling, and acting. These adaptations are natural, inevitable, and forced on prisoners by the very circumstances under which they live. Former prisoners do not easily relinquish these patterns once they have been released from prison. But no program that we might fashion to ease the transition from prison to home or to minimize the negative impact of imprisonment on the families and children of the incarcerated can succeed without taking into account the nature and consequences of institutionalization.

Although none of these problems is insurmountable or intractable, the scope and magnitude of the task—and, therefore, the resistance that will be encountered in some quarters if a serious attempt is made to complete it—should not be underestimated. We *do* have ways of minimizing these negative psychological changes in the first place and ways of helping people to overcome them even after they have taken place. As I have suggested, no significant amount of progress can be made in easing the transition from prison to home until and unless significant changes are made in the normative structure of prison life in the United States and the normative policies by which we have come to drastically overuse incarceration as a strategy of crime control.

Beyond that difficult but important policy change, clear recognition and legitimacy must be given to the proposition that persons who return home from prison face significant personal, social, and structural challenges that many are unable to overcome entirely on their own. In part because of what they experience during incarceration, and in part because of the unique social and structural burdens they must shoulder once released, the postrelease success of formerly incarcerated persons is always in jeopardy. This success broadly depends on the nature and quality of the services and support available to former prisoners in the communities to which they return.

NOTES

1. These rates include persons incarcerated in local jails. When jail inmates are excluded from the calculations, and only prisoner data are reported, the incarceration rate is lower. In terms of historical change, the rate of incarceration of prisoners was relatively stable between 1925 and 1975, remaining at around 105 prisoners per 100,000 persons in the population through this 50-year period. Between 1975 and 1995, however, it quadrupled to 411 per 100,000. See Maguire and Pastore (1997).

2. In California, for example, see *Dohner v. McCarthy* [United States District Court, Central District of California, 1984–1985; 635 F. Supp. 408 (C.D. Cal. 1985)] (examining the effects of overcrowded conditions in the California Men's Colony); *Coleman v. Wilson,* 912 F. Supp. 1282 (N.D. Cal. 1995) (challenge to grossly inadequate mental health services throughout the state prison system). In Texas, see the long-lasting *Ruiz* litigation in which the federal court has monitored and attempted to correct unconstitutional conditions of confinement throughout the state's sprawling prison system for more than 20 years. Current conditions and the most recent status of the litigation are described in *Ruiz v. Johnson* [United States District Court, Southern District of Texas, 37 F. Supp. 2d 855 (S.D. Texas 1999)].

These two states were not unique. According to the American Civil Liberties Union's National Prison Project, in 1995 there were fully 33 jurisdictions in the United States under court order to reduce overcrowding or improve general conditions in at least one of their major prison facilities. Nine were operating under court orders that covered their entire prison system (National Prison Project 1995).

3. One of the most skeptical reviews of the effects of prison can be found in Bonta and Gendreau (1990). However, even these authors concede the following: "physiological and psychological stress responses . . . were very likely [to occur] under crowded prison conditions"; "when threats to health come from suicide and self-mutilation, then inmates are clearly at risk"; "in Canadian penitentiaries, the homicide rates are close to 20 times that of similar-aged males in Canadian society"; "a variety of health problems, injuries, and selected symptoms of psychological distress were higher for certain classes of inmates than probationers, parolees, and, where data existed, for the general population"; studies show long-term incarceration to result in "increases in hostility and social introversion . . . and decreases in self-evaluation and evaluations of work"; imprisonment produced "increases in dependency upon staff for direction and social introversion," a tendency for prisoners to prefer "to cope with their sentences on their own rather than seek the aid of others," "deteriorating community relationships over time," and "unique difficulties" with "family separation issues and vocational skill training needs"; and some researchers have speculated that "inmates typically undergo a 'behavioral deep freeze'" such that "outside-world behaviors that led the offender into trouble prior to imprisonment remain until release" (Bonta and Gendreau 1990, 353–59).

4. Again, precisely because they represent themselves as highly skeptical about whether the pains of imprisonment have very many significant negative effects on prisoners, Bonta and Gendreau are worth quoting. They concede that there are "signs of pathology for inmates incarcerated in solitary for periods up to a year"; anxiety levels in inmates are higher after eight weeks in jail than they are after one week; increases in psychopathological symptoms occur after 72 hours of confinement; and death row prisoners

have been found to have "symptoms ranging from paranoia to insomnia," "increased feelings of depression and hopelessness," and feel "powerlessness, fearful of their surroundings, and . . . emotionally drained" (Bonta and Gendreau 1990, 361–62).

5. A distinction is sometimes made in the literature between institutionalization—psychological changes that produce more conforming and institutionally "appropriate" thoughts and actions—and prisonization—changes that create a more oppositional and institutionally subversive stance or perspective. I use both terms more or less interchangeably here to denote the totality of the negative transformation that may take place before prisoners are released back into free society.

6. These two categories of special-needs prisoners are discussed together simply because they constitute the two largest disability groups. Obviously, they differ in many important respects.

7. I refer often to California not only because, as my home state, I am most familiar with its prison system, but also because of its sheer size—what happens in California by definition affects a large number of people. In addition, its historical reputation as a state in which corrections-related issues were once taken seriously, funded reasonably well, and approached for the most part with a modern and humane perspective makes it something of a correctional bellwether. If chronic and egregious problems exist in California, it is reasonable to assume that they are relatively widespread in prison systems across the United States.

8. Specifically, these were prisoners who "at the survey point experienced at least some identifiable symptoms from a disorder that was once sufficiently severe to meet full DSM criteria" (Cotton and Associates 1989, 34).

9. "Undetected" was defined as suffering from one of the four major mental illnesses but not having been placed in any of the prison system's psychiatric classification categories. It was unclear exactly why there were so many undetected mentally ill prisoners in the California system. However, the authors of the study concluded generally that "the prevalence findings suggest an estimated 60 percent of the prison population have not been screened, identified, and/or treated" (Cotton and Associates 1989, 107), and that "it is clear that intensified screening efforts would be likely to uncover a very large number of disordered individuals in the general institutions" (Cotton and Associates 1989, 13).

10. The mere fact that prisoners had been identified or detected by prison authorities as suffering from mental disorders did not mean that their problems were being handled appropriately. In fact, despite their psychiatric classification status, fully 64 percent of the *identified* group reported that they had not received mental health professional services at *any* time during their present incarceration.

11. The change in policy and sudden willingness to commence such screening occurred in response to the threat of litigation. See Haney and Specter (2001).

12. Using the only California-specific empirical data to appear anywhere in the literature—Brown and Courtless's (1971) albeit dated figure of 5.4 percent of California prisoners—would lead to a present-day estimate of more than 8,600 mentally retarded prisoners, far more than the handful estimated by prison officials and certainly more than the very small number who had been placed in the appropriate prison habilitation programs.

13. For example, according to a Department of Justice census of correctional facilities across the country, there were approximately 200,000 mentally ill prisoners in the

United States in midyear 2000. This represented approximately 16 percent of prisoners nationwide. See Bureau of Justice Statistics (2001).

14. Some scholars have made the reasonable argument that the high number of special-needs prisoners in the criminal justice system can be attributed to the deinstitutionalization movement of the 1970s and the reduction in community treatment resources and social services that continued throughout much of the 1980s and 1990s. In past times, people with mental health problems, especially, would have been handled through other means. Now they are likely to find themselves being processed by the criminal justice system and incarcerated. In light of this, many commentators have emphasized the importance of making increased treatment services available to persons being released from prison. For example, see Lurigio (2001).

15. A detailed discussion of this issue is beyond the scope of this chapter. However, note that in the mid-1990s, the rate of incarceration of African-American men approached 7,000 per 100,000, over seven times the rate for white men and far higher than the rate of incarceration for blacks in South Africa (Bureau of Justice Statistics 1997).

REFERENCES

Bartollas, Clemens, Stuart Miller, and Simon Dinitz. 1976. *Juvenile Victimization: The Institutional Paradox.* New York: Halsted.

Bonta, James, and Paul Gendreau. 1990. "Reexamining the Cruel and Unusual Punishment of Prison Life." *Law and Human Behavior* 14: 347–72.

Brown, Bertram, and Thomas Courtless. 1971. *The Mentally Retarded Offender.* DHEW Pub. No. (HSM) 72-90-39. Washington, D.C.: U.S. Government Printing Office.

Bureau of Justice Statistics. 1996. *Sourcebook of Criminal Justice Statistics, 1996.* Washington, D.C.: U.S. Department of Justice.

———. 1997. *Correctional Populations in the United States, 1995.* Washington, D.C.: U.S. Department of Justice.

———. 2000. *Correctional Populations in the United States, 1997.* Washington, D.C.: U.S. Department of Justice.

———. 2001. *Mental Health Treatment in State Prisons, 2000.* Washington, D.C.: U.S. Department of Justice.

California Department of Corrections. 2002. *Historical Trends, 1981–2001.* Sacramento: Author.

Chambliss, William. 1994. "Policing the Ghetto Underclass: The Politics of Law and Law Enforcement." *Social Problems* 41: 177–94.

Clemmer, Donald. 1958. *The Prison Community.* New York: Rinehart.

Cotton, Norman, and Associates. 1989. *Current Description, Evaluation, and Recommendations for Treatment of Mentally Disordered Offenders.* San Rafael, Calif.: Author.

Cullen, Francis. 1995. "Assessing the Penal Harm Movement." *Journal of Research in Crime and Delinquency* 32: 338–58.

Dutton, Donald G., and Stephen D. Hart. 1992. "Evidence for Long-Term, Specific Effects of Childhood Abuse and Neglect on Criminal Behavior in Men." *International Journal of Offender Therapy and Comparative Criminology* 36 (2): 129–37.

Ekland-Olson, Sheldon, William R. Kelly, and Michael Eisenberg. 1992. "Crime and Incarceration: Some Comparative Findings from the 1980s." *Crime and Delinquency* 38 (3): 392–416.

Forer, Lois. 1994. *A Rage to Punish: The Unintended Consequences of Mandatory Sentencing.* New York: W.W. Norton.

Goffman, Erving. 1961. *Asylums: Essays on the Social Situation of Mental Patients and Other Inmates.* New York: Anchor.

Goodstein, Lynne. 1979. "Inmate Adjustment to Prison and the Transition to Community Life." *Journal of Research on Crime and Delinquency* 16: 246–72.

Greene, Susan, Craig Haney, and Aida Hurtado. 2000. "Cycles of Pain: Risk Factors in the Lives of Incarcerated Women and Their Children." *Prison Journal* 80: 3–23.

Haney, Craig. 1995. "The Social Context of Capital Murder: Social Histories and the Logic of Capital Mitigation." *Santa Clara Law Review* 35: 547–609.

———. 1997. "Psychology and the Limits to Prison Pain: Confronting the Coming Crisis in Eighth Amendment Law." *Psychology, Public Policy, and Law* 3: 499–588.

———. 1998. "Riding the Punishment Wave: On the Origins of Our Devolving Standards of Decency." *Hastings Women's Law Journal* 9: 27–78.

———. 2003. "Mental Health Issues in Solitary and 'Supermax' Confinement." *Crime and Delinquency* 49: 144–76.

Haney, Craig, and Mona Lynch. 1997. "Regulating Prisons of the Future: A Psychological Analysis of Supermax and Solitary Confinement." *New York University Review of Law and Social Change* 23: 477–570.

Haney, Craig, and Donald Specter. 2001. "Vulnerable Offenders and the Law: Treatment Rights in Uncertain Legal Times." In *Treating Adult and Juvenile Offenders with Special Needs,* edited by Jose Ashford, Bruce Sales, and William Reid (51–79). Washington, D.C.: American Psychological Association.

Haney, Craig, and Philip Zimbardo. 1998. "The Past and Future of U.S. Prison Policy: Twenty-Five Years after the Stanford Prison Experiment." *American Psychologist* 53: 709–27.

Harrison, Paige, and Allen Beck. 2002. "Bureau of Justice Statistics Bulletin: Prisoners in 2001." NJC 195189. Washington, D.C.: U.S. Department of Justice.

Herman, Judith. 1992. "A New Diagnosis." In *Trauma and Recovery,* edited by Judith Herman (115–32). New York: Basic Books.

———. 1995. "Complex PTSD: A Syndrome in Survivors of Prolonged and Repeated Trauma." In *Psychotraumatology: Key Papers and Core Concepts in Post-Traumatic Stress,* edited by George S. Everly Jr. and Jeffrey M. Lating (87–100). New York: Plenum.

Homant, Robert. 1984. "Employment of Ex-Offenders: The Role of Prisonization and Self-Esteem." *Journal of Offender Counseling, Services, and Rehabilitation* 8: 5–23.

Huff-Corzine, Lin, Jay Corzine, and David C. Moore. 1991. "Deadly Connections: Culture, Poverty, and the Direction of Lethal Violence." *Social Forces* 69 (3): 715–32.

Human Rights Watch. 2000. "Out of Sight: Super-Maximum Security Confinement in the United States." *Human Rights Watch* 12 (1): 1–9.

Inciardi, James, and Steven Martin. 1993. "Drug Abuse Treatment in Criminal Justice Settings." *Journal of Drug Issues* 23: 1–6.

Irwin, John. 1970. *The Felon.* Englewood Cliffs, N.J.: Prentice-Hall.

Jose-Kampfner, Christina. 1990. "Coming to Terms with Existential Death: An Analysis of Women's Adaptation to Life in Prison." *Social Justice* 17 (2): 110–24.

Keve, Paul. 1974. *Prison Life and Human Worth.* Minneapolis: University of Minnesota Press.

King, Anthony. 1993. "The Impact of Incarceration on African American Families: Implications for Practice." *Families in Society: The Journal of Contemporary Human Services* 74: 145–53.

Levenson, Hannah. 1975. "Multidimensional Locus of Control in Prison Inmates." *Journal of Applied Social Psychology* 5: 342–47.

Lipton, Douglas. 1995. "The Effectiveness of Treatment for Drugs Abusers under Criminal Justice Supervision." *NIJ Research Report.* Washington, D.C.: U.S. Department of Justice.

Lo, Celia, and Richard Stephens. 2000. "Drugs and Prisoners: Treatment Needs on Entering Prison." *American Journal of Drug and Alcohol Abuse* 26: 229–45.

Long, Lydia M., and Allen D. Sapp. 1992. "Programs and Facilities for Physically Disabled Inmates in State Prisons." *Journal of Offender Rehabilitation* 18 (1, 2): 191–204.

Lurigio, Arthur. 2001. "Effective Services for Parolees with Mental Illnesses." *Crime and Delinquency* 47 (3): 446–61.

Maguire, Kathleen, and Ann Pastore. 1997. *Sourcebook of Criminal Justice Statistics, 1996.* NCJ 165361. Washington, D.C.: U.S. Department of Justice.

Masten, Ann, and Norman Garmezy. 1985. "Risk, Vulnerability and Protective Factors in Developmental Psychopathology." In *Advances in Clinical Child Psychology,* edited by Benjamin Lahey and Alan Kazdin (1–52). New York: Plenum.

Mauer, Marc. 1992. "Americans Behind Bars: A Comparison of International Rates of Incarceration." In *Cages of Steel: The Politics of Imprisonment in the United States,* edited by Ward Churchill and James J. Vander Wall (22–37). Washington, D.C.: Maisonneuve Press.

———. 1995. "The International Use of Incarceration." *Prison Journal* 75: 113–23.

McCord, Joan. 1991. "The Cycle of Crime and Socialization Practices." *Journal of Criminal Law and Criminology* 82: 211–28.

McCorkle, Lloyd, and Richard Korn. 1954. "Re-socialization within Walls." *Annals of the American Academy of Political Science* 293: 88–98.

McCorkle, Richard. 1992. "Personal Precautions to Violence in Prison." *Criminal Justice and Behavior* 19: 160–73.

Morash, Merry, Robin N. Haarr, and Lila Rucker. 1994. "A Comparison of Programming for Women and Men in U.S. Prison in the 1980s." *Crime and Delinquency* 40 (2): 197–221.

Mumola, Christopher, and Allen Beck. 1997. *Prisoners in 1996.* Washington, D.C.: U.S. Department of Justice, Bureau of Justice Statistics.

National Prison Project. 1995. *Status Report: State Prisons and the Courts.* Washington, D.C.: American Civil Liberties Union.

Peat, Barbara, and Thomas Winfree. 1992. "Reducing the Intra-Institutional Effects of 'Prisonization': A Study of a Therapeutic Community for Drug-Using Inmates." *Criminal Justice and Behavior* 19: 206–25.

Petersilia, Joan. 1992. "California's Prison Policy: Causes, Costs, and Consequences." *The Prison Journal* 72: 8–36.

Sampson, Robert, and John Laub. 1993. *Crime in the Making: Pathways and Turning Points through Life.* Cambridge, Mass.: Harvard University Press.

Sapsford, Roger. 1978. "Life Sentence Prisoners: Psychological Changes during Sentence." *British Journal of Criminology* 18: 128–45.

Specter, Donald. 1994. "Cruel and Unusual Punishment of the Mentally Ill in California's Prison System: A Case Study of a Class Action Suit." *Social Justice* 21: 109–16.

Streeter, Patricia A. 1998. "Incarceration of the Mentally Ill: Treatment or Warehousing?" *Michigan Bar Journal* 77: 167.

Sykes, Gresham. 1958. *The Society of Captives: A Study of a Maximum Security Prison.* Princeton, N.J.: Princeton University Press.

Taylor, A. J. W. 1961. "Social Isolation and Imprisonment." *Psychiatry* 24: 373–76.

Texas Department of Criminal Justice (TDCJ). 1997. "Report on TDCJ Offender Bed Management." Huntsville: TDCJ Internal Audit.

Thomas, Charles W., and David M. Peterson. 1981. "A Comparative Organizational Analysis of Prisonization." *Criminal Justice Review* 6: 36–43.

Tittle, Charles. 1972. "Institutional Living and Self Esteem." *Social Problems* 20: 65–77.

Tonry, Michael. 1995. *Malign Neglect: Race, Crime, and Punishment in America.* New York: Oxford University Press.

Travis, Jeremy, and Sarah Lawrence. 2002. "California's Parole Experiment." *California Journal* (August): 2–7.

Veneziano, Louis, and Carol Veneziano. 1996. "Disabled Inmates." In *Encyclopedia of American Prisons,* edited by Marilyn McShane and Frank Williams (157–61). New York: Garland.

Veneziano, Louis, Carol Veneziano, and Charles Tribolet. 1987. "The Special Needs of Prison Inmates with Handicaps: An Assessment." *Journal of Offender Counseling, Services and Rehabilitation* 12: 61–72.

Widom, Cathy. 1989. "The Cycle of Violence." *Science* 244: 160–66.

Wright, Kevin. 1991. "The Violent and Victimized in a Male Prison." *Journal of Offender Rehabilitation* 16: 1–25.

Zalman, Martin. 1987. "Sentencing in a Free Society: The Failure of the President's Crime Commission to Influence Sentencing Policy." *Justice Quarterly* 4: 545–69.

3

A Woman's Journey Home
Challenges for Female Offenders

Stephanie S. Covington

O
ver the past 25 years, our knowledge and understanding of women's lives have increased dramatically—in part because of the influence of the women's movement. New information has impacted and improved services for women, particularly in the areas of health, education, employment, mental health, substance abuse, and trauma treatment. At present, however, both a need and an opportunity exist to bring knowledge from other fields into the criminal justice system to develop effective programs for women. Until recently, theory and research on criminality focused on crimes perpetrated by men, with male offenders viewed as the norm. Historically, correctional programming for women has thus been based on profiles of male criminality or paths to crime. However, the policies, services, and programs that focus on the overwhelming number of men in the corrections system often fail to identify gender- and culturally responsive options for women's specific needs. While men and women face some similar challenges upon returning to the community, the intensity, multiplicity, and specificity of their needs, and the most effective ways for addressing those needs, are very different.

Profile of Women in the Criminal Justice System

Clinical work seeks to know who the client is and what she brings into the treatment setting. As such, in order to design systemwide services that match women's specific strengths and needs, it is important to consider the demographics and history of the female offender population, and how various life factors impact women's patterns of offending.

In recent decades, the number of women under criminal justice supervision has increased dramatically. Although the rate of incarceration for women continues to be far lower than the rate for men (51 of every 100,000 women vs. 819 of every 100,000 men), since 1980 the number of women imprisoned in the United States has increased at a rate nearly double the rate for men (Greenfeld and Snell 1999). In 2000, there were 162,026 women incarcerated in jails and prisons across the country (Beck and Karberg 2001).

However, most female offenders are under community supervision. In 2000, 844,697 women were on probation, representing 22 percent of all probationers (up from 18 percent in 1990); 87,063 women were on parole, representing 12 percent of all parolees (up from 8 percent in 1990) (Bureau of Justice Statistics 2002).

Women are arrested and incarcerated primarily for property and drug offenses. A recent study conducted by the Bureau of Justice Statistics indicates that drug offenses represented the largest share of growth in the number of female offenders (38 percent, compared with 17 percent for males) (Greenfeld and Snell 1999). Between 1995 and 1996, female drug arrests increased by 95 percent, while male drug arrests increased by 55 percent. In 1979, approximately 1 in 10 women in U.S. prisons was serving a sentence for a drug conviction; by 1999, however, this figure had grown to approximately 1 in 3 women (Beck 2000).

While the rate of female incarceration has risen, there has not been a corresponding rise in violent crime among female offenders. In fact, the proportion of women imprisoned for violent crimes continues to decrease as the proportion of women incarcerated for drug offenses increases. The women in state prisons in 1998 represented 14 percent of all violent offenders (Greenfeld and Snell 1999). Many of the violent crimes committed by women are against a spouse, ex-spouse, or partner; women often report having been physically and/or sexually abused by the person they assaulted.

The increased incarceration of women appears to be the outcome of forces that have shaped U.S. crime policy over the past two decades: government policies prescribing simplistic, punitive enforcement responses for complex social problems; federal and state mandatory sentencing laws; and the public's fear of crime (even though crime in this country has been on the decline for nearly a decade). Included in these forces are the war on drugs and the shift in legal and academic realms toward a view of lawbreaking behavior as individual pathology, a view that discounts the structural and social causes of crime.

Most women in the criminal justice system are poor, undereducated, and unskilled, and they are disproportionately women of color. Many come from impoverished urban environments and were raised by single mothers or in foster homes. Women are more likely than men to have committed crimes to obtain money to purchase drugs. Although it is widely assumed that female addicts typically engage in prostitution as a way to support a drug habit, it is more common for these addicts to engage in property crimes (Sanchez and Johnson 1987).

Important documented differences exist between female and male drug offenders, differences with implications for their incarceration, treatment, and reentry. A recent study of 4,509 women and 3,595 men in 15 prison-based drug treatment programs found that drug-dependent women and men differ with regard to employment histories, substance abuse problems, criminal involvement, psychological functioning, and sexual and physical abuse histories (Messina, Burdon, and Prendergast 2001). Cocaine/crack was the most prevalent drug problem reported by women, while methamphetamine use was a more prevalent problem among men. While men had more severe criminal histories, many men and women reported that their last offense was drug related. Women had more severe substance abuse histories (e.g., more frequent usage, intravenous drug use). Women reported more co-occurring psychiatric disorders and were more likely to use prescribed medications. They also reported lower self-esteem and more extensive sexual and physical abuse histories. Although income levels for both sexes were, for the most part, below the federal poverty level, the women reported earning only half as much as the men reported earning.

The Importance of Acknowledging Gender

To create appropriate services and treatment for women in the criminal justice system, we must first acknowledge and understand the importance of gender differences as well as the gender-related dynamics inherent in any society. "Despite claims to the contrary," comments one expert, "masculinist epistemologies are built upon values that promote masculinist needs and desires, making all others invisible" (Kaschak 1992, 11). Women are often invisible in the many facets of the correctional system. This invisibility, in turn, can act as a form of oppression.

Where sexism is prevalent, frequently something declared genderless or gender neutral is, in fact, male oriented. The same phenomenon occurs in terms of race in a racist society, where the term "race neutral" generally means white (Kivel 1992). The stark realities of race and gender disparity touch the lives of all women and appear throughout the criminal justice process (Bloom 1996).

Understanding the distinction between sex differences and gender differences is vital. While sex differences are biologically determined, gender differences are socially constructed—they are assigned by society and relate to expected social roles. Gender differences are neither innate nor unchangeable. Gender is about the reality of women's lives and the contexts in which women live. "If programming is to be effective, it must . . . take the context of women's lives into account" (Abbott and Kerr 1995, 7).

Race and socioeconomic status or class can also determine views of gender-appropriate roles and behavior. And regardless of women's differences in these categories, all women are expected to incorporate the gender-based norms, values, and behaviors of the dominant culture into their lives. As Kaschak points out,

> The most centrally meaningful principle on our culture's mattering map is gender, which intersects with other culturally and personally meaningful categories such as race, class, ethnicity, and sexual orientation. Within all of these categories, people attribute different meanings to femaleness and maleness (Kaschak 1992, 5).

Gender stereotypes influence both our beliefs about the appropriate roles for women and men in our society and our behaviors toward women and men. Stereotypes also influence how we perceive people who violate the law, and stereotypes often have a differential impact on women. A convicted female offender may automatically be labeled a bad mother, while a male offender may not necessarily be labeled a bad father.

Research on women's pathways into crime indicates that gender matters. Steffensmeier and Allen (1998) note how the "profound differences" between the lives of women and men shape their patterns of criminal offending. Many women on the social and economic margins struggle to survive outside of legitimate enterprises, engaging in a lifestyle that brings them into contact with the criminal justice system. Because of their gender, women are also at greater risk for experiencing sexual abuse, sexual assault, and domestic violence. Among women, the most common pathways to crime are characterized by issues of survival (of abuse and poverty) and substance abuse. Pollock (1998) points out that women offenders have histories of sexual and/or physical abuse that appear to be precursors to subsequent delinquency, addiction, and criminality.

The link between female criminality and drug use is very strong, with research indicating that women who use drugs are more likely to be involved in crime (Merlo and Pollock 1995). Of female offenders in state prisons, approximately 80 percent have substance abuse problems (Center for Substance Abuse Treatment 1999), and about 50 percent had been using alcohol, drugs, or both at the time of their offense (Greenfeld and Snell 1999). Nearly one in three women serving time in state prisons report having committed their offenses in order to obtain money to support a drug habit. Furthermore, about half of the incarcerated women describe themselves as daily drug users.

Abusive families and battering relationships are also typical in the lives of female offenders (Chesney-Lind 1997; Owen and Bloom 1995). Frequently, adult female offenders had their first encounter with the justice system as juveniles—often after running away from home to escape situations involving violence and sexual or physical abuse. In such situations, prostitution, property crime, and drug use become a way of life. Not surprisingly, addiction, abuse, economic vulnerability, and severed social relations often result in homelessness, another frequent complication in the lives of women in the criminal justice system (Bloom 1998).

Studies of female offenders point to yet another gender difference— the importance of relationships and the criminal involvement that often results from relationships with family members, significant others, or friends (Chesney-Lind 1997; Owen 1998; Owen and Bloom 1995; Pollock 1998). Women are often first introduced to drugs by their partners, and these partners frequently continue to supply drugs. Women's attempts to get off drugs and their failure to supply partners with drugs through prostitution or other means often elicit violence from their partners. However, many women remain attached to their partners despite neglect and abuse. These issues have significant implications for therapeutic interventions addressing the impact of relationships on women's current and future behavior.

The gender differences inherent in all of these issues—invisibility, stereotypes, pathways to crime, addiction, abuse, homelessness, and relationships—need to be addressed at all levels of criminal justice. Such issues significantly affect female offenders' successful transition to the community, in terms of both programming needs and successful reentry. Unfortunately, these issues have until now been addressed separately at best, even though they are crucial in the lives of most women in the system. Without a holistic perspective on women's lives in any discussion of criminal justice, appropriate policy, planning, and program development is impossible.

Relational Theory

Various theories explain human psychological growth and development. One such premise, the relational theory, is a developmental theory stemming from an increased understanding of gender differences, specifically the different ways in which females and males develop psychologically. We need to understand relational theory in order to develop effective services and to avoid re-creating, in correctional settings, the same kinds of growth-hindering and/or violating relationships that women experience in society at large. It is also important to consider how women's life experiences may affect how they will function both within the criminal justice system and during the process of their transition and successful reentry into the community.

Traditional theories of psychology have described development as a progression from childlike dependence to mature independence. According to these theories, an individual's goal is to become a self-sufficient, clearly differentiated, autonomous self. Therefore, a person should spend his or her early life separating and individuating in a process leading to maturity, at which point he or she will be equipped for intimacy. Jean Baker Miller (1976, 1986) challenged this assumption, however. She suggested that these accepted theories describe men's experience, while a woman's path to maturity is different. A woman's primary motivation, said Miller, is to build a sense of connection with others. Women develop a sense of self and self-worth when their actions arise out of, and lead back into, connections with others. Connection, not separation, is the guiding principle of growth for women.

Miller's work led a group of researchers and practitioners to create the Stone Center at Wellesley College in 1981. The center was established to examine the qualities of relationships that foster growth and development. The Stone Center relational model defines connection as "an interaction that engenders a sense of being in tune with self and others and of being understood and valued" (Bylington 1997, 35). According to this model, such connections are so crucial that many of women's psychological problems can indeed be traced to disconnections or violations within their family, personal, or societal relationships.

In relational theory, mutual, empathic, and empowering relationships produce five psychological outcomes: (1) increased zest and vitality, (2) empowerment to act, (3) knowledge of self and others, (4) self-worth, and (5) a desire for more connection (Miller 1986). These outcomes constitute psychological growth for women. Therefore, mutuality, empathy, and power with others are essential qualities of an environment that will foster growth in women. By contrast, Miller (1990) has described the outcome of disconnections—that is, nonmutual or abusive relationships that become what she terms a "depressive spiral." The psychological outcomes of a "depressive spiral" are (1) diminished zest or vitality, (2) disempowerment, (3) unclarity or confusion, (4) diminished self-worth, and (5) a turning away from relationships.

The recurring themes of relationship and family seen in the lives of female offenders underscore the importance of understanding relational theory. Disconnection and violation rather than growth-fostering relationships characterize the childhood experiences of most women in the correctional system. In addition, these women have often been marginalized, not only because of race, class, and culture, but also by political decisions that criminalize their behavior (e.g., the war on drugs). "Females are far more likely than males to be motivated by relational concerns. . . . Situational pressures such as threatened loss of valued relationships play a greater role in female offending" (Steffensmeier and Allen 1998, 16).

Many women in prison have lost family members and/or experienced abuse in family or other relationships. Of 82 women surveyed in a Massachusetts prison, 38 percent had lost parents in childhood, 69 percent had been abused as children, and 70 percent had left home before the age of 17. Seventy percent of women had been repeatedly abused verbally, physically, and/or sexually as adults (Garcia Coll and Duff 1996). Further compounding the sense of loss and disconnection, the majority of women in the criminal justice system are mothers who may be at risk of losing their children during their incarceration.

Although Gilligan, Lyons, and Hanmer (1990) report that girls are socialized to be more empathic than boys, incarcerated women have been exposed repeatedly to nonempathic relationships. As a result, they may lack empathy for both themselves and others, or they may be highly empathic toward others but lack empathy for themselves. To create change in their lives, incarcerated women need to experience relationships that do not repeat their histories of loss, neglect, and abuse.

Risk, Need, and Level of Burden

Any discussion of women's services and the reentry process must consider the roles of classification and assessment (Covington and Bloom 1999). Throughout the 1990s, much of the research on correctional interventions was conducted by a group of Canadian psychologists who argued that it was possible to target the appropriate group of offenders with the appropriate type of treatment. Gendreau, Andrews, Bonta, and others in the "Ottawa school" developed a theory they called "the psychology of criminal conduct." The premise of this theory is that correctional programming should focus on criminogenic risks and needs directly related to recidivism; for example, interventions should be concentrated on those offenders who represent the greatest risk. This theory focuses on developing effective methods of assessing and managing risk factors—personal characteristics that can be assessed prior to treatment and used to predict future criminal behavior (Andrews, Bonta, and Hoge 1990).

The assessment of risk continues to play a critical role in correctional management, supervision, and programming. At the community corrections level, classification and assessment involve calculating the degree of risk an offender represents and, increasingly, determining service and program needs as well. (This approach is often referred to as "risk and needs" assessment.) In the community, these calculations are designed not only to assess the level of threat from the prisoner, typically as it relates to violence, but also to evaluate the risk of the prisoner absconding from parole supervision.

Canadian academics in particular, however, have raised concerns about the reliability and validity of risk-assessment instruments as these relate to women and to people of color (Hannah-Moffat 2000; Kendall 1994; McMahon 2000). Hannah-Moffat (2000) argues that the concept of risk is not neutral for gender or race. Most risk-assessment instruments are developed for white males, and using these tools with women and nonwhite offender populations raises empirical and theoretical questions. In fact, justification for using the risk-needs framework for women is based on a meta-analysis of 26 studies conducted from 1965 to 1997. More than 70 percent of these studies were conducted before 1985, and some focused on delinquent girls (Dowden and Andrews 1999). Therefore, given the age and paucity of the data, the validity of these instruments for women is questionable.

In addition, as Hannah-Moffat and Shaw state:

> Classification systems that prioritize risk often give limited consideration to needs. When needs are considered in the context of risk, they are often redefined as risk factors that must be addressed. If the current risk paradigm does not seem to work well for women, then why keep it? (Hannah-Moffat and Shaw 2001, 59).

In other words, why should we keep trying to fit women into a preexisting mold? Another academic researcher asks:

> Does women's offending relate to criminogenic risks and needs or to the complex interconnection of race, class, gender, and trauma, or does it relate to both? The philosophy of criminogenic risks and needs does not consider factors such as economic marginalization, the role of patriarchy, sexual victimization, or women's place in society. Nor does the existing "What Works?" body of literature address the concerns of those scholars who study women offenders (B. Bloom 2000, 128).

As Nancy Stableforth, Deputy Commissioner for Women, Correctional Service of Canada, asserts:

> There are respected and well-known researchers who believe that criminogenic needs of women offenders is a concept that requires further investigation; that the parameters of effective programs for women offenders have yet to receive basic validation; that women's pathways to crime have not received sufficient research attention; and that methodologies appropriate for women offender research must be specifically developed and selected to be responsible not only to gender issues, but also to the reality of the small number of women (Stableforth 1999, 5).

Another approach to the assessment of female offenders is based on the concept of "level of burden," which is defined as the number and severity of problems experienced by the women themselves, by the staff, and by the community. Brown, Melchior, and Huba (1995, 1999) found that exploring the level of burden from the client's perspective is important for several reasons. First, individuals with three or four disorders, such as alcohol and/or other drug abuse, mental illness, cognitive impairment, and HIV/AIDS and/or other health problems experience continuous challenges to their self-esteem from associated negative images and social stigmas. Second, understanding how the level of burden impacts a woman may help caregiving staff to understand how to intervene when a woman is noncompliant with treatment or exhibits a poor connection with treatment providers. Third, this understanding can also contribute to the development of interventions for helping staff, family members, and the larger community.

Specific Issues of Female Offenders

Policymakers and corrections officials planning for and providing gender-responsive services for female offenders need to consider two main concerns: (1) the role of motherhood and (2) the interrelationship between substance abuse, trauma, and mental health issues.

The Role of Motherhood

A major difference between female and male offenders involves their relationships with their children. The Bureau of Justice Statistics reports that in 1997, 65 percent of the women in state prisons and 59 percent of the women in federal prisons had minor children. The majority were single mothers, with an average of two children. About two-thirds of women in state prisons and one-half of women in federal prisons lived with their young children before entering prison. Furthermore, the number of children with incarcerated mothers nearly doubled between 1991 and 1999—from 64,000 to 126,000. Currently, it is estimated that 1.3 million minor children have a mother who is under some form of correctional supervision (Mumola 2000).

Incarcerated women are mostly portrayed as inadequate, incompetent mothers who are unable to provide adequately for the needs of their children (Garcia Coll et al. 1998). In reality, separation from and concern about the well-being of their children are among the most damaging aspects of prison for women, and the problem is exacerbated by a lack of contact (Baunach 1985; Bloom and Steinhart 1993). "One of the greatest differences in stresses for women and men serving time is that the separation from children is generally a much greater hardship for women than for men" (Belknap 1996, 105). For many incarcerated mothers, their relationships—or lack thereof—with their children can profoundly affect how they function in the criminal justice system. Often, behaviors such as negativism, manipulation, rule breaking, and fighting among incarcerated women are signs of what Garcia Coll et al. (1998) have described as "resistance for survival" in response to the grief, loss, shame, and guilt these women feel about their roles as mothers.

Grandparents most frequently care for the children of female offenders, while approximately 10 percent of these children are in foster care or group homes. According to the Bureau of Justice Statistics, 54 percent of mothers in state prisons as of 2000 had had no personal visits with their children since their admission (Mumola 2000). Geographical distance, lack of transportation, the prisoner-caregiver relationship, and the caregiver's inability to bring a child to a correctional facility represent the most common reasons for a lack of visits. In some cases, the forced separation between mother and child can result in permanent termination of the parent-child relationship (Genty 1995). In addition, passage of the Adoption and Safe Families Act (ASFA) in 1997 increased the risk of such termination. This legislation allows states to file for termination of parental rights if a child has been in foster care for 15 or more of 22 consecutive months.

Even when a child is able to visit an incarcerated mother or father, the event is often not a positive experience. Few correctional programs assess themselves through the eyes of children. Prison visiting facilities are created solely to address the issues of safety and security, without consideration for how a child experiences the prison environment. Such issues as travel logistics, clearance processes, noise levels and distractions in visiting rooms, privacy, and the availability of toys or other child-friendly resources—any or all of which can have a profound impact on the visiting child's experience—are most often ignored. What should be an experience fostering family support and connection is instead often an unpleasant or traumatic occasion for both the child and the parent.

The only source of hope and motivation for many women during their involvement with the criminal justice system and their transition back to the community is a connection with their children. When asked why some women return to prison, one mother commented:

> Many women that fall [back] into prison have the problem that their children have been taken away. When they go out to the street, they don't have anything, they have nothing inside. Because they say, "I don't have my children, what will I do? I'll go back to the drug again. I will go back to prostitution again. And I'll go back to prison again. Why fight? Why fight if I have nothing?" (Garcia Coll et al. 1998, 266).

Recognizing the centrality of women's roles as mothers provides an opportunity for criminal justice, medical, mental health, legal, and social service agencies to include this role as an integral part of program and treatment interventions for women.

The invisibility of women in the criminal justice system often extends to their children. And this situation is exacerbated by the fact that there are few, if any, sources of data about offenders' children. However, one study (Johnston 1995) identified three factors that were consistently present in the lives of the children of incarcerated parents: parent-child separation, enduring traumatic stress, and inadequate quality of care. Not surprisingly, these factors can have a profound impact on children's ability to successfully progress through the various developmental stages of childhood. For instance, children born to women in the criminal justice system experience a variety of prenatal stressors (e.g., a mother's drug or alcohol use, poor nutrition, and high levels of stress associated with criminal activity and incarceration). Better outcomes can be achieved if mothers can adopt more stable lifestyles and receive adequate nutrition and proper medical care. There is a clear need for a range of prenatal services for women during both their incarceration and their transition back to the community (Johnston 1995).

Parental crime and incarceration continues to impact children throughout adolescence. These children are subjected to unique stressors because of their parents' involvement with the criminal justice system. Johnston (1995) has identified higher rates of troubling behaviors, including aggression, depression, anxiety, parentified behaviors, substance abuse, and survivor guilt among these children, as well as an increased risk that they, too, will become involved with the criminal justice system. It is important that gender-responsive interventions for women in the system better address the effects of parental incarceration on children.

Substance Abuse, Trauma, and Mental Health Issues

Looking at the profile of women in the system, the differences between women and men, and the concept of level of burden reveals three critical and interrelated issues in women's lives: substance abuse, trauma, and mental health. These issues affect a female offender's transition back into the community in terms of both programming needs and the success of reentry. Historically, however, these three issues have been treated separately. Both the training of professionals and the categorical funding of services have helped to create and maintain this separation. Yet substance abuse, trauma, and mental health are generally related issues for women in the system.

Gender differences exist in the behavioral manifestations of mental illness; men generally turn anger outward and women turn it inward. Men tend to be more physically and sexually threatening and assaultive, while women tend to be more depressed, self-abusive, and suicidal. Women engage more often in self-mutilating behaviors, such as cutting, as well as in verbally abusive and disruptive behaviors.

In terms of substance abuse, female offenders are more likely to have used drugs (e.g., cocaine and heroin), to have used them intravenously, and to have used them more frequently before being arrested. Women are also more likely to have a coexisting psychiatric disorder and to exhibit lower self-esteem (Bloom and Covington 2000). In one study of both men and women in the general population, 23 percent of those surveyed reported a history of psychiatric disorders; of this group, 30 percent also reported having had a substance abuse problem at some time in their lives (Daley, Moss, and Campbell 1993). These co-occurring issues are more prevalent among women, with depression, anxiety, and other mood disorders more common among substance-abusing women than among men. A study by Blume (1990) found that major depression co-occurred with alcohol abuse in 19 percent of women (almost four times the rate for men); phobic disorder co-occurred with alcohol abuse in 31 percent of women (more than twice the rate for men); and panic disorder co-occurred with alcohol abuse in 7 percent of women (three and one-half times the rate for men).

With regard to the issue of trauma, one of the most important developments in health care over the past several decades is the recognition that many people have a history of serious traumatic experiences that play a vital and often unrecognized role in the evolution of physical and mental health problems. According to the Bureau of Justice Statistics, nearly 8 of every 10 female offenders with a mental illness report having been physically or sexually abused (Greenfeld and Snell 1999). A 1994 study of women in U.S. jails found that approximately 22 percent had been diagnosed with posttraumatic stress disorder (PTSD) (Vesey 1997). Another study found that nearly 80 percent of female prisoners had experienced some form of abuse either as children or as adults (Bloom, Chesney-Lind, and Owen 1994). Browne, Miller, and Maguin

(1999) found that 70 percent of incarcerated women interviewed in a New York prison reported physical abuse, and nearly 60 percent reported sexual abuse.

A history of abuse drastically increases the likelihood that a woman will also abuse alcohol and/or other drugs. In one of the earliest comparison studies of addicted and nonaddicted women (Covington and Kohen 1984), 74 percent of the addicts reported sexual abuse (vs. 50 percent of the nonaddicts); 52 percent (vs. 34 percent) reported physical abuse; and 72 percent (vs. 44 percent) reported emotional abuse. The connection between addiction and trauma for women is complex and often includes the following dynamics: (1) substance-abusing men are often violent toward women and children; (2) substance-abusing women are vulnerable targets for violence; and (3) both childhood abuse and current abuse increase a woman's risk for substance abuse (Miller 1991).

The risk of physical and sexual abuse continues to be higher for women than for men throughout life. "While both male and female children are at risk for abuse, females continue to be at risk for interpersonal violence in their adolescence and adult lives. The risk of abuse for males in their teenage and adult relationships is far less than that for females" (Covington and Surrey 1997, 341). In a study of participants in prison-based treatment programs, Messina et al. (2001) found that women reported childhood abuse at a rate almost twice that of men. Abuse of women as adults was reported at a rate eight times higher than the rate for men. It is important to note that abuse statistics may reflect the possibility that women are more willing than men to report victimization. The traumatization of women is not limited to interpersonal violence, however. It also includes witnessing violence, as well as stigmatization stemming from gender, race, poverty, incarceration, and/or sexual orientation (Covington 2002).

Posttraumatic stress disorder is common among survivors of abuse. A survey of female pretrial jail detainees found that more than 80 percent of the women in the sample met the *Diagnostic and Statistical Manual of Mental Disorders* criteria for one or more lifetime psychiatric disorders (American Psychiatric Association 1994). "The most common disorders were drug abuse or drug dependence (63.6 percent), alcohol abuse or alcohol dependence (32.3 percent), and post-traumatic stress disorder (33.5 percent)" (Teplin, Abram, and McClelland 1996, 508). Sixty percent of the subjects had exhibited drug or alcohol abuse or dependence within six months of the interview. In addition, 17 percent met the criteria for a major depressive episode. Najavits (1998) reviewed studies that examined the combined effects of PTSD and substance abuse on women and found more comorbid mental disorders, medical problems, psychological symptoms, inpatient admissions, interpersonal problems, lower levels of functioning, difficulties in compliance with aftercare and motivation for treatment, and other significant life problems (such as homelessness, HIV, domestic violence, and loss of custody of children).

PTSD and co-occurring substance abuse disorders can have devastating effects on women's ability to care for their children properly. PTSD symptoms include flashbacks, hypervigilance, and dissociation. Because of the unpredictable, volatile, and depressive behaviors associated with PTSD, women with this disorder may be viewed as unfit or inadequate mothers, putting them at risk for the removal of their children or loss of custody (Garcia Coll et al. 1998). Additionally, if women have co-occurring substance abuse problems, their focus on dealing with addiction can impact their ability to adequately care for their children. As Garcia Coll et al. point out:

> This is a tragedy for them, their children, and society. We need to recognize both their good intentions and their bad judgments that led them into this destructive pathway at the expense of other, more crucial relationships in their lives, including those with their children (Garcia Coll et al. 1998, 205).

As noted earlier, women who have been exposed to trauma and who are also addicted to drugs or alcohol are at higher risk for other mental disorders. The rate of major depression among alcoholic women was almost three times the rate of the general female population, and the rate for phobias was almost double. The rate of antisocial personality disorder (ASPD)—a disorder that can often result in criminal justice involvement—was 12 times higher among alcoholic women than among the general female population (Blume 1990, 1997).

Co-occurring disorders are complex, and the prevalence of dual diagnoses for women with both substance abuse and another psychiatric disorder has not been well studied. Women in early recovery often show symptoms of mood disorders, but these can be temporary conditions associated with withdrawal from drugs. Also, it is difficult to know whether a psychiatric disorder existed for a woman before she began to abuse alcohol or other drugs, or whether the psychiatric problem emerged after the onset of substance abuse (Institute of Medicine 1990). Research suggests that preexisting psychiatric disorders improve more slowly for recovering substance abusers and need to be addressed directly in treatment.

Women with serious mental illness and co-occurring disorders experience significant difficulties in criminal justice settings. As a study by Teplin et al. reported:

> The American Bar Association recommends that persons with mental disorders who were arrested for misdemeanors be diverted to a mental health facility instead of [being] arrested. With appropriate community programs, nonviolent felons also could be treated outside the jail after pretrial hearings. . . . Unfortunately, community-based programs are rarely available for released jail detainees, who often have complex diagnostic profiles and special treatment needs (Teplin et al. 1996, 511).

With the higher rate of mental illness among female offenders, higher rates of medication can be expected. However, there is a rush to over-medicate women both in society at large and in correctional settings. The use of psychotropic drugs is ten times higher in women's prisons than in men's prisons (Culliver 1993). Leonard (2002) notes the overuse of psychotropic drugs (e.g., tranquilizers), which she refers to as "chemical restraints," as a means of institutional social control. Leonard also states that many of her interviewees reported that psychotropic drugs directly interfered with their ability to participate in the preparation of their defense cases.

RETRAUMATIZATION VIA OPERATING/MANAGEMENT PRACTICES
Standard policies and procedures in correctional settings (e.g., searches, restraints, and isolation) can profoundly affect women with histories of trauma and abuse, often acting as triggers to retraumatize women already suffering from PTSD. These issues clearly have implications, therefore, for service providers, corrections administrators, and staff.

Many forms of custodial misconduct have been documented, including verbal degradation, rape or other sexual assault, unwarranted visual supervision, denial of goods and privileges, and the use or threat of force (Amnesty International USA 1999; GAO 1999; Human Rights Watch 1996). For example, female prisoners are generally strip-searched after prison visits (as well as at other times), and these searches can be used punitively. In light of the large percentage of incarcerated women who have been sexually abused, strip searches can be traumatic personal violations. Furthermore, many jails and state prisons require that pregnant women about to give birth be shackled as they are transported to hospitals (Amnesty International USA 1999). This procedure can be traumatic for a woman already in labor, especially since the escape risk in such a situation is minimal.

Sexual misconduct by staff is a serious issue in women's prisons. "Male correctional officers and staff contribute to a custodial environment in state prisons for women that is often highly sexualized and excessively hostile" (Human Rights Watch 1996, 2). Reviewing the situation of incarcerated women in five states (California, Georgia, Michigan, Illinois, and New York) and the District of Columbia, Human Rights Watch concluded:

> Our findings indicate that being a woman prisoner in U.S. state prisons can be a terrifying experience. If you are sexually abused, you cannot escape from your abuser. Grievance or investigatory procedures, where they exist, are often ineffectual, and correctional employees continue to engage in abuse because they believe that they will rarely be held accountable, administratively or criminally. Few people outside the prison walls know what is going on or care if they do know. Fewer still do anything to address the problem (Human Rights Watch 1996, 1).

As criminal justice researchers and practitioners begin to acknowledge the interrelationship among the multiple issues facing female offenders, the need for gender-specific treatment programming that is both comprehensive and integrated becomes clearly evident. In the past, women have often been expected to seek help for addiction, psychological disorders, and trauma from separate sources and to somehow incorporate on their own what they have learned from a recovery group, a counselor, and/or a psychologist. These unrealistic expectations obviously can lead to relapse and/or recidivism. A longitudinal study conducted by Gil-Rivas, Fiorentine, and Anglin determined that:

> Assessment of sexual and physical abuse as well as PTSD, along with the delivery of services dealing with these issues, should be a routine feature of effective drug-abuse treatment programs. Indeed, there is some evidence that women are more likely to participate in drug-abuse treatment programs that offer services addressing emotional and family problems (Gil-Rivas et al. 1996, 96).

THE IMPORTANCE OF ENVIRONMENT
The development of effective gender-responsive services should provide for an environment that understands the realities of women's lives and addresses the participants' issues. This environment should comprise

such integral elements as appropriate site selection, staff selection, and program development, content, and material (Covington 2001).

In reality, the culture of corrections (i.e., the environment created by the criminal justice system) is often in conflict with the culture of treatment. The corrections culture is based on control and security, and thus discourages women from coming together, trusting others, speaking about personal issues, or forming bonds. Women who leave prison are often discouraged from associating with other women who have been incarcerated. Treatment, however, is necessarily based on concern for the women's safety and on the need to assist them in making life changes. One way to alter the corrections aspect of treatment is to apply relational theory on a systemwide basis.

If women in the system are to change, grow, and recover, they must be involved in programs and environments that foster relationships and mutuality. We therefore need to provide settings that enable women to experience healthy relationships both with staff and with one another. A pilot project in a Massachusetts prison found that women benefited from being in a group in which members both received information and had the opportunity to practice mutually empathic relationships with others (Garcia Coll and Duff 1996). Women also need respectful, mutual, and compassionate relationships with correctional staff. In a study done in Ohio, young women in detention reported their need for respect from correctional staff (Belknap, Dunn, and Holsinger 1997). Finally, women will benefit if relationships among staff and between staff and administration are mutual, empathic, and respectful.

Work with trauma victims has shown that social support is critical for recovery, and the lack of that support results in damaging psychological and social disruptions. Trauma always occurs within a social context, and social wounds require social healing (S. Bloom 2000). The growing awareness of the long-term consequences of unresolved traumatic experience, combined with the disintegration or absence of communities for individuals in the criminal justice system (e.g., neighborhoods, extended families, occupational identities), has encouraged corrections researchers and practitioners to take a new look at the established practice and principles of the therapeutic milieu model.

The term "therapeutic milieu" refers to a carefully arranged environment designed to reverse the effects of exposure to interpersonal violence. The therapeutic culture contains the following five elements, all of them fundamental both in institutional settings and in the community:

- *Attachment:* a culture of belonging
- *Containment:* a culture of safety
- *Communication:* a culture of openness
- *Involvement:* a culture of participation and citizenship
- *Agency:* a culture of empowerment (Haigh 1999)

Any teaching and reorientation process will be unsuccessful if its environment mimics the dysfunctional systems female prisoners have already experienced. Rather, program and treatment strategies should be designed to undo some of the prior damage. Therapeutic community norms are consciously designed to be different: safety with oneself and with others is paramount, and the entire environment is designed to create living and learning opportunities for everyone involved—staff and clients alike (S. Bloom 2000).

A Plan for Reentry

If women are to be successfully reintegrated back into society after serving their sentences, there must be a continuum of care that can connect them to a community. In addition, the planning process must begin as soon as women begin serving their sentences, rather than during the final 30 to 60 days of a prison term (the current practice). In fact, very few inmates report receiving prerelease planning of any kind in prisons and jails (Lynch and Sabol 2001). However, women reentering the community after incarceration require transitional services from the institution to help them reestablish themselves and their families. These former prisoners also need transitional services from community corrections and supervision to assist them as they begin living on their own again.

Ideally, a comprehensive approach to reentry services for women would include a mechanism to allow community-based programs to enter institutional program settings. At the women's prison in Rhode Island, Warden Roberta Richman has opened the institution to the community through the increased use of volunteers and community-based programs. This policy allows the women to develop connections with community providers as a part of their transition process. It also creates a mutual accountability between the prison and the community (Richman 1999).

The restorative model of justice is yet another means for assisting female offenders as they prepare to reintegrate themselves into their neighborhoods and communities. The framework for restorative justice involves relationships, healing, and community, a model in keeping with female psychosocial developmental theory. To reduce the likelihood of future offending among known lawbreakers, official intervention should emphasize restorative rather than retributive goals. Offenders should be provided opportunities to increase their "caring capacity" through victim restitution, community service, and moral development opportunities, rather than be subject to experiences that encourage violence and egocentrism (as do most prisons and juvenile institutions in the United States) (Pollock 1999, 250). In turn, this process provides yet another mechanism to link women with support and resources.

Transition to the Community

There is a critical need to develop a societal support system that provides assistance to women transitioning from jails and prisons back into the community. The need to navigate a myriad of systems that often provide fragmented services can impede successful prisoner reintegration. For example, released women must comply with conditions of probation or parole, achieve financial stability, access health care, locate housing, and attempt to reunite with their families (Bloom and Covington 2000). In addition, they must obtain employment (often with few skills and a sporadic work history), find safe and drug-free housing, and, in many cases, maintain recovery from addiction. However, many women find themselves either homeless or in environments that do not support sober living. Without strong community support in dealing with multiple systems and agencies, many offenders fall back into a life of substance abuse and criminal activity.

Community-based programs offer other benefits, not only to female offenders and their children, but also to society. One survey compared the average annual cost of an individual's probation with the costs of jailing or imprisoning that person. While the cost of probation is roughly $869, the cost for jail is $14,363 and for prison, $17,794 (Phillips and Harm 1998). Community sanctions are less disruptive to women than incarceration and subject them to less isolation. Furthermore, community corrections potentially create far less disruption in the lives of female offenders' children.

Most women in the correctional system are mothers, and a major consideration for these women is reunification with their children.

Because of ASFA stipulations, the time frame for reunification is now critical. These conditions add what Brown et al. (1999) identify as an additional level of burden for mothers who must provide safe housing, economic support, medical services, and so on for their children also. Because these children have specific needs, being the custodial parent potentially brings women returning from prison into contact with more agencies, which may have conflicting or otherwise incompatible goals and values. At present, few treatment programs address the needs of women, especially those with minor children.

Much has been learned about community-based services for women from the work done through the Center for Substance Abuse Treatment (CSAT) grants and models. Treatment programs must not only offer a continuum of services, but they must also integrate these services within the larger community. The purpose of comprehensive treatment, according to a model developed by CSAT, is to address a woman's substance use in the context of her health and her relationship with her children and other family members, the community, and society. An understanding of the interrelationships among the client, the treatment program, and the community is critical to the success of the comprehensive approach (Reed and Leavitt 2000). Few treatment programs can respond to all the identified needs of substance-abusing women; therefore, these programs need to include referral mechanisms and collaborative agreements to further assist women in their recovery process (CSAT 1994, 1999; Covington 1999). Furthermore, CSAT's knowledge base can be applied not only to substance abuse treatment programs, but also to the development of other programs for transitioning women.

A study by Austin, Bloom, and Donahue (1992) identified effective strategies for working with women offenders in community correctional settings. Austin et al. found that the most promising community-based programs for female offenders do not employ the medical or clinical model of correctional treatment. Effective programs enable clients to broaden their range of responses to various types of behavior and needs. Their coping and decisionmaking skills can be enhanced by using an "empowerment" model designed to promote self-sufficiency. In addition, effective therapeutic approaches are multidimensional and deal with specific women's issues, including chemical dependency, domestic violence, sexual abuse, pregnancy and parenting, relationships, and gender bias.

Another study of community-based drug treatment programs for female offenders concluded that success appears to be positively related to the amount of time women spend in treatment, with more lengthy programs having greater success rates (Wellisch, Anglin, and Prendergast 1994). The authors noted that the services women need are more likely to be found in programs for women only, rather than in coed programs. The study also concluded that improving client needs assessment is necessary in order to develop better programs that deliver a range of appropriate services. The assessment process should provide the basis for developing individual treatment plans, establishing a baseline from which progress in treatment can be monitored; the process should also generate data for program evaluation.

Wraparound Services

Each transitioning woman clearly needs a holistic and culturally sensitive plan that draws on "wraparound services"—a coordinated continuum of services located within a community. As Jacobs notes, "Working with women in the criminal justice system requires ways of working more effectively with the many other human service systems that are involved in their lives" (Jacobs 2001, 47). The types of organizations that must work as partners to assist women's reentry into the community include mental health systems; alcohol and other drug programs; programs for survivors of family and sexual violence; family service agencies; emergency shelter, food, and financial assistance programs; educational, vocational, and employment services; health care services; the child welfare system; transportation; child care; children's services; educational organizations; self-help groups; organizations concerned with subgroups of women; consumer advocacy groups; organizations that provide leisure options; faith-based organizations; and community service clubs.

Wraparound models and other integrated and holistic approaches can be very effective because they address multiple goals and needs in a coordinated way and facilitate access to services (Reed and Leavitt 2000). Wraparound models stem from the idea of "wrapping necessary resources into an individualized support plan" (Malysiak 1997, 12) and stress both client-level and system-level linkages. The need for wraparound services is highest for clients with multiple and complex needs that cannot be addressed by limited services from a few locations in the community.

Community-based wraparound services can be particularly useful for two primary reasons:

1. Women have been socialized to value relationships and connectedness and to approach life within interpersonal contexts (Covington 1998a, b). Service-delivery approaches that are based on ongoing relationships, that make connections among different life areas, and that work within women's existing support systems are especially congruent with female characteristics and needs.
2. More female offenders than male offenders are the primary caregivers of young children. These children have needs of their own and require other caregivers if their mothers are incarcerated. Support for parenting, safe housing, and an appropriate family wage level are crucial when the welfare of children is at stake.

Programming that is responsive in terms of both gender and culture emphasizes support. Service providers need to focus on women's strengths, and they need to recognize that a woman cannot be treated successfully in isolation from her social support network (e.g., relationships with her partner, family, children, and friends). Coordinating systems that connect a broad range of services will promote a continuity-of-care model. Such a comprehensive approach provides a sustained continuity of treatment, recovery, and support services, beginning with incarceration and continuing through the full transition to the community.

Gender-Responsive Models for a Community Approach

Effective, gender-responsive models do exist for programs and agencies that provide for a continuity-of-care approach. The models described below are examples of interventions that can be used at various points within the criminal justice system and in community-based services, and respond to the needs of women transitioning back to their communities.

Program Models

1. *Helping Women Recover: A Program for Treating Substance Abuse* is a unique, gender-responsive treatment model designed especially for women in correctional settings. It is currently in use in both

institutional and community-based programs. The program provides treatment for women recovering from substance abuse and trauma by dealing with their specific issues in a safe and nurturing environment based on respect, mutuality, and compassion. This program addresses the issues of self-esteem, parenting, relationships, sexual concerns, and spirituality that have been identified by the Center for Substance Abuse Treatment (CSAT 1994, 1999) in its guidelines for comprehensive treatment. Helping Women Recover integrates the theoretical perspectives of addiction, women's psychological development, and trauma in separate program modules of four sessions each (Covington 1999, 2000). Using a female facilitator, the modules address the issues of self, relationships, sexuality, and spirituality through the use of guided discussions, workbook exercises, and interactive activities. According to recovering women, addressing these four areas is crucial to preventing relapse (Covington 1994).

2. *Beyond Trauma: A Healing Journey for Women* is an integrated, theoretically based, gender-responsive treatment approach that consists of 11 sessions (Covington 2003). This program has been developed for use in residential, outpatient, and correctional settings in a group format (it can be adapted for individual work). Beyond Trauma has a psychoeducational component that teaches women what trauma is, its process, and its impact on both the inner self (thoughts, feelings, beliefs, values) and the outer self (behavior and relationships, including parenting). The major emphasis is on coping skills with specific exercises for developing emotional wellness. The curriculum includes a facilitator guide, participant workbook, and videos. These items can be used alone or as a continuation of the trauma work in the Helping Women Recover curriculum (Covington 1999).

3. The *Sanctuary Model* is an example of an institutional-based and community milieu program that addresses the issues of mental health, substance abuse, and trauma. The sanctuary model focuses on safety, affect management, grieving, and emancipation (SAGE) in the treatment of trauma (Foderaro and Ryan 2000). This model provides for either an inpatient or outpatient environment in which trauma survivors are supported in a process to establish safety and individual empowerment.

4. *Seeking Safety* is a cognitive-behavioral program for women who have substance dependence and co-occurring PTSD. It is based on five key elements: (1) safety (the priority of this "first stage" treatment); (2) integrated treatment of PTSD and substance abuse; (3) a focus on ideals; (4) cognitive, behavioral, and interpersonal therapies, along with case management; and (5) attention to therapist processes (Najavits 2002).

5. The *Addiction and Trauma Recovery Integration Model (ATRIUM)* is a psychoeducational program with expressive activities designed for a 12-week period. It is an assessment and recovery model designed to intervene on the levels of body, mind, and spirit (Miller and Giudry 2001).

6. The *Trauma Recovery and Empowerment Model (TREM)* is a psychoeducational group approach that includes survivor empowerment, techniques for self-soothing, secondary maintenance, and problem solving, in 33 sessions over a nine-month period (Harris and Anglin 1998).

Agency Models

The two agency models described below share a similar conceptual basis—the settlement house. Social worker Jane Addams opened the first settlement house in the United States in 1886 with the aim of providing multiple services to "strangers in a new land" (Elshtain 2001). This concept of resettlement is particularly applicable to the experiences of women with multiple challenges who are returning to their communities. Recently, several women who had had lengthy incarcerations and who were preparing to leave institutions expressed fears about "being a stranger," "feeling alone," and feeling "overwhelmed by changes in the community."[1]

1. *Our Place, D.C.,* located in Washington, D.C., is an example of a community-based organization that provides a continuum of services and addresses the important issue of family reunification. The organization's mission is to empower women who are or have been in the criminal justice system by providing them with the support and resources they need to resettle in the community, reunite with their families, and find decent housing and jobs. The

center also supports incarcerated women by providing prerelease classes, a family support program, family transportation to the prisons, and a quarterly newsletter called *Finding Our Place.* When women are released, the center assists them in finding housing, employment, clothing, substance abuse treatment, mental and physical health care services, HIV services, legal services, and support groups. Support is ongoing, with no time limits. Over 90 percent of the women who utilize the center have done so voluntarily.

2. The *Refugee Model* provides a well-coordinated, comprehensive example of a community response to the issue of prisoner reentry that could be made applicable to women. This process would entail appropriate site and staff selection, a focus on women's specific issues, and the use of gender-responsive materials. For the past 30 years, the Catholic Church has resettled tens of thousands of refugees from all over the world. Through local parishes, this practice has been expanded to assist parolees as well. Using the refugee model, Catholic dioceses work to promote the coordination of services and supportive relationships for parolees transitioning to the community. In turn, the church believes this experience enriches its parishes. Using the refugee model reflects an understanding of the complexity of reentry issues and acknowledges the similarities between refugees' needs and those of offenders. However, while this model provides an excellent conceptual foundation for reentry, it has yet to be redesigned for gender specificity.

Recommendations

All offenders have similar categories of needs. Both women and men transitioning from prison back to the community typically require substance abuse treatment and vocational and educational training. Family and community reintegration issues are also shared, as are physical and mental health care concerns. However, the research on differences between women and men suggests that the degree or intensity of these needs and the ways in which they should be addressed by the criminal justice system are quite different.

In planning for gender-responsive policies and practice, it is necessary to consider gender differences in terms of both behavior under correctional supervision and responses to programs and treatment. We must also understand the current social climate, which is reflected in policies and legislation, and the differential impact of that climate on women and men. For example, the following provisions have a greater negative impact on women transitioning to their communities (and, subsequently, their children) than they do on men:

- Drug policy
  The War on Drugs has had a particularly devastating impact on women. As previously mentioned, drug offenses have accounted for the largest proportion of growth in the numbers of women prisoners. In fact, women are more likely than men to be incarcerated for drug offenses. Furthermore, society's emphasis on punishment rather than treatment has brought many low-income women and women of color into the criminal justice system (The Sentencing Project 2001).
- Welfare benefits
  Section 115 of the Welfare Reform Act, Temporary Assistance for Needy Families (TANF), stipulates that persons convicted of using or selling drugs are subject to a lifetime ban on receiving cash assistance and food stamps. No other offenses result in a loss of benefits (Allard 2002).
- Drug treatment
  Access to drug treatment is frequently impeded for women who lose welfare benefits because of drug offense convictions. Since these women are denied the cash assistance and food stamps so critical to their successful recovery, they may be required to go to work and thereby are prevented from participating in treatment. In addition, programs that accommodate women with children are limited (Legal Action Center 1999).
- Housing
  Federal housing policies permit (and, in some cases, require) public housing authorities, Section 8 providers, and other federally assisted housing programs to deny housing to individuals who have engaged in drug-related activity (Legal Action Center 1999).
- Education
  Although correctional institutions are now offering more general education programs, there are still fewer programs for women than there are for men. As of 1996, only 52 percent of correctional facil-

ities for women offered postsecondary education. Access to college education was further limited in 1994, when prisoners were declared ineligible for college Pell Grants (Allard 2002).

• Reunification with children

The 1997 Adoption and Safe Families Act (ASFA) allows states to file for termination of parental rights once a child has been in foster care for 15 or more of 22 consecutive months. It is difficult enough for single mothers with substance abuse problems to meet ASFA requirements when they live in the community, but the short deadline has particularly severe consequences for incarcerated mothers, who serve an average of 18 months (Jacobs 2001).

Clearly, women's inability to access various social entitlements critical to successful reentry into the community undermines their efforts to recover, care for their children, and become full, productive members of their communities. Our current policies and legislation must be reviewed and revised to prevent harmful short- and long-term consequences for both women and their children.

A gender-responsive approach includes services that in content and in context (i.e., structure and environment) are comprehensive and relate to the reality of women's lives. While the overarching standard for gender-responsive practice is to do no harm, the specific guidelines that follow can be used in the development of services in both institutional and community-based settings (Bloom and Covington 1998):

1. The theoretical perspectives used consider women's particular pathways into the criminal justice system, fit their psychological and social needs, and reflect their actual lives (e.g., relational theory, trauma theory).
2. Treatment and services are based on women's competencies and strengths and promote self-reliance.
3. Programs use a variety of interventions—behavioral, cognitive, affective/dynamic, and systems perspectives—in order to fully address women's needs.
4. Homogeneous groups are used, especially for primary treatment (e.g., trauma, substance abuse).
5. Services/treatment address women's practical needs, such as housing, transportation, child care, and vocational training and job placement.

6. Participants receive opportunities to develop skills in a range of educational and vocational (including nontraditional) areas.
7. Staff members reflect the client population in terms of gender, race/ethnicity, sexual orientation, language (bilingual), and ex-offender and recovery status.
8. Female role models and mentors are provided who reflect the racial/ethnic/cultural backgrounds of the clients.
9. Cultural awareness and sensitivity are promoted using the resources and strengths available in various communities.
10. Gender-responsive assessment tools and individualized treatment plans are utilized, with appropriate treatment matched to each client's identified needs and assets.
11. Programs emphasize parenting education, child development, and relationships/reunification with children (if relevant).
12. The environment is child friendly, with age-appropriate activities designed for children.
13. Transitional programs are included as part of gender-responsive practices, with a particular focus on building long-term community support networks for women.

Because of the high rates of violence against women and children, it is imperative that all services become trauma informed. Trauma-informed services are services that have been created to provide assistance for problems other than trauma, but in which all practitioners have a shared knowledge base and/or core of understanding about trauma resulting from violence. Knowledge about violence and the impact of trauma helps providers avoid both the triggering of reactions to trauma and retraumatization. Such information also allows women to manage their trauma symptoms successfully so that they are able to benefit from these services (Harris and Fallot 2001).

Conclusion

A look at the principal themes and issues affecting women in the criminal justice system reveals that women's issues are also society's issues: sexism, racism, poverty, domestic violence, sexual abuse, and substance abuse. While the impact of incarceration and reentry sets the stage and defines the individual experiences of female prisoners, their children and families, and their communities, what is required is a social response. Agencies and actions are not only about the individual; they are also, unavoidably, about family, institutions, and society. "Each of us is inextricably bound to others—in relationship. All human action (even the act of a single individual) is relational" (Gilligan 1996, 7).

If we expect women to successfully return to their communities and avoid rearrest, community conditions must change. A series of in-depth interviews with women produced the following conclusion:

> They need families that are not divided by public policy, streets and homes that are safe from violence and abuse, and health and mental health services that are accessible. The challenges women face must be met with expanded opportunity and a more thoughtful criminal justice policy. This would require a plan for reinvestment in low-income communities in this country that centers around women's needs for safety and self-sufficiency (Richie 2001, 386).

Communities need to increase their caring capacity and create a community response to the issues that negatively impact women's lives and increase their incarceration and recidivism risks.

> We have become a careless society. . . . Care is the consenting commitment of citizens to one another. . . . Care is the manifestation of a community. The community is the site of the relationships of citizens. And it is at this site that the primary work of a caring society must occur (McKnight 1995, x).

A series of focus groups conducted with women in the criminal justice system asked this question: How could things in your community have been different to help prevent you from being here? The respondents identified a number of factors whose absence they believed had put them at risk for criminal justice involvement: housing, physical and psychological safety, education, job training and opportunities, community-based substance abuse treatment, economic support, positive female role models, and a community response to violence against women (Bloom, Owen, and Covington 2003). These are the critical components of a gender-responsive prevention program.

Perhaps we can begin to learn from other nations, applying in our own communities the knowledge we gain. Poor countries around the world have found that spending money on health, education, and income-generation programs (such as microcredit for women) is the most efficient way to reduce poverty because a woman's progress also helps her family—women spend their money on their children. As women receive education and health care, and as they enter the work force and increase their power both in the family and in society, they have fewer and healthier children. Also, because women are poorer than men, each dollar spent on them means proportionally more (*New York Times* 2001).

In conclusion, the true experts in understanding a woman's journey home are women themselves. Galbraith (1998) interviewed women who had successfully transitioned from correctional settings to their communities. These women said that what had really helped them do this were

- relationships with people who cared and listened, and who could be trusted,
- relationships with other women who were supportive and who were role models,
- proper assessment/classification,
- well-trained staff, especially female staff,
- proper medication,
- job training, education, substance abuse and mental health treatment, and parenting programs,
- inmate-centered programs,
- efforts to reduce trauma and revictimization through alternatives to seclusion and restraint,
- financial resources, and
- safe environments

As we saw earlier, the reasons why the majority of criminal justice programming is still based on the male experience are complex, and the primary barriers to providing gender-responsive treatment are multi-layered. These barriers are theoretical, administrative, and structural, involving policy and funding decisions. There are, therefore, many of us in a diversity of professions who play a role within the continuum of care for women in the criminal justice system and who can do more.

NOTE

1. These statements were made by female inmates of a large East Coast correctional institution during interviews with the author in June 2000. These women were serving sentences of 15 years or more, and their comments came as they were preparing to be part of a one-day program sponsored by community providers and held in the prison.

REFERENCES

Abbott, Beverly, and Donna Kerr. 1995. *Substance Abuse Program for Federally Sentenced Women.* Ottawa, Ontario, Canada: Correctional Services of Canada.

Allard, Patricia. 2002. *Life Sentences: Denying Welfare Benefits to Women Convicted of Drug Offenses.* Washington, D.C.: The Sentencing Project.

American Psychiatric Association. 1994. *Diagnostic and Statistical Manual of Mental Disorders,* 4th ed. Washington, D.C.: Author.

Amnesty International USA. 1999. *Part of My Sentence: Violations of the Human Rights of Women in Custody.* New York: Author.

Andrews, Don, Jim Bonta, and Robert Hoge. 1990. "Classification for Effective Rehabilitation: Rediscovering Psychology." *Criminal Justice and Behavior* 17: 19–52.

Austin, James, Barbara Bloom, and Trish Donahue. 1992. *Female Offenders in the Community: An Analysis of Innovative Strategies and Programs.* Washington, D.C.: National Institute of Corrections.

Baunach, Phyllis Jo. 1985. *Mothers in Prison.* New York: Transaction Books/Rutgers University Press.

Beck, Allen J. 2000. *Prisoners in 1999.* Bureau of Justice Statistics Bulletin. Washington, D.C.: U.S. Department of Justice.

Beck, Allen J., and Jennifer C. Karberg. 2001. *Prison and Jail Inmates at Midyear 2000.* Bureau of Justice Statistics Bulletin. Washington, D.C.: U.S. Department of Justice.

Belknap, Joanne. 1996. *Invisible Woman: Gender, Crime, and Justice.* Belmont, Calif.: Wadsworth.

Belknap, Joanne, Melissa Dunn, and Kristi Holsinger. 1997. *Moving toward Juvenile Justice and Youth-Serving Systems That Address the Distinct Experience of the Adolescent Female.* A Report to the Governor. Columbus, Ohio: Office of Criminal Justice Services.

Bloom, Barbara. 1996. "Triple Jeopardy: Race, Class, and Gender." Ph.D. diss., University of California, Riverside.

———. 1998. "Women with Mental Health and Substance Abuse Problems on Probation and Parole." *Offender Programs Report: Social and Behavioral Rehabilitation in Prisons, Jails and the Community* 2 (1): 1–13.

———. 2000. "Beyond Recidivism: Perspectives on Evaluation of Programs for Female Offenders in Community Corrections." In *Assessment to Assistance: Programs for Women in Community Corrections,* edited by Maeve McMahon (107–38). Latham, Md.: American Correctional Association.

Bloom, Barbara, and Stephanie Covington. 1998. "Gender-Specific Programming for Female Offenders: What Is It and Why Is It Important?" Paper presented at the 50th annual meeting of the American Society of Criminology, Washington, D.C., November 11–14.

———. 2000. "Gendered Justice: Programming for Women in Correctional Settings." Paper presented at the 52nd annual meeting of the American Society of Criminology, San Francisco, November 15–18.

Bloom, Barbara, and David Steinhart. 1993. *Why Punish the Children? A Reappraisal of the Children of Incarcerated Mothers in America.* San Francisco: National Center on Crime and Delinquency.

Bloom, Barbara, Meda Chesney-Lind, and Barbara Owen. 1994. *Women in California Prisons: Hidden Victims of the War on Drugs.* San Francisco: Center on Juvenile and Criminal Justice.

Bloom, Barbara, Barbara Owen, and Stephanie Covington. 2003. *Gender-Responsive Strategies: Research, Practice, and Guiding Principles for Women Offenders.* Washington, D.C.: National Institute of Corrections.

Bloom, Sandra. 2000. "The Sanctuary Model." *Therapeutic Communities* 21 (2): 67–91.

Blume, Sheila. 1990. "Alcohol and Drug Problems in Women: Old Attitudes, New Knowledge." In *Treatment Choices for Alcoholism and Substance Abuse,* edited by Harvey Milkman and Lloyd Sederer. New York: Lexington.

———. 1997. "Women: Clinical Aspects." In *Substance Abuse: A Comprehensive Textbook,* edited by Joyce Lowinson, Pedro Ruiz, Robert Millman, and John Langrod (645–54). Baltimore, Md.: Lippincott Williams and Wilkins.

Brown, Vivian, Lisa Melchior, and George Huba. 1995. "Level of Burden: Women with More Than One Co-occurring Disorder." *Journal of Psychoactive Drugs* 27 (4): 339–46.

———. 1999. "Level of Burden among Women Diagnosed with Severe Mental Illness and Substance Abuse." *Journal of Psychoactive Drugs* 31 (1): 31–40.

Browne, Angela, Brenda Miller, and Eugene Maguin. 1999. "Prevalence and Severity of Lifetime Physical and Sexual Victimization among Incarcerated Women." *International Journal of Law and Psychiatry* 22: 301–22.

Bureau of Justice Statistics. 2002. *Correctional Populations in the United States.* Washington, D.C.: U.S. Department of Justice.

Bylington, Diane. 1997. "Applying Relational Theory to Addiction Treatment." In *Gender and Addictions: Men and Women in Treatment,* edited by Shulamith Lala Ashenberg Straussner and Elizabeth Zelvin (33–45). Northvale, N.J.: Jason Aronson.

Center for Substance Abuse Treatment. 1994. *Practical Approaches in the Treatment of Women Who Abuse Alcohol and Other Drugs.* Rockville, Md.: U.S. Department of Health and Human Services, Public Health Service, Substance Abuse and Mental Health Services Administration.

———. 1999. *Substance Abuse Treatment for Women Offenders: Guide to Promising Practices.* Rockville, Md.: U.S. Department of Health and Human Services, Public Health Service, Substance Abuse and Mental Health Services Administration.

Chesney-Lind, Meda. 1997. *The Female Offender: Girls, Women and Crime.* Thousand Oaks, Calif.: Sage Publications.

Covington, Stephanie. 1994. *A Woman's Way through the Twelve Steps.* Center City, Minn.: Hazelden.

———. 1998a. "The Relational Theory of Women's Psychological Development: Implications for the Criminal Justice System." In *Female Offenders: Critical Perspectives and Effective Intervention,* edited by Ruth T. Zaplin (113–31). Gaithersburg, Md.: Aspen.

———. 1998b. "Women in Prison: Approaches in the Treatment of Our Most Invisible Population." *Women and Therapy* 21 (1): 141–55.

———. 1999. *Helping Women Recover: A Program for Treating Substance Abuse* (Special edition for the criminal justice system). San Francisco: Jossey-Bass.

————. 2000. "Creating Gender-Specific Treatment for Substance-Abusing Women and Girls in Community Correctional Settings." In *Assessment to Assistance: Programs for Women in Community Corrections,* edited by Maeve McMahon (171–233). Latham, Md.: American Correctional Association.

————. 2001. "Creating Gender-Responsive Programs: The Next Step for Women's Services." *Corrections Today* 63 (1): 85–87.

————. 2002. "Helping Women Recover: Creating Gender-Responsive Treatment." In *The Handbook of Addiction Treatment for Women,* edited by Shulamith Lala Ashenberg Straussner and Stephanie Brown. San Francisco: Jossey-Bass.

————. 2003. "Beyond Trauma: A Healing Journey for Women." Center City, Minn.: Hazelden.

Covington, Stephanie, and Barbara Bloom. 1999. "Gender-Responsive Programming and Evaluation for Women in the Criminal Justice System: A Shift from What Works? to What Is the Work?" Paper presented at the 51st annual meeting of the American Society of Criminology, Toronto, Ontario, Canada, November 17–20.

Covington, Stephanie, and Janet Kohen. 1984. "Women, Alcohol, and Sexuality." *Advances in Alcohol and Substance Abuse* 4 (1): 41–56.

Covington, Stephanie, and Janet Surrey. 1997. "The Relational Model of Women's Psychological Development: Implications for Substance Abuse." In *Gender and Alcohol: Individual and Social Perspectives,* edited by Sharon and Richard Wilsnack (335–51). New Brunswick, N.J.: Rutgers Center of Alcohol Studies.

CSAT. See Center for Substance Abuse Treatment.

Culliver, Concetta. 1993. *Female Criminality: The State of the Art.* New York: Garland.

Daley, Dennis, Howard Moss, and Frances Campbell. 1993. *Dual Disorders: Counseling Clients with Chemical Dependency and Mental Illness.* Center City, Minn.: Hazelden.

Dowden, Craig, and Don Andrews. 1999. "What Works for Female Offenders: A Meta-analytic Review." *Crime and Delinquency* 45 (4): 438–52.

Elshtain, Jean. 2001. *Jane Addams and the Dream of American Democracy.* New York: Basic Books.

Foderaro, Joseph, and Ruth-Ann Ryan. 2000. "SAGE: Mapping the Course of Recovery." *Therapeutic Communities* 21 (2): 91–104.

Galbraith, Susan. 1998. *And So I Began to Listen to Their Stories. . . : Working with Women in the Criminal Justice System.* Delmar, N.Y.: Policy Research, Inc.

GAO. See U.S. General Accounting Office.

Garcia Coll, Cynthia, and Kathleen Duff. 1996. *Reframing the Needs of Women in Prison: a Relational and Diversity Perspective.* Project report. Wellesley, Mass.: Stone Center, Wellesley College.

Garcia Coll, Cynthia, Janet Surrey, Phyllis Buccio-Notaro, and Barbara Molla. 1998. "Incarcerated Mothers: Crimes and Punishments." In *Mothering against the Odds,* edited by Cynthia Garcia Coll, Janet Surrey, and Kathy Weingarten. New York: Guilford.

Genty, Philip. 1995. "Termination of Parental Rights among Prisoners: A National Perspective." In *Children of Incarcerated Parents,* edited by Katherine Gabel and Denise Johnston (167–82). New York: Lexington Books.

Gilligan, Carol, Nona P. Lyons, and Trudy J. Hanmer, eds. 1990. *Making Connections.* Cambridge, Mass.: Harvard University Press.

Gilligan, James. 1996. *Violence: Our Deadly Epidemic and Its Causes.* New York: Putnam.

Gil-Rivas, Virginia, Robert Fiorentine, and Douglas Anglin. 1996. "Sexual Abuse, Physical Abuse, and Posttraumatic Stress Disorder among Women Participants in Outpatient Drug Abuse Treatment." *Journal of Psychoactive Drugs* 28 (1): 95–102.

Greenfeld, Lawrence A., and Tracy L. Snell. 1999. *Women Offenders.* Bureau of Justice Statistics Special Report. Washington, D.C.: U.S. Department of Justice.

Haigh, Rex. 1999. The Quintessence of a Therapeutic Environment: Five Universal Qualities. In *Therapeutic Communities: Past, Present and Future,* edited by Penelope Campling and Rex Haigh (246–57). London: Kingsley.

Hannah-Moffat, Kelly. 2000. *Punishment in Disguise.* Toronto: University of Toronto Press.

Hannah-Moffat, Kelly, and Margaret Shaw. 2001. *Taking Risks: Incorporating Gender and Culture into the Classification and Assessment of Federally Sentenced Women in Canada.* Ottawa: Status of Women Canada, Policy Research Fund.

Harris, Maxine, and Jerri Anglin. 1998. *Trauma Recovery and Empowerment: A Clinical Guide for Working with Women in Groups.* New York: Free Press.

Harris, Maxine, and Roger Fallot. 2001. *Using Trauma Theory to Design Service Systems.* San Francisco: Jossey-Bass.

Human Rights Watch. 1996. *All Too Familiar: Sexual Abuse of Women in U.S. State Prisons.* New York: Author.

Institute of Medicine. 1990. "Populations Defined by Functional Characteristics." In *Broadening the Base of Treatment for Alcohol Problems* (381–98). Washington, D.C.: National Academy Press.

Jacobs, Ann. 2001. "Give 'Em a Fighting Chance: Women Offenders Reenter Society." *Criminal Justice Magazine* 45 (Spring).

Johnston, Denise. 1995. "Effects of Parental Incarceration." In *Children of Incarcerated Parents,* edited by Katherine Gabel and Denise Johnston (59–88). New York: Lexington Books.

Kaschak, Ellen. 1992. *Engendered Lives: A New Psychology of Women's Experience.* New York: Basic Books.

Kendall, Katherine. 1994. "Therapy behind Prison Walls: A Contradiction in Terms?" *Prison Service Journal* 96: 2–22.

Kivel, Paul. 1992. *Men's Work: Stopping the Violence That Tears Our Lives Apart.* Center City, Minn.: Hazelden.

Legal Action Center. 1999. *Steps to Success: Helping Women with Alcohol and Drug Problems Move from Welfare to Work.* New York: Author.

Leonard, Elizabeth, D. 2002. *Convicted Survivors: The Imprisonment of Battered Women Who Kill.* Albany: State University of New York Press.

Lynch, James, and William Sabol. 2001. *Prisoner Reentry in Perspective.* Crime Policy Report, vol. 3. Washington, D.C.: The Urban Institute.

Malysiak, Rosalyn. 1997. "Exploring the Theory and Paradigm Base for Wraparound Fidelity." *Journal of Child and Family Studies* 7 (1): 11–25.

McKnight, John. 1995. *The Careless Society: Community and Its Counterfeits.* New York: Basic Books.

McMahon, Maeve. 2000. "Assisting Female Offenders: Art or Science?" In *Assessment to Assistance: Programs for Women in Community Corrections,* edited by Maeve McMahon (300–16). Lanham, Md.: American Correctional Association.

Merlo, Alida, and Joycelyn Pollock. 1995. *Women, Law, and Social Control*. Boston: Allyn and Bacon.

Messina, Nena, William Burdon, and Michael Prendergast. 2001. *A Profile of Women in Prison-Based Therapeutic Communities*. Draft. Los Angeles: UCLA Integrated Substance Abuse Program, Drug Abuse Research Center.

Miller, Dusty. 1991. "Are We Keeping Up with Oprah? A Treatment and Training Model for Addictions and Interpersonal Violence." In *Feminism and Addiction*, edited by Claudia Bepko (103–26). New York: Haworth Press.

Miller, Dusty, and Laurie Giudry. 2001. *Addictions and Trauma Recovery: Healing the Body, Mind and Spirit*. New York: W.W. Norton.

Miller, Jean Baker. 1976. *Toward a New Psychology of Women*. Boston: Beacon Press.

———. 1986. *What Do We Mean by Relationships?* Work in Progress no. 22. Wellesley, Mass.: Stone Center, Wellesley College.

———. 1990. *Connections, Disconnections, and Violations*. Work in Progress no. 33. Wellesley, Mass.: Stone Center, Wellesley College.

Mumola, Christopher J. 2000. *Incarcerated Parents and Their Children*. Bureau of Justice Statistics Special Report. Washington, D.C.: U.S. Department of Justice.

Najavits, Lisa. 1998. "Seeking Safety: A New Cognitive-Behavioral Therapy for PTSD and Substance Abuse." *Journal of Traumatic Stress* 11 (3): 437–56.

———. 2002. *Seeking Safety*. New York: Guilford Press.

New York Times. 2001. "Liberating the Women of Afghanistan." Editorial, 24 November.

Owen, Barbara. 1998. *In the Mix: Struggle and Survival in a Women's Prison*. New York: State University of New York Press.

Owen, Barbara, and Barbara Bloom. 1995. *Profiling the Needs of California's Female Prisoners: A Needs Assessment*. Washington, D.C.: National Institute of Corrections.

Phillips, Susan, and Nancy Harm. 1998. "Women Prisoners: A Contextual Framework." In *Breaking the Rules: Women in Prison and Feminist Therapy*, edited by Judy Harden and Marcia Hill (1–9). New York: Haworth.

Pollock, Joycelyn. 1998. *Counseling Women Offenders*. Thousand Oaks, Calif.: Sage Publications.

———. 1999. *Criminal Women*. Cincinnati, Ohio: Anderson Publishing.

Reed, Beth Glover, and Maureen E. Leavitt. 2000. "Modified Wraparound and Women Offenders in Community Corrections: Strategies, Opportunities and Tensions." In *Assessment to Assistance: Programs for Women in Community Corrections*, edited by Maeve McMahon (1–106). Lanham, Md.: American Correctional Association.

Richie, Beth. 2001. "Challenges Incarcerated Women Face As They Return to Their Communities: Findings from Life History Interviews." *Crime and Delinquency* 47 (3): 368–89.

Richman, Roberta. 1999. "Women in Prison: Are Anybody's Needs Being Met?" Paper presented at the 24th annual conference of the Association of Women in Psychology, Providence, R.I., March 6–9.

Sanchez, Jose, and Bruce Johnson. 1987. "Women and the Drugs-Crime Connection: Crime Rates among Drug Abusing Women at Rikers Island." *Journal of Psychoactive Drugs* 19 (2): 200–216.

Sentencing Project, The. 2001. *Drug Policy and the Criminal Justice System*. Washington, D.C.: Author.

Stableforth, Nancy. 1999. "Effective Corrections for Women Offenders." *Forum on Corrections Research* 11 (3): 3–5.

Steffensmeier, Darrell, and Emilie Allen. 1998. "The Nature of Female Offending: Patterns and Explanations." In *Female Offenders: Critical Perspectives and Effective Intervention,* edited by Ruth Zaplin. Gaithersburg, Md.: Aspen.

Teplin, Linda, Karen Abram, and Gary McClelland. 1996. "Prevalence of Psychiatric Disorders among Incarcerated Women." *Archives of General Psychiatry* 53: 505–12.

U.S. General Accounting Office. 1999. *Women in Prison: Sexual Misconduct by Correctional Staff.* Washington, D.C.: Author.

Vesey, Bonnie. 1997. *Specific Needs of Women Diagnosed with Mental Illnesses in U.S. Jails.* Delmar, N.Y.: Policy Research, Inc.

Wellisch, J., Douglas M. Anglin, and Michael Prendergast. 1994. "Treatment Strategies for Drug-Abusing Women Offenders." In *Drug Treatment and the Criminal Justice System,* edited by James Inciardi (5–25). Thousand Oaks, Calif.: Sage Publications.

4

The Skill Sets and Health Care Needs of Released Offenders

Gerald G. Gaes and Newton Kendig

An unprecedented number of offenders are being released from prison and returning to our communities. How do we maximize their chances for success and minimize our exposure to criminal victimization? Preparation for reentry begins in prison. This chapter updates the previous literature about inmate needs and the programs designed to address those needs (Gaes et al. 1999). Instead of referring to inmate "deficits" or "needs," however, we will use a more neutral term—"skill sets"—for the different domains. A skill implies mastery and competence rather than personal liability. Although this orientation to inmate skills is somewhat symbolic, it emphasizes the interaction of training or teaching with the individual's proficiency and achievement. This is a small step away from the medical model toward a paradigm that emphasizes the role of the offender in his or her own successful reentry. This chapter also discusses the medical/mental health needs of reentering inmates and the barriers they encounter both within the criminal justice system and the community, as well as obstacles to productive prison programming. The skill and medical/mental health needs of reentering offenders are viewed here as complementary and overlapping issues that require integration.

This chapter is organized into six sections. The first section briefly reviews some of the literature on skill sets and introduces a classification (taxonomy) of these skills as a framework for understanding, assessing, and remediating skill deficiencies. The second section reviews the literature on in-prison programs designed to address these deficiencies. A number of recent, systematic reviews are more focused on these deficiencies than are previous meta-analyses of prison programs; the results of these research syntheses are reviewed and incorporated into the skill sets taxonomy. In this section, we also discuss the value of cost-benefit analyses and review in great detail a report by Aos et al. (2001) that has been the most comprehensive attempt to assign cost-benefit calculations to criminal justice programs. The third section, drawing upon data from the Bureau of Prisons and a recently completed study by the National Commission on Correctional Health Care (2002), outlines the health and mental health needs of returning prisoners. The fourth section discusses the barriers the criminal justice system and communities face in addressing inmate skill deficiencies and medical needs. The fifth section considers the role of the prisoner as parent in the reintegration process, a skill domain for which little research exists. The last section introduces a "self help" model that integrates concepts in both the medical and skill set literature. We also recognize and discuss the limitations of the "what works" model, which focuses on interventions that address primarily the propensity to commit crime. What is needed is a coherent theory that relates the skills/needs literature to other theories about crime that consider social context, opportunity, and social embeddedness. Social embeddedness refers to the extent to which an individual considers herself or himself a member of a family, group, or community.

Defining and Assessing Skill Deficiencies of the Returning Prison Population

There is no uniform way to categorize and define inmate skills, and we propose the following classification more as a heuristic than an attempt to finalize some taxonomy:[1] academic skills, vocational skills/correctional work, interpersonal skills, leisure time skills, cognitive skills, spirituality/ethical skills, daily living skills, wellness skills, mental health skills, and accountability skills (table 4.1). The goal here is to develop a more nuanced understanding of the factors that may contribute to criminal behavior as a starting point to providing interventions most effective in producing behavioral change. A number of researchers would probably

Table 4.1. *Categories and Definitions of Individual Skill Sets*

Reentry skills	Definitions/outcomes
Academic skills	Participates and progresses in educational activities commensurate with ability and occupation to serve as foundational skills for other reentry skills. Reads, writes, and utilizes basic arithmetic at a level necessary to function in a correctional environment and in society.
Vocational skills/ correctional work	Acquires and maintains employment in order to fulfill financial obligations, engages in purposeful activity, develops abilities useful in the acquisition and maintenance of postrelease employment and pursuit of career goals.
Interpersonal skills (parenting, normative relationships)	Relates appropriately and effectively with staff, peers, visitors, family, coworkers, neighbors, and members of the community, observing basic social conventions and rules. Maintains healthy family and community ties. Avoids negative interpersonal influences.
Leisure time skills	Engages in meaningful recreational activities and hobbies, making positive use of free time and facilitating stress management and favorable peer affiliations.
Cognitive skills	Engages in accurate self-appraisal and goal setting. Solves problems effectively, maintains self-control, and displays prosocial values.
Spirituality/ethical skills	Displays capacity for self-reflection and consideration of meaning in life in relation to a particular faith or personal philosophy.
Daily living skills	Displays independent living skills commensurate with institution or community opportunities to include maintenance of a clean residence, a responsible budget to include a savings account, meal preparation, appropriate personal hygiene and appearance, and proper etiquette. Obtains and maintains a legal residence and any necessary transportation. Obeys institution rules and regulations and local, state, and federal laws.
Wellness skills (self-help model)	Maintains physical well-being through health promotion and disease prevention strategies, such as healthy life-style habits and routine medical care. Obtains necessary treatment for acute and chronic medical conditions.
Mental health skills (substance abuse, sexual predation)	Maintains sound mental health through avoidance of substance abuse/dependence and other self-destructive behaviors and through use of effective coping techniques. Participates in appropriate medication and/or treatment regime as necessary to address any acute or chronic mental health issues.
Accountability skills	Assumes responsibility for own behaviors. Recognizes and accepts the short-term and long-term consequences of actions.

take issue with some of the categories appearing in table 4.1. For example, does it really make sense to define mental health as a skill? Should spirituality/ethical practices be considered a skill or should this be a private matter left up to the individual and his or her conscience? And while substance abuse and sexual predation fall in the mental health category, these problems could merit separate categorization. Nonetheless, this taxonomy is a starting point for defining skill sets that will ultimately lead to thorough assessment and intervention, and act as a kind of ongoing "report card" for an individual's ability to integrate back into the community.

By creating a taxonomy, we also have a way of categorizing research on the relationship between skills and postrelease outcomes. There have been at least two attempts to demonstrate this relationship: Gendreau, Little, and Goggin's (1996) summary of the literature on predictors of adult recidivism;[2] and Lipsey and Derzon's (1998) summary of the predictors of violent or serious youth delinquency. Table 4.2 compares the reentry skills and risk factor data for these two studies. The "predictors of recidivism" column refers to the individual inmate characteristics that increase the likelihood of postrelease recidivism. Gendreau et al. refer to these characteristics as risk factors and point out that "the design of effective offender treatment programs is highly dependent on knowledge of the predictors of recidivism" (Gendreau et al. 1996, 575). To the extent possible, we have tried to place these predictors in the table's reentry skills categories where they seem most appropriate. For instance, while parent or sibling criminality is a predictor of recidivism, we assume that prisoners' past associations can be addressed by helping them develop interpersonal skills focusing on prosocial values.

Andrews and Bonta (1998) distinguish between two kinds of predictors—dynamic and static (table 4.2). Dynamic predictors (in bold type) are theoretically amenable to treatment, training, and program interventions. In contrast, static predictors are not modifiable and are either historical, such as a person's past criminal behavior, or immutable individual characteristics, such as age, sex, and race. Table 4.2 lists only historical static predictors, since such predictors usually suggest interventions that can interrupt a cycle of crime. For example, an individual's criminal history does not automatically prevent that individual from overcoming such a tendency by learning new skills.

The correlations in table 4.2 indicate the relationship between the predictors and recidivism.[3] The value of the correlation coefficient (r) theoretically can vary from 0 to 1; however, because recidivism is usually

Table 4.2. Comparison of Postrelease Success/Failure Rates for Reentry Skill Sets

Reentry skills	Predictors of recidivism[a]	
	Gendreau, Little, and Goggin (1996)	Lipsey and Derzon (1998)
Academic skills	**Lack of education or employment skills (67 studies, average $r = .18$)** Intellectual functioning (32 studies, average $r = .07$)	**School aptitude/performance ($r = .13$)** IQ ($r = .12$)
Vocational skills/correctional work	**Lack of education or employment skills (67 studies, average $r = .18$)**	—
Interpersonal skills (parenting, normative relationships)	**Conflicts with family and significant others (28 studies, average $r = .15$)** Parent or sibling criminality (35 studies, average $r = .12$) Family rearing practices (31 studies, average $r = .15$) Separation from parents, broken home (41 studies, average $r = .10$)	**Parent-child relationship ($r = .15$)** **Social ties ($r = .15$)** Other family characteristics ($r = .12$) **Antisocial peers ($r = .04$)** Broken home ($r = .09$) Abusive parents ($r = .07$) Antisocial parents ($r = .23$)
Leisure time skills	**Identification/close relationship with criminal peers (27 studies, average $r = .18$)**	—
Cognitive skills	**Attitudes supportive of a criminal lifestyle (67 studies, average $r = .18$)** **Antisocial personality (63 studies, average $r = .18$)** **Identification/close relationship with criminal peers (27 studies, average $r = .18$)**	General offenses ($r = .38$) IQ ($r = .12$)

(continued)

Table 4.2. Continued

Reentry skills	Predictors of recidivism[a]	
	Gendreau, Little, and Goggin (1996)	Lipsey and Derzon (1998)
	Adult criminal history and prison misconduct (64 studies, average r = .18) History of antisocial behavior before adulthood (119 studies, average r = .13)	
Spirituality/ethical skills	—[b]	—[b]
Daily living skills	—[b]	—[b]
Wellness skills	—	Medical/physical characteristics (r = .13)
Mental health skills	**Anxiety, depression, neuroticism, psychiatric symptomatology (66 studies, average r = .05)** **Substance abuse (60 studies, average r = .14)**	**Substance abuse (r = .30)**
Accountability skills	**Attitudes supportive of a criminal lifestyle (67 studies, average r = .18)** **Antisocial personality (63 studies, average r = .18)** Adult criminal history and prison misconduct (64 studies, average r = .18) History of antisocial behavior before adulthood (119 studies, average r = .13)	General offenses (r = .38) **Aggressive behavior (r = .21)**

Notes: **Bold** type indicates dynamic risk predictors; roman type indicates historical static predictors.

a. The correlation *r* represents the strength of association between a predictor (e.g., antisocial personality) and recidivism. The larger the value of *r*, the stronger the association.

b. There were no predictors of recidivism that could be categorized within this reentry skill.

measured as yes or no, r cannot reach 1, and its maximum value is probably much less than 1. Some of the predictor domains, such as attitudes supportive of a criminal lifestyle, are listed under more than one skill, such as cognitive and accountability skills. Most of the relationships depicted in table 4.2 are modest. The strongest predictors of recidivism among adults are criminal history, prison misconduct, identification or close relationship with criminal peers, attitudes supportive of a criminal lifestyle, and lack of education or employment skills.[4] For youth, the strongest predictors are general offenses, substance abuse, antisocial parents, and aggressive behavior.

One of the weakest relationships for adults exists between recidivism and mental health measures of anxiety, depression, neuroticism, and psychiatric symptomology. Using meta-analytic techniques, Bonta, Law, and Hanson (1998) compared predictors of criminal and violent recidivism for mentally disordered and nondisordered offenders and found they were the same. Criminal history variables were the best predictors, and the clinical variables had the weakest relationship. Thus, although it appears future offending may be influenced by mental illness, the dominant factors are other actuarial and predisposing characteristics that are essentially the same regardless of mental illness diagnosis.

While this modest taxonomy suggests a way of categorizing skills, it would be important to know the extent to which inmates lack such skills and the extent to which those who have a skill deficit are allowed to participate in programs that can help them achieve those skills. Unfortunately, systematic program participation data for prisons or jails are sparsely reported and rarely collected. The most relevant data collection available is the Bureau of Justice Statistics' inmate survey, conducted every five or six years. This survey uses inmate interviews to discover important facts about their incarceration, their criminal and civil life prior to incarceration, and issues pertinent to their release. Lynch and Sabol (2001) used the 1991 and 1997 surveys to analyze inmate program participation and found that most prisoners do not participate in inmate programs, such as education and vocational programs, and the rate of participation has declined over the years. About 13 percent of "soon-to-be-released" inmates reported participating in a prerelease program in both 1991 and 1997. In 1997, 27 percent of soon-to-be-released inmates participated in vocational training programs, down from 31 percent in 1991. Educational programs also saw reductions— 35 percent in 1997, compared with 43 percent in 1991.

One essential element missing in these kinds of analyses is an accurate, systematic, and consistent estimate of the magnitude of need. Understanding the level of unmet need in skills development is just as important as knowing whether the percentage of inmates completing these programs is increasing or decreasing. Ideally, a baseline of a prisoner's skill sets (see table 4.1) would be assessed at prison intake and subsequently tracked and updated throughout incarceration. Not only might we measure and monitor inmate proficiencies in these skill sets, but we could chart inmates' progress over the course of their prison stay and just prior to release. Consider school achievement, for example. At what grade level do inmates enter prison? What is their progress throughout their prison stay? And what is their grade level at the time of release? This kind of monitoring and measurement not only helps inmates assess their level of achievement, but it also informs the institution and community case managers of the remaining work that needs to be done. Furthermore, such assessment serves as a kind of management barometer, gauging how well prison program providers are achieving their goals.

Education assessment may lead the way. The 1992 National Adult Literacy Survey (NALS) evaluated a sample of state and federal prisoners in addition to a large community sample (Haigler et al. 1994). The NALS results showed that 70 percent of prisoners scored at the two lowest levels of proficiency on the prose, document, and quantitative literacy scales, compared with 50 percent of the general population. Assessments such as the NALS can provide a standardized way of monitoring literacy, informing educators on their progress in improving inmate literacy during imprisonment. While some jurisdictions use standardized assessments for education level, there is no one national barometer for skill level. Tests such as the NALS that would focus on a broader set of skills and deficiencies, including cognitive, interpersonal, and wellness skills, would be complicated to develop. Furthermore, there are some skill sets for which there may never be a satisfactory assessment, such as ethical and leisure time skills. However, in order to know how to promote criminal desistance effectively, we must also know how interventions affect underlying deficiencies.

Addressing inmates' skill needs does not ensure that inmates will be motivated to learn and change, nor does achieving certain skill levels guarantee their postrelease success. Social settings; economic, familial, and neighborhood context; and peer relationships all affect the offender's opportunity and engagement in crime independent of the factors that affect propensity. The skill sets taxonomy proposed here, however, establishes a framework for understanding and addressing criminal propensity or the "psychology" of criminal conduct. The overall goal of classifying skill sets is to decompose propensity to crime into some of its component parts, thereby laying the groundwork for changing criminal behavior without losing sight of the fact that prisoners are not the fractured representation of skills depicted in table 4.1.

An Update on the "What Works" Literature and Recent Extensions to Cost-Benefit Considerations

Recent Meta-analyses on Inmate Intervention

Table 4.3 summarizes recent meta-analyses on inmate interventions, updating the last synopsis by Gaes et al. (1999). More focused than previous studies, these recent meta-analyses tend to address specific domains or skill sets (such as the ones outlined in table 4.1). Prior meta-analyses tended to cross many of these domains (see Gaes et al. 1999 for a summary of those meta-analyses). Meta-analysis methodology is evolving and increased rigor will lead to a more systematic and enriched understanding of these interventions. Nonetheless, the studies that form the basis of these research syntheses are still fraught with methodological problems. Meta-analyses conducted since we last reviewed them in 1999 cover more specific domains, such as cognitive skills, drug treatment, treatment for violent offenders, and work programs.[5] Results from the Aos et al. (2001) meta-analysis are interspersed throughout the table; however, the study itself is considered in more depth below because it was also combined with a rigorous cost-benefit analysis of the interventions.

According to Gaes et al. (1999), the meta-analysis literature in its entirety indicated that prison programs, on average, reduced recidivism; the likelihood of arrest fell from 55 percent to 45 percent.[6] Recent meta-analyses continue to show treatment effectiveness, particularly for academic instruction, vocational training, cognitive skills, sex offender programs, and substance abuse interventions. However, the results of these meta-analyses are not always definitive. For example, three meta-analyses and a fourth research review of sex offender treatment differ in their conclusions. Sex-offending intervention is particularly difficult

Table 4.3. *Postrelease Success/Failure Rates for Interventions Designed to Address Specific Skill Sets*

Reentry skills	*Meta-analyses results*
Academic skills	*Aos et al. (2001)* In-prison adult basic education: 3 studies; effect size = .11 *Pearson and Lipton (1999a)* Literacy training/reading education: 4 studies; r = .06; not significant. Authors conclude that a credible test of these programs cannot be conducted until better studies are done. Literacy and general equivalency diploma (GED) studies: 8 studies; r = .10; program = 45 percent; comparison = 55 percent College course work: 12 studies; r = .03; no effect *Wilson, Gallagher, and MacKenzie (2000)* For the adult basic education and GED programs, the odds were 1.44, and the contrast between program and comparison groups was 41 percent versus 50 percent. Postsecondary education: odds = 1.74; program = 37 percent; comparison = 50 percent
Vocational skills	*Aos et al. (2001)* In-prison vocational education: 2 studies; effect size = .13; program = 43.5 percent; comparison = 56.5 percent *Wilson, Gallagher, and MacKenzie (2000)* Vocational training: odds = 1.55; program = 39 percent; comparison = 50 percent
Correctional work (job training, job seeking, job placement programs)	*Aos et al. (2001)* Correctional industries programs: 3 studies; effect size = .08; program = 46 percent; comparison = 54 percent *Pearson and Lipton (1999a)* Job seeking and job training programs: 26 studies; r = .03; not significant

Interpersonal skills (parenting, normative relationships)	*Wilson, Gallagher, and MacKenzie (2000)* Correctional work: odds = 1.48; program = 40 percent; comparison = 50 percent Multicomponent/other: odds = 1.39; program = 43 percent; comparison = 50 percent The weighted odds ratios were not significantly different from zero. However, there were only 4 comparisons in the correctional work category and 5 comparisons in the multicomponent/other category. The cognitive skills results should apply here; however, there are no meta-analyses on parenting programs.
Leisure time skills	—
Cognitive skills	*Wilson, Allen, and MacKenzie (2000)* Average effect size, d = .36. This means that the treatment group recidivates at about 36 percent and the comparison group at 50 percent. *Aos et al. (2001)* Moral reconation therapy (ethics training): Average effect size, d = .08; not significant
Spirituality/ethical skills	— —
Daily living skills	
Wellness skills	
Mental health skills	*Aos et al. (2001)* Cognitive-behavioral sex offender treatment: 7 studies; effect size = .11; program = 44.5 percent; comparison = 55.5 percent *Gallagher, Wilson, and MacKenzie (2002)* Sex offender studies: Found 22 studies having 25 independent effect sizes, average d = .43. The treatment group on average demonstrated a sexual recidivism rate of about 12 percent while the comparison group was at 22 percent. In-prison therapeutic community (TC), with community aftercare: 11 studies; effect size = .08; program = 46 percent; comparison = 54 percent

(continued)

Table 4.3. *Continued*

Reentry skills	Meta-analyses results
	In-prison nonresidential substance abuse treatment: 5 studies; effect size = .09; program = 45.5 percent; comparison = 54.5 percent
	Pearson and Lipton (1999b)
	Drug abuse studies: Only the TC average effect size reached significance. The average correlation was .13. This translates to a failure rate of 43.5 percent for TC treatment groups and 56.5 percent for comparison groups. Outpatient counseling and boot camp drug treatments were not effective.
Accountability skills	—

Notes: The effect sizes have been represented in their original format as well as the percentage recidivating during the postrelease period. Effect sizes are typically represented as correlations (r), the difference in means measured in standard deviation units (Cohen's d), and in odds ratios. Where it was possible, effect sizes are converted to percent recidivating among program participants and percent recidivating among those who did not participate in the program. For some reentry categories, there are no meta-analysis results that apply to the particular reentry skill.

to deliver and assess, so it is not surprising that no uniformity exists among the conclusions about the interventions. The purpose for introducing the controversy here is to point out that treatment syntheses, even with better analytic techniques, still require a close reading of the evidence. Nonetheless, on the whole, these studies give us reason to be optimistic about the effectiveness of institutional interventions for returning prisoners.

Although these studies point to the success of prison intervention programs, it is important to note that there has been little recognition and analysis of the studies' external validity and generalizability. Most program interventions still depend on volunteer participants rather than random assignment. Therefore, the program may attract the most motivated individuals, making it difficult to tell whether the outcomes are due to the program itself or individual characteristics. In addition to the problem of selection bias inherent in these research designs, there is the difficulty of estimating how many inmates would or could be affected by these interventions. If only a few inmates volunteer and thus benefit from these interventions, it is easy to exaggerate the benefit to all inmates being released from our correctional systems. In fact, existing data suggest that many inmates do not participate in such programs, especially programs that will prepare them for community integration.

There is no reason to be particularly pessimistic about the impact of in-prison programs on postrelease success. However, researchers must still measure or estimate the degree to which offenders with skill deficits are able to participate in these programs. We then need to understand completion and dropout rates, a prerequisite to understanding the ultimate cost-benefit of program interventions. We discuss cost-benefit analysis as the next step in evaluating in-prison and community interventions.

Cost-Benefit Analyses of Treatment Interventions

Cost-benefit analysis is the economic realization of a program. It assigns a dollar value to all intervention benefits and costs. And converting benefits and costs to one dimension enables us to evaluate if that intervention yields a net benefit relative to its cost. Yet as Brown (2000) noted, cost-benefit or efficiency evaluations are missing from most program evaluations. This is probably true because assigning monetary values to program outcomes interpreted as intervention benefits is difficult. Specifically, computing "downstream" estimates of crime trajectories requires a great deal of data; gathering data on marginal costs of criminal justice resources is difficult; and controversies surround many of the intangible benefits resulting from these interventions (e.g., safety, family stability). Since these latter benefits are not traded in the marketplace (Laplante and Durham 1983), one has to impute their value. Recent work by Cohen and colleagues (Cohen 1988, 1998; Cohen, Miller, and Rossman 1994) has tried to explain the direct, indirect, tangible, and intangible costs of crime. Direct costs and benefits are those that can be anticipated, such as a crime victim's lost salary because of work absences resulting from the need to attend court dates or disability due to injuries. On the other hand, indirect costs and benefits are unanticipated, such as increases in insurance costs resulting from the victimization. While most costs are tangible, intangible costs—such as the pain, suffering, and fear a victim may experience following an armed robbery—are the most difficult of all costs to estimate.

Recognizing that cost-benefit analysis adds an additional perspective to program evaluation, one research team combined elements of meta-analyses with rigorous cost-benefit analyses. Aos et al. (2001) of the Washington State Institute for Public Policy (hereafter called the Institute) created a model for future approaches to cost-benefit analyses of program interventions. Their report, mandated by the Washington state legislature, used a meta-analysis to evaluate more than 400 research studies conducted in the United States and Canada. In addition, they produced a cost-benefit evaluation of most of these juvenile and adult interventions. The researchers asked, from the taxpayer's perspective, whether the savings in "downstream criminal justice costs" (Aos et al. 2001, 2) were more than the costs of the program.

The Institute primarily evaluated programs that had been conducted in other jurisdictions; however, the dollar values of costs and benefits were those expected to occur in Washington. Aos et al. took a conservative approach to the cost-benefit analyses by deflating the value of effects associated with evaluations demonstrating weak research designs. Although the Institute started with over 400 studies, about one-fourth did not meet the minimum research design criteria and were not included in the cost-benefit analysis.[7] The authors presented their results as dollars spent on programs versus dollars saved (returned) or dollars lost (wasted). Among their conclusions: even if a program leads to a reduction in criminality (positive average effect size), if it costs more than the value of crime reduction, it may not be economical.

The economic perspective adds a policy dimension missing from most of the program evaluation literature. It does, however, raise the level of uncertainty for policymakers. Programs must now be viewed in the context of assumptions about program content, program effect sizes, program costs, downstream criminal justice costs, and victim costs. All of these characteristics have their own sources of error. The interventions may vary because of differences in program implementation and organizational endorsement. The community outcomes depend on the amount of postrelease supervision, criminal opportunity, and the social dimensions of the ex-offenders' postrelease environment. Costs and benefits will depend on the circumstances of local economies. While it is true that all of these dimensions complicate the analysis, they have always been present, although often unrecognized or disregarded. Thus, the Institute's program analysis strategy engages the research community and policymakers in a more deliberate and systematic appraisal of the value of an intervention.

The Institute's report presented data on four domains: early childhood programs (8 studies), middle childhood and adolescent (non–juvenile offender) programs (6 studies), juvenile offender programs (85 studies), and adult offender programs (157 studies). While the non–criminal justice prevention programs will not be discussed here, it should be noted that the average highest economic benefits, according to this report, actually result from juvenile programs conducted *within* the criminal justice setting. Table 4.4 summarizes the average effect sizes and net benefits per participant reported by the Institute for each juvenile and adult offender program.

Unlike most meta-analyses of intervention studies, the Institute combined treatment completers and dropouts to get an unbiased assessment of treatment effects. If a particular study reported only treatment completers, then that study received the second lowest quality rating, and the effect sizes were adjusted based on the quality of the research design.[8] The research quality was judged on a five-point scale, with 5 representing the highest quality, and 1 representing the lowest quality. The Institute excluded any study it assessed at a value of 1. Studies receiving a value of 2 did not enter the cost-benefit calculations. A study receiving a quality rating of 3 was discounted by a factor of 0.5, which means its effect size counted 50 percent of the value of a study with a quality rating of 5. Studies with a rating of 4 received a 0.25 discount, and studies with a rating of 5 received no discount. In addition, the Institute also

Table 4.4. Results from the Aos et al. (2001) Cost-Benefit Analysis of Prisoner Treatment Programs

	Number of program effects in the statistical summary	Average effect size[a]	95% confidence intervals (table VI-A)[b]		Homogeneity test Q (table VI-A)	Net direct cost of the program per participant ($) (table I)	Net benefits per participant (Benefits minus costs) ($) (table I)	
							Lower end of range: taxpayer benefits only	Upper end of range: taxpayer and crime victim benefits[c]
Juvenile offender programs								
Specific "off-the-shelf" programs								
Multisystemic therapy	3	0.31	.111 to .517		1.91	4,743	31,661	131,918
Functional family therapy	7	0.25	.067 to .442		2.31	2,161	14,149	59,067
Aggression replacement training	4	0.18	−.097 to .457	Y	0.26	738	8,287	33,143
Multidimensional treatment foster care	2	0.37	−.006 to .746	Y	0.14	2,052	21,836	87,622
Adolescent diversion program	5	0.27	.133 to .413		16.8*	1,138	5,720	27,212
General types of treatment programs								
Diversion with services (vs. regular juvenile court processing)	13	0.05	.006 to .090		3.24	−127	1,470	5,679
Intensive probation (vs. regular probation caseloads)	7	0.05	−.073 to .168	Y	4.28	2,234	176	6,812
Intensive probation (as alternative to incarceration)	6	0.00	−.095 to .099	Y	4.89	−18,478	18,586	18,854
Intensive parole supervision (vs. regular parole caseloads)	7	0.04	−.075 to .156	Y	4.20	2,635	−117	6,128

Coordinated services	4	0.14	−.048 to .326	Y	1.66	603	3,131	14,831
"Scared Straight"–type programs	8	−0.13	−.249 to −.007	Y	6.38	51	−6,532	−24,531
Other family-based therapy approaches	6	0.17	.031 to .200		0.06	1,537	7,113	30,936
Juvenile sex-offender treatment	5	0.12	−.081 to .328	Y	2.76	9,920	−3,119	23,602
Juvenile boot camps	10	0.10	−.181 to −.018	Y	16.88*	−15,424	10,360	−3,587
Adult offender programs								
Adult offender drug treatment programs (compared with no treatment)								
In-prison therapeutic community (TC), no community aftercare	5	0.05	−.043 to .138	Y	1.27	2,604	−899	2,365
In-prison TC, with community aftercare	11	0.08	.031 to .128		5.77	3,100	−243	5,230
Non-prison TC (as addition to an existing community residential facility)	2	0.17	−.021 to .363	Y	0.18	2,013	4,110	15,836
In-prison nonresidential substance abuse treatment	5	0.09	.024 to .153		2.94	1,500	1,672	7,748
Drug courts	27	0.08	.032 to .119		23.08	2,562	−109	4,691
Case management substance abuse programs	12	0.03	−.021 to .089	Y	37.14*	2,204	−1,050	1,230
Community-based substance abuse programs	3	0.07	−.024 to .169	Y	1.09	2,198	237	5,048
Drug treatment programs in jails	7	0.05	−.05 to .145	Y	4.21	1,172	373	3,361
Adult sex-offender treatment programs								
Cognitive-behavioral sex-offender treatment	7	0.11	.013 to .200	Y	3.11	6,246	−778	19,354
Adult offender intermediate sanctions								
Intensive supervision (surveillance oriented)	19	0.03	−.032 to .097	Y	19.5	3,296	−2,250	−384
Intensive supervision (treatment oriented)	6	0.10	−.004 to .212	Y	0.37	3,811	−459	5,520
Intensive supervision (diversion from prison)	3	0.00	−.153 to .162	Y	1.41	−5,925	6,083	6,386
Adult boot camps	11	0.00	−.058 to .062	Y	4.64	−9,725	9,822	10,011
Adult boot camps (as partial diversion from prison)	11	0.00	—		—	−3,380	3,477	3,666

(*continued*)

Table 4.4. *Continued*

	Number of program effects in the statistical summary	Average effect size[a]	95% confidence intervals (table VI-A)[b]		Homogeneity test Q (table VI-A)	Net direct cost of the program per participant ($) (table I)	Net benefits per participant (Benefits minus costs) ($) (table I)	
							Lower end of range: taxpayer benefits only	Upper end of range: taxpayer and crime victim benefits[c]
Cognitive-behavioral programs								
Moral reconation therapy (ethics training)	8	0.08	−.012 to .167	Y	4.44	310	2,471	7,797
Reasoning and rehabilitation	6	0.07	−.011 to .159	Y	3.15	308	2,202	7,104
Other programs								
Work release programs (vs. in-prison incarceration)	2	0.03	−.184 to .237	Y	0.58	456	507	2,351
Job counseling/search for inmates leaving prison	6	0.04	−.006 to .084	Y	4.03	772	625	3,300
In-prison adult basic education	3	0.11	0.00 to .214		0.39	1,972	1,852	9,176
In-prison vocational education	2	0.13	.061 to .207		0.02	1,960	2,835	12,017
Correctional industries programs	3	0.08	.045 to .124		2.18	1,800	1,147	9,413

a. Positive effect size means lower crime.

b. Confidence interval spans $0 = Y$, or negative impact of program $= Y$. If the confidence interval spans zero (0), then there was no statistically significant effect of the program. If the confidence interval is negative, then the program increases recidivism.

c. Miller, Cohen, and Wiersema (1996).

*$P < .05$, indicating heterogeneity.

added a 0.5 discount for programs instituted by researchers or program developers because Institute researchers believe programs implemented and evaluated by program developers do not achieve the same magnitude of effect once they are implemented by line staff.[9] Aos et al. are not suggesting that researchers and developers who evaluate a study also subtly and unintentionally influence study outcomes, although this issue has been raised by Gaes et al. (1999).

Table 4.4 also includes the Q statistic (homogeneity test), which aids analysts in determining if all of the studies come from the same "population" of studies. When Q is large, indicating heterogeneity, analysts then use other factors to discern why the effect sizes are so discrepant. Unlike many meta-analyses reported in the criminal justice program evaluation literature, the Institute's method correctly computes the average effect size.[10]

Many of the 95 percent confidence intervals shown in table 4.4 span zero (0), indicating that those programs have no effect. Furthermore, many of the Q statistics indicate heterogeneity of variance among the effect sizes. These situations call for recomputing the effect size using a different approach and assessing those factors that contribute to the large differences in effect sizes.[11] Note also that the results of the Institute's meta-analysis contradict other meta-analysis results in some domains. For example, the average effect sizes for cognitive skills were not significant in the Aos et al. analysis, but were significant in the meta-analysis conducted by Wilson, Allen, and MacKenzie (2000). One of the reasons that the results of the Institute's meta-analysis differ from other meta-analyses is the discounting described above.

For each program listed in table 4.4, the Institute computed the per capita net direct cost. It is a net cost because some programs displace other programs that no longer have to be funded. For example, an improved work skills program could replace a different program and one would calculate the net cost as the cost of the new program less the cost of the prior intervention. Some programs have a negative net cost because they are cheaper to run than the ordinary criminal justice program. For example, boot camps are cheaper than prison stays for juveniles and adults because the participants spend much less time in a boot camp than they would in a normal correctional regime.

The downstream costs/savings were also calculated using the long-term reconviction rates of program and comparison participants. We have so far described steps 1 (compute the program effect) and 2 (estimate the long-term reconviction rates) in a five-part estimation process. The first two steps are used to estimate, according to the analysts, "the number of crimes that can be avoided with a program over a long time frame" (Aos et al. 2001, 46). In their model, Institute analysts estimate avoided crime, arrests, or convictions. Then, in steps 3, 4, and 5, they calculate and compare program costs and benefits (table 4.4). Of the two cost-benefit analyses provided, the first incorporates only the direct costs and benefits (savings) of a program, while the latter incorporates victim effects, such as lost wages and pain and suffering. The costs of the programs are based on the marginal operating and capital costs of a program in the State of Washington (see "Net Direct Cost of the Program per Participant" column in table 4.4). The benefits accrue from reductions in the marginal operating and capital costs of criminal justice resources, including police and sheriffs' offices; superior courts; county prosecutors; juvenile detention, probation, and institutions; and adult jails, prisons, and supervision.

The crime victims' cost savings used in table 4.4 were taken from Miller, Cohen, and Wiersema (1996), who defined monetary and quality-of-life costs, the most controversial elements of the cost-benefit analysis. Monetary costs include medical expenses, property damages, and reduction in future earnings incurred by crime victims. Quality-of-life costs put an estimate on crime victims' pain and suffering. In the Miller et al. analysis, pain and suffering costs were based on jury awards. In reporting program net benefits, Aos et al. provided a lower bound based on the taxpayer benefits only (the criminal justice costs—see "Lower End of Range" column in table 4.4) and an upper bound based on the taxpayer costs and victim benefits (see "Upper End of Range" in table 4.4). For example, in-prison vocational training costs $1,960 per participant. The net benefit of this program based on taxpayer expenses was $2,835 per participant, while the net benefit including victim costs was $12,017. As table 4.4 illustrates, some of the net benefits are very large. Multisystemic therapy for juveniles cost the taxpayer $4,743 per participant; however, the taxpayer's net savings was $31,161 per participant in downstream criminal justice costs and including victim benefits resulted in a combined savings of $131,918 per participant.

The Aos et al. methodology is the most comprehensive evaluation of juvenile and prison interventions available to date, combining some of the best elements of meta-analysis with a solid framework for cost-benefit methods.[12] This work also provides a model for how cost-benefit analyses can be an important means for advancing policy discussions. Cost-benefit analysis results may be more persuasive to policymakers, especially those who control the public purse, than are other summaries of program evaluations. Each step in the analysis process makes the results more concrete and meaningful to the consumer. To say a program reduces recidivism by 15 percent relative to a comparison group is less convincing than the implication that the program will reduce crime and cost the taxpayer less in the long run.

Cost-benefit analysis also advances the idea of program efficiencies. Since the calculations involve both the cost of the program and the benefit through crime reduction, programs can be compared not only on the basis of their potential to reduce crime, but also on the basis of the operational resources required. A cognitive skills program that costs only $500 per participant and reduces recidivism by 10 percent may be much more economical than a multisystemic therapy that costs $10,000 per participant and reduces recidivism by 11 percent.

The Medical/Mental Health Needs of Released Offenders

The National Commission on Correctional Health Care (NCCHC) has completed a congressionally mandated study entitled *The Health Status of Soon-to-Be-Released Inmates* (National Commission on Correctional Health Care 2002). Key data from the report are compiled in table 4.5 and suggest that the prevalence of certain infectious diseases, mental health disorders, and substance abuse problems is remarkably greater in inmate populations than in the overall U.S. population. The report argues that U.S. correctional systems serve as a strategic venue for diagnostic, treatment, and prevention initiatives among populations in need of health services that otherwise elude traditional public health providers.

The potential for enhanced control of communicable diseases in the United States through correctional systems is obvious. Serodiagnostic studies and tuberculin skin test data indicate that most inmates with communicable diseases enter prisons already infected with human immunodeficiency virus (HIV), hepatitis C virus (HCV), hepatitis B virus (HBV), and *M. tuberculosis* (Glaser and Griefinger 1993; Ruiz, Mokitor, and Sun 1999; Vlahov, Brewer, and Castro 1991; Vlahov et al. 1993). The recent success of U.S. tuberculosis (TB) control efforts is, in part, the result of correctional programs that have aggressively identified and treated inmates with active TB disease and latent TB infection as

Table 4.5. *Summary Information on Disease among Inmates from* The Health Status of Soon-to-Be-Released Inmates *and Other Sources*

Disease	Estimates of prevalence within correctional institutions (CIs), both prisons and jails, and among released inmates	Relation to U.S. population
Communicable disease[a,b,c,d]		
AIDS	Prevalence in prisons and jails: 0.5% 8,900 inmates with AIDS in CIs 38,500 inmates with AIDS released from CIs	Prevalence in U.S. population: 0.9%; 229,000 individuals Released inmates in 1996 represented 17% of all 229,000 U.S. AIDS patients.
HIV	Prevalence in prisons: 2.3–2.9% Prevalence in jails: 1.2–1.8% 35,000–47,000 inmates infected within CIs 98,500–145,000 HIV-positive inmates released from CIs	Prevalence in U.S. population: 0.3%; 750,000 individuals Released inmates in 1996 represented 13.1–19.3% of all U.S. HIV-positive individuals.
Sexually transmitted diseases (STDs) (syphilis, chlamydia, gonorrhea)	Prevalence of syphilis in prisons and jails: 2.6–4.3% Prevalence of chlamydia in prisons and jails: 2.4% Prevalence of gonorrhea in prisons and jails: 1.0% 107,000–137,000 infected with STDs inside CIs 465,000–595,000 inmates with STDs released from CIs	—
Current or chronic Hepatitis B infection	Prevalence in prisons and jails: 2.0% 36,000 inmates in CIs 155,000 inmates released from CIs	In 1996, 12.4–15.5% of all individuals with current or chronic Hepatitis B infection in the United States spent time in a CI.

Hepatitis C	Prevalence in prisons and jails: 17–18.6%	In 1996, 29–32% of the estimated 4.5 million individuals with Hepatitis C infection in the United States spent time in a CI.
	303,000–332,000 inmates inside CIs	
	1.3–1.4 million inmates released from CIs	
Tuberculosis (TB) disease	Prevalence in prisons: 0.04%	In 1996, there were 12,200 cases of TB disease among people who had spent time in a CI. This figure represented 35% of active TB cases in the United States.
	Prevalence in jails: 0.17%	
	1,400 inmates in CIs	
	12,000 inmates released from CIs	
Tuberculosis (TB) infection	Prevalence in prisons: 7.4%	—
	Prevalence in jails: 7.3%	
	130,000 inmates tested positive for latent TB	
	566,000 inmates released from CIs	
Chronic disease[c, d, e]		
Asthma	Prevalence: 8.5%; 140,738 cases	Prevalence in U.S. population: 7.8%
Diabetes	Prevalence: 4.8%; 73,947 cases	Prevalence in U.S. population: 7.0%
Hypertension	Prevalence: 18.3%; 283,105 cases	Prevalence in U.S. population: 24.5%
Mental health[f, g, h]		
Schizophrenia/other psychotic disorders	Six-month prevalence, jails: 1.0–1.1% (4,955–5,589 inmates)	Six-month prevalence in U.S. population: 0.4%
	Lifetime prevalence, state prisons: 2.3–3.9% (22,994–39,262 inmates)	Lifetime prevalence in U.S. population: 0.8%
	Lifetime prevalence, federal prisons: 0.8–2.5% (763–2,326 inmates)	
	Ohio = 1.5%; California = 3.4%; Michigan = 2.8%; Canada = 4.4%	Total ECA[i] = 1.5%

(continued)

Table 4.5. *Continued*

Disease	*Estimates of prevalence within correctional institutions (CIs), both prisons and jails, and among released inmates*	*Relation to U.S. population*
Major depressions	Six-month prevalence, jails: 7.9–15.2% (39,690–76,229 inmates)	Six-month prevalence, U.S. population: 8.4%
	Lifetime prevalence, state prisons: 13.1–18.6% (132,619–188,259 inmates)	Lifetime prevalence, U.S. population: 18.1%
	Lifetime prevalence, federal prisons: 13.5–15.7% (12,378–14,363 inmates)	
	Ohio = 12.7%; California = 7.3%; Michigan = 11.3%; Canada = 13.6%	Total ECA = 6.4%
Anxiety disorders	Six-month prevalence, jails: 14.01–20.0% (70,613–100,098 inmates)	—
	Lifetime prevalence, state prisons: 22.0–30.1% (222,147–303,936 inmates)	
	Lifetime prevalence, federal prisons: 18.2–23.0% (16,638–21,079 inmates)	
Bipolar (manic) disorder	Six-month prevalence, jails: 1.5–2.6% (7,755–12,920 inmates)	Six-month prevalence, U.S. population: 1.0%
	Lifetime prevalence, state prisons: 2.1–4.3% (21,468–43,708 inmates)	Lifetime prevalence, U.S. population: 1.5%

	Lifetime prevalence, federal prisons: 1.5–2.7% (1,393–2,475 inmates)	Total ECA = 1.5%
	Ohio = 2.8%; California = 2.9%; Michigan = 2.7%; Canada = 1.6%	
Posttraumatic stress disorder	Six-month prevalence, jails: 4.0–8.3% (19,770–41,509 inmates)	Six-month prevalence, U.S. population: 3.4%
	Lifetime prevalence, state prisons: 6.2–11.7% (62,388–118,071 inmates)	Lifetime prevalence, U.S. population: 7.2%
	Lifetime prevalence, federal prisons: 4.9–6.8% (4,466–6,257 inmates)	
Dysthymia (less severe depression)	Six-month prevalence, jails: 2.7–4.2% (13,644–21,040 inmates)	Six-month prevalence, U.S. population: 2.0%
	Lifetime prevalence, state prisons: 8.4–13.4% (85,018–135,121 inmates)	Lifetime prevalence, U.S. population: 7.1%
	Lifetime prevalence, federal prisons: 6.8–11.6% (6,253–10,652 inmates)	
	Ohio = NA; California = 3.8%; Michigan = 6.4%; Canada = 7.9%	Total ECA = 3.3%

(continued)

Table 4.5. *Continued*

Disease	*Estimates of prevalence within correctional institutions (CIs), both prisons and jails, and among released inmates*		*Relation to U.S. population*
Alcohol abuse/ dependence	Ohio = NA; California = 55.1%; Michigan = 46.5%; Canada = 47.4%	Total ECA = 2.6%	
Drug abuse/ dependence	Ohio = NA; California = 50.9%; Michigan = NA; Canada = 41.6%	Total ECA = 13.8%	

Note: NA = not available.

a. *Source:* National Commission on Correctional Health Care (2002), vol. 1, table 3-1. Most of the estimates in this table are from National Commission on Correctional Health Care (2002), vol. 2, Theodore M. Hammett, Patricia Harmon, and William Rhodes, "The Burden of Infectious Diseases among Inmates and Releasees from Correctional Facilities."

b. In 1996, 3 percent of the U.S. population spent time in a CI; however, 12–35 percent of the total number of people with these selected communicable diseases passed through a CI during that year.

c. Communicable disease estimates within prison and jails: applied national prevalence estimates to total number of inmates in prisons and jails on June 30, 1997.

d. Communicable disease estimates among persons released from prisons and jails: applied national prevalence estimates to total number of unduplicated inmates released from prisons and jails during 1996.

e. *Source:* National Commission on Correctional Health Care (2002), vol. 1, table 3-2. Most of the estimates in this table are from National Commission on Correctional Health Care (2002), vol. 2, Carlton A. Hornung, Robert B. Greifinger, and Soniya Gadre, "A Projection Model of the Prevalence of Selected Chronic Diseases in the Inmate Population."

f. *Source:* National Commission on Correctional Health Care (2002), vol. 1, table 3-3. Most of the estimates in this table are from National Commission on Correctional Health Care (2002), vol. 2, Bonita M. Veysey and Gisela Bichler-Robertson, "Prevalence Estimates of Psychiatric Disorders in Correctional Settings."

g. Estimates for 1995.

h. The mental illness estimates for specific state jurisdictions are from Diamond et al. (2001), table 3.

i. Total ECA sample refers to the community-based epidemiological study of mental illness, the Epidemiological Catchment Area program (Robins and Regier 1991). The sample size for that study was 19,182.

they passed through U.S. jails and prisons. The NCCHC report helps quantify the potential scope of correctional involvement in controlling communicable diseases. The report estimates that 98,500 to 145,000 inmates with HIV infection were released from prisons and jails in 1996, representing 13.1 to 19.3 percent of all HIV-infected persons living in the United States; furthermore, between 29 to 32 percent of the estimated 4.5 million individuals with HCV infection spent time in a correctional institution during 1996. These remarkable turnover rates support a public health role for U.S. jails and prisons that involves not only containing infectious diseases, but also decreasing the spread of disease through prevention efforts involving infected inmates prior to release.

The NCCHC report also recognizes mental illness and substance abuse as two of the most prevalent health conditions affecting inmate populations. Additional data from the Bureau of Justice Statistics reveals that 1.6 percent of all inmates received 24-hour care in a special housing or psychiatric unit, and that 13 percent received mental health therapy or counseling (Beck and Maruschak 2000). However, these estimates of the level of mental illness in the nation's prisons and jails have limitations. Perhaps the most critical review of prevalence data on mental illness in correctional populations comes from Diamond et al. (2001). They identify weaknesses in certain studies that depend on self-reporting, record reviews, and other nonstandard diagnostic techniques. The stronger studies, on the other hand, use diagnostic assessments with clear definitions and known reliabilities.[13] Diamond et al. compared the results of individual studies conducted within the nation's prison systems with the Epidemiological Catchment Area program (ECA) (Robins and Regier 1991), a large community-based study of mental illness. Compared with the community study, the studies using standard diagnostic instruments generally found higher lifetime and current prevalence rates for many psychiatric disorders in the prisoner samples.

Despite the availability of prevalence reports on mental illness in correctional populations, the number of inmates with mental illnesses pending release is rarely reported. In a review of automated records of 43,187 inmates released to the community in 2000, the Bureau of Prisons Office of Research identified 1,135 offenders (2.63 percent) with a diagnosed mental disorder. Inmates with the following conditions were considered mentally ill: bipolar disorder, delusional disorder, presenile dementia, major/nonpsychotic depression, major/psychotic depression, mania, organic mental disorders, schizoaffective disorder, schizophrenia (delusional), and schizophreniform disorder. The estimate does not include released inmates with mental illnesses that were undiagnosed at the time of release.

The large number of inmates released to the community with contagious diseases, chronic medical and mental health problems, and histories of substance abuse will require coping skills to maintain long-term health. Furthermore, there is an important overlap in the health/mental health needs of released offenders and the skill deficits outlined in table 4.1. Many of the skill sets depicted in the table refer to self-regulating behaviors, the ability to limit and control impulsive behavior, and the facility to think through and anticipate the consequences of one's actions. The risk-taking behavior that results from the inability to control impulsive behavior overlaps with some of the same behavior associated with infectious disease. Acquiring new skills could control such behavior as, for example, intravenous drug use, thereby decreasing the probability that blood-borne infectious diseases would be transmitted to others. The proposed skill sets outlined in table 4.1 provide a useful construct for release-planning programs designed for inmates with serious health problems.

Although each inmate possesses a unique health status and previously acquired skill set, most patients generally benefit from taking greater responsibility for their own health, improving communication with their primary care provider, establishing personal wellness goals, regulating impulsive and risk-taking behaviors, and improving interpersonal skills that strengthen family and social support systems (see especially Sbarbaro [1990] on medication compliance). Those inmates with histories of chronic addiction and mental illness require particularly intensive and targeted skill-building efforts because of the complexity of these problems and their known association with criminal behavior. Including inmates with serious health problems in proven skill-building programs will not only promote the long-term health of released offenders but will also serve as an effective strategy for improving our nation's public health.

External and Internal Barriers to In-Prison Preparation and Successful Transitions

In addition to enhancing skills, removing barriers to needed resources and services is also essential for improving community reentry for high-risk inmate populations. Barriers, both external and internal to the correctional environment, must be bridged. This section reviews obstacles reentering inmates encounter as they seek out medical and other services. These barriers primarily result from the fact that the different agencies that provide services and supervision for these offenders focus on their own internal missions and not on the offenders' broader reintegration needs.

External Barriers to Health Care Provision for Released Offenders

In a special issue of *Crime and Delinquency,* Hammett, Roberts, and Kennedy (2001) outline the following five important research areas that should be studied and developed to improve the medical needs of reentering inmates: (1) discharge planning, community linkages, continuity of care; (2) adherence to treatment regimens; (3) availability of transitional and permanent housing; (4) quick access to Medicaid, AIDS drug assistance, and other benefit programs; and (5) needs of dually and triply diagnosed individuals.

Most jurisdictions and communities have marginally addressed the important issue of linking in-prison and community-based health service providers. Model programs in Rhode Island, Hampden County (Massachusetts), and New York City are highlighted in the NCCHC report as well as in Hammett et al. (2001). These programs are successful because of strong cooperation between community health care providers and prison and jail administrators. In the most integrated programs, the same local health care worker who delivers medical care to inmates during incarceration also provides services upon inmates' release to the community.

Successful programs linking at-risk inmates to necessary health care and support services are exceptions rather than the norm, largely because of agency, policy, and logistical barriers that affect discharge planning and continuity of care. The logistical obstacles are formidable. Inmates often come from many different jurisdictions and are frequently housed in remote locations far from their homes. Ensuring chronically ill inmates access to resources and support services in distant communities requires inordinate planning and coordination. Thus, ensuring that a specific prisoner's medical needs are addressed in the community to which he or she will return represents an enormous management problem. Inmates in most states and federal prisons receive direct medical care from onsite prison providers through public funding appropriated specifically for prison health care. However, inmates are usually ineligible for federally funded dollars for health care maintenance once they are released (Ryan White funds for HIV-infected inmates may soon be an exception).

Maintaining continuous medical care is most critical for inmates with serious health needs. Slight interruptions in medications can be serious and in certain situations may have significant public health consequences. For example, treatment interruptions in the management of TB and HIV infection may lead to resistant illnesses that in turn may be transmitted to other persons. Obtaining fiscal resources for such patients is essential. However, released offenders may not have ready access to third-party benefits, such as Social Security, Medicaid, or the AIDS Drug Assistance Program (ADAP), and most offenders do not have private medical insurance. Ex-offenders find that qualifying for public funds is often difficult and tedious. Even with aggressive discharge planning, some inmates will experience a gap in their benefits while their eligibility is reinstated, while others will not qualify for either private or publicly funded medical insurance and fall to the bottom rung of available medical care—typically community health centers and local emergency rooms.

Perhaps the most basic need among released offenders is affordable housing (Hammett et al. 2001, 401). Returning offenders are frequently faced with a short supply of available housing and are unable to establish a stable "home base" that would help ensure continued medical treatment and community reintegration. Overcoming these external barriers to continuity of care is daunting but not insolvable. Telemedicine, a technique that allows a health care provider to interact with a patient with televideo equipment, is one solution. Its sophisticated technology can be used to enhance images and transmit diagnostic information during screening and follow-up interactions. Telemedicine holds the promise of allowing community medical practitioners to contact and even evaluate offenders before they are released. Increasingly, federal funding of community-based health care requires such formal connections with correctional systems. In addition, certain jurisdictions are also allowing offenders to "pre-qualify" for public health insurance benefits in anticipation of release (see, for example, Project Greenlight in New York City).

The largest impediments to continuity of care, however, are the lack of interagency collaboration and institutional compartmentalization. Customarily, prison administrators focus primarily on safely housing inmates under their custody. And parole and other postrelease supervision agencies view their role narrowly as monitoring the offenders under their custody. Furthermore, community service providers do not enroll ex-offenders until these released inmates somehow come to their attention. Therefore, cross-jurisdictional, cross-agency cooperation must be nurtured and developed. Recognizing the problem is the first step to recovery or, in this case, solutions.

The Impact of Criminal Justice Policies on In-Prison Preparation

While correctional systems aim to promote skills that foster reentry, they must also ensure public, prisoner, and staff safety. These goals are complementary when prisoners' programs provide a constructive environment compatible with day-to-day security needs. Thus, keeping prisoners occupied and focused on their long-term reintegration goals can dramatically impact the institution's safety and security. Unfortunately, because the bar has been set so high for most correctional systems to maintain institutional and public safety, prison order is often viewed as the primary mission, with almost a zero tolerance for escapes, homicides, and other threatening events. This attitude results in regimentation, close monitoring, and highly structured environments that are discouraging to inmate self-regulation and self-control, and represents one of the primary barriers to skill building. In addition, these structured environments often lead to a clash between the program providers and security staff.

Consider the following two examples. In one situation, medical staff members encourage a prisoner to monitor and control her diabetes. The inmate is taught how to monitor her blood glucose levels and to inject insulin by herself. However, in a prison environment, hypodermic needles are tightly controlled. Thus, there is conflict between the need to provide a reentry skill that should become a habit and the need to control a contraband item. In another situation, an inmate wants to acquire Internet skills. However, he is not permitted to use the Internet for fear he will misuse it to commit a crime. These examples may seem like simple mundane activities that should have solutions, and typically there are solutions. However, tension always exists between those employees who specialize in prison order—the security staff—and those employees who specialize in promoting prisoner skills—the programming staff. Ann Chih Lin (2000) has discussed this tension, proposing that program implementation in a prison depends on the collective efforts and good will of the line staff. Line staff members include both those who deliver the programs and those who are responsible for day-to-day operations of the prison, mostly security staff. Lin's ethnography examines the structure of program implementation, framing the problem as an extension of the "street level bureaucrat" concept. In his classic, *Street-Level Bureaucracy,* Michael Lipsky argued that line staff, rather than policy-makers or agency directors, actually make policy. "They exercise wide discretion in decisions about citizens with whom they interact. Then, when taken in concert, their individual actions add up to agency behavior" (Lipsky 1980, 13).

According to Lin, successful program implementation depends on the attitudes and the cultural context of the entire prison, both inmates and staff. Her analysis suggests that there are two dimensions of prison culture: prison-centered needs and institutional values. Prison-centered needs enhance the management of an institution. To the extent prison programs promote or are complementary to the primary needs of a prison, both the administration and the line staff will accept those programs. As Lin and others have noted, the prison's primary need is order. Rules and routines help to establish expectations about behavior so that prison is safe for both inmates and staff.

The second dimension, institutional values, has two poles. At one pole is an institution where the overriding ethos is for staff to support one another—the notion of staff solidarity. At the other pole, the institution emphasizes staff and inmate communication. In the former culture, the administration backs up staff members even when they are wrong. The term "staff solidarity" is shorthand for a culture characterized by an "us versus them" mentality and "for many staff, the two actions—backing each other and running to help when a colleague's life is threatened—are morally equivalent. Any relaxation of solidarity leads to a slippery slope. There must never be any doubt about where one's loyalty lies" (Lin 2000, 51).

Alternatively, in a culture of communication, staff members interact with inmates by openly trying to understand the inmate's point of view, by encouraging inmate participation in programs, and by seeking to understand the inmate's dilemma. These are, of course, idealized abstractions. Because prisons are about order, there will always be a sense of staff solidarity—"us against them." However, it does not take long for both staff and inmates to learn that communication and problem solving can preclude violent interactions, defusing situations before they get out of control.

Lin used these two dimensions to characterize and categorize five institutions, four federal and one state facility, at which she conducted site visits. "Successful implementation" occurred in institutions where the culture endorsed communication and programs met the needs of the institution. In these institutions, Lin observed variety and flexibility in the programs, staff that encouraged program participation, an emphasis on staff-prisoner communication, and an acknowledgment by staff that the institution had a reputation of excellence—which in turn encouraged staff to support programs. In the institution where Lin observed "neglected implementation," programs did not meet prison-centered needs even though there was a culture of communication. In this facility, too few inmates were enrolled in programs to contribute to prison order and programs seemed like an extra burden; however, because the prison demonstrated a history of quality programs and good relationships between staff and prisoners, there was still a tolerance for program innovation. The institution displaying "subverted implementation" conducted programs that met the needs of the prison; however, the prison culture emphasized solidarity. In prisons like this one, staff maximize program enrollment to solve the problem of prisoner supervision; however, prisoners resent staff and are not interested in programs. And because of the emphasis on staff solidarity, employees modify programs to serve institutional rather than inmate needs. Facilities demonstrating "abandoned implementation" are characterized by a culture of solidarity where the prison programs do not meet prison-centered needs. In such an institution, staff members emphasize solidarity among themselves and social distance from prisoners. A reputation of excellent custody means program employees have no leverage to ask for changes that might benefit programs, and prisoners avoid participation out of resentment.

Lin's analysis gives us a theoretical model by which to understand and minimize the barriers to successfully implementing in-prison programming and bringing community providers into the institution. If prison administrators can promote a culture that embraces programs while encouraging order, then the tension between the guards, on the one hand, and the educators, psychologists, doctors, and counselors, on the other, may be minimized. A culture based on security and custody is a culture based on regimentation, unquestioned authority, simplicity/uniformity, repetitive routines, rules, conformity, and an autocratic structure. A culture of rehabilitation, on the other hand, offers choices, the opportunity to affect one's surroundings, the ability to challenge authority, complexity/ individuality, scheduling flexibility, consideration of exceptions, unconventional approaches, and a democratic/participatory structure. Unfortunately, prison administrators are subject to social, legal, and political pressures that, for the most part, promote an environment in which these administrators are held accountable more for security and custody than for prisoner reintegration.

Involving Families of Incarcerated Parents

Interpersonal skills, one of the reentry skill sets outlined in our taxonomy, include the prisoner's interaction with his or her family and children. This section focuses on family interaction, an area in which research evaluating its impact on the offender's release success has been minimal. In order to understand the scope of the parenting problem, however, we first review data from a Bureau of Justice Statistics report. We then examine the few studies that evaluate parenting programs and discuss an article in which the authors tried to lay out some of the parenting issues facing incarcerated men.

The Role of Families

According to a report from the Bureau of Justice Statistics (BJS) (Mumola 2000), 2.1 percent of the nation's 72 million minor children had a parent in a state or federal prison during 1999. This percentage represented 721,500 parents (667,900 fathers and 53,600 mothers), and about 1.5 million children.[14] Only 23 percent of parents in state prison were married at the time of the BJS interview, 28 percent were divorced or separated, and 48 percent had never been married. Among federal prisoner-parents, 36 percent reported they were married, 25 percent were divorced or separated, and 38 percent had never been married.

Among these children of incarcerated parents, the typical caregiver was primarily the child's other parent, who was not in prison. However, as one might expect, this was much more true of male incarcerated parents than female prisoners (table 4.6.) Among state male inmate parents, the child's caregiver was primarily the other parent (89.6 percent). This was followed by the grandparent (13.3 percent), other relatives

Table 4.6. *Children's Caregivers during Parental Incarceration*

	Inmate parents (%), 1997								
	State				Federal			
Child's current caregiver	*Total*	*Males*	*Females*		*Total*	*Males*	*Females*
Other parent of child	85.0	89.6	28.0		87.6	91.7	30.7
Grandparent of child	16.3	13.3	52.9		12.2	9.8	44.9
Other relatives	6.4	4.9	25.7		6.2	4.2	33.9
Foster home or agency	2.4	1.8	9.6		1.3	1.1	3.2
Friends, others	5.3	4.9	10.4		6.8	6.4	11.9

Source: Mumola (2000), p. 3, table 4.

(4.9 percent), friends/others (4.9 percent), and foster home or agency (1.8 percent). These numbers do not add up to 100 percent because some inmates reported multiple children living with multiple providers. This pattern of caregiving was similar for male imprisoned parents in federal facilities. For incarcerated female parents, the differences were quite dramatic. The child's caregiver while these women were in prison was primarily the grandparent.

In the month prior to their arrest, 35.6 percent of male state inmate parents and 47.2 percent of male federal inmate parents claimed they lived with their children. For women, these percentages were 58.5 percent (state female parents) and 73.4 percent (federal female parents), respectively. The BJS report shows that only 19.6 percent of state inmate parents and 32.2 percent of federal inmate parents lived with their children in a two-parent household prior to their incarceration.

The BJS survey also assessed the extent to which inmate parents remained in contact with their children during their period of incarceration. Overall, 10.1 percent of the incarcerated parents said they kept in contact with their children on a daily basis; 31.2 percent kept in contact at least once a week; 22.2 percent kept in contact once a month; 16.1 percent had contact less than once a month; and 20.4 percent had no contact with their children. The primary method of contact was mail, closely followed by telephone, and least of all by personal contact. Females were more likely to keep in contact than males, and federal inmates were more likely to keep in contact than state inmate parents (table 4.7). These data underscore the compelling need for prison systems to enhance the communication between incarcerated parents and their children, except in those cases where the contact is inappropriate (e.g., cases of abuse). The majority of state male inmates (60.3 percent) and a large plurality of federal male inmates (42 percent) had very infrequent contact with their children (once a month or less). Even among female incarcerated parents, 39.9 percent of state and 30.3 percent of federal inmates had contact with their children once a month or less. Personal visits, not surprisingly, were not very common. Overall, among all incarcerated parents, 92.6 percent had seen their children once a month or less. In fact, 56.6 percent had never seen their children. A study by Hairston (1995) found that most incarcerated men neither were married to their child's mother nor had an ongoing relationship with her. Therefore, part of the problem in the parent-child dyad, especially for men, is the lack of any ongoing relationship between the parent and child that would foster familial, social support.

Table 4.7. *Frequency of Contact with Children by Parents in State and Federal Prisons, 1997*

| | Inmate parents (%), 1997 | | | | | |
| | State | | | Federal | | |
Frequency and type of contact with children	Total	Males	Females	Total	Males	Females
Any type of contact[a]						
Daily or almost daily	10.1	9.5	17.8	15.1	14.6	21.1
At least once a week	31.2	30.3	42.4	43.7	43.4	48.5
At least once a month	22.2	22.6	18.0	23.8	23.9	22.0
Less than once a month	16.1	16.6	9.7	10.0	10.3	5.0
Never	20.4	21.1	12.2	7.5	7.8	3.3
Telephone						
Daily or almost daily	6.6	6.2	11.3	13.0	12.8	15.0
At least once a week	19.8	19.2	27.0	36.3	35.9	41.2
At least once a month	16.5	16.6	15.3	23.2	23.1	24.9
Less than once a month	15.4	15.5	13.8	11.3	11.4	9.2
Never	41.8	42.5	32.6	16.2	16.7	9.7
Mail						
Daily or almost daily	4.8	4.4	9.6	4.3	3.9	9.5
At least once a week	23.2	22.2	35.6	30.4	30.0	35.9
At least once a month	23.1	23.3	20.6	30.4	30.5	27.8
Less than once a month	18.2	18.6	13.2	18.9	19.2	14.5
Never	30.8	31.6	21.0	16.1	16.4	12.3
Personal visits						
Daily or almost daily	0.8	0.7	1.1	0.4	0.3	0.9
At least once a week	6.6	6.5	8.0	7.1	7.1	6.6
At least once a month	13.9	13.8	14.7	15.1	15.3	12.0
Less than once a month	22.2	22.2	22.1	33.4	33.0	38.5
Never	56.6	56.8	54.1	44.1	44.2	42.0

Source: Mumola (2000), p. 5, table 6.
a. Telephone, mail, or personal visit.

Surveyed inmate parents, on average, expected to serve 80 months in prison; however, 42.2 percent expected to serve less than 4 years. Because the BJS survey is a cross section of inmates, the data emphasize longer sentences because prisoners with shorter lengths of stay move through the system more quickly. Nonetheless, 20.2 percent of incarcerated parents expected to serve at least 10 years in prison, typically having limited contact with their children as they mature into adults.

Furthermore, there is some indication that the incarcerated parents should have their own needs attended to as well. Over 75 percent reported a prior conviction, 56 percent reported a prior incarceration, 58.1 percent reported using drugs in the month before their arrest, and 33.6 percent reported using drugs at the time of their arrest. Nonparents were slightly less likely to report using drugs. Mothers reported more serious drug use than did fathers and were more likely to commit a crime to acquire drugs. Twenty-nine percent of females and 19.0 percent of males reported intravenous drug use before their arrest, and 32.2 percent of women and 18.5 percent of men claimed they committed an offense to acquire money for drugs. Furthermore, 25 percent of incarcerated parents reported behavior consistent with a history of alcohol dependence. Further underscoring these parents' needs, the BJS data indicate that 70.9 percent were employed in the month prior to their arrest, 46 percent reported income of at least $1,000 in the month prior to their arrest (mostly wages or transfer payments [72.8 percent], but also illegal sources [27.2 percent]), and 9.2 percent were homeless in the year previous to their incarceration (women more so than men).

In summary, it appears that there are quite a few incarcerated fathers whose child's welfare depends on the mother; in addition, there are many mothers whose child's welfare depends primarily on the grandparents. Among these parents, contact with children is limited, especially for men. Their financial resources are meager, and their skill deficits are great. In addition to attending to these prisoners' individual skill deficits, many correctional systems offer parenting programs. Unfortunately, no evidence apparently exists showing what proportion of inmate parents are able to participate in these programs. In addition, there is also no meta-analysis indicating the degree to which the programs that promote parenting or normative family interaction demonstrate effects on the parent-child relationship, the parent, or the child. Furthermore, there is no meta-analysis that we could locate that showed the effect of parenting on postrelease recidivism, much less the quality of the parent-child interaction. There is evidence, however, that marital stability and family relationships decrease the likelihood of postrelease recidivism and desistance from crime (Harer 1994; Laub, Nagin, and Sampson 1998; Pelissier et al. 2001; Rhodes et al. 2001). But few studies focus on the effect of parenting programs on the postrelease outcomes of incarcerated parents.

We found a few studies of in-prison parenting programs and two reviews of the literature (Lanier 2001; Magaletta and Herbst 2001). Marsh (1983) found that a parenting program in the Idaho State Correctional Institution improved parent communication and child management. Hairston and Lockett (1987) examined a parenting intervention intended to reduce neglect and abuse of children after the incarcerated parent's release. However, the authors were unable to establish whether there was any program effect. Lanier and Fisher (1990) described a parenting program based on support meetings, seminars, and a parenting education course; however, the program collapsed before it could be evaluated. Genisio (1996) used anecdotal reports to demonstrate that a book-reading program to improve the relationships between father and child was a success. Harrison (1997) found that parent training led to improved child-rearing attitudes. Landreth and Lobaugh (1998) evaluated "filial therapy," which promoted parent-child interactions. They found that as a result of the intervention, participants enjoyed greater acceptance by their children than did control group fathers. The intervention group fathers had fewer problems with their children's behavior and the children's self-concepts were significantly higher. Wilczak and Markstrom (1999) investigated the impact of parenting education on self-reported measures of satisfaction and knowledge. Even though they could demonstrate that the program could enhance parents' interactions with their children, there was no effort to assess any impact on the postrelease success of the incarcerated parent.

Magaletta and Herbst (2001) discuss the chaotic family structure of many incarcerated men, taking a psychological, therapeutic perspective that focuses on the father and the child. They also offer practical suggestions on improving the quality and amount of contact through the use of videotapes and televideo. However, these authors caution that, as with personal visits, televideo interactions should be structured. Magaletta and Herbst refer to resources that are already available to enhance these remote visits, including letter writing. These authors also point out that families may hide bad news from the incarcerated parent to avoid further distress. Yet the incarcerated parent eventually learns of the news, often in a distorted fashion, and the communication may be more distressing in its filtered form. Magaletta and Herbst suggest a four-step process based on cognitive skills that helps address some of the problems that arise between incarcerated parents and their children: (1) admission/grieving, (2) confrontation/disclosure, (3) forgiveness/reconciliation, and (4) restoration/healing.

The little evidence that exists supports the effectiveness of parenting programs in improving the parent-child relationship for those who can participate. However, while we can theoretically expect that the enhancement of the parent role should increase the parent's postrelease success, there is no systematic evidence to support that supposition. In fact, there is no assessment of either the extent to which such programming is available or the level of prisoner participation. While parenting programs involve efforts to bring the inmate's family into the institution while fostering family bonds, there is also a rationale for bringing other resources from the community into the prison. At the same time that corrections officials and inmates must be looking forward to preparation for release, corrections officials and community service providers must be looking backward from the community context into the institution in an effort to establish connections between the inmate and his family, his work environment, and his civic responsibilities.

A Self-Help Model, an Agenda for Future Theory and Research, and Policy Implications

A Self-Help Model of Behavior

If there is a prerequisite skill among all of the skills discussed in this chapter, it is accountability. We defined this as assuming responsibility for one's own behaviors and recognizing and accepting the short-term and long-term consequences of one's actions. This was categorized as a skill, even though it may be more appropriately thought of as a requisite disposition. This thinking extends to health care as well. Teaching inmates to monitor their own health and become informed citizens in their own care and maintenance encourages them to pursue a lifestyle inconsistent with substance abuse and other deleterious habits and behaviors. Furthermore, by making inmates advocates of their own health maintenance, we encourage their relationships with community resources and providers. Within the context of health decisions, inmates can enhance the quality of their own health care by becoming informed resources for the community health care provider. This process may extend to other positive lifestyle choices as well. We call this the "self-help" model of behavior.

The self-help model is also consistent with a strength-based reentry philosophy (Maruna and LeBel 2001), which emphasizes the individual as an asset to his or her community. Maruna and LeBel contrast their strength-based model to the current public policy themes of supervision/control and welfare/service, which they characterize as the "needs" model. The inmate builds his skills under the direction of service provision agents (e.g., drug counselors, therapists) while being monitored by control agents. The control agents are prison security officers and probation or parole officers providing postrelease supervision. However, Maruna and LeBel characterize these approaches as incompatible with the goal of becoming self-sufficient. Under this regime, responsibility for inmate skill-building rests on those monitoring the inmate's behavior and those providing treatment or services. The strength-based model, however, locates the locus of control in the individual. According to Maruna and LeBel, the message of the needs model is "You have problems and need our help," while the strengths model says "You are needed in your community" (Maruna and LeBel 2001, 16). Maruna and LeBel argue that the needs and strength-based models are incompatible because the essential problem ex-offenders face on reentry is the stigma associated with the conviction. Skill deficits or needs defined by social control agents reinforce that stigmatization.

Duguid (2000) makes a parallel argument in his discussion of the difference between the opportunities model and treatment model within the prison. The opportunities model is based on the presumption that the inmate is a free actor and should choose among the prison's alternative programs offered in an effort to increase skills and knowledge. The new treatment model, according to Duguid, is a disguised form of the medical model; it gives correctional psychologists and staff authority to decide what a specific prisoner needs since these "experts" know how to assess (diagnose) the inmate's problems and have the insight required to train the inmate.

Without trying to referee the choice of one model over the other, we see components of both models as important. The needs model says the community and agents of control have a plan for reintegration that recognizes the offender's strengths and weaknesses. The strength-based model recognizes the potential contribution the ex-offender can make to the community.

The self-help model is more difficult to implement in prison than in the community. However, it could work in a prison framework if inmates could work themselves down to lower security levels by demonstrating productive use of their time. As they moved downward, they would be given more opportunities to make personal decisions and more control over their daily activities. At the lowest security level, inmates would be responsible for a making a budget, preparing their own meals, participating in their health care, and perhaps making decisions governing their daily routines. This would be a huge policy shift in the context of American prisons. While there is certainly some risk in providing these freedoms, piloting more "open" institutions could test such a construct while limiting the risk.

Future Directions for Assessment and Interventions

As the "what works" literature has reemerged, resurrected by meta-analyses of program evaluations (Cullen and Gendreau 2001; MacKenzie 2000), we should recognize the limitations of this orientation toward the psychology of criminal behavior (Andrews and Bonta 1998). There is plenty of room for further development of theories based upon a psychological model to improve assessment and enhance programs. However, this work ought to be embedded within a broader framework that recognizes social context. The work by Laub and Sampson (2001), Uggen and Massoglia (2003), Bushway et al. (2001), and Nagin (1999) on the life course of criminality is an exciting step in that direction. Desistance from criminality is recognized as the process by which the individual ends a criminal career, and that career can be very brief or quite long. Moffit's (1993) theory distinguishing between patterns of crime that are limited to adolescence or that persist through life is one step in recognizing a developmental theory that includes psychology and social context. We envision future theoretical developments that integrate a taxonomy of skill deficiencies with a developmental theory explaining how these deficiencies arise, a life course model showing how criminal propensity can change over time, and an understanding of the social institutions and other social contexts that make this possible. There is a great deal of work yet to do on these theoretical developments while other criminal justice researchers try to grasp how to change policy and make successful reintegration work.

Policy Implications

While policy implications of the research reviewed in various sections of this chapter have already been noted, we close with some of the more important suggestions:

- Correctional institutions should begin the reentry process on the first day of an offender's imprisonment by assessing the individual's shortcomings and providing programs to address skill deficits. For example, a plan to maintain quality family interaction should be initiated soon after incarceration begins.
- As inmates demonstrate they can be productive within prison, they should be given opportunities to exercise more discretion over their lives. For example, prisoners could manage a budget, proactively manage their health care, and determine and follow through on their daily activities. However, this policy would stretch prison resources and is antithetical to the culture of most prison systems; furthermore, it may be possible only at low-security prisons.
- The data on infectious disease prevalence among returning ex-offenders demonstrates that transitional and community health care for these returning inmates should be funded, to promote not only their health but also the health of the larger community.
- Prison programs designated as cost-effective by cost-benefit analyses should be funded to cover as many inmates as possible; however, funding should also be set aside for the development and cost-benefit analyses of new and innovative programs.
- To effectively introduce policy changes, administrators should anticipate how line staff would react to program implementations and the extent to which the staff culture might subvert the designed policy change. Administrators should find innovative ways to develop a prison culture based on successful inmate reintegration rather than safety and security alone.

NOTES

The opinions expressed in this chapter are those of the authors and do not represent the views or policies of the Federal Bureau of Prisons or the U.S. Department of Justice.

1. Patti Butterfield, Bureau of Prisons psychologist, developed the classification scheme during her work on a reengineering workgroup on inmate reintegration.

2. The Gendreau et al. (1996) meta-analysis of the factors that predict recidivism summarized research from a number of studies in which a given predictor of recidivism was but one among many covariates. One of the problems in using such covariates in a meta-analysis is that it does not take account of the implication of other covariates in the equation. Thus, studies with different specifications may have different effect sizes by virtue of the covariate pattern.

3. The correlations for the Lipsey and Derzon article are for the predictors at ages 6–11, rather than ages 12–14. Furthermore, unlike the Gendreau, Little, and Goggin representation, these correlations are adjusted for methods features of the different studies.

4. We have left out of table 4.2 the risk scales, such as the Salient Factor Score (SFS) and Level of Supervision Inventory (LSI), which were assessed by Gendreau, Little and Goggin. These scales are composites of many of the individual predictors already represented in the table.

5. Meta-analyses completed since the Gaes et al. (1999) review include effective programs for women (Dowden and Andrews 1999); treatment for violent offenders (Dowden and Andrews 2000); treatment of sex offenders (Furby, Weinrott, and Blackshaw 1989; Gallagher et al. 1999; Gallagher, Wilson, and MacKenzie 2002; and Hall 1995), boot camps (MacKenzie, Wilson, and Kidder 2001); drug treatment programs (Pearson and Lipton 1999b); structured cognitive behavioral programs (Wilson, Allen, et al. 2000); education, vocational training, and work programs (Pearson and Lipton 1999a; Wilson et al. 1999; and Wilson, Gallagher, and MacKenzie 2000); and a systematic coverage of many of these skill domains (Aos et al. 2001). Some of these are not represented in table 4.3 because they do not fit in very well. For example, the boot camp program is composed of many of the elements found in table 4.1 within a regimented structure.

6. This is equivalent to an effect size of .10.

7. The appendix to the Institute's report lists every study and the research design rating it received.

8. Effect sizes were also adjusted to remove bias (Hedges 1981).

9. This so-called "non–real world" discount, represented on page 41 of the report, was noted as 25 percent, a factor of 0.75. However, on page 81 of the report, table IV-C, the authors list model parameters and indicate that the non–real world programs discount was 50 percent, a factor of .50. One of the studies depicted in table IV-K (page 109) indicates an effect size of .30, a design score of 5 (no discount), and a researcher role of 1 indicating researcher participation. The discounted effect size for this study was .15, implying that the Institute's analysis included a 50 percent discount for non–real world programs.

10. The inverse variance method of weighting was used to calculate the average effect size. Confidence intervals were computed and the Q test for homogeneity of variance was calculated. We have added the 95 percent confidence intervals and the Q statistic test results to table 4.4. These come from the original report's table IV-A. We have reoriented the data because, in most meta-analyses, an effect size showing a positive benefit is usually recorded as a positive effect size. The Institute chose the opposite way to represent the data, and to reduce confusion for the reader, we have transposed the effect sizes.

11. Analysts are supposed to use a random effects model to recompute the weighted average effect size.

12. While the Aos et al. methodology is a model for future cost-benefit analyses for prison- and community-based programs, as a research community we will have to decide how to treat study discounting. We will also have to consider what to do about costs when the meta-analysis indicates a lack of statistical significance and possible study heterogeneity. The purist will argue that in order to proceed with the cost-benefit portion, the effect sizes ought to be significant. This may be appropriate in intervention domains where there is a clear conclusion about the effect sizes. But, there are a number of program intervention domains where the conclusions are, at best, ambiguous and the cost-benefit may still be worthwhile. Finally, some consensus on benefits will have to be reached, especially on how we treat intangible victim costs.

13. These diagnostic instruments included the Diagnostic Interview Schedule III (DIS) (Robins and Helzer 1985), the Psychiatric Epidemiology Research Interview (PERI) (Dohrenwend et al. 1980), and the Structured Clinical Interview for the DSM (SCID) (Spitzer et al. 1990).

14. These data were based on the 1997 Survey of Inmates in State and Federal Correctional Facilities.

REFERENCES

Andrews, Don A., and James Bonta. 1998. *The Psychology of Criminal Conduct,* 2nd ed. Cincinnati, Ohio: Anderson.

Aos, Steve, Polly Phipps, Robert Barnoski, and Roxanne Lieb. 2001. *The Comparative Costs and Benefits of Programs to Reduce Crime.* Olympia: Washington State Institute for Public Policy.

Beck, Allen J., and Laura M. Maruschak. 2000. *Mental Health Treatment in State Prisons, 2000.* Bureau of Justice Statistics Special Report. Washington, D.C.: U.S. Department of Justice.

Bonta, James, Moira Law, and Karl Hanson. 1998. "The Prediction of Criminal and Violent Recidivism among Mentally Disordered Offenders: A Meta-analysis." *Psychological Bulletin* 123 (2): 123–42.

Brown, Shelley L. 2000. "Correctional Program Evaluation: An Economic Perspective." In *Compendium 2000 on Effective Programming.* Ottawa: Correctional Services of Canada.

Bushway, Shawn D., Alex R. Piquero, Lisa M. Broidy, Elizabeth Cauffman, and Paul Mazerolle. 2001. "An Empirical Framework for Studying Desistance As a Process." *Criminology* 39 (2): 491–515.

Cohen, Mark A. 1988. "Pain, Suffering, and Jury Awards: A Study of the Cost to Crime Victims." *Law and Society Review* 22 (3): 537–55.

———. 1998. "The Monetary Value of Saving a High-Risk Youth." *Journal of Quantitative Criminology* 14 (1): 5–33.

Cohen, Mark A., Ted R. Miller, and Shelli B. Rossman. 1994. "The Costs and Consequences of Violent Behavior in the United States." In *Consequences and Control of*

Understanding and Preventing Violence, edited by Albert J. Reiss and Jeffery A. Roth. Washington, D.C.: National Research Council and National Academy Press.

Cullen, Francis T., and Paul Gendreau. 2001. "From Nothing Works to What Works." *The Prison Journal* 81 (3): 313–38.

Diamond, Pamela M., Eugene W. Wang, Charles E. Holzer III, Christopher R. Thomas, and des Agnes Cruser. 2001. "The Prevalence of Mental Illness in America's Prisons: Review and Policy Implications." *Administration and Policy in Mental Health* 29 (1): 21–40.

Dohrenwend, Bruce P., Patrick Shrout, Gladys Egri, and Frank Mendelsohn. 1980. "Measures of Non-specific Psychological Distress and Other Dimensions of Psychopathology in the General Population." *Archives of General Psychiatry* 37: 1229–36.

Dowden, Craig, and Donald A. Andrews. 1999. "What Works for Female Offenders: A Meta-analytic Review." *Crime and Delinquency* 45 (4): 438–52.

———. 2000. "Effective Correctional Treatment and Violent Reoffending: A Meta-analysis." *Canadian Journal of Criminology* 42 (4): 449–67.

Duguid, Stephen. 2000. *Can Prison Work? The Prisoner as Object and Subject in Modern Corrections.* Toronto: University of Toronto Press.

Furby, Lita, Mark R. Weinrott, and Lyn Blackshaw. 1989. "Sex Offender Recidivism: A Review." *Psychological Bulletin* 105 (1): 3–30.

Gaes, Gerald G., Timothy J. Flanagan, Laurence L. Motiuk, and Lynn Stewart. 1999. "Adult Correctional Treatment." In *Prisons: Crime and Justice: A Review of Research,* edited by Michael Tonry and Joan Petersilia (361–426). Chicago: University of Chicago Press.

Gallagher, Catherine A., David B. Wilson, and Doris L. MacKenzie. 2002. *Effectiveness of Sex Offender Treatment Programs,* University of Maryland, College Park, Md.

Gallagher, Catherine A., David B. Wilson, Paul Hirschfield, Mark B. Coggeshall, and Doris L. MacKenzie. 1999. "A Quantitative Review of the Effects of Sex Offender Treatment on Sexual Reoffending." *Corrections Management Quarterly* 3 (4): 19–29.

Gendreau, Paul, Tracy Little, and Claire Goggin. 1996. "A Meta-analysis of the Predictors of Adult Recidivism: What Works." *Criminology* 34 (4): 575–607.

Genisio, Margaret H. 1996. "Breaking Barriers with Books: A Father's Book-Sharing Program from Prison." *Journal of Adolescent and Adult Literacy* 40 (2): 92–100.

Glaser, John B., and Robert B. Griefinger. 1993. "Correctional Health Care: A Public Health Opportunity." *Annals of Internal Medicine* 118: 139–45.

Haigler, Karl O., Caroline Harlow, Patricia O'Connor, and Anne Campbell. 1994. *Literacy behind Prison Walls: Profiles of the Prison Population from the National Adult Literacy Survey.* Princeton, N.J.: Educational Testing Service.

Hairston, Creasie. 1995. "Fathers in Prison." In *Children of Incarcerated Parents,* edited by Katherine Gabel and Denise Johnston (31–40). New York: Lexington Books.

Hairston, Creasie, and Patricia Lockett. 1987. "Parents in Prison: New Directions for Social Services." *Social Work* 32 (2): 162–64.

Hall, Gordon C. Nagayama. 1995. "Sexual Offender Recidivism Revisited: A Meta-analysis of Recent Treatment Studies." *Journal of Consulting and Clinical Psychology* 63 (5): 802–9.

Hammett, Theodore M., Cheryl Roberts, and Sofia Kennedy. 2001. "Health-Related Issues in Prisoner Reentry." *Crime and Delinquency* 47 (3): 390–409.

Harer, Miles. 1994. *Recidivism among Federal Prisoners Released in 1987.* Washington, D.C.: Office of Research, Federal Bureau of Prisons.

Harrison, Kim. 1997. "Parental Training for Incarcerated Fathers: Effects on Attitudes, Self-Esteem, and Children's Self-Perceptions." *The Journal of Social Psychology* 137 (5): 588–93.

Hedges, Larry V. 1981. "Distribution Theory for Glass's Estimator of Effect Size and Related Estimators." *Journal of Educational Statistics* 6: 107–28.

Landreth, Garry L., and Alan F. Lobaugh. 1998. "Filial Therapy with Incarcerated Fathers: Effects on Parental Acceptance of Child, Parental Stress, and Child Adjustment." *Journal of Counseling and Development* 76 (2): 157–65.

Lanier, Charles S. 2001. *Who's Doing the Time Here, Me or My Children? Addressing the Issues Implicated by Mounting Numbers of Fathers in Prison,* School of Criminal Justice, State University of New York at Albany.

Lanier, Charles S., and Glenn Fisher. 1990. "A Prisoner's Parenting Center (PPC): A Promising Resource Strategy for Incarcerated Fathers." *Journal of Correctional Education* 41 (4): 158–65.

Laplante, Josephine M., and Taylor R. Durham. 1983. *An Introduction to Benefit-Cost Analysis for Evaluating Public Expenditure Alternatives.* Croton-on-Hudson, N.Y.: Council on International and Public Affairs.

Laub, John H., and Robert J. Sampson. 2001. "Understanding Desistance from Crime." In *Crime and Justice: A Review of Research,* edited by Michael J. Tonry (1–69). Chicago: University of Chicago Press.

Laub, John H., Daniel S. Nagin, and Robert J. Sampson. 1998. "Trajectories of Change in Criminal Offending: Good Marriages and the Desistance Process." *American Sociological Review* 63: 225–38.

Lin, Ann Chih. 2000. *Reform in the Making: The Implementation of Social Policy in Prison.* Princeton, N.J.: Princeton University Press.

Lipsey, Mark W., and James H. Derzon. 1998. "Predictors of Violent or Serious Delinquency in Adolescence and Early Adulthood: A Synthesis of Longitudinal Research." In *Serious and Violent Juvenile Offenders: Risk Factors and Successful Interventions,* edited by Rolf Loeber and David P. Farrington (86–105). Thousand Oaks, Calif.: Sage Publications.

Lipsky, Michael. 1980. *Street-Level Bureaucracy: Dilemmas of the Individual in Public Services.* New York: Russell Sage.

Lynch, James P., and William J. Sabol. 2001. *Prisoner Reentry in Perspective.* Crime Policy Report, vol. 3. Washington, D.C.: The Urban Institute.

MacKenzie, Doris L. 2000. "Evidence-Based Corrections: Identifying What Works." *Crime and Delinquency* 46: 457–71.

MacKenzie, Doris L., David B. Wilson, and Suzanne B. Kidder. 2001. "Effects of Correctional Boot Camps on Offending." *Annals of the American Academy of Political and Social Science* 578: 126–43.

Magaletta, Phillip R., and Dominic Herbst. 2001. "Fathering from Prison: Common Struggles and Successful Solutions." *Psychotherapy* 38 (1): 88–96.

Marsh, Robert L. 1983. "Services for Families: A Model Project to Provide for Services for Families of Prisoners." *International Journal of Offender Therapy and Comparative Criminology* 27 (2): 156–62.

Maruna, Shadd, and Thomas P. LeBel. 2001. "Ex-convict Re-entry: A Slogan in Search of a Narrative." Paper presented at the meeting of the American Society of Criminology, Atlanta, November 6–10.

Miller, Ted R., Mark A. Cohen, and Brian Wiersema. 1996. *Victim Costs and Consequences: A New Look.* Washington, D.C.: National Institute of Justice.

Moffit, Terrie E. 1993. " 'Life-Course Persistent' and 'Adolescent-Limited' Antisocial Behavior: A Developmental Taxonomy." *Psychological Review* 100: 674–701.

Mumola, Christopher J. 2000. *Incarcerated Parents and Their Children.* Bureau of Justice Statistics Special Report. Washington, D.C.: U.S. Department of Justice.

Nagin, Daniel S. 1999. "Analyzing Developmental Trajectories: A Semi-parametric, Group-Based Approach." *Psychological Methods* 4: 139–57.

National Commission on Correctional Health Care. 2002. *The Health Status of Soon-to-Be-Released Inmates.* 2 volumes. Washington, D.C.: Author.

Pearson, Frank S., and Douglas S. Lipton. 1999a. *The Effectiveness of Educational and Vocational Programs: CDATE Meta-analyses.* Paper presented at the meeting of the American Society of Criminology, Toronto, November 16–20.

———. 1999b. "A Meta-analytic Review of the Effectiveness of Corrections-Based Treatment for Drug Abuse." *The Prison Journal* 79 (4): 384–410.

Pelissier, Bernadette, Sue Wallace, Joyce A. O'Neil, Gerald G. Gaes, Scott Camp, William R. Rhodes, and William G. Saylor. 2001. "Federal Prison Residential Drug Treatment Reduces Substance Use and Arrests after Release." *The American Journal of Drug and Alcohol Abuse* 27 (2): 315–37.

Rhodes, William, Bernadette Pelissier, Gerald G. Gaes, William Saylor, Scott Camp, and Susan Wallace. 2001. "Alternative Solutions to the Problem of Selection Bias in an Analysis of Federal Residential Drug Treatment Programs." *Evaluation Review* 25 (3): 331–69.

Robins, Lee N., and John E. Helzer. 1985. *Diagnostic Interview Schedule (DIS), Version III-A,* Department of Psychiatry, Washington University School of Medicine, St. Louis, Mo.

Robins, Lee N., and Darrel Regier. 1991. *Psychiatric Disorders in America: The Epidemiological Catchment Area Study.* New York: Free Press.

Ruiz, Juan D., Fred Mokitor, and Richard K. Sun. 1999. "Prevalence and Incidence of Hepatitis C Virus Infection among Male Prisoners Entering the California Correctional System." *Western Journal of Medicine* 170: 156–60.

Sbarbaro, John A. 1990. "The Patient-Physician Relationship: Compliance Revisited." *Annals of Allergy* (April): 325–31.

Spitzer, Robert L., Janet B. W. Williams, Miriam Gibbon, and Michael B. First. 1990. *Structured Clinical Interview for DSM-III-R.* Washington, D.C.: American Psychiatric Press, Inc.

Uggen, Christopher, and Michael Massoglia. 2003. "Desistance from Crime and Deviance As a Turning Point in the Life Course." In *Handbook of the Life Course,* edited by Jeylan T. Mortimer and Michael Shanahan. New York: Kluwer Academic/Plenum Publishers.

Vlahov, David, T. Fordham Brewer, and Kenneth G. Castro. 1991. "Prevalence of Antibody to HIV-1 among Entrants to U.S. Correctional Facilities." *Journal of the American Medical Association* 265: 1129–32.

Vlahov, David, Kenrad E. Nelson, Thomas C. Quinn, and Newton E. Kendig. 1993. "Prevalence and Incidence of Hepatitis C Virus Infection among Male Prison Inmates in Maryland." *European Journal of Epidemiology* 9: 566–69.

Wilczak, Ginger L., and Carol A. Markstrom. 1999. "The Effects of Parent Education on Parental Locus of Control and Satisfaction of Incarcerated Fathers." *International Journal of Offender Therapy and Comparative Criminology* 43 (1): 90–102.

Wilson, David B., Leana C. Allen, and Doris L. MacKenzie. 2000. *A Quantitative Review of Structured, Group-Oriented Cognitive-Based Programs for Offenders,* University of Maryland, College Park.

Wilson, David B., Catherine A. Gallagher, and Doris L. MacKenzie. 2000. "A Meta-analysis of Corrections-Based Education, Vocation, and Work Programs for Adult Offenders." *Journal of Research in Crime and Delinquency* 37 (4): 347–68.

Wilson, David B., Catherine A. Gallagher, Mark B. Coggeshall, and Doris L. MacKenzie. 1999. "A Quantitative Review and Synthesis of Corrections-Based Education, Vocation, and Work Programs." *Corrections Management Quarterly* 3 (4): 8–18.

PART II
The Impact of Incarceration and Reentry on Children and Families

5

From One Generation to the Next

How Criminal Sanctions Are Reshaping Family Life in Urban America

Donald Braman and Jenifer Wood

Davida's first memory of her father's return home from prison is vivid. She was getting off the school bus and saw him waiting for her outside her grandmother's house. "I just looked, and I was, like, 'Daddy!' And I just ran. . . . At that time," she says, crossing her fingers, "we was like this, you know?" Thinking back on the time when she, her father, and her grandmother all lived together, she smiles, shaking her head: "I mean, it was just so much that me and my father did. I missed that when he got locked back up." Her father's subsequent arrest remains a vivid memory:

> I remember the night the police came. They chased him in the house, and I was sitting there screaming, like, "Daddy! Daddy!" And he ran to the back door, but the back door was locked. The police came, and they pushed him down on the floor. He got up and pushed them off and ran through the front door, so I ran behind him, and I was just running right behind him . . . running right behind him. I seen the police behind me, and my father ran in through the alley. And I came, and I seen the police coming, so I ran behind the gate, by where my father was at. They didn't see us. My father, they came and pulled my father from under the car and started beating him. And I was standing there looking at them beating my father with night sticks, and they dragged him through the alley and put him in the paddy wagon. So they took my father.[1]

The effect on Davida was, by her own assessment, powerful: "I was *upset* by that. I started hanging out more, started drinking. I wasn't going to school. I was, like, 'Forget school.' In sixth grade I dropped out of school completely, I didn't want to go no more."

In the next four years, Davida would be sexually assaulted by her stepfather, serve time in a juvenile facility for girls, sell her body to help support herself and her grandmother, and be confined in a psychiatric institution. She would hide what she could from her father, knowing that there was little he could do while he was in prison. Now at age 16, Davida watches incredulously as her grandmother's landlord removes all their furniture from their apartment, surprised not so much by their eviction as by her entire life:

> My father is very important to me and grandmother, because by me not being old enough to get a regular job that maintains a stable place for us to stay, and my grandmother's retired, she only gets one check a month, we don't have much money to do this, or, you know, food or whatever. She's not with Section 8 yet, public housing, food stamps, so it's, like, my father needs to be here. . . . I'm bending over backwards trying to keep everything intact while he's not here, and by me being my age it's hard, you know? I'm going through a hell of a life while he's not home.

Davida and millions of families like hers are now suffering effects from the unprecedented expansion of our criminal justice system over the past two decades—effects reaching far beyond criminal offenders themselves. For an increasing number of families, incarceration and reentry are parts of everyday life. Today, millions of children have fathers in jail or prison, and millions more have fathers who have returned home in recent years.[2] By all measures, these families are typically among the most fragile and these children among the most vulnerable in our society. Unfortunately, the experience of reentry for most families is, as it was for Davida, just a prelude to the experience of rearrest and reincarceration[3]— a cycle that can have devastating effects on family life and, more specifically, child development.

This chapter discusses findings from a three-year ethnographic study of families of male prisoners in Washington, D.C.,[4] and examines the accounts of families like Davida's to shed light on how incarceration and reentry are reshaping family life. This study's findings suggest that our current criminal justice policies significantly strain family systems, often derailing children of offenders from their normal developmental trajectories. Through its impact on the families and communities from which prisoners are taken and to which they return, mass incarceration is having significant negative intergenerational effects.

Because reentry must be understood in the context of family history, including history with the criminal justice system, we begin our discussion with the familial experience of incarceration. The many problems that families face—from economic strain and parental conflict to maternal depression and familial isolation—have specific and well-documented sequelae for children but have been largely absent from discussions of criminal justice policy. We then describe families trying to cope with reentry and reincarceration, including the difficulties that offenders and their families face when reunited. The chapter concludes with a summary of how current and common criminal justice policies are affecting family life and, in particular, child development and children's mental health.

Incarceration and Family Life

Incarceration reaches more deeply into the substance of family and community life than standard accounts of criminal sanctions suggest. Forcefully transforming the material and social lives of families, incarceration creates a set of concurrent problems, which, in combination, strain relationships and break apart fragile families. The accounts of families attempting to cope with incarceration, typically missing from criminal justice and child development literatures, illustrate a broad array of consequences for families as a whole and for children in particular.

"Everything Piling Up"

Shabaka, age 8, and Tyrone, age 9, have lived with their paternal grandmother, Edwina, and—prior to his incarceration—their father, Kenny, for most of their lives. Kenny and Edwina share custody of the boys because their mother was, as Kenny put it, "in the drug life," and Edwina often had to sign school papers as a legal guardian. The boys can visit their mother whenever they want, but over the years they have asked less and less because her addiction has made her life and her living arrangements increasingly unpleasant.

For several years leading up to Edwina's retirement, the family had been carefully planning a return to their hometown in rural Alabama. Although

Kenny and his two boys lived with her in the District of Columbia, most of their extended family still lived in Alabama, and Edwina was eager to return to a simpler life near her kin. Shabaka and Tyrone, like their father, spent part of their childhood in Alabama and also enjoyed being close to the extended family. Kenny and Edwina thought that, as the boys got older, country life might do them some good. Managing two pre-adolescent boys in the city was already proving challenging, and Kenny and Edwina worried about how they would shepherd the boys through to adulthood.

Prior to his incarceration, Kenny had a job as a computer technician at a local TV station that paid reasonably well. He was able to help Edwina with her expenses while she helped him to care for his children. His income helped Edwina to buy groceries, make mortgage payments, and cover whatever bills she had trouble paying. Over the years, they accrued a fair amount of equity in the house, enough to aid the family's return to Alabama.

The End of a Dream

"That seems like a long time ago," Edwina says now, looking around at her untidy house. Her son was arrested a year ago on a murder charge (he claims he was defending himself) and has been awaiting trial since. Edwina has decided to stay in the area "until Kenny is out and situated." She has cared for the boys and, while it would be far less expensive to care for them in Alabama, she thinks they need to be near their father. Unable to afford retirement, Edwina works part-time at a staffing agency for nursing homes. At the age of 62, she is solely responsible for her two grandsons and her granddaughter, Tasha, who recently moved in with the family after having a baby of her own.

While Kenny was worried about his sons seeing him in jail, Edwina felt that they needed to see him. The boys wanted to know where their father was, and she did not feel she could keep the truth from them much longer. "They had a bond between them where they were very close to him, you know. It was 'Daddy! Daddy! Daddy!' " She told Kenny that he would have to tell them over the phone what was going on, and eventually she convinced him to let the boys visit.

> I told him . . . "I just want the boys to see you, and they need to see you." The only problem I have when I go see him is the youngest one—he gets upset and he wants to know, "Why you can't go home with us? How much longer you gonna be here?" You know?

Incarceration can be confusing for children who have difficulty comprehending the workings of the criminal justice system. Shabaka and Tyrone's grandmother was at a loss to explain to them exactly how to predict what would happen to their father.

> They keeps on saying—I think it was just last night, the youngest one asked me, "Grams, how many more years Daddy got to do," you know? And I say, "I don't know." I say, "We just praying every day that it don't be too much more longer." And then they worry about, you know, how old they're gonna be when he comes.

This was a common complaint from those caring for children of prisoners: the family never knew for sure if or when their father would be home.

Their father's absence has had a significant impact on the boys' behavior. Kenny worries about this a good deal:

> Sometimes they get mad because I'm not there. I can sense they're getting a[n] attitude even when I talk to 'em on the telephone. Usually, they're very well mannered, you know, and like, it's that they display this attitude when they can't have their way, or something is out of the norm, then they show up for attention, and I can see it. My mother, now she does as well as she can but she's a grandmother to them, so she spoils 'em. They start to think they can just get away with things, you know, just skimping by on their homework or talking back.

Of the effects that incarceration may have on the boys, the hardest to gauge is also the one that worries their father and grandmother the most: the stigma of their father's imprisonment. According to Kenny, "That's what I worried most about. . . . I cried a lot over that . . . thinking how they will grow up and what it will do to them." While the boys are acting out and their schoolwork is suffering, the effects of this stigma run deeper. Tyrone and Shabaka rarely invite friends over to the house now and have withdrawn from many of the social relationships they had at school. Kenny doesn't believe the boys talk to anyone about their family situation. "The boys, no, they don't speak to no one about it. My family wears it more as a badge of shame. It's not like we're proud, so we just keep it to ourselves." Edwina agrees. "No, I don't think they'd tell a person. They get real quiet when people talk about fathers."

HARSH REALITY
While parental incarceration and the stigma associated with it are difficult for any family to confront, many practical and material consequences compound the problem for families and children. Kenny had not only served as his children's primary caretaker, but also he had

helped Edwina with mortgage payments and other bills. Having lost one major provider, his family finds it difficult to make ends meet and is quickly losing many of the practical and symbolic rewards earned by years of hard work.

Instead of enjoying retirement, Edwina now cares for Kenny's sons and assists his daughter. She hires a babysitter when necessary, and while the children's maternal grandmother helps out once in a while, Kenny's incarceration has been disruptive and costly. To make ends meet, Edwina works and has taken out a second mortgage on the home that was her nest egg for retirement. "You just have to hope something will work out," she says, "but it's not easy." Edwina and Kenny now worry a good deal more about their finances than before. "I don't even know where it all goes. The boys, my granddaughter, the house, just everything piling up." After a moment's reflection, she adds, "It's a good thing we had the house, though, or I don't know how we'd manage."

Even in this brief period, Edwina has had to put off moving, return to work, remortgage her house, and assume increased responsibility for the care of Kenny's children. The effect of this financial strain has, by her own account, not been good for her or the kids. "Sometimes I just give up," she says, "or otherwise I get snappy." Kenny has noticed how the strain has affected his mother as well: "She used to be very good-natured. I don't think I ever heard her cuss. But now she swears left and right, she's yelling at the kids. But I can't do a thing to help, so I don't criticize. But that worries me a lot, both for my mother's sake and the boys'."

The potential long-term effects of this kind of increased emotional and financial hardship on Shabaka and Tyrone are, sadly, well documented in the child development literature.[5] According to many studies, economic strain negatively affects caretaker behavior in a significant way, for example, harsh and inconsistent parenting—problems that both Edwina and Kenny describe. These parenting behaviors, in turn, bring about a range of emotional and behavioral problems among children (McLoyd 1998).

Kenny's case shows what can happen when a family encounters incarceration. Kenny's family felt the effects of his absence quickly, and the effects have been extensive. In the brief time since their father's arrest, incarceration has transformed not only Shabaka and Tyrone's household, but also the current and prospective material resources available to them. Indeed, incarceration has drained their family of both material and emotional resources remarkably fast.

Kenny's case also suggests the difficulties that many returning offenders face. Two points are worth noting in this regard. First, prisoners' families confront a broad array of problems simultaneously, and these problems, including emotional loss, stigma, diminished care, and economic strain, can have a cumulative impact. All of these factors contribute to the difficulties these families encounter and in aggregate diminish the families' ability to cope with any one of them.

Second, few families in this study had significant stores of capital that they could draw upon. On the other hand, Shabaka and Tyrone's family has considerable resources—at least relative to most prisoners' families. While Kenny's incarceration is straining relationships within the family, it has not yet broken them. The next two accounts examine the transformation in many inner-city families when they exhaust the resources available to them.

"Where Is Your Dad?"

Prison makes it difficult for people to maintain close relationships. While few family members cut ties altogether, an attenuated reduction of the intensity of family relationships with the incarcerated family member is common. In this case, Murielle has been raising her two daughters—Janise, age 10, and Chriselle, age 14—on her own for some time because both fathers are incarcerated. She was married to Dale, Janise's father, until their divorce last year.

Murielle struggled with the economic burden and stigma of Dale's incarceration for most of their marriage, and has not told Janise that her father is incarcerated:

> What I'd learned to do with my first daughter when her father became incarcerated, I told her that he was away at school to make it a lot easier for her to accept, and if anybody asked her, you know, "Where is your dad?" . . . "He's away at school." That pretty much worked for a while, and then when the kids get older they become more inquisitive, and. . . . "Well, if he's at school, why can't he come home?" And the couple of times that I did take her down, she couldn't understand why . . . both of them pretty much the same, the same attitude, and I guess it's the same with any kid. They want to know why they can't come. When you get to that door and you have to say good-bye, they want to know why you can't get on the van or the bus. And they turn around with this look on their face. "Isn't he coming, Mom?" "No, he's not coming, he has to stay here."

While Murielle told Chriselle about her father's incarceration when she was about age 12, Janise still doesn't know. The family has carefully kept the information from outsiders and from the young girls. Even though Chriselle knows the truth now, she still tells her friends that her father is away at school.

> The hardest part is bringing my children [up] by myself. . . . Doing birthdays for my kids by myself. Inviting children that come with their father and their mother, seeing the two parent . . . the two-parent thing. Even now for Chriselle with her classmates, for her it sometimes becomes difficult when she goes on a field trip and I come along, and some of the children have their mother and their father come along. Or the first day of school, I'm the one that shows up, and it's not her father and me, it's just me. Seeing my daughter knowing that another child over there has her father here on family day, or first day, but my father isn't here on first day. So the most difficult time for me—birthdays, holidays, family days. Walking down the street or walking in the mall and seeing the father, mother, child kind of circle would get to me.

While Murielle maintained her relationship with Dale for a decade, she described herself as consistently "unhappy" and "financially stressed." She did love him and still does, but the relationship simply became too much for her. They would argue over her commitment to him because she insisted that their daughter not know about his status and refused to bring Janise to visit with him once she was old enough to understand that her father was in a prison. Murielle has tried to find a middle ground that she and her daughters can manage, though it has not been easy. Most prisoners' families have very limited financial resources, making the choice between phone calls and visits on the one hand, and phone service and rent on the other, a very real one.

> You get so frustrated with the traveling, the costs of the calls. From Sussex, Virginia, it costs you 10 dollars for 10 minutes, so it's a dollar a minute. So with Chriselle's father I had to put my foot down, and I told him that he couldn't call for awhile, because it became too expensive for me. . . . Because it becomes so expensive, and the cost becomes so enormous that it takes away other things that you could be doing with your money. . . . I have to look out for my well-being and my children's well-being, because I'm the only source of income they have.[6]

Dale felt that Murielle was slowly cutting him off from her life, and he asked her for a divorce last year. Shaking her head, she recalls that Dale "couldn't understand why I didn't put up a fight." Murielle told him that she couldn't afford to stay with him. "I have to take care of your daughter," Murielle explained. While that was certainly true, the underlying explanation, one she didn't discuss with him, was that, as a wife, she felt obligated to bring their daughter to visit him, and she didn't want to confront her daughter with his criminality so directly. "To be honest . . . I did not take and expose my daughter to that a lot, because I didn't want her to see the environment, and I didn't want her to see her father incarcerated."[7] For her, managing both her own relationship with Dale and the threat of stigma for her daughters was just too much.

> When I called downtown last year to find out when the divorce became final, and the girl told me it was final on December 23rd, I took a deep breath . . . and it was almost as if a great burden had been lifted from my shoulders, because trying to be the wife of somebody incarcerated . . . it's like you are not just you, you are you and them, and you can't say "That's not me. I'm somebody else."

As much as she is relieved to be divorced, Murielle knows that she has really just made a transition into another kind of relationship with her daughters' fathers. She still believes it is important to keep her daughters' fathers involved in their lives, a sentiment commonly expressed by women with children by prisoners and one of the reasons many women stay involved with their ex-husbands and ex-boyfriends.

While Murielle has tried to maintain positive relationships with both of her daughters' paternal families, she still feels that her "exes'" incarceration has limited her social world considerably, forcing her to guard against the stigma that attaches to criminality:

> My friends for me are very limited. I don't have a lot of friends or associations at work, because too many people are in your business, who will turn it against you. . . . You've got a whole bunch of people that are always trying to find out somebody's business, so I choose not to share it, you know. And that's why I say, I have, like, few friends, period.

Because of the stigma associated with incarceration, many close relatives of prisoners, like Murielle, diminish their social ties, both by avoiding friendships and sharing less information within their friendships. Although divorce has made things easier for Murielle emotionally and financially, managing the impact on her daughters is a difficult balancing act.

> It's hardest, I think, around about the holidays. My youngest daughter just celebrated her 10th birthday, and her father wrote her a letter, and she read it, and she started crying. Holidays—Christmas and Thanksgiving. I really see it now in Janise, you know. I used to see it in Chriselle a lot. I don't see it in her that much anymore. But with [Janise], I guess you can see the sensitivity in her, and she'll look at me, and these big tears will be in her eyes, and she'll go, "Mom, I really miss my daddy." I said, "I know you do." She'll say, "I wish he was home." And I say, "He'll be home."

Many women are in the same predicament—they've moved on from their former relationships, but can't put them behind them entirely.

GOING IT ALONE

Murielle tries to maintain and encourage Chriselle's and Janise's positive relationships with their fathers. However, shielding them from their fathers' status brings about consequences as well, fostering a family secret that causes Murielle and her daughters significant discomfort. As the accounts of many of the couples in this study illustrate, the significant financial costs and stigma of incarceration bear down heavily on those left behind, and few families survive extended prison terms intact. The costs are not trivial to a single working mother of two like Murielle.

Many of the families in this study have found that incarceration pits family relationships and financial welfare against one another in ways that are exceedingly difficult to manage. Although Murielle loved Dale, she found that her marriage had become a liability she could no longer afford. There was simply no way for Murielle to shield her daughters entirely from all the risks related to incarceration, and she had to assess how to balance the girls' separation from their fathers, economic hardship, and other ongoing life stressors (Thompson 1998). She is doing the best she can, trying to make the least damaging sacrifices. Unfortunately, her marriage has not survived.

"It's Like You Dying"

DJ's parents, Denise and Dante, met in tenth grade and have been together, on and off, since then. Both came from abusive families and, partly because they are able to discuss their physical and sexual abuse with each other, Denise feels that they share a special bond. "That's why I love Dante, I do. I love him a lot." In the beginning, Dante gave Denise the kind of support she had never had before. No one in her family had ever encouraged her, but Dante was different. Unlike anyone else she knew, claims Denise, "He used to defend me. I liked that."

After Denise and Dante graduated from high school, Dante's uncle got him involved in dealing drugs, and soon after that Dante began using drugs heavily himself.

> Right after we got out of school, '86 and '87, he started getting locked up in '88. From there on—before we even had the baby—from there on, he has been in for six months, come out three months, back in for maybe eight months, back in for one year.

Looking back, Denise describes the early years as good ones. "That was back before the drugs and the booze started. I never really did much of that, but Dante got into it hard."

Dante's descent into addiction is a familiar story, starting out as occasional use and becoming increasingly serious. Incarcerated several times without treatment, he would stay clean for a short time after release from prison but eventually fall back into his addiction. This current incarceration, his fifth, is serious. At his last arrest, Dante was standing in the middle of an intersection near the housing project where he and Denise lived, wearing only underwear, yelling incoherently, and waving a gun. The gun violation was a felony, and he is now four years into a six-to-eight-year sentence. Again, he was not sentenced to drug treatment.

Moving On?

While Denise still loves Dante, she is trying to move on with her life after struggling with his addiction for years. Her social world, already quite limited, has been further reduced by tensions between her and Dante. Although she used to visit him frequently, years of struggling to cope with his drug addiction have made her less interested in sustaining their relationship. This, in turn, has created problems with Dante's family members, who now openly disparage Denise in front of her son for "abandoning" Dante. As a result, Denise avoids bringing her son to visit his father's family.

Given Denise's financial status, familial strife has brought about dire consequences. Dante's family no longer helps Denise with her rent or groceries, and she has taken full responsibility for DJ's child care. Unemployed, she is now receiving job training. Her welfare benefits amount to only $268 per month. Because of her family history of sexual abuse, Denise does not like to ask her own family members for assistance.[8] This pattern is consistent with findings that the benefits of social support do not always outweigh the costs when support providers can also be "sources of distress" (Ceballo and McLoyd 2002).

Denise's isolation from both families may be nearly as damaging as her exposure to them. Asked to describe how she has survived, she describes the painful experience of selling her body to pay the bills:

> I'll go to the streets if I have to. Maybe $300 or whatever I had to do—I mean, it wasn't a stranger, like a person on 14th Street. It would be like a person I already know, a drug dealer, but he got money, you know. I need $300 or I need $800, and I am going to get it. So then my rent was paid. I had food. . . . I just cry or bite my hands after. Like just really bite my hands with my teeth like . . . I can't stand it. It's not like they was gross, but it was somebody I didn't care about. I had to get my son stuff. His shoes or whatever. I used to, I used to go there. And I don't want to do that no more.

Having limited resources can impact mothers' psychological well-being as well as their parenting behavior (Shonkoff and Phillips 2000), and this seems to be the case for Denise. Her depression has increased significantly, and she spends a good deal of her day inside, either cleaning or listening to gospel music. The music helps, but many days she cannot get out of bed.

> Every time I get up in the morning, when I look at myself, I'll be saying, "Yeah. I think it's gonna be a great day." But it's just like a line or something I say. And then I be like, I can't do nothing. I just can't move sometimes. I just be consumed, like it's like eating me up. I don't know. It's like you dying.

Nearly without exception, the wives, girlfriends, mothers, and sisters closest to the prisoners in this study experienced depression and blamed their depression, at least in part, on their loved ones' incarceration.[9]

Denise's depression feeds her feelings of guilt about her failure as a mother. She recognizes that her depression has made it harder for her to be the mother that she wants to be for DJ.

> I have been a bad mother, though, as far as growing up in an affectionate way, I have rejected him a lot. . . . He would need me to feed him and—I used to let him just stay in the room, just cry. I just—I couldn't take it. . . . Sometimes, I still can't be a mother.

The emotional withdrawal and irritability that Denise describes are symptomatic of her depression. The impact of maternal depression on child development and child and adolescent mental health is largely mediated by its effects on parents' parenting behavior, including an increased likelihood of child abuse and neglect (Bifulco et al. 2002; Oyserman, Bybee, and Mowbray 2002). Studies of parenting under conditions of economic hardship in particular show that increased parental depression and irritability result in more punitive, erratic, and "generally nonsupportive" behavior toward children (McLoyd 1990). Maternal depression has also been linked to risky behaviors, such as smoking and failing to use car seats—behaviors that present direct physical health risks for children (Leiferman 2002). Furthermore, parental depression can create a chronically stressful family environment; for example, Denise's depression has resulted in unpredictable behavior and mood swings, failure to look after DJ's basic needs, and ongoing conflict with neighbors and extended family members. How children like DJ cope with the stress of living with a depressed parent can affect their long-term outcomes.[10]

DJ is coping with his mother's depression and his father's absence as well as he can, but he struggles in school, gets into frequent fights, and has few friends. Many of DJ's fights stem from his family situation; when other students and even teachers make comments about his mother's appearance or unusual behavior, DJ becomes aggressive. His cycle of victimization and aggressive behavior has nearly overwhelmed Denise, and she recognizes that he needs someone in the community to mentor him. "He don't have a father, and he ain't got no male, nobody to talk to. So we go to church and try to get the male people to talk to him, but it has not really worked too much."

Children like DJ face a cascade of risks, because economic strain, paternal drug use, and lack of community supports compound his exposure to maternal depression. Children of depressed parents are at risk for poor outcomes in both behavioral and emotional domains (Langrock et al. 2002) and, in fact, are at greater risk than children of parents with other psychiatric or medical conditions (Lee and Gotlib 1989). A recent study estimated that children of depressed parents are eight times more likely to experience a childhood-onset major depressive disorder themselves and are at significantly increased risk of experiencing a number of other psychiatric disorders (Wickramaratne and Weissman 1998). Depression that begins in childhood or adolescence is likely to continue into adulthood and result in a range of interpersonal, occupational, and other difficulties (Weissman and Jensen 2002). Viewed in this light, the potential costs of Dante's incarceration to society are quite substantial.

Rethinking Incarceration

Many of the difficulties that families face during prisoner reentry are, in fact, related to the experience of incarceration itself. Indeed, many of the families in this study described the hardships that incarceration imposed on other family members—particularly on children—as acute. A number of these consequences create immediate obstacles to family functioning, present long-term risks for children, and may ultimately serve as barriers to successful offender reentry.

The economic strain described by nearly every family in this study is perhaps the least understood of the major stressors related to incarceration. Much of the previous research on economic strain has investigated parental unemployment resulting from layoffs and plant closures (Conger et al. 1994, 1999; Elder 1999).[11] Parental incarceration as a precipitating factor, however, has received little attention, in part because studies have typically underestimated the economic contributions of incarcerated family members (Braman 2002; Western, Petit, and Guetzkow 2002).

The economic consequences of incarceration are also substantial. For example, although Kenny's incarceration has directly affected Shabaka and Tyrone, who have become socially withdrawn and understandably anxious about their father's return, the unraveling of the family's financial security could have even more devastating long-term effects. The signs of economic strain are already beginning to show on Edwina, who has become uncharacteristically unpredictable and punitive with the boys. As Kenny's story suggests, economic strain—whatever its cause— has negative emotional and behavioral effects on the adults in a family; these changes in adult behavior, in turn, affect the children. Financial losses, such as those Kenny describes resulting from his arrest, tend to accrue over the course of incarceration, leaving reentering offenders struggling to dig themselves out of debt and restore, if possible, their families' former financial status.

Along with significant economic and practical consequences, incarceration has a powerfully corrosive effect on family structure. Murielle's desire to distance herself and her children from the hardships and stigma resulting from paternal incarceration eventually led to divorce. The kind of separation—temporary or permanent—brought about by incarceration can negatively affect not only children, but also prisoners themselves when they attempt to reenter the community without socially supportive relationships. Murielle has struggled (with some success) to ease the impact of paternal absence on Chriselle and Janise; but for many families, interparental conflict spills over into parent-child relationships. It is both striking and disturbing that reducing family ties, in Murielle's case through divorce, is a common way of coping with incarceration.

The economic strain, increased daily hassles, and pervasive sense of loss (of companionship, of family integrity, of hope for the future) that result from incarceration contribute to feelings of depression among many of the women left behind. Denise's account suggests that parental depression has an insidious, trickle-down effect on families. The consequences and social costs of parental depression for children have been well documented and are clearly evident in Denise's case. Her depression has had an impact not only on her ability to parent DJ—putting him at risk for such poor childhood outcomes as childhood onset depression, externalization (e.g. fighting, aggression), and diminished social competence—but also on her ability to hold a job and to forge sustaining social ties in the community.

As evidenced in each of these stories and those that follow, incarceration powerfully affects a family's material welfare, structure, and mental health, all of which have significant consequences for children. The impact of parental incarceration on the children in this study was, though sometimes indirect, always significant.

Release and Reincarceration

While the criminal justice system has expanded dramatically in the past 20 years, recidivism has increased as well. This trend is troubling, not only because it indicates that increasingly harsh criminal penalties are failing to reform offenders, but also because it means that families are increasingly confronting extended cycles of release and incarceration. Indeed, for most of the families in this study, the current incarceration or release was just one in a series.

Back to Basics

With the best of intentions, Clinton returned to the community after serving time for dealing drugs. He moved in with his sister, Zelda, toward whom he had always been protective, and her two daughters. After a lifetime of physical and sexual abuse by men in her extended family, Zelda had come to view Clinton and his girlfriend, Pat, as something like adoptive parents—her only "real" family.[12] Clinton intended not only to support Zelda, but also to help out Pat financially. Although years of cycling in and out of prison had damaged Clinton and Pat's relationship, he still felt an obligation to her and to their grown daughter, Janet, who had a new baby of her own.

After his release, Clinton took a low-paying job at a department store and started helping Zelda, who was receiving public assistance, make ends meet. Zelda earned extra money cutting hair, but after paying the rent, buying food, and paying the phone bill, she had little money left over to buy her growing daughters' shoes, clothing, and school supplies. Clinton helped out with these expenses while he was employed. "He would pay my phone bill, take my kids shopping, give me a little money here and there to buy something for myself." In addition to providing some financial help, Clinton also supported Zelda by picking up the kids or taking them out on weekends while she cut hair. This arrangement worked well for about six months until the store where he worked closed, and his income vanished with it. According to Clinton and his family, he applied for a number of jobs, but no one wanted to hire him. He blames his lack of success in part on his candor about his criminal record.

> I couldn't lie. I feel as though that if . . . if I lied and the next thing you know it came out, it's embarrassing. I can't be on a job and then when you work a job, and you get used to the job, you get competent at that job, you and your peers start to clicking together like a family, you start to liking the peoples on the job you're associating with—man, this is your second family—and all of a sudden, the man walk in one day and say, "You're fired. We have to terminate you because we found out that you had a record and you did not mention it on your application."

Clinton's job loss and resulting inability to provide for his family the way he could while selling drugs weighed heavily on him. He tried to reassure his sister and himself, but instead began becoming a source of financial strain rather than support.

> I would tell [Zelda] that I might not get another job right away, but I'm gonna keep trying. But I felt good, 'cause . . . I'm looking at these certificates [from prison programs]. All my accomplishments, all of the things I achieved while I was in there, and I think about how I eventually pursued them to achievement, so I feel good. So when I go and apply for a job I'm feeling good. Then when it get around to about the fifteenth or twentieth application and no one calling, now I go into a slump. I don't have no finance. My family keeps giving me money. Then, now, they short, 'cause they're saying that the bills is catching up on them because they have to provide for me.

After a few months without pay, he went back to his old neighborhood and decided to start hustling again, telling his family he'd gotten work as a day laborer.

> See, it's . . . just certain things just don't sit right with you. If you know you accomplished a certain degree, you feel as though "I'm supposed to be able to give my child some money from working on a job from the experience that I learned." . . . I would look at [my degree], and it made me feel good. And then when I looked around [after losing the job at the clothing store] and said, "But I can't get a damn job!" Back to basics. And what that does, it makes you resort back to what you do best—what you feel as though you do best, what you know, and that is to break the law. . . . You know, even though you can try and try and try and try and try not to, there you are.

For Clinton, despite his family's desire for him to stay straight, it was the feeling of obligation to them that weighed on him and made him decide to look for "easy money." However, even while he made a lot of money selling drugs, he felt bad about that, too: "I started selling drugs, but then, when I started to take the proceeds from that and go give them little things, buy them little things, I didn't feel good about it, because I knew I was not doing it right."

Financially, Clinton's reincarceration has had significant consequences for Zelda. Although she was clear that she never wanted him to sell drugs again, the two fathers of her children were not helping her to raise them, and Zelda acknowledged that her brother felt pressure to earn or otherwise get money to assist her. Zelda is unhappy that Clinton gave up on going straight, not only because she loves her brother and wants to see him free, but also because she was depending on him to get a job and help out with the kids. Clinton had not only helped her to pay her bills, but had promised to take her daughters shopping for back-to-school supplies and clothes just before he was arrested. Now, instead of receiving Clinton's help, Zelda is working extra hours to send him money until he gets a job inside.

Zelda knows that Clinton's commitment to help out is part of what drove him once again to sell drugs. His desire to help his younger sister and her desire to provide a decent living environment for her children were both powerful and helped push Clinton back into the informal drug economy. Now, because of Clinton's incarceration, Zelda must turn to the family that abused her. This outcome is particularly painful for her and gives some indication of the social consequences of financial difficulties. In times of need, people are often forced to make use of resources they might otherwise refuse. While this is true for everyone, most Americans have a far wider and far more attractive array of options than those available to Zelda.

As recent research has indicated, reduced financial resources can lead to increased exposure to abuse (Albeda 1997; Edin and Lein 1997; Lyon 2000).[13] Women without their own resources are more likely to make use of other sources of support, usually family and friends. This situation forces some women to maintain certain relationships or reopen relationships that they had left with good reason. In Zelda's case, material resources as well as available social resources have been diminished. She is left with two undesirable options: returning to her abusive family or making do on her own.

Now, instead of receiving Clinton's help, Zelda is working extra hours and sending him money until he gets a job inside. The private prison he is in prohibits inmates from receiving personal items through the mail; underwear, undershirts, soap, toothpaste, toothbrushes, antifungal powder,[14] and deodorant must all be purchased at the private canteen operated by the corporation that owns and manages the facility. The prices are high, but inmates have no alternative. Zelda also has trouble staying in touch with Clinton. Collect phone calls from his facility are priced at a flat rate of $9.00 for 10 minutes.[15] For this reason, she limits her phone calls with him to once a month.

Perhaps most significantly, Zelda feels that even if she had needed to reach out to her extended family while Clinton was outside but unemployed, she would not have been nearly as fearful of doing so with him around. Now she has lost not only a material resource, but also one of her closest friends—the person who she feels understands her complicated family situation best, and who would have protected her and her daughters should they need protection.

During her last interview, Zelda seems exhausted and overwhelmed. She has struggled with depression before and is having difficulty following her brother's reincarceration. She is less hopeful about Clinton's return since he was recently denied parole and shipped out of state. She describes herself as tired out, saying that she does not leave the apartment much any more, "just to shop, really." She spends most of her days dressing hair in the middle of her living room and cleaning. She says she is trying to work harder now so she will not have to rely on her family, and she hopes she will not have to ask them for help. Her goal, she says, is to save enough so that her daughters will have what she did not have, or "all the things that they can have, you know, once it's over for me." When asked what she means by "over," she shrugs and puts her face down into her hands.

Trying to Focus on the Family

Sharon, Cooper, and Derrick's father has been in and out of prison and drug addiction for over a decade—something their mother, Londa, views as the central struggle of their marriage.[16] Both Cooper (age 4) and Derrick Jr. (Little Derrick, age 1) have had irregular contact with their father, who is currently serving a long sentence in an out-of-state facility. Their father, Derrick Sr., describes the challenges of parenting on the inside:

> See, now I have two boys. One of them knows me but the other one was born while I was in here, and when I got out I only picked him up one time when he was a baby. And he's named after me, you know, but he don't know me from

Adam. His mother may show him some pictures and things and say, "This is your father," or whatever. Maybe, I don't know. But I think my oldest son, he do know me a little bit. He's four years old now, so he may not know me as well, or maybe my face or something, you know, remember it. Well, now since I'm in here, I try to be a father to them, sending them money, you know, to be able to help the mother out. . . . I try to do that, you know. So if I keep up the job, I can send back money, keep Londa a little more happy, keep the kids knowing me. But then I just go in circles. The judge said I have to do the treatment here before I go for parole. . . . I mean, I look at it and it would have been so easy to be a father out there. Maybe not easy, but it's like it's impossible here.

Like most of the inmates added to our criminal justice system in recent years, Derrick is a nonviolent offender (Mauer 1999). Like most offenders who use drugs, he has neither been sentenced to nor received anything approaching serious treatment. As a result, like most prisoners, he is also a repeat offender (Langan and Levin 2002).

Early in Derrick and Londa's relationship, Derrick earned a reliable income working construction and other odd jobs. Londa had been a good student and, after high school, was able to get work as a secretary. Londa became pregnant with Sharon when she was 21 and Derrick was 22. Not long afterwards, Derrick's drug use, once limited to the occasional party, became more serious. By the time their daughter was born, Londa could see changes in Derrick as he began hiding his growing addiction. Anyone who has experienced addiction within a family will know the litany of problems that Londa encountered: mood swings, dishonesty, erratic behavior, late night disappearances, pleas for money, and eventually theft.

As Londa realized how serious things had become, she tried to hold Derrick accountable as a parent, something she felt that she deserved and their daughter needed. Londa told Derrick, "You get yourself together [and you can see her, but] I don't think she should get less from you and more from me. . . . The best you can do is to come over here like that? No. I'm sorry, she deserves more than that." Shortly after Londa prohibited Derrick from seeing their daughter, he was arrested and sentenced to 18 months on a possession charge.

Although Derrick did not enter drug treatment while incarcerated, he managed to stay off drugs and felt as though he had recovered from his addiction. When Derrick was released, he married Londa and resumed working hard to provide for his family. Unfortunately, his recovery lasted a little less than a year. Then he was back on drugs and back in jail, a cycle that he would repeat several times. He would attend Narcotics Anonymous meetings for a while, work hard, pay the bills, and then one day he would run into some "friends" and his recovery was over—it was on to another binge and another set of broken promises.

Londa has struggled to hold her family together, financially and emotionally. As hard as the cycle of addiction and incarceration has been for her, she recognizes that it has been far harder for Sharon, who still has trouble understanding why her father could be loving and responsible one month, but manipulative and reckless the next. "Trying to explain to a kid why her father left with her radio and why he's not allowed in the house at the moment," says Londa, ". . . that's just not something a kid can really understand." The fact that drug-free Derrick was a good father made the times that he was using drugs all the harder. Londa does not think that Sharon ever forgot what life was like when Derrick was drug free. "She really misses that, because when she was little they were really, really close."

In addition to missing her father and coping with her own ambivalence toward him, Sharon has also had to manage the information about her father in her encounters with friends and teachers. Londa believes that Derrick's incarceration has led her daughter, already a quiet girl, to become increasingly private and withdrawn.

> It bothers her because, you know, everybody is dealing with their fathers and school and their mothers. They come see them in shows and stuff. . . . You could see the hurt. I mean it's not more or less she's gonna come out say it. She's gonna keep everything in 'til she can decide, "Okay, who do I want to talk to?" You know. Other than that, she really is very private. But I could see it. She has girlfriends and stuff, but they don't know.

> And then her school work. It showed in her school work. And my daughter is a brain. You know . . . "A's" ever since she made kindergarten. She's never gotten a "C." Never. Fifth grade everything just went [downhill]. He went to jail and everything just . . . she just really went down this [year]. . . . I receive[d] her report card and they said she had to repeat a grade, I cried, I . . . I hurt. It bothers me now. It still bothers me. You just think, you know, there is nothing that you can do. What can you do?

Londa looks back on the times that she had nothing and was not sure how she would feed her kids, often sending them to stay with relatives while she went to look for work. She feels like she has been torn between wanting to be a supportive wife and being a good mother to her children, often feeling like she failed at the latter.

> I feel like I let my kids down. I feel like I really, really let them down. And [this last time] I was out of work. I didn't have no money. I felt like I was just getting exactly what I deserved . . . you know. Even all the good I did, it didn't outweigh

the bad or something. I just felt like I was just getting everything that I was supposed to get. I was bitter. I didn't want to talk to nobody.

Derrick, on the other hand, is torn between helping to meet his family's
immediate financial needs and making a commitment to drug treatment
that might benefit them all over the long run. The structure of the correctional system makes this an either/or proposition for Derrick.

> My problem now is this. I got to choose between the treatment route, the educa-
> tion route, and the job route. Now on the treatment route, I'll get nothing [in the
> way of money]. Doing school, maybe just enough to cover cosmetics, but that's it.
> I go the job route, and I can send home some money and, see, that helps out Londa
> and keeps the family intact. The point is, though, that they ain't coming to see me
> here and ain't taking my calls 'cause they can't afford the collect. But if I take the
> job, I don't get the drug treatment. So I'm trying to focus on the family, but I'm also
> kinda trying to get out of here. But it's also, too, I want to get back with them.

These issues weigh heavily on Londa as she considers how much her
commitment to Derrick has cost her. Perhaps the greatest loss she has
suffered is not material at all; it is the loss of her faith in the family itself.
Looking back on her relationship with Derrick, she describes what many
young women in her situation dream of:

> I always thought that, "Okay, we want to raise our kids together." There's not too
> many [families], there's not any that I can think of at this time that's not a single-
> parent family. I never wanted that for my kids. I wanted them to have something
> that I didn't have. So you try to give them this and you try to give them that. But
> to me it is more important to have both your parents there. And I've always
> thought, you know, "Okay, that will happen." I always thought that would happen.

While she still holds out some faint hope that Derrick might be released
early to a treatment program, she is exhausted from years of trying to
work it out with him. After this last incarceration, Londa reluctantly
began considering filing for divorce.

> I mean, at first when we was dating, I could just walk away. But now, you know,
> I put a ring on my finger, and I'm married, and so it's more difficult now
> because I'm married to him. And I have more kids. I already had one, but I have
> more kids now. It would be a lot less pressure on me to stay, by me not being
> married to him.

As the stories of other families in this study indicate, Londa is not alone in
feeling the pressure to leave the father of her children. That marriage and
coparenting are far less common and single female–headed households
are far more common in areas where incarceration rates are high is no
surprise. Indeed, for the 10 percent of families in the District of Colum-

bia that live in neighborhoods with the highest male incarceration rates, over 75 percent are without fathers (Braman 2002).

"Behind Bars with My Father"

Davida, whose account opened this chapter, has a half brother whose life, like hers, has been upset by their father's repeated arrests and incarcerations. Charles is 13 and gets straight A's in school. Like his sister, he is clearly intelligent, but is small for his age and more soft spoken. Despite his academic potential, Charles has had a host of problems with the criminal justice system, having been arrested three times for auto theft and once for shoplifting. After Charles stole his first car at age 6, his mother, Carla, took him to a psychiatrist. Reports Carla, "[The psychiatrist] told me that his badness was inherited. She didn't say it in front of Charles. She said 'Charles has the trait of a bad child, but it was inherited from his father.' "

Over time Carla has come to agree, and now sees her own child as a "bad seed," because, as she puts it, "In my heart [I think] he really do act like David, and I don't want him to act like him, because David been incarcerated from the age of 12. And his son moving in the same footsteps, just that Charles started off six years earlier." As another piece of evidence that Charles's problems are mostly because he is David's child, she notes that Davida is having problems, too.

> All of them got big issues, you know. My son got the main problems. He running 'round here just doing any and everything. He think the world of David. He already act like David, stealing cars, stealing bikes. I had a three-story; he burnt that house to the ground. That's why I'm over here in this apartment. He took some matches and lit his curtain on fire, and then the curtain fell onto the bed, and he shut the bedroom door and by the time the smoke detector went off the fire was already spread. You know, I have a lot a problems out of Charles. He do, he act just like his father's family, he act just like them. Another one of his children running around selling her body. I be real worried about her. She's not my child, but I be worried about her.

But when asked directly how his father's incarceration has affected Charles, Carla tells a different story. Charles, she explains, usually gets into trouble as soon as his father gets arrested. "If his father was here he wouldn't be acting like that. Because when David is on the street, he don't act like that because he know that you could page David, and David going to be right here."

Carla lost custody of Charles, a situation that can also be linked to David's incarceration. After David's arrest, Carla found a new boyfriend who became increasingly violent, beating Carla regularly and sometimes Charles as well. Carla said she wanted to report him but stated "I was scared of him for real." Finally, Carla's daughter told her grandmother, who then called the police. When Child Protective Services found out that Carla had failed to report the abuse of her son, she lost custody. "I know how my son was hurting, you know," she says, crying. "I think about that. My son took a[n] ass whipping for me, and I should have been in there for him."

It is impossible to know whether the prospect of David's intervention would have deterred Carla's boyfriend, but it very well may have. The absence of a biological father is one of the strongest predictors of abuse (Margolin 1992; Wilson and Daly 1987), due in no small part to strong norms against disciplining other men's children. As one father put it:

> The thing is, that the child isn't yours. I don't want no one laying a hand on my child, so I'm not going to lay a hand on no one else's child. You're not supposed to lay a hand on that child because that's that parent's responsibility. But, now, that may be true, but when the parent is not around, you might have to take that role.

David's absence may well have diminished whatever risk Carla's live-in boyfriend perceived in beating her and Charles.

For now, Charles and Carla's 11-year-old son, Anthony, live with their maternal grandmother, Dora, who has custody of them until Carla completes a parenting class. Dora has trouble explaining his behavior at school. "He can go to school, be an honor roll and model student, and then he goes over to his friend's house and he's just like a model person to them. Yet, when he get[s] home, he wants to act crazy."

When Charles is asked what he wants to be when he grows up, his answer is immediate: "I really want to be a surgeon. I'm not saying I want to be a doctor for the money, I just want to do what I like and make good money for it, too." His other dream is to have a car—"one like my Dad's." Most of the time that he spent with his father, in fact, was in his father's car. When Charles was younger, David would let him steer, and when Charles got old enough to reach the pedals, David would give him driving lessons in an abandoned parking lot.

Charles reports that when he gets in trouble, which he says happens only when his father is locked up, the only thing David can do to discipline him is call home and talk to him on the phone. "But my grandmother don't accept the calls any more because they're expensive." Charles used to go visit his father in prison, but his grandmother stopped taking him because she did not want to expose him to the prison environment any longer.

Charles thinks often of his father. Although he is angry with his father for not being around to raise him or help him in his daily life, he believes his father loves him and he often thinks about what his father's life is like. When asked if he ever thinks he might end up in jail, Charles responds, "Uh-huh." When asked what he thinks about ending up in jail, Charles answers, "That's when I started thinking about him. I always thought about how would I look if I was in the jail cell with my father, if I was behind bars with my father."

Rethinking Reentry

These stories show how difficult it can be for families to cope, not only with incarceration, but also with reentry. In Clinton's family, we can see how release and reincarceration are bound up with a host of family concerns. Clinton's diminished ability to obtain employment and help provide for his family led him back to the only trade he knew well—hustling. While his story and those of the millions of repeat offenders who cycle through the criminal justice system each year should be of concern to policymakers interested in lowering recidivism rates, the consequences for his family are just as important. Although Clinton's daughter grew up without her father present, dropped out of high school, and now, at age 17, has a child by a man who is also incarcerated, Clinton's sister and nieces have felt his recent incarceration most keenly. The financial and emotional strain that Zelda has experienced as a result of both Clinton's release and reincarceration has, as many women in this study reported, contributed to a significant decline in her mental health. And this decline, as we noted above, is strongly correlated with diminished child welfare.

Though rarely mentioned in discussions about family integrity or family values, a growing body of evidence shows that over the past 20 years, incarceration has been pulling apart the most vulnerable families in our society.[17] However, as stories like Londa's indicate, incarceration not only alters family structures in ways that traditional studies measure, increasing the number of single female–headed households, but it also significantly impacts family relationships by straining resources and diminishing both physical and emotional health. Without drug treatment for Derrick, Londa and their children have had to cope not only with significant financial hardship, but also, in a deeper sense, with the loss of faith in family itself. So alongside incarceration's impact on household composition, legal ties, and health outcomes runs its effect on the norms of trust and reciprocity that families share and model for succeeding generations.

We can see in Charles's example how cycles of release and reincarceration affect succeeding generations. Paternal absence is one of the strongest predictors we have for a host of negative sequelae for children, including—as Charles experienced—parental distress, economic hardship, and child abuse. Thus, parental incarceration is also one of the strongest predictors we have for a child's involvement in the criminal justice system—a fact that is, sadly, also borne out in Charles's case.

Conclusion

As the accounts in this chapter suggest, the widespread incarceration of fathers has numerous pernicious consequences for families in poor, inner-city communities already facing an array of stresses and challenges. The material and structural changes resulting from incarceration reverberate through family relationships, including the relationships between spouses and between children and their caregivers. The removal of a parent like Kenny creates an economic burden on remaining family members who are trying to make ends meet. For many mothers, like Denise, who are struggling on their own, a sense of isolation and feelings of depression can color their relationships with their children. Marital relationships, such as Derrick and Londa's, are strained, and important connections between children and their incarcerated fathers are at risk. While some parents are successful in buffering incarceration's impact on their children, for others, the accumulation of stressors and challenges in their lives can overwhelm their abilities to cope.

For many families, incarceration adds to and exacerbates a host of other risk factors that families and children face on a daily basis, many of which also persist after a parent's return to the community. These, in turn, contribute to many of the ongoing difficulties associated with reentry that children and families experience. Changes to the family system resulting from incarceration can create obstacles for prisoners and their families as they seek to adjust to reentry.

Following reentry, many ex-prisoners are not prepared to assume the role of a financial provider, caregiver, and relationship partner. Moreover, they return to families that are already under significant stress and children who are beginning to act out the effects of conflictual, chronically stressed family relationships. Returning to an extended family with economic difficulties, for example, Clinton feels pressure to be a breadwinner, even though his criminal record is an obstacle to employment. For Derrick, returning to the community without having received drug treatment virtually ensures his family's disappointment and his eventual reincarceration. Davida and Charles, like many children of prisoners, face immense challenges with few resources.

In each case, a cascade of risks for children follows from criminal justice practices that ignore family needs. Whether a parent is incarcerated, has returned to the community after an incarceration, or is repeatedly cycling through the justice system, criminal justice practices disrupt family life in ways that can produce lasting negative consequences for children. During parental incarceration, children are exposed to strained family relationships and economic and emotional deprivation. Caregivers often describe children as being in a state of extended uncertainty, waiting for their parents' unpredictable return. Parents who are unprepared for reentry create disappointment and even disaster for their children, who are expecting their parents' return to bring stability and an improvement to their home life.

The role of parental incarceration in predicting poor child outcomes has been largely hidden in the child development literature. By deconstructing the effects of incarceration and reentry—whether they are economic, structural, emotional, or interpersonal—we can better document the nature and scope of the problems that families of prisoners confront and develop appropriate strategies for preventing or remediating the effects of criminal justice sanctions on children.

While the effects of incarceration are necessarily specific to each family, the mass incarceration of young fathers is, on the whole, distorting family life and undermining child welfare in many minority and low-income communities. This situation has disturbing implications not only for the health and welfare of those families, but also for the way the disproportionate incarceration of poor and minority men is shaping our public understanding of social welfare generally. As mass incarceration undermines family life in our inner cities, poor and minority families increasingly look like the stereotypes that inform the very criminal justice policies that imprison so many young men and women.

While there is a great deal we do not know about incarceration and family life, it is becoming increasingly clear that our current correctional practices are dismantling many of the most vulnerable families in our society and putting children at great risk. While policymakers have, out of ignorance, created policies that are devastating to family systems, this need not be so.

A number of policy options can strengthen families and enhance child welfare. According to many studies, mandatory, long-term inpatient drug treatment followed by careful transitioning to outpatient drug treatment and close supervision can have significant positive effects on recidivism, and the accounts of families highlighted in this chapter suggest that these programs could help to prevent the deterioration of family life that often accompanies addiction and incarceration. Where incarceration is necessary, correctional drug treatment, parenting classes, job training, and correctional industries can significantly reduce the problems that families face both during incarceration and, more significantly, following release. Despite the presence of significant risk in their lives, children of criminal offenders are capable of being resilient as long as their primary protective systems, particularly the parent-child relationship, remain intact (Masten 2001).

We do not expect that reform in the criminal justice system will fully answer the problems that these families confront, nor do we underestimate the difficulty of restructuring our criminal justice system. Many of our correctional practices are so well entrenched that it may be decades before we can turn them to better use. Incarcerated fathers are often unprepared not only for reentry into society, but also for reentry into their families. They have little understanding of how to manage their relationships with their children, let alone provide for them. But the sooner we begin thinking about how we can hold offenders accountable to their families—particularly their children—the better.

NOTES

We thank the families that participated in this study for sharing their experiences. We also thank Michael Bryant, Kathryn Dudley, Ryan Goodman, Eleanor Judah, Dan Kahan, Linda-Anne Rebhun, Harold Scheffler, Charles Sullivan, Pauline Sullivan, Paul Wood, and reviewers at the Urban Institute for their help and advice. This research was funded by the National Institute of Justice (Award Number 98-CE-VX-0012), the National Science Foundation (Award Number SBR-9727685), the Wenner-Gren Foundation for Anthropological Research, and the Yale Center for the Study of Race, Inequality, and Politics. This research also could not have been conducted without the cooperation of the District of Columbia, Virginia, and Maryland Departments of Correction, and the various federal agencies working with District inmates.

1. The accounts in this chapter are transcriptions of taped interviews. Identifying information has been omitted or altered. Fifty families of male prisoners participated in

the study. Twenty families were part of a preliminary snowball sample, and an additional 30 families were randomly selected from the District of Columbia Department of Corrections population.

2. Mumola (2000) estimates that, on any given day, 1,372,700 children have a father who is incarcerated, a majority (667,900) of prisoners are fathers, and over 60 percent of incarcerated fathers have at least monthly contact with their children.

3. Bureau of Justice Statistics data (Langan and Levin 2002) indicate that 67.5 percent of all released offenders are rearrested within three years.

4. The study is briefly reported in Braman (2002). A book describing the study in detail will be published in 2004 by the University of Michigan Press.

5. See McLoyd (1990) describing the adverse effects of economic hardship on children's socioemotional development; Shonkoff and Phillips (2000) commenting that understanding poverty's effects requires examining how poverty "manifests itself in young children's lives, how it affects the extent to which their basic needs are met, and through what processes it promotes or undermines their capacity to accomplish the basic developmental tasks" (268); and Evans and English (2002) noting that stress associated with economic hardship can have a long-term impact on children's ability to self-regulate and delay gratification.

6. Telephone charges are the expense that families complain about most often. Most correctional facilities contract out phone services for profit. Phone companies compete for contracts, and the key criterion is not low price, but how much revenue the service will return to the Department of Corrections in each state. Because phone conversations are often time-limited, many families are required to accept several calls to complete a single conversation, with connection charges applying to each call. While there are no data on overall phone costs for D.C. inmates, the costs are high locally and nationally, as several news accounts have noted:

> In Florida, where the state prison system collected $13.8 million in commissions in fiscal 1997–98, a legislative committee found that big prison systems in 10 other states took in more than $115 million in the same budget year. New York topped the list with $20.5 million. In Virginia, MCI gave the state $10.4 million, or 39 percent of the revenue from prison calls. Maryland receives a 20 percent commission on local calls by inmates, which must be made through Bell Atlantic, and gets 42 percent of revenue from long-distance calls, all of which are handled by AT&T (Duggan 2000, A03).

As a result, collect calls from prisons can be up to 20 times as expensive as standard collect calls.

7. The issue is difficult for many women and, in some cases, for the judges. See Sims (2001).

8. Unfortunately, as sexual abuse is not uncommon, about a quarter of the women in this study were reluctant to ask the abusive relatives for assistance, preferring to reduce their contact with them entirely.

9. While not all of them have described themselves as "depressed," they described feelings and patterns of behavior consistent with the symptoms of clinical depression. These include a persistent sad, anxious, or "empty" mood; too much or too little sleep; middle-of-the-night or early-morning waking; reduced appetite and weight loss or

increased appetite and weight gain; loss of interest or pleasure in activities, including sex; irritability; restlessness; persistent physical symptoms that do not respond to treatment (such as chronic pain or digestive disorders); difficulty concentrating, remembering, or making decisions; fatigue or loss of energy; feelings of guilt, hopelessness, or worthlessness; and thoughts of death or suicide. See National Mental Health Association (2003).

One of the difficulties in discussing depression with African-American women is that many are reluctant to use clinical language or to admit that they were defeated by a psychiatric illness. This point is further supported by the recent Surgeon General's Report on Mental Health:

> Mental illness is at least as prevalent among racial and ethnic minorities as in the majority white population. Yet many racial and ethnic minority group members find the organized mental health system to be uninformed about cultural context and, thus, unresponsive and/or irrelevant. It is partly for this reason that minority group members overall are less inclined than whites to seek treatment, and to use outpatient treatment services to a much lesser extent than do non-Hispanic whites (Satcher 1999).

10. Among the well-established risk factors for mental health problems in children are parental depression and stressful life events. See Satcher (1999, 124).

11. See, for example, the work of Rand Conger and his colleagues investigating the impact of economic strain on intact, predominantly Caucasian families in the rural Midwest (Conger et al. 1994, 1999). Glen H. Elder Jr. also examined the economic changes caused by the Great Depression and its impact on families and children's development (Elder 1999).

12. Clinton is the oldest and Zelda the youngest of 13 children. Clinton was raised separately for most of his childhood and came to know Zelda only after both became adults.

13. See, for example, Edin and Lein (1997): "Mothers who relied on boyfriends for income sometimes had to choose between danger and destitution. . . . Many mothers reported that they or their children had been physically or sexually abused by their domestic partners at some point in the past. . . . [Some] ignored the abuse because they were so desperate for their boyfriends' money" (158); Lyon (2000); Albeda (1997): "Twenty percent of all welfare recipients are recent [within the previous 12 months] victims of domestic violence and two-thirds have been abused by a husband or boyfriend sometime in their adult lives. The limited choices and terms of welfare reform will likely mean that many women choose to return to an abusive situation to make ends meet" (A23).

14. In the correctional setting, foot fungus is a significant problem. Several inmates told me about the importance of obtaining and guarding one's own cosmetic products. "In this type of environment you got people coming from the street . . . they got all kinds of fungus because they been smoking crack."

15. See note 6 and accompanying text (discussing phone rates).

16. This family's story is described in more detail in Braman (2003).

17. See Western and McLanahan (2000, 322) (citing evidence that the incarceration has a "large destabilizing effect" on low-income families). See also Testa and Krogh (1995); and Sampson (1995) (describing the influence of incarceration on joblessness and sex ratios). These findings logically reverse the causal relationship implicit in many other studies that describe familial environment as influencing rather than being influenced by involvement in the criminal justice system. See, e.g., Taylor et al. (1997, 46) (reviewing the literature on female-headed households and crime).

REFERENCES

Albeda, Randy. 1997. "What Has Happened to Those Who Left the Massachusetts Welfare Rolls?" *Boston Globe,* 30 October, A23.

Bifulco, Antonia, Patricia M. Moran, Caroline Ball, Catherine Jacobs, Rebecca Baines, Amanda Bunn, and James Cavagin. 2002. "Childhood Adversity, Parental Vulnerability and Disorder: Examining Inter-generational Transmission of Risk." *Journal of Child Psychology and Psychiatry* 43 (8): 1075–86.

Braman, Donald. 2002. "Families and Incarceration." In *Invisible Punishment: The Collateral Consequences of Mass Imprisonment,* edited by Marc Mauer and Meda Chesney-Lind (117–35). New York: The New Press.

———. 2003. "The Moral Economy of Incarceration." *Social Thought,* in press.

Ceballo, Rosario, and Vonnie C. McLoyd. 2002. "Social Support and Parenting in Poor, Dangerous Neighborhoods." *Child Development* 73 (4): 1310–21.

Conger, Rand, Katherine Conger, Lisa Matthews, and Glenn Elder Jr. 1999. "Pathways of Economic Influence on Adolescent Adjustment." *American Journal of Community Psychology* 27 (4): 519–41.

Conger, Rand, Xiaojia Ge, Glenn Elder Jr., Frederick Lorenz, and Ronald Simons. 1994. "Economic Stress, Coercive Family Process, and Developmental Problems of Adolescents." *Child Development* 65 (2): 541–61.

Duggan, Paul. 2000. "Captive Audience Rates High; Families Must Pay Dearly When Inmates Call Collect." *Washington Post,* 23 January, A03.

Edin, Kathryn, and Laura Lein. 1997. *Making Ends Meet: How Single Mothers Survive Welfare and Low-Wage Work.* New York: Russell Sage Foundation.

Elder, Glen H., Jr. 1999. *Children of the Great Depression: Social Change in Life Experience.* Boulder, Colo.: Westview Press.

Evans, Gary W., and Kimberly English. 2002. "The Environment of Poverty: Multiple Stressor Exposure, Psychophysiological Stress, and Socioemotional Adjustment." *Child Development* 73 (4): 1238–48.

Langan, Patrick A., and David J. Levin. 2002. *Recidivism of Prisoners Released in 1994.* Bureau of Justice Statistics Special Report. Washington, D.C.: U.S. Department of Justice.

Langrock, Adela M., Bruce E. Compas, Gary Keller, Mary Jane Merchant, and Mary Ellen Copeland. 2002. "Coping with the Stress of Parental Depression: Parents' Reports of Children's Coping, Emotional, and Behavioral Problems." *Journal of Clinical Child and Adolescent Psychology* 31 (3): 312–24.

Lee, Christine M., and Ian H. Gotlib. 1989. "Clinical Status and Emotional Adjustment of Children of Depressed Mothers." *American Journal of Psychiatry* 146 (4): 478.

Leiferman, Jenn. 2002. "The Effect of Maternal Depressive Symptomatology on Maternal Behaviors Associated with Child Health." *Health Education and Behavior* 29 (5): 596–607.

Lyon, Eleanor. 2000. "Welfare, Poverty, and Abused Women: New Research and Its Implications." Building Comprehensive Solutions to Domestic Violence Policy and Practice Paper No.10. Harrisburg, Pa.: National Resource Center on Domestic Violence.

Margolin, Leslie. 1992. "Child Abuse by Mothers' Boyfriends: Why the Overrepresenta-
tion?" *Child Abuse and Neglect* 16 (4): 541–51.

Masten, Ann S. 2001. "Ordinary Magic: Resilience Process in Development." *American
Psychologist* 56 (3): 227–38.

Mauer, Marc. 1999. *Race to Incarcerate.* New York: The New Press.

McLoyd, Vonnie C. 1990. "The Impact of Economic Hardship on Black Families and
Children: Psychological Distress, Parenting, and Socioemotional Development."
Child Development 61 (2): 311–46.

———. 1998. "Socioeconomic Disadvantage and Child Development." *American Psychologist* 53 (2): 185–204.

Mumola, Christopher J. 2000. *Incarcerated Parents and Their Children.* Bureau of Justice
Statistics Special Report. Washington, D.C.: U.S. Department of Justice.

National Mental Health Association. 2003. "Depression: What You Need to Know."
http://www.nmha.org/infoctr/factsheets/21.cfm. (Accessed February 2003.)

Oyserman, Daphna, Deborah Bybee, and Carol T. Mowbray. 2002. "Influences of Maternal Mental Illness on Psychological Outcomes for Adolescent Children." *Journal of
Adolescence* 25 (6): 587–602.

Sampson, Robert J. 1995. "Unemployment and Imbalanced Sex Ratios." In *The Decline
in Marriage among African Americans,* edited by M. Belinda Tucker and Claudia
Mitchell-Kernan (229–54). New York: Russell Sage Foundation.

Satcher, David. 1999. *Mental Health: A Report of the Surgeon General.* Washington, D.C.:
U.S. Department of Health and Human Services.

Shonkoff, Jack P., and Deborah A. Phillips, eds. 2000. *From Neurons to Neighborhoods: The
Science of Early Childhood Development.* Washington, D.C.: National Academy Press.

Sims, Rachel. 2001. "Can My Daddy Hug Me? Deciding Whether Visiting Dad in a Prison
Facility Is in the Best Interest of the Child." *Brooklyn Law Review* 66: 933.

Taylor, Robert Joseph, M. Belinda Tucker, Linda M. Chatters, and Rukmalie Jayakody.
1997. "Recent Demographic Trends in African American Family Structure." In *Family Life in Black America,* edited by Robert Joseph Taylor, James S. Jackson, and
Linda M. Chatters (14–62). Thousand Oaks, Calif.: Sage Publications.

Testa, Mark, and Marilyn Krogh. 1995. "The Effect of Employment on Marriage among
Black Males in Inner-City Chicago." In *The Decline in Marriage among African
Americans,* edited by M. Belinda Tucker and Claudia Mitchell-Kernan (59–95). New
York: Russell Sage Foundation.

Thompson, Patricia. 1998. "Adolescents from Families of Divorce: Vulnerability to Physiological and Psychological Disturbances." *Journal of Psychosocial Nursing and Mental Health Services* 36 (3): 34–39.

Weissman, Myrna, and Peter Jensen. 2002. "What Research Suggests for Depressed
Women with Children." *Journal of Clinical Psychiatry* 63 (7): 641–47.

Western, Bruce, and Sara McLanahan. 2000. "Fathers behind Bars: The Impact of Incarceration on Family Formation." In *Families, Crime and Criminal Justice,* edited by
Greer Litton Fox and Michael L. Benson (307–22). New York: JAI/Elsevier.

Western, Bruce, Beck Petit, and Josh Guetzkow. 2002. "Back Economic Progress in the
Era of Mass Imprisonment." In *Invisible Punishment,* edited by Marc Mauer and
Meda Chesney-Lind (165–80). New York: The New Press.

Wickramaratne, Priya J., and Myrna M. Weissman. 1998. "Onset of Psychopathology in Offspring by Developmental Phase and Parental Depression." *Journal of the American Academy of Child and Adolescent Psychiatry* 37 (9): 933–42.

Wilson, Margo, and Martin Daly. 1987. "Risk of Maltreatment of Children Living with Stepparents." In *Child Abuse and Neglect,* edited by Richard J. Gelles and Jane B. Lancaster (215–32). New York: Aldine de Gruyter.

6

The Effects of Parental Incarceration on Children

Perspectives, Promises, and Policies

Ross D. Parke and K. Alison Clarke-Stewart

One of the greatest punishments for imprisoned mothers is separation from their children. As one mother put it, "I can do time alone okay. But it's not knowing what's happening to my son that hurts most" (Baunach 1985, 121). When parents are incarcerated, "what's happening" to their children is of great concern. This issue is a concern for citizens and policymakers as well. This chapter examines how parental incarceration affects children's well-being and development, analyzing what is happening to these children during and after their parents are in prison.

Several assumptions guided our examination of this problem:

1. The child is located in a family system, and to understand incarceration's impact on the child, we should consider the network of relationships within the family system (Belsky 1984; Sameroff 1994).
2. The child's developmental level at the time of parental incarceration and the quality of the child's relationship with the incarcerated parent are important (Bowlby 1973).
3. The incarcerated parent's gender should be considered, because separation from a mother may affect a child differently than separation from a father (Parke 2002).

4. The characteristics of the extended kin network in which the family is located are relevant (Cochran and Brassard 1979).
5. The nature and availability of formal institutional supports for the family should be examined (Bronfenbrenner and Morris 1998).

This chapter describes the psychological theories that formed the basis for these assumptions. It also outlines the scope of the problem of parental incarceration and examines available research documenting the short- and long-term effects of parental incarceration on children. Variables that might moderate the effects of incarceration on children are explored and research on programs for children, parents, and families aimed at ameliorating the negative effects of parental incarceration on children are summarized. Finally, the chapter ends with a discussion about policy implications and suggests topics for future research.

A caveat is in order. Mounting successful interventions and designing effective policies for dealing with parental incarceration requires extensive, longitudinal studies that go beyond demonstrating that "parental incarceration is bad for children." We need a rich database that allows us to answer descriptive questions (How many children have parents whose crimes would seriously undermine their ability to have a positive effect on their children?) and process questions (How does parental incarceration generate effects on children?). We need to gather information about the many events and conditions that contribute to children's well-being before, during, and after parental incarceration. A solid scientific base documenting this complex and multifaceted issue is absent; therefore, much of our discussion is speculative and preliminary. In fact, our review rests upon research limited in both scope and quality. Many studies are atheoretical, cross-sectional in design, and insensitive to developmental issues. They use small samples that are not necessarily representative of the incarcerated population, employing nonstandardized measures or relying on single and potentially biased reporters.

In light of this fragile empirical foundation, we offer our overview with caution—in the interest of stimulating better research. At the same time, we attempt to weave together the existing, albeit flawed, strands of evidence into a coherent and useful picture that can serve as a preliminary guide to policy decisionmakers and program designers. To achieve this coherence, we examine the existing literature in the light of our knowledge of children's development and especially their stress and coping skills.

Scope of the Problem

According to recent estimates, nearly 3.6 million parents in the United States are under some form of correctional supervision, including parole (Mumola 2000), and of these, almost 1.1 million are incarcerated in federal or state prisons or local jails. These parents have an estimated 2.3 million children. Alarmingly, the rate of parental incarceration has gone up sharply in the past decade. In 1991, there were 452,500 parents of 936,500 minor children in state and federal prisons. By 2000, the number of parents in prisons had nearly doubled to 737,400, and the number of children affected rose by over one-half to 1,531,500 (Mumola 2000). Although the percentage of state and federal prisoners with minor children has not changed over this period (56 percent), absolute numbers have increased, and this fact makes the issue all the more urgent.

Parent gender is a major factor in incarceration; 90 percent of incarcerated parents are fathers. However, over the past decade, the number of mothers in prison has grown at a faster rate than the number of incarcerated fathers. Between 1990 and 1999, there was a 98 percent increase in the number of incarcerated mothers, compared with a 58 percent increase in incarcerated fathers (Mumola 2000). Hagan and Dinovitzer (1999) suggest that incarceration is being used more frequently, for longer terms, and with declining prospects for parole because federal sentencing guidelines have reduced judges' discretion, particularly when it comes to drug-related offenses. These guidelines have especially contributed to increased incarceration rates among women, who are more likely to be incarcerated for economic offenses and drug-related crimes.

In addition, clear differences exist in the ethnic make-up of incarcerated parents. More African-American (47 percent) than Hispanic (19 percent) or white non-Hispanic parents (29 percent) are incarcerated in state prisons. As a result, of the total population of minor-age children in the United States, nearly 7 percent of African-American, 3 percent of Hispanic, and 1 percent of white children have a parent in prison (Mumola 2000).

In terms of age, 58 percent of children with incarcerated parents are under 10 years of age, with 8 years being the mean age (Mumola 2000). In terms of marital status, less than one-quarter (23 percent) of parents in state prisons were married at the time of their incarceration. Furthermore, nearly half (48 percent) of the parents in state prisons have never been married. In terms of education, 60 percent of the parents in state facilities have a high school diploma; 13 percent report some college education (Mumola 2000).

To understand the impact of parental incarceration, it is important to know the nature of family living arrangements prior to incarceration. Before incarceration, mothers (64 percent) are more likely than fathers (44 percent) to be living with their children (Mumola 2000). Unfortunately, the nature of such prior living arrangements is not generally considered in assessments of incarceration's impact on children; however, incarceration likely carries different meanings and produces different consequences for children depending on whether or not they live with their parents before incarceration. As we know from other research literatures, meaningful social relationships may or may not exist between children and their nonresident parent (Furstenberg, Morgan, and Allison 1987; Garfinkel et al. 1998). The extent to which incarceration disrupts the contact patterns between these nonresidential parents and their children and the effects of incarceration on children who were living with their parent at the time of imprisonment are both issues that merit examination.

The question of who cares for the children when parents are incarcerated is yet another important issue. Again, the answer varies with the parent's gender. Incarcerated fathers report that, before their arrest, their child's mother was the usual caregiver, and 90 percent report that, after their imprisonment, these mothers continue the caregiving responsibility. On the other hand, when mothers are put in prison, only about 30 percent of fathers assume parental responsibility. Instead, most commonly, the grandparent becomes the caregiver (53 percent). In addition, other relatives in the kin network pick up the parenting role for another 30 percent of the cases, and friends step in about 10 percent of the time. Fewer than 10 percent of mothers in state prisons report that their children were placed in foster care (Mumola 2000). These disparities in parenting responsibilities reflect our society as a whole, in which mothers assume the largest share of parenting among intact families (Coltrane 1996; Parke 1996, 2002) and post-divorce families (Hetherington and Kelley 2002).

On average, mothers and fathers in prison also spend different lengths of time away from their children. Fathers serve an average of 82 months in state prison, whereas mothers serve an average of 49 months (Mumola 2000). Clearly, length of time in prison needs to be considered as a factor that may account for the different effects of children's separations from mothers and fathers. Shorter separation periods make it more likely that mothers will retain custody and maintain their parent-child relationships—two factors critical to successful reunion upon release. At the same time, the lengthier period of separation from fathers may bode poorly for father-child ties (Gadsden and Rethemeyer 2001). The lengths of incarceration reflect the nature of the different offenses committed by males and females. Fathers are more likely than mothers to be in prison for violent crimes (45 vs. 26 percent in state prison). Mothers, on the other hand, are more likely to be incarcerated for drug-related offenses (35 vs. 23 percent) and fraud (11 vs. 2 percent) (Mumola 2000). Therefore, we must consider these gender-related patterns of incarceration when addressing the question of incarceration's impact on mother-child versus father-child relationships.

Theoretical Perspectives to Guide Research and Policy

A variety of theoretical perspectives are relevant to parental incarceration and provide useful guidelines for the design of future research, intervention, and policy. These theoretical perspectives include developmental and ecological contexts and cross-level analyses of the individual child and parent, the parent-child dyad, the family network, the community, the institution, and the culture.

Developmental Theory

From a developmental perspective, several theories aid our understanding about the consequences of parental incarceration. Bowlby's (1973) attachment theory, for example, serves as a framework for grasping the importance of the development of the parent-infant or parent-child relationship. According to Bowlby, the lack of regular and sustained contact between an infant and parent will prevent the development of the infant's attachment to the parent. Once an attachment has developed, however, separation from the parent can generate a set of adverse emotional reactions ranging from sadness to anger, which, in turn, will interfere with the child's optimal development (Sroufe 1988). At the same time, children can form multiple attachments, including attachments to fathers and other nonmaternal caregivers, as well as to mothers. That infants can develop strong attachments to their fathers (Parke 2002) underscores the importance of assessing children's reactions to separation from their incarcerated fathers as well as reactions to the loss of their incarcerated mothers. It also suggests that a secure attachment relationship with another caregiver helps children who "lose" their relationship with an incarcerated parent. For example, Howes and Hamilton (1993) found that children with an insecure attachment to their mother but a secure attachment to a day care provider tended to be more socially competent than were insecurely attached children who had not formed a strong compensatory relationship outside the family. This work underscores the need to assess the quality of children's attachment relationships with alternative caregivers, such as grandparents, when the parent is unavailable because of incarceration. Finally, Bowlby's theory alerts us to the fact that, like children, mothers experience anxiety when separated from their children.

Life-Span Theory

According to the life-span theory of development (Baltes 1987; Elder 1998), development is a process that continues throughout the life cycle into adulthood. Childhood is important, but other ages also significantly shape later stages of development. Experts are recognizing the importance of examining developmental change in adults and now appreciate that parents continue to change and develop during their adult years. For example, age at the onset of parenthood can have important implications for how women and men manage their maternal and paternal roles. In the current context, how parents and their children adjust to the parent's incarceration will vary greatly depending on the parent's age as well as the child's developmental level. According to life-span theory, change over time can be traced to three sets of causes. First, there are normative events and experiences, such as starting school, reaching menarche, and graduating from college, that most children and adults undergo at roughly the same ages. Second, there are unexpected events, such as job loss, divorce, death of a family member, or incarceration, that push development in a new direction. For incarcerated parents, living in a violent, inhumane, and dangerous environment will inevitably affect their attitudes and behavior in ways that are likely to persist after the incarceration. The implications for family life can be profound. Parents who return from prison dependent on institutional structures and routines will not likely be able to effectively organize the lives of their children or behave with the autonomy parenting requires. Those who learn to be distrusting in prison will find it difficult to promote trust in their children (or perhaps to trust them) and they may remain alienated and unable to nurture. (See chapter 2 in this volume for more on this topic.)

Historical time periods and social trends constitute the third set of events that can influence individual development. Historical periods provide the social conditions for individual and family transitions, and across these periods, incarceration, its consequences, and policies may vary. Over the past several decades, a number of secular changes have occurred that could affect American families' reactions to and experiences with incarceration. These changes include declining fertility and family size, increasing female participation in the workforce, the rising number of divorces and single-parent families, and, most recently, changes in the welfare system and child welfare laws. These societal trends and the historical era in which the incarceration takes place can profoundly shape child-rearing experiences and subsequent developmental outcomes.

Systems Theory

Developmental analyses need not be restricted to the individual, either parent or child, but, as suggested by systems theory, include dyadic and family levels as well (Minuchin 2002). At the dyadic level, relationships (between husband and wife, mother and child, and father and child) may follow separate and partially independent developmental courses over childhood (Belsky, Rovine, and Fish 1989; Parke 1988). At the family level, changes in structure (e.g., through the removal of the incarcerated member or the addition of the child to a foster family or a grandparent-headed household) also occur over time, with implications for both children and caregivers. The mutual impact of different sets of relationships varies as a function of the nature of all these developmental trajectories. Systems theory alerts us to the interdependence among these various family subsystems. When a parent is incarcerated, the loss of that parent has implications for the remaining parent in a two-parent family as well as for extended family members, such as grandparents. This perspective is helpful in understanding how families adapt to the temporary or permanent loss of a parent through incarceration.

Risk and Resilience Theories

Other theorists (e.g., Luthar, Cicchetti, and Becker 2000; Rutter and Sroufe 2000) have recognized that children's successful adaptation in the face of such stressful life events as parental incarceration varies as a function of two components: the form and frequency of the risks and the protective or resilience factors that buffer the child from the adverse events. Individual children respond to risks in a variety of ways. Some suffer permanent developmental disruptions and delays. Others show sleeper effects; they appear to cope well initially but exhibit problems later in development. Still others exhibit resilience under the most difficult circumstances and may even be strengthened by adversity. Moreover, when they confront new risks later in life, these children seem better able to adapt to challenges than do children who have experienced little or no risk—a kind of inoculation effect (Hetherington 1991; Rutter and Rutter 1993).

Three sets of protective factors appear to buffer children from risk and stress and promote coping and good adjustment in the face of adversity. The first set of factors consists of positive individual attributes. Children who exhibit easy temperaments, high self-esteem, intelligence, and independence are more adaptable in the face of stressful life experiences (Rutter 1987; Werner 1993). Compared with boys and men, girls and women have a slight edge as well. The second set of protective factors is found in a supportive family environment. A parent's encouragement can help buffer the adverse effects of poverty, divorce, or incarceration (Luthar et al. 2000). The final set of factors involves people outside the family, for example, individuals in the school system, peer groups, or churches who support children's and parents' coping efforts.

Cumulative Risk Models

Cumulative risk represents a closely related theoretical perspective with clear relevance to the issue of incarceration's effects on children (Rutter 1987; Sameroff et al. 1998). According to this perspective, risks often co-occur and are best understood not as single events but as sets or combinations of events. Children are most likely to suffer when multiple risks co-occur. Moreover, the nature of the particular risk may be less critical than the number of risks that the child encounters. In fact, any attempt to attribute specific child outcomes to parental incarceration alone might be incomplete because many events before, during, and after the incarceration co-occur and contribute to overall child adjustment and well-being. For example, children who suffer the loss of a parent through imprisonment may also be at risk because of poverty, family violence, substance abuse, changes in residence, shift in caregivers, and stigmatization by peers and community. Moreover, all of these factors, especially poverty, substance abuse, and family violence (including child abuse), result in major negative consequences for children. Although reviews of these risk factors are beyond the scope of this chapter (see Duncan and Brooks-Gunn 1997), experts recognize that incarceration's effects can only be understood adequately by considering the family ecology of incarcerated parents and their children. Realizing the multiple risks that children of incarcerated parents experience is critical to gaining a better understanding of the multiple factors that contribute to children's adjustment; policymakers should consider these risks when designing interventions and crafting social policy.

Putting the Pieces Together

No single theoretical perspective adequately encompasses the complexity of the parental incarceration problem. Instead, a framework integrating these perspectives into a unified theoretical whole is necessary. Figure 6.1 shows a transactional model of risks and supports associated with parental incarceration. Incarceration and reentry increase the probability of parents and children encountering a set of interrelated risks. These risks interact in a variety of complex ways, just as they do in such transitions as divorce and remarriage or job loss (Conger and Elder 1994; Hetherington, Bridges, and Insabella 1998). According to our model, incarceration leads to changes in family composition and shifts in caregiving arrangements. The ability of alternative caregivers to cope adequately and to avoid depression will affect children indirectly through the caregiving processes. However, the extent to which these caregiving processes affect the child's adjustment will also be determined by the child's coping strategies. Similarly, the opportunity parents and children have to maintain contact during the separation will affect the nature of their relationships, and this, in turn, will affect the children's adjustment.

Different variables may play different roles at various points across time. For example, the quality of caregiving processes (e.g., the child's

Figure 6.1. *A Transactional Model of the Predictors of Children's Adjustment following Parental Incarceration and Reunion*

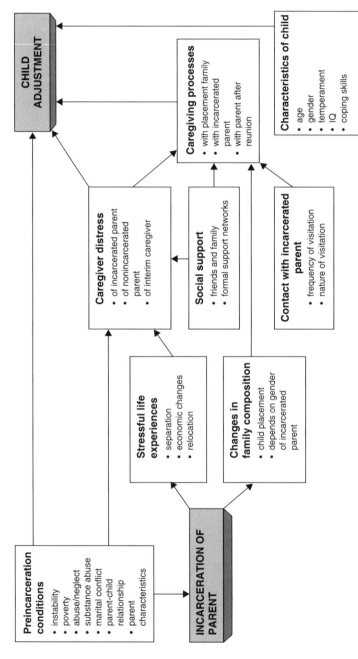

Source: Adapted from Conger and Elder (1994) and Hetherington et al. (1998).

relationship with the alternative caregiver) may play a protective role during parental incarceration but present a risk to successful reunion with the incarcerated parent after the separation period is over. As the risk and resilience perspective suggests, the balance between risks and resources might determine the impact of parental incarceration and reentry on children. Static and cross-sectional slices out of the lives of parents and children present a misleading picture of how risk and protective factors operate across time to affect children's adjustment to parental incarceration. As figure 6.1 suggests, only by examining this issue in a dynamic and transactional framework will we fully appreciate the complexities of the interacting trajectories that parents, alternative caregivers, and children follow across time and the roles that risks and protective factors play in determining children's outcomes.

Finally, in evaluating this literature, we need to understand how selection factors may affect the differences between children of incarcerated and nonincarcerated parents (Hagan and Dinovitzer 1999). Imprisoned parents and their children might differ from their nonincarcerated peers long before the incarceration occurs, and this perspective needs to be included as a theoretical caveat that permeates all of the other theoretical viewpoints. Similar arguments have been made with regard to other complex issues, such as the effects of day care (Clarke-Stewart and Allhusen 2002) and divorce (Cherlin 1992) on children.

The Impact of Incarceration on Children

Incarceration is not a single or discrete event, but a dynamic process that unfolds over time. Understanding the impact of the incarceration process on children requires considering separately the short-term effects of the parent's arrest and the removal of the child from the parent, the impact of the parent's unavailability to the child during the period of incarceration, and the effects—both positive and negative—of reunion after the incarceration period. Observing events preceding and circumstances surrounding the arrest is also critical—whether the child was living with the parent, whether a single or two-parent household is involved, and, in the case of a two-parent household, which parent is incarcerated. As we have noted, only a small percentage of children live with their father as the sole caregiver; children are usually living with a single mother prior to parental incarceration. The most recent figures (Mumola 2000) indicate that

36 percent of inmate mothers in state prison were not living with their children at the time of admission. In contrast, 56 percent of state inmate fathers were not living with their children at the time of their incarceration. Thus, when a parent is incarcerated, it is more likely that children will experience separation from a mother than separation from a father. Moreover, single women are at increased risk of losing their parental rights after incarceration (Genty 1995; Hagan and Dinovitzer 1999).

Short-Term Effects

THE ARREST PHASE

Unfortunately, our picture of how initial arrest affects children is incomplete. According to Johnston (1991), one in five children of incarcerated parents witnesses his or her mother's arrest, and more than half of the children who witness this traumatic event are under age 7 and in the sole care of their mother. Jose-Kampfner (1995) interviewed 30 children who witnessed their mother's arrest and reported that these children suffered nightmares and flashbacks to the arrest incident. Children in middle childhood who are in school at the time of the arrest may return to an empty residence, unaware of their mother's fate (Fishman 1983). The impact of father's versus mother's arrest is unknown and needs to be assessed in future research, as does the effect of variability in how police handle arrests.

THE MANAGEMENT OF THE EXPLANATION

Controversy surrounds the wisdom of providing children with information concerning the arrest and the reasons for their parent's incarceration. Some experts argue that children ought to be protected from the knowledge that their parents are incarcerated as a way of minimizing the trauma associated with the separation (Becker and Margolin 1967). Others argue that the unwillingness of family, friends, or caregivers to discuss parental incarceration exacerbates children's emotional distress (Snyder-Joy and Carlo 1998). This failure to disclose has been variously termed the "conspiracy of silence" (Jose-Kampfner 1995) or "forced silence" (Johnston 1995). Mothers are usually the ones who take responsibility for explaining the situation to the children—regardless of whether or not they are the incarcerated parent. For example, Sack, Seidler, and Thomas (1976) found that in only 7 of 31 cases did the father or both parents together explain the situation to the child. Moreover, when explanations were provided, they were often vague and general; one typical mother told her children that their father "did wrong and had to be punished." Other explanations were distorted or deceitful. Deception took a variety of forms, from total lies to strong shading of the truth, in which prison was referred to as an army camp, a hospital, or a school. Total deception occurred in 4 of the 31 families in the study, and partial deception occurred in another 6 families. In other words, nearly one-third of the families engaged in some form of deception. Similarly, in a much larger study carried out in England, Morris (1965) reported that 38 percent of the families used partial or total deception in explaining a parent's incarceration to children.

How does this "conspiracy of silence" or deception affect children? In light of the literature on children's coping (Ayers et al. 1996; Compas 1987)—which suggests that uncertainty and lack of information undermine children's ability to cope—it is not surprising that children who are uninformed about their parent's incarceration are more anxious and fearful (Johnston 1995). Although the situation of a parent lost through death is more extreme, this literature offers some instructive insights concerning ways of helping children cope with loss. As Nolen-Hoeksema and Larson (1999) argue, children need honest, factual information, and they need to have their experience validated. Providing children with reliable information allows them to begin to make sense of their situation and begin the dual processes of grieving the loss of their parent and coping with their new life circumstances. On the other hand, silence about parental incarceration often results not from a deliberate attempt to deceive children but from an effort to avoid other complications. As Johnston notes, "There may be a very good reason for such a forced silence; family jobs, welfare payments, child custody, and even housing may be jeopardized when others become aware of the parents' whereabouts. However, children of prisoners are more likely to have negative reactions to the experience when they cannot talk about it" (Johnston 1995, 74).

Long-Term Effects

Researchers and practitioners have identified a variety of negative long-term effects for children stemming from parental incarceration. These effects vary depending on a number of factors. First, incarceration is often preceded by a period of familial instability, poverty, poor parenting, child abuse or neglect, marital discord and conflict, or paternal absence. A combination of these conditions may have already increased the base rates of children's problem behaviors. Consequently, without measures of the child's environment and behavior prior to incarceration, it is difficult to attribute the problem behaviors to incarceration per se. Second, other events also transpiring during incarceration could account for some of the negative effects on children. For example, relocation and placement with alternative caregivers both represent major disruptions in these children's lives, which past research has shown to be detrimental (Rutter 1987). A similar set of interpretative problems has plagued the literature on the effects of other kinds of stress, such as divorce, on children's functioning (Hetherington and Kelley 2002; Hetherington et al. 1998). These limitations must be kept in mind in reviewing the research linking parental incarceration with child outcomes.

INCARCERATION AND INFANTS
A small number of women (6 percent; U.S. Department of Justice 1994) are pregnant at the time of their incarceration, but few prisons in the United States permit mothers to keep their infants with them during incarceration (Gabel and Girard 1995). In most cases, the mother of a newborn infant is permitted only a few days of contact before she must relinquish her infant and return to prison. As a result, there is little opportunity for the mother to bond with her baby or for the baby to form an attachment to the mother. As Myers et al. (1999) note, when the mother is released, she comes home to an infant or young child with whom she has not developed an emotional bond and who is not emotionally attached to her. The immediate consequences of this will depend on the mother's sensitivity and the infant's adaptability. Without an effort on both their parts, the child will likely develop emotional and behavioral problems. Caution is in order, however, in assigning a causal role to separation- and attachment-related problems since there are a variety of other factors such as poverty, multiple residential changes, and quality of relationship with the interim caregiver that could account for child difficulties.

INCARCERATION AND YOUNG CHILDREN
Even if a child-parent attachment bond has already developed, as in the case of infants who have been in the care of their mother or father for the first 9 to 12 months of life, the disruption associated with parental incarceration will likely adversely affect the quality of the child's attachment to

the parent. Even less drastic changes, such as job loss, divorce, or residential relocation, have been found to negatively affect child-parent attachment (Thompson 1998; Thompson, Lamb, and Estes 1982; Vaughn et al. 1979). Insecure attachments—a consequence of adverse shifts in life circumstances—in turn, have been linked to a variety of child outcomes, including poorer peer relationships and diminished cognitive abilities (Sroufe 1988). In light of this research, it is not surprising that when their parents are incarcerated, young children (age 2 to 6 years) have been observed to suffer a variety of adverse outcomes that are consistent with the research on the effects of insecure attachments (Johnston 1995). In fact, according to one estimate (Baunach 1985), 70 percent of young children with incarcerated mothers had emotional or psychological problems. Children exhibit internalizing problems, such as anxiety, withdrawal, hypervigilance, depression, shame and guilt (Bloom and Steinhart 1993; Dressel et al. 1992). They also exhibit somatic problems, such as eating disorders. And, perhaps most clearly, young children exhibit externalizing behaviors, such as anger, aggression, and hostility toward caregivers and siblings (Fishman 1983; Gaudin 1984; Johnston 1995; Jose-Kampfner 1995; Sack et al. 1976). Poehlmann's study (2001) of 37 incarcerated mothers, their 3- to 6-year-old children, and their children's caregivers demonstrates incarceration's effects on children's attachment relationships. Children were interviewed using the Attachment Story Completion Task (Bretherton, Prentiss, and Ridgeway 1990) to assess how they represented their attachment relationships with their mothers and their alternate caregivers. Representations of relationships with caregivers were more positive and coherent than were representations of relationships with mothers. Representations of mothers mixed nurturance with violence—a profile that suggests that these children's attachments to their mothers were ambivalent. These findings suggest that children who undergo separation due to incarceration do indeed have less healthy attachment relationships with their incarcerated parents and imply that these children may be less well adapted to deal effectively with other social relationships (Cassidy et al. 1996).

INCARCERATION AND SCHOOL-AGE CHILDREN

School-age children of incarcerated parents exhibit school-related problems and problems with peer relationships. Sack et al. (1976) reported that over 50 percent of the children of incarcerated parents had school problems, such as poor grades or instances of aggression, albeit many of these problems were temporary. Among the younger children (6 to 8 years old) in the study, 16 percent exhibited transient school phobias and were unwilling to go to school for a four- to six-week period after their parents' incarceration. In another report, Stanton (1980) found even higher rates of school problems: Of 166 children of incarcerated mothers, 70 percent showed poor academic performance and 50 percent exhibited classroom behavior problems. Furthermore, children in school are sometimes teased or ostracized by their peers as a result of their parents' incarceration (Jose-Kampfner 1991). In addition, as Eddy and Reid (chapter 7) note, suspension and dropout rates are higher for these children as they reach adolescence (Trice 1997).

INCARCERATION EFFECTS BY CHILDREN'S GENDER
Although we would expect that boys would be more adversely affected by the stress of separation from parents—especially in the light of evidence that boys are, in general, more vulnerable to stressful changes than girls are (e.g., Hetherington et al. 1998)—the evidence on this issue is unclear. Instead, the most likely scenario is that both boys and girls are adversely affected by parental incarceration, but their modes of expressing their reactions may differ. Boys are more likely to exhibit externalizing behavior problems (aggression, defiance, disobedience), while girls are more likely to display internalizing problems (depression, anxiety, withdrawal) (Cummings, Davies, and Campbell 2000). However, these sets of symptoms or problems often co-occur and are evident in children of both sexes (Russo and Beidel 1994).

Modifiers of Children's Reactions to Incarceration

Children's reactions to parental incarceration are likely to be modified by a number of factors occurring before and during the incarceration and during the reunion phase.

PREINCARCERATION CONDITIONS
The quality of the parent-child relationship is the most important predictor of how well the child will adjust to the immediate separation. Theoretically, a high-quality parent-child relationship should serve as a protective or buffering factor in helping the child cope with the temporary loss of a parent (Myers et al. 1999; Thompson 1998). Unfortunately, however, many parents who end up in prison have limited parenting

abilities, and thus this potential protective factor is unavailable to their children (Johnston 1991). Moreover, research to empirically establish whether children with a closer relationship with their incarcerated parents are able to transcend the separation period with greater ease is not available. Other factors associated with the parent's history may increase the risk of insecure parent-child attachments. For example, nearly 75 percent of incarcerated mothers use drugs prior to incarceration and many end up in prison for drug-related crimes or for crimes that were committed to support their drug use (Mumola 2000; Snell 1994). Repeated separations due to multiple prior incarcerations may also undermine attachment quality (Mumola 2000; Poehlmann 2001).

Yet another predictor of how well children adjust to parental incarceration is likely to be the quality of relationships within their extended families and their nonfamily informal social networks. This support is especially relevant when the father is incarcerated and the mother must cope as a single parent. There is an extensive literature suggesting that the quality of family ties within the extended family network affects mothers' parenting attitudes and behavior (Cochran and Brassard 1979; Cochran and Niego 1995). In addition, Crnic et al. (1983) reported that mothers with higher levels of informal social support were more responsive and affectionate with their infants. More recently, Goldstein, Diener, and Mangelsdorf (1996) similarly found that women with larger social networks were more sensitive in interactions with their infants. In turn, the children of parents who receive more social, emotional, and physical support are better adjusted than children of parents with limited kin or network support (Thompson 1995). Moreover, in the case of incarcerated mothers, extended family members such as grandmothers often assume the role of primary caregiver (Mumola 2000). Children who have already established close emotional relationships with their extended families will experience less trauma in transitioning to grandmother care (Bloom and Steinhart 1993).

FACTORS DURING INCARCERATION

In the light of earlier work on the importance of the parent-child relationship and the impact of separation on children's adjustment (Bowlby 1980), it is important to examine how (1) the nature and quality of the alternative caregiving arrangements and (2) the opportunities to maintain contact with the absent parent affect children's adjustment during parental incarceration.

As we have noted, the incarcerated parent's gender is a major determinant of the type of alternative care arrangement. When fathers are incarcerated, the mother generally continues to be responsible for child care; when mothers are incarcerated, grandmothers most likely assume that responsibility (Bloom and Steinhart 1993; Mumola 2000). The latter arrangement provides greater continuity for the child relative to foster care because the child is with a familiar caregiver. Moreover, this arrangement permits more frequent and consistent contact with the incarcerated parents as well as with siblings. Kinship placements tend to be more stable and avoid transethnic discontinuities that are likely to occur in the foster care system. However, while experts assume that children make better adjustments in kinship homes, comparative studies of kinship versus foster care placements are not available. Moreover, there are problems with kinship arrangements as well. For one, kinship families are not likely to be connected with the formal child welfare system and therefore may not be receiving financial or health care assistance (Seymour 1998). Young and Smith (2000) cite a range of challenges grandparents face in raising grandchildren, including emotional difficulties (increased depression), physical difficulties (poorer physical health), and financial difficulties (added expense), which, in turn, may undermine their effectiveness as substitute caregivers. As in the case of grandmothers raising infants for their teenage daughters (Brooks-Gunn and Chase-Lansdale 1995), the relationship between the grandmother and the incarcerated mother is often strained and characterized by a range of negative feelings, such as resentment, anger, guilt, or disappointment (Bloom and Steinhart 1993; Young and Smith 2000). In turn, this situation complicates decisionmaking on the child's behalf, a process that requires cooperation across generations if the child's best interests are to be served.

Parallel problems are evident in joint custody arrangements after divorce (Hetherington and Kelley 2002; Maccoby and Mnookin 1993). Grandmothers serve as gatekeepers in terms of children's access to their parents, just as divorced mothers regulate fathers' access to their children (Braver and O'Connell 2000). In spite of this potential barrier, 94 percent of caregivers surveyed by the National Counsel on Crime and Delinquency endorsed the idea that contact between mother and child is important, and 97 percent helped promote contact during incarceration (Bloom and Steinhart 1993). At the same time, for some children who have experienced unstable, chaotic home lives, the shift to a more predictable and stable child-rearing environment may be beneficial—in spite of the loss of contact with the incarcerated parent.

A second potential determinant of children's adjustment to parental incarceration is the degree of regular contact they have with their incarcerated parents. Institutional, attitudinal, and practical barriers make this contact difficult to maintain. As Young and Smith (2000) note, correctional policies regarding visitation and phone use make it difficult for mothers to stay in touch with their children. Facilities are typically located in remote areas, often long distances from where children and caregivers live, making visitation extremely difficult for families with limited resources; furthermore, visitation hours are scheduled for specific times each week without regard for would-be visitors' schedules (Kaplan and Sasser 1996). The problem of prison access is especially acute for incarcerated mothers because there are fewer prisons for women. According to one estimate, incarcerated females are, on average, 160 miles farther away from their families than are incarcerated males (Coughenour 1995). In addition, rules about who is eligible to visit, the number of visitors allowed at one time, appropriate behavior during the visit, along with lack of privacy, harsh treatment of visitors by correctional staff, and the physical layout of the visiting room often deter visits by family members and caregivers. Other problems include child-unfriendly visiting rooms and increased anxiety on the part of the visiting child (Bloom and Steinhart 1993; Simon and Landis 1991). These conditions, in part, flow from cultural and institutional beliefs that incarcerated individuals, including parents, do not deserve such privileges as family visitation. As Clark (1995) notes, the children become the "unseen victims" of a mother's incarceration.

Parents', caregivers', and social workers' attitudes also play a role in visitation patterns. Some resist the idea of visitation by children either because of the unpleasant and inhospitable visiting conditions (Hairston 1991) or because they believe visitation will produce negative reactions in the children (Bloom and Steinhart 1993). However, Johnston (1995) found that the excitability and hyperactivity associated with children's visitation were relatively short-lived and there was no evidence of long-term negative responses. Visiting can calm children's fears about their parent's welfare as well as their concerns about the parent's feelings for them (Sack 1977). Investigations of the patterns of visitation reveal that approximately half of incarcerated parents do not receive any visits from their children (Snell 1994). Children are most likely to visit their mother in the first year and less likely to do so after this initial period. Moreover, even when children do visit, they do not visit often. According to one large-scale survey of state prison inmates, only 8 percent of the incarcerated mothers saw their children as often as once a week; 18 percent were visited once a month; and 74 percent saw their children less than once a month (U.S. Department of Justice 1993).

Programs for Incarcerated Parents

Programs to aid incarcerated parents and their children take a variety of forms and are targeted at several different audiences—imprisoned parents, alternative caregivers, and the children themselves. Moreover, these programs are delivered by a range of agencies, including prisons, social work agencies, schools, and clinics. In addition, goals and timing of interventions vary. Some aim to increase contact between incarcerated parents and their children; some attempt to improve the structure of visits and facilitate family interactions; others seek to improve parenting skills of incarcerated parents; still others seek to ease the inmate parents' reentry into society and the parental role by offering postincarceration training, job placement services, and housing assistance.

Unfortunately, although such programs exist, information about which approaches, if any, are most effective is limited. Furthermore, numerous problems characterize research in this area—lack of comparison groups, failure to carry out systematic evaluations of the impact of the interventions, use of nonstandardized measurement instruments, and limited follow-up assessing the long-term effects of the interventions. Generally atheoretical, these programs do not include all relevant parties, are narrow in scope, vary in length, do not provide postincarceration services, and, because clients are self-selected volunteers, probably exclude those most in need of intervention.

Interventions for Parents

In light of the well-documented finding that many incarcerated mothers have limited parenting skills (Johnston 1991), several programs have been developed to provide parent education for these mothers. This development seems particularly appropriate because, according to one recent survey (Kazura 2001), incarcerated parents—fathers as well as mothers—are motivated to gain more information to improve their parenting skills. Improvements in parenting practices are beneficial to the extent that they result in improvements in children's adjustment to parental incarceration (which is dependent upon regular, unsupervised contact during the period of incarceration) and improvements in children's adjustment to parental reentry after incarceration (which is dependent upon the parent resuming his or her parental role in the family).

Educational programs vary in their samples, their assessment methods, and their training strategies. In one model program, Showers (1993) compared 203 women who completed a parent education curriculum based on the Systematic Training for Effective Parenting (STEP) program (Dinkmeyer and McKay 1982) with 275 women who were being released without such training. The intervention involved 15 hours of instruction over a 10-week period. Women in both groups completed a 36-item Child Management Behavior Survey, which assessed their knowledge about child development and child behavior management techniques, either before and after the educational intervention or, in the case of the comparison group, on two occasions without any intervening educational program. Compared with the control group, women in the intervention group demonstrated significant improvements. Moreover, the effect held for both Caucasian and African-American women. Recidivism rates were altered, too: The reincarceration rate for the intervention group was 1 percent, compared with 19 percent for the comparison group.

In a similar effort on a smaller scale, Moore and Clement (1998) provided 20 mothers with 18 hours of parenting instruction over 9 weeks and compared these mothers with 20 waiting-list control mothers. Mothers in the treatment group, compared with those in the control group, showed a significant increase in knowledge about positive management techniques from pre- to post-test periods. Another study reported significant improvements in parenting as a result of educational interventions, but lacked a comparison group and therefore is more difficult to interpret. Harm and Thompson (1997) provided weekly parent education classes over a 15-week period and reported improvements in self-esteem, increases in positive attitudes about parenting, and self-reported improvements in the quality of the mothers' relationships with their children. On the other hand, although mothers in a study by Browne (1989) reported improved self-esteem after 96 hours of instruction over a 24-week course, they also reported increased endorsement of physical punishment and increased inappropriate expectations.

These studies do not make an unequivocal case for this approach to intervention, although the overall picture is positive. However, the success of training programs with nonincarcerated parents in modifying parent-child interaction patterns and parental behavior and, in turn, improving children's adjustment suggests that continuing to develop parent educational intervention for incarcerated parents is worthwhile. Examples of recent well-designed and carefully evaluated parent education interventions include programs for single mothers (Forgatch and DeGarmo 1999), for parents of children making the transition to school (Cowan and Cowan 2002), and for parents of high-risk children (Ramey et al. 2001). It is unfortunate that studies of incarcerated mothers have focused more on the well-being and attitudes of incarcerated parents than on the intervention's impact on the parents' behavior and parent-child interaction patterns. Our assumption that these programs will, in fact, benefit the children of incarcerated parents as well as the parents themselves remains untested.

Many experts believe that fathers as well as mothers could benefit from parent-education intervention. Growing evidence suggests that non-incarcerated fathers of various types—single, married, noncustodial—improve their parenting skills and their relationships with their offspring as a consequence of parent education programs (see Fagan and Hawkins 2001). Support for the effectiveness of parent education for inmate fathers comes from one recent study by Wilezck and Markstrom (1999). Compared with their scores before the class, the fathers scored higher on parental knowledge and parental efficacy and lower on the belief that fate or chance influenced their parenting after they participated in an eight-session STEP parenting class. They also reported higher overall satisfaction with their parenting. Inmate fathers in the control group did not show any significant changes. As in the studies of interventions with incarcerated mothers, the impact of the parental intervention on the children was not evaluated. In a related project, Harrison (1997) found that, compared with fathers in a control group, male inmates who participated in a six-week program including parent education and behavior management training improved their attitudes toward appropriate parenting. Harrison did measure children's perceptions of their own self-worth in this study and found no differences between children of fathers in the experimental and control groups. However, there was little visitation between fathers and their children in either condition and, therefore, limited opportunity for fathers to demonstrate their improved attitudes or for children to benefit from them.

More evidence of how father-oriented intervention influences children comes from a study of the effects of "filial therapy" training on the father-child relationship. According to Landreth and Lobaugh (1998), filial therapy training teaches parents basic child-centered play therapy skills and helps them learn how to create an accepting environment in which their children feel safe enough to express and explore their thoughts and feelings. Compared with fathers in a control group, the fathers in the 10-week training program scored significantly higher on both their acceptance of and empathic behavior toward their children. In addition, these fathers scored significantly lower than control fathers on parenting stress and on perceptions of problem behavior in their children. Their children showed a significant improvement in their self-concept relative to children of control fathers. The relative success of this approach in promoting positive change in the children stems, in part, from the fact that both fathers and their children participated in the program, not just fathers alone. As Cowan, Powell, and Cowan (1998) argue, programs that focus on both partners in a relationship are often more effective than those that focus on only one member of the dyad. The success of this program was due, in part, to the availability of the children to participate in weekly sessions with their fathers. In many families with incarcerated parents, practical constraints, such as long distances between home and prison, limit children's participation in such programs.

In brief, although these parent intervention efforts show promise, their limited follow-up, small sample sizes, and failure to systematically isolate effective components of the intervention severely restrict our conclusions. Widespread adoption of existing interventions requires carefully designed and monitored programs based on sound theory and empirical evaluation.

Beyond the Incarcerated Parent: The Family Unit as a Focus of Intervention

Most programs have focused their efforts on the incarcerated parent and given less attention to the needs of the nonincarcerated partner or the couple. The importance of including the entire family stems from claims that postrelease success is higher among inmates who have maintained family ties during incarceration (Clements 1986; Hairston and Lockett 1987). Interventions can be directed to the family unit, which is often strained by the incarceration. Experts suggest that such mechanisms as conjugal visits, furloughs, and family and marital counseling strengthen family relationships. The United States lags behind other countries (e.g., Mexico, Sweden, Denmark, and Canada) in providing those conjoint family services when one parent is incarcerated. In view of the clear links between the quality of the marital relationship and child outcomes— either directly or indirectly through parenting—it is critical that more effort be devoted to this form of intervention (Grych and Fincham 2000).

Another form of conjoint family intervention involves providing services to all family members. In a promising but extremely small-scale demonstration, Marsh (1983) offered parent education aimed at improving communication and child management skills to three couples in which the father was incarcerated. Both the inmate father and his wife attended eight weekly classes. Communication skills increased in all parents, and child management skills increased in two of the three families, as evidenced by observations of parent-child interactions at home. Providing services to help the nonincarcerated parent deal with the problems of temporary single parenthood could enhance the children's adjustment and stabilize the couple's relationship.

We acknowledge the difficulties of implementing family programs. Families take many forms in this population. Families include single-parent family units with and without an identified father who may or may not have lived with the mother and child (Hairston 1995), as well as cases where one incarcerated male may have fathered multiple children with different partners. In a survey of state prisoners, less than one-quarter of inmates with children reported that they were married; nearly 60 percent had never been married (Mumola 2000). The task of identifying the family unit that ought to be targeted is, in itself, a challenging problem.

Visitation Programs

In spite of the problems associated with child visitation noted earlier, many parents feel that, on balance, visits are worthwhile. Both men and women express strong desires to have the opportunity for regular family visits (Kazura 2001). As one incarcerated mother put it, "The main advantages of the visits are tightening up the relationship, watching your children grow, [seeing] how you've changed, being able to love one another" (Datesman and Cales 1983, 147, cited by Block and Potthast 1998). In light of sentiments such as these, several women's institutions have developed visiting programs featuring special play areas for parents and children, extended visits, more flexible scheduling, and special housing of children in the institution (Clement 1993). Evaluations of visitation programs underscore the benefits of these efforts. For example, Snyder-Joy and Carlo (1998) initiated a mother-child visitation program for 40 mothers and their children, which provided special monthly visits in addition to regular visits. Activities (crafts, games, reading, etc.) were encouraged in a room set aside for these programs, and transportation was provided as well. Based on interviews with 31 mothers and 27 waiting-list control mothers, Snyder-Joy and Carlo found that program mothers had more frequent contact with their children and spent more time discussing such important issues as behavior and feelings with their children. The mothers' fears about their parenting abilities decreased, and they viewed their children as doing better than control mothers did. Mothers in both groups, however, felt the same about the quality of their relationships with their children.

A second visitation program of note is the Sesame Street program (Fishman 1983). In an effort to alleviate congestion in the visiting room, to let parents communicate without interruption by young children, and to provide children with an accepting environment in which to express their feelings about the prison, a number of prisons have opened special playrooms adjacent to their visiting rooms. Children can visit with their incarcerated parent and then go to the playroom when they get restless. There they participate in educational and entertaining activities. Parents indicate that children are eager to visit the prison; inmates and their families find visiting more rewarding; and correctional administrators have accepted the project as an important service to the institution.

The Girl Scouts Beyond Bars (GSBB) program is yet another example of parent-child visitation (Block and Potthast 1998). This program was designed to provide enhanced visitation between mothers and daughters so as to preserve or enhance the mother-daughter relationship, reduce the stress of being apart, enhance the daughter's sense of self, reduce reunification problems, and ultimately help improve the likelihood of a successful reintegration upon release to the community. To achieve these goals, the program provides transportation and regular Scout troop meetings for mothers and daughters at the prison. Outside the prison setting, the girls participate in other regular Girl Scout activities (field trips, meetings) without their mothers. In addition, some GSBB programs offer both parenting programs for mothers and counseling for their daughters. Evaluations indicate that the GSBB program increases the frequency of daughter-mother visitation and improves the quality of the visits and the mother-daughter relationship. Moreover, studies found that the program enhanced daughters' self-esteem, encouraged them to form new friendships with peers, and lessened the problems associated with separation from their mothers. Daughters became less sad, angry, and worried about their mothers, and, in most cases, their grades improved as well. Further work is needed to disentangle which of the multiple program components—such as increased visitation, involvement in organized activities, new friendships, or exposure to nonparental adult mentors—were responsible for these positive outcomes.

Co-detention: Raising Children in Prison

A central assumption underlying our review is that the separation of parent and child during incarceration is detrimental to the parent-child relationship and to the child's adjustment. (Of course, there may be exceptions in which it is better for the child not to have contact with the parent during incarceration—for example, if the parent is abusive, is not being rehabilitated, and the child will not be resuming a relationship with him or her after the period of incarceration.) Several innovative programs in the United States and Europe have been designed to allow the mother and child to remain together during some portion of the incarceration period.

Prison nurseries, in which the mother gives birth in prison and raises the infant in the institution, have a long history in the United States. Since 1901, the nursery program in the Bedford Hills correctional facility in New York, the oldest such program in the country, has housed female inmates who have given birth during their prison stay. Mothers and infants are permitted to stay together until the child's first birthday, and a parenting program is provided as part of the program. Unfortunately, this effort has received no formal evaluation. A similar program developed in the Nebraska Center for Women provides a live-in nursery for infants up to 18 months of age. Only mothers who are eligible for release within 18 months of giving birth can participate in the program, which also includes parenting and child development classes. In a preliminary evaluation of 11 women, Carlson (1998) found that 8 mothers believed that the program increased mother-child bonding, and all of them felt that the parenting classes improved their parenting skills. Moreover, misconduct reports for these women decreased relative to rates observed prior to their entry into the program, and recidivism rates after they were released were lower.

The latter finding, if it is confirmed by further investigation, is of great importance for children's adjustment. If recidivism can be reduced, children will be spared the trauma of repeated periods of separation, which, in turn, will improve their psychological adjustment. Furthermore, co-detention allows the mother and child to develop a close emotional attachment or to maintain the relationship that they have already formed. However, prison-based co-detention has several negative aspects. Restricted freedom and exposure to the prison's impoverished environment may impair young children's cognitive development. European countries avoid these problems by offering a variety of approaches to co-detention. In Hungary, for example, pregnant women's sentences are often delayed up to a year to enable them to give birth and care for their children at home (Jaffe, Pons, and Wicky 1997). In France and Switzerland, co-detention programs have been organized to permit mother and child to be together for a two- to three-year period in a special prison section adapted to children's needs and to provide an enriched prison milieu and opportunities to experience life outside prison (Jaffe et al. 1997).

Alternatives to Incarceration

Many of the problems associated with either separation from the parent or co-detention can be avoided through some form of community-based sentencing instead of prison-based incarceration (Myers et al. 1999). These alternatives include house arrest, halfway houses where mother and children reside, and day programs in which mothers attend programs in a correctional institution during the day but are permitted to return home at night. Devine (1997) surveyed 24 community-based programs for mothers and children in 14 states. Community sentencing programs yielded reduced recidivism and increased family preservation— outcomes that have positive implications for children's adjustment. In view of the cost-effectiveness achieved by reducing the number of incarcerated women, it is surprising that these types of programs are available to only a small percentage of women violators. Because most offenses committed by women are relatively minor and nonviolent (e.g., drugs, prostitution), alternatives to regular incarceration merit more consideration (Jaffe et al. 1997). These sentencing alternatives may be especially relevant for women in light of recent evidence that women are more amenable to nonincarceration alternatives and more willing to endure them for longer periods than men, especially if they are their children's primary caregivers (Wood and Grasmick 1999).

Programs for Children of Incarcerated Parents

Although most intervention programs are designed for the incarcerated adults rather than their offspring, some interventions deal directly with the children. These interventions can take various forms, including individual counseling or therapy, family therapy, or group therapy located in schools, clinics, or prisons. We have already reviewed Girl Scouts Beyond Bars, a program that includes not only visitation opportunities, but also nonprison group activities as well. Experts have long believed that a group approach is most effective for children of incarcerated parents (e.g., Konopka 1949). Group treatment can address the need for social support and provide a structured setting for children to express their concerns (Springer, Lynch, and Rubin 2000). Groups can diffuse the sense of shame that often accompanies parental incarceration, as children learn that other group members have similar experiences (Kahn 1994). Springer et al. (2000) conducted a small-scale intervention program for children with incarcerated parents. A group of Hispanic fourth and fifth grade children met for a six-week period under the guidance of two adult leaders. Compared with children in a waiting-list control group, children in the intervention group exhibited increased self-esteem, while the control children showed a slight decrease in self-esteem over the six-week period (effect size = .57). These results were similar to those in studies of group treatment for children and adolescents of nonincarcerated parents, according to a meta-analysis by Hoag and Burlingame (1997; effect size for differences between group treatment and wait-list and placebo control groups = .61). The Springer et al. study does suggest that sons and daughters of incarcerated parents can benefit from a time-limited group intervention; however, the small sample size ($N = 10$) and the sample's restriction to only Hispanic children limit the generality of their results.

The Youth Advisory Program, yet another promising approach to intervening directly with the children of incarcerated parents, is aimed at adolescents. It addresses issues of the adolescents' feelings of isolation, self-esteem, and shame; helps them deal with their peers regarding their absent parent; directs them in making positive choices, setting goals, and developing support systems; and promotes an understanding of the corrections system (Weissman and La Rue 1998). Adolescents in the program report a sense of relief at being able to express their emotions about the trauma of losing their parents. This approach could be modified for use with younger children and pre-adolescents. Because evidence shows that children who begin a deviant path early in childhood are more likely to develop stable, serious criminal patterns (Moffitt 1993; Patterson, DeBaryshe, and Ramsey 1989), interventions designed to help individuals avoid a deviant life trajectory should begin in childhood.

Parental Reentry: The Implications for Children

Incarceration's impact on children does not end with the parents' release. Children as well as parents face a range of problems, challenges, and opportunities when reuniting after incarceration. In addition to the problems a reentering parent faces, such as finding a job and housing and reintegrating into the community, the child and parent must also tackle the formidable task of reestablishing their relationship. This task is complex because the child has likely established new relationships while the incarcerated parent was absent. The parent is reentering a revised family system, one that was formed or stabilized without clear roles or responsibilities for the returning parent.

As Sullivan (1993) observed in his ethnographic studies of both incarcerated and nonincarcerated young unwed African-American fathers, family members may limit a returning father's access to his children. Or a mother may have begun a new relationship during the incarcerated father's absence, and that situation may discourage the reentering father's involvement with her or the child (Furstenberg 1995; Nurse 2001). Perhaps most critical, the child may have developed close ties with a substitute parent, such as a grandmother or foster care parent. The process of shifting focus from this caregiver to a long-absent, returning parent may be disruptive for the child and present another stressful transition that further undermines the child's adjustment. Moreover, the experiences that the incarcerated parent has suffered in prison may affect his or her ability to reintegrate into the family. Male veterans returning to their families after military deployment experience guilt feelings, emotional withdrawal, and elevated levels of aggression, making it difficult—even impossible—for them to fully resume their former roles as fathers, husbands, and breadwinners (Solomon 1988). Inmates' experiences in prison may lead to comparable outcomes for their families. To date, little is known about either the short-term consequences of the reunion process or the long-term effect of that process on the child's well-being. Many factors likely affect the transition, including the quality and duration of the parent-child relationship prior to incarceration; the nature and extent of the contact between parent and child during incarceration; the quality, stability, and duration of the new caregiver-child relationship developed during incarceration; and the management of the transition back to the original parent-child caregiving arrangement. In addition, the extent to which the child maintains ties with multiple caregivers—the parent and the substitute caregiver—after the reentry of the incarcerated parent likely further determines adjustment.

Finally, the implications of nonreunion for the child's adjustment merit examination. The 1997 Adoption and Safe Families Act mandates termination of parental rights in the case of a child in foster care more than 15 of 22 consecutive months (Genty 1998). This legislation often has consequences for children of incarcerated mothers, because over two-thirds of these women spend more than 15 months in prison (Mumola 2000). Thus, many children are deprived of their right to reunite with their mother, even in the absence of any allegations of abuse or neglect. Although the reunion process is a complex one, it is unclear whether permanent foster care is preferable, especially in the light of the relative instability of foster home placements (Beckerman 1998; Genty 1998). On the other hand, some recent evidence (Horowitz, Balestracci, and Simms 2001) suggests that children's functioning in foster care improves over time. Obviously, the debate over permanent placements for children of incarcerated parents is far from settled (Beckerman 1998).

Problems Associated with Intervention and Evaluation Efforts

In formulating an agenda for future efforts in this area, it is important to recognize the difficulties of conducting theory-based intervention with this population (Eddy et al. 2001). According to Eddy et al., several problems limit the scope and type of interventions that can be implemented. One problem is the high prevalence of mental impairment among incarcerated parents and the concomitant difficulty these parents have with reading. It is critical that intervention materials be written and administered at an appropriate level or that programs not require reading. Second, barriers to acceptance by prison staff have to be overcome. As Hairston (1991) found in a survey of prison policies and practices, correctional institutions are not generally supportive of inmate-family relationships or family-oriented services. A third set of problems relates to the dynamic nature of inmates' families. As Eddy et al. found, families of inmates exhibit frequent changes in roles and relationships. Some male inmates may be involved with multiple families as a result of having children with several women. The nature of these family ties, including the amount and frequency of contact, the quality and quantity of parenting, and even the parent's knowledge of children's living arrangements varies across inmates. This family instability both during and after incarceration presents serious problems for any longitudinal research design. Transience among inmates' partners and children and among prisoners after their release poses an additional problem for follow-up research. Whereas 16 percent of Americans move in a given year, Eddy et al. report that 62 percent of the inmates participating in their study moved at least once in the previous year. Six months later, only 5 percent of the subjects were still residing at their pre-arrest residence.

Research and Policy Issues: A Look Ahead

Research Issues

Parental incarceration and reentry involves a dynamic set of processes that unfold over time. Only by designing and executing prospective, longitudinal studies of the effects of parental incarceration on children will we be able to trace the various pathways followed by different children and begin to describe the nature of the changes that affect children's functioning. Only in this way will we be able to make empirically grounded policy. Although it is not uncommon to make policy in the absence of data, the lack of data in this case is critical. Policies that rely solely on anecdotal or limited information are unlikely to be effective.

Comprehensive longitudinal research on incarcerated parents and their children requires, first of all, identifying parents at risk for incarceration before the period of incarceration occurs so that preexisting conditions and relationships can be described. This design would be a step toward disentangling the impact of incarceration per se from the impact of preexisting family conditions on children's subsequent adjustment. These children and their incarcerated parents would then be followed during the period of incarceration through the postprison reunion period. Recognizing the difficulty of this type of prospective approach, careful retrospective interviews with the incarcerated parent, the child, and informed kin could begin to provide a profile of life in these families before incarceration.

Second, designs should include developmentally sensitive measures that have been not only well standardized but also demonstrate adequate psychometric properties. Multimeasure and multi-informant designs are needed. Researchers must complete direct assessment of children, as much of the literature relies on parental reports, which are potentially biased (Myers et al. 1999). Observing children in different contexts (home, school, playground) with a variety of interactive partners (parents, substitute caregivers, siblings, peers) would begin to provide solid descriptive data. Careful evaluations of children's psychological functioning and patterns of coping are also needed.

Third, more attention needs to be given to the unique effects of the incarceration of fathers versus mothers. Experts have paid less attention to paternal incarceration than to maternal imprisonment, but the father-child relationship is an important focus for future research and policy efforts (see Gadsden and Rethemeyer 2001), particularly because most parents in prison are fathers.

Fourth, social scientists are recognizing more and more that cultural background plays a major role in shaping children's reactions to various types of family transitions and stressors and in developing the coping strategies children and families use in the face of adversity (Demo, Allen, and Fine 2000; Parke and Buriel 1998). Therefore, future research must give more attention to the role of incarcerated parents' cultural and ethnic backgrounds.

Fifth, in research, we must move beyond simple descriptions of differences in children to explanations of processes in the individual, family, context, and culture that account for children's adjustment. Only when we have begun to identify these processes will we be positioned to design meaningful interventions. Our interventions need to be theoretically guided and should be viewed not simply as a plan to help children and/or their families but as an opportunity to evaluate the adequacy of our theories as well. Progress is likely to flow from recognizing the need for interdisciplinary research teams. Disciplinary specialists, including child developmentalists, family psychologists, social workers, criminologists, and organizational and community social scientists, offer important and distinctive perspectives and need to work cooperatively in the design and evaluation of research and intervention efforts.

Finally, we need applied research in which the interventions that flow from theory and research are stringently evaluated using designs that include random assignment to treatments and careful, systematic follow-up assessments. We need research in which observers document actual behavior change in parents and children (not just changes on paper-and-pencil measures), and we need interventions replicated across various populations.

Policy Implications

Deriving policy implications in this area requires guidance from prior theory and empirical evidence. Our review suggests that policies should address three aspects of incarceration. First, generally speaking, separation from the parent injures children and, therefore, policies aimed at minimizing periods of separation and maintaining parent-child contact during incarceration should be encouraged. (Again, there are exceptions in which children may be better off when an abusive or disruptive parent is no longer a part of their lives.) Second, discontinuity in all its forms, including shifts in residence, changes in schools and peer groups, and disruptions in caregiving arrangements, can harm children with incarcerated parents. Policies to increase stability for the child should be encouraged. Third, economic stress often accompanies parental incarceration and has negative effects on children; policies aimed at minimizing the economic hardship surrounding incarceration should be advocated.

FAMILIES

Policies should be developed to facilitate healthy connections between incarcerated parents and their children (and the nonincarcerated parent or other child caregiver). Contact can be maintained in a variety of ways, including visitation, furloughs, and telephone and electronic communication. This is particularly important if the parent is to take an active role with the children after release. In some cases, however, the reasons that men are imprisoned do not recommend continued contact. If the father is imprisoned for domestic abuse or for any kind of crime that involved the child, such as child molestation, the goal should not be to facilitate continued contact, but to rehabilitate the father or to sever contact with him so that the child and mother can move on to a more positive family situation. Policies to maintain children's contact with their incarcerated parents should discriminate between those situations in which reunion would be a positive outcome and those in which it would not. If it is not possible to make such decisions on a case-by-case basis, then at least there should be a policy that rules out contact with parents who have committed certain types of offenses.

Whatever the nature of the incarcerated parent's crime, a variety of types of support ought to be provided to the nonincarcerated parent to ensure high-quality care for the child while the other parent is in prison. Social and emotional support as well as parenting guidance would all be potentially helpful. But most critical, perhaps, are economic supports to minimize disruptions in the child's life associated with residence changes and to keep the nonincarcerated family out of poverty. The negative effects of poverty on child development are well documented (Duncan and Brooks-Gunn 1997). Policies that decrease the likelihood that families will be in poverty—before, during, or after incarceration—help children. For example, in some states, incarcerated men are still responsible for paying child support while they are in prison. That debt accumulates while they are in prison, and when these men get out they are required to pay the state this debt. This obligation compromises their ability to get involved in their children's lives and leads many men back to illicit activities that can separate them from their families altogether. Policies like this one do not seem to be positive for children in the long run. A more humane policy would be one in which fathers are offered a grace period and a gradual repayment schedule.

SOCIAL SERVICE AGENCIES
These agencies are often the main source of support for nonincarcerated parents, and policies and resources to allow them to provide support ser-

vices are a critical part of our policy agenda. In addition, agencies should develop policies that encourage placement decisions minimizing the potential disruptions for children. Social services need to develop programs to promote parent-child contact during incarceration that include providing transportation, coordinating with prison officials, and working with prison personnel to develop appropriate visitation conditions for children. Finally, social services need to increase their commitment to ease the postincarceration transition not only by assisting the incarcerated adult with employment and housing, but also by supporting the nonincarcerated family members—adults as well as children—when the absent adult rejoins the family unit. Programs that alert all parties to the stresses and strains of reentry and that provide guides to easing the problems are needed.

LAW ENFORCEMENT AND PRISONS

Police need to be trained to handle parental arrests in which children are present more sensitively to minimize the negative impact on the children. Policies that educate prison officials about the importance of maintaining contact between children and incarcerated parents need to be developed. Pro-family policies that encourage parent-child visits are needed. These policies would include providing appropriate and inviting spaces for visits, education for inmates and staff, and incentives for parents to participate.

CRIMINAL JUSTICE SYSTEM

Sentencing policies for parents who are nonviolent offenders need to be critically examined, and alternative sentencing guidelines for parents, such as community service option, work-related programs that permit a parent to live at home or visit children on a regular basis, merit consideration. The punitive value of imprisonment for noncriminal offenses, such as drug possession, need to be weighed against the human costs (specifically, the cost to the parents and their children).

SCHOOLS

To ease children's adjustment to the loss of a parent through incarceration, it would be beneficial to make teachers and school administrators aware of the special needs of these children. Programs need to be developed for educators to help them combat victimization and stigmatization of these children by their peers.

CONNECTING THE SYSTEMS

Even if measures at these different levels are implemented, there remains a need to "connect the systems" (Adalist-Estrin 1994). If we want to design policies that are at the intersection between social services and the criminal justice system, we need to balance the goals of each system. The goal of the criminal justice system is to punish offenders; the goal of social services is to promote people's welfare. To come up with a policy that meets both needs, both systems have to articulate a combined set of goals. The criminal justice system is fraught with problems of its own, which include variability of laws from state to state and lack of funds for rehabilitative programs. How can this system promote people's welfare? In many states, fragmented services and agencies result in service gaps, unmet needs, and overlapping or conflicting service delivery agendas (Phillips and Bloom 1998). The systems that provide services for children and families affected by incarceration need to coordinate their efforts across time to permit continuity of services. For example, decisions and services on behalf of family members during incarceration need to be recognized in the planning of postincarceration services to ensure continuity across the transition from prison to home. The criminal justice system, including correctional officers and prison administrators, needs to be involved in decisionmaking about family contacts and family support. The social welfare system needs to be involved with the family members of incarcerated parents to provide coordination between their services and the needs of the imprisoned parent (visitation, reentry services), and, in turn, these activities need to be coordinated with the criminal justice system, including prison and later parole systems. Schools need to be partners in the support provision process so that children's needs beyond the family setting are recognized. Only when all the various players—courts, prisons, community and social service agencies, schools, and policymakers—begin to coordinate their efforts will we be able to develop and implement programs that will maximally support children, families, and kin of incarcerated parents.

CHANGING CULTURE; RESPECTING CULTURES

Equally important, social policy needs to address the issue of public attitudes toward incarcerated individuals and their families. By educating the wider community about the needs of incarcerated parents, their children, and their families, more humane policies may emerge and the difficulties faced by these individuals will be better appreciated. In recognition of the diversity in our society and the disproportionate numbers of minority group members who are incarcerated, social policies should be made more culturally sensitive. For example, recognition of the historically important role played by extended family networks in the care of children in African-American families (Gadsden 1999) should guide placement policies of social service agencies as a way of maintaining continuity for children of incarcerated parents. If they are to be maximally effective, social policies, social services, and intervention programs need to be tailored to the needs of different cultural groups.

Concluding Thoughts

When parents are incarcerated, children often become the unintended victims. To build a reliable empirical foundation for effective programs and policies, researchers must carefully and rigorously evaluate such damage. Only through a better understanding of these issues will we be able to break the intergenerational cycle of incarceration and misery that characterizes these families. Intervening to prevent the negative consequences of parental incarceration will help children. Encouraging and facilitating parental involvement during incarceration may also serve parents. In short, better understanding and improved programs will benefit children and their parents and, in the final analysis, society as well.

REFERENCES

Adalist-Estrin, Ann. 1994. "Family Support and Criminal Justice." In *Putting Families First: America's Family Support Movement and the Challenge of Change,* edited by Sharon L. Kagan and Bernice Weissbourd (161–85). San Francisco: Jossey-Bass.

Ayers, Tim S., Irwin N. Sandler, Stephen G. West, and Mark W. Roosa. 1996. "A Dispositional and Situational Assessment of Children's Coping: Testing Alternative Models of Coping." *Journal of Personality* 64 (4): 923–58.

Baltes, Paul B. 1987. "Theoretical Propositions of Life-Span Developmental Psychology: On the Dynamics Between Growth and Decline." *Developmental Psychology* 23 (5): 611–26.

Baunach, Phyllis J. 1985. *Mothers in Prison.* New Brunswick, N.J.: Rutgers University Press.

Becker, Diane, and Faith Margolin. 1967. "How Surviving Parents Handled Their Young Children's Adaptation to the Crisis of Loss." *American Journal of Orthopsychiatry* 37 (4): 753–57.

Beckerman, Adela. 1998. "Charting a Course: Meeting the Challenge of Permanency Planning for Children with Incarcerated Mothers." *Child Welfare* 77 (5): 513–29.

Belsky, Jay. 1984. "The Determinants of Parenting: A Process Model." *Child Development* 55 (1): 83–96.

Belsky, Jay, Michael Rovine, and Margaret Fish. 1989. "The Developing Family System." In *Systems and Development,* edited by Megan R. Gunnar and Esther Thelen (119–66). Hillsdale, N.J.: Lawrence Erlbaum Associates.

Block, Kathleen J., and Margaret J. Potthast. 1998. "Girls Scouts beyond Bars: Facilitating Parent-Child Contact in Correctional Settings." *Child Welfare* 77 (5): 561–78.

Bloom, Barbara, and David Steinhart. 1993. "Why Punish the Children? A Reappraisal of the Children of Incarcerated Mothers in America." Paper presented at the National Council on Crime and Delinquency, San Francisco, November 15.

Bowlby, John. 1973. *Attachment and Loss: Separation,* vol. 2. New York: Basic Books.

———. 1980. *Attachment and Loss: Loss, Sadness, and Depression,* vol. 3. New York: Basic Books.

Braver, Sanford L., and Diane O'Connell. 2000. *Divorced Dads: Shattering the Myths.* New York: Tarcher/Putnam.

Bretherton, Inge, Charlynn Prentiss, and Doreen Ridgeway. 1990. "Family Relationships as Represented in a Story-Completion Task at Thirty-seven and Fifty-four Months of Age." *New Directions for Child Development* 48 (Summer): 85–105.

Bronfenbrenner, Urie, and Pamela A. Morris. 1998. "The Ecology of Developmental Processes." In *Handbook of Child Psychology, vol. 1: Theories of Human Development,* 5th ed., edited by William Damon and Richard M. Lerner (993–1028). New York: Wiley.

Brooks-Gunn, Jeanne, and Lindsay Chase-Lansdale. 1995. "Adolescent Parenthood." In *Handbook of Parenting,* edited by Marc H. Bornstein (113–49). Mahwah, N.J.: Lawrence Erlbaum Associates.

Browne, Dorothy H. 1989. "Incarcerated Mothers and Parenting." *Journal of Family Violence* 4 (2): 211–21.

Carlson, John R. 1998. "Evaluating the Effectiveness of a Live-in Nursery Within a Women's Prison." *Journal of Offender Rehabilitation* 27 (2): 73–85.

Cassidy, Jude, Steven Kirsh, Krista Scolton, and Ross D. Parke. 1996. "Attachment and Representations of Peer Relationships." *Developmental Psychology* 32 (5): 892–904.

Cherlin, Andrew. 1992. *Marriage, Divorce, Remarriage,* rev. ed. Cambridge, Mass.: Harvard University Press.

Clark, Judith. 1995. "The Impact of the Prison Environment on Mothers." *The Prison Journal* 75 (4): 306–29.

Clarke-Stewart, Alison, and Virginia Allhusen. 2002. "Nonparental Caregiving." In *Handbook of Parenting,* 2d ed., edited by Marc H. Bornstein (251–52). Mahwah, N.J.: Erlbaum.

Clement, Mary J. 1993. "Parenting in Prison: A National Survey of Programs for Incarcerated Women." *Journal of Offender Rehabilitation* 19 (2): 89–100.

Clements, Carl B. 1986. *Offender Needs Assessment.* College Park, Md.: American Correctional Association.

Cochran, Moncrieff, and Jane A. Brassard. 1979. "Child Development and Personal Social Networks." *Child Development* 50 (3): 601–16.

Cochran, Moncrieff, and Starr Niego. 1995. "Parenting and Social Networks." In *Handbook of Parenting, vol. 4: Status and Social Conditions of Parenting,* edited by Marc H. Bornstein (123–248). Hillsdale, N.J.: Erlbaum.

Coltrane, Scott. 1996. *Family Man.* New York: Oxford University Press.

Compas, Bruce E. 1987. "Coping with Stress During Childhood and Adolescence." *Psychological Bulletin* 101 (3): 393–403.

Conger, Rand, and Glen H. Elder Jr. 1994. *Families in Troubled Times.* Hawthorne, N.Y.: Aldine de Gruyter.

Coughenour, John C. 1995. "Separate and Unequal: Women in the Federal Criminal Justice System." *Federal Sentencing Reporter* 8 (2): 142–44.

Cowan, Philip A., and Carolyn P. Cowan. 2002. "What an Intervention Design Reveals about How Parents Affect Their Children's Academic Achievement and Behavior Problems." In *Parenting and the Child's World,* edited by John G. Borkowski, Sharon L. Ramey, and Marie Bristol-Power (75–98). Mahwah, N.J.: Erlbaum.

Cowan, Philip A., Douglas Powell, and Carolyn P. Cowan. 1998. "Parenting Interventions: A Family Systems Perspective." In *Handbook of Child Psychology, vol. 4: Child Psychology in Practice,* 5th ed., edited by William Damon, Irving E. Sigel, and K. Ann Renninger (3–72). New York: Wiley.

Crnic, Keith, Mark Greenberg, Arlene S. Ragozin, Nancy M. Robinson, and Robert B. Bashman. 1983. "Effects of Stress and Social Support on Mothers and Premature and Full-term Infants." *Child Development* 54 (1): 209–17.

Cummings, E. Mark, Patrick T. Davies, and Susan B. Campbell. 2000. *Developmental Psychopathology and Family Process.* New York: Guilford Press.

Demo, David H., Katherine R. Allen, and Mark A. Fine, eds. 2000. *Handbook of Family Diversity.* New York: Oxford University Press.

Devine, Kevin. 1997. *Family Unity: The Benefits and Costs of Community-Based Sentencing Programs for Women and Their Children in Illinois.* Chicago: Chicago Legal Aid to Incarcerated Mothers.

Dinkmeyer, Don C., and Gary D. McKay. 1982. *The Parent's Handbook: Systematic Training for Effective Parenting.* Circle Pines, Minn.: American Guidance Service.

Dressel, Paula L., Sandra K. Barnhill, Anne Chambers, Craig Gardner, Richard Harris, and Barbara Jones. 1992. *Three Generations at Risk: A Model Intergenerational Program for Families of Imprisoned Mothers.* Atlanta, Ga.: Aid to Children of Imprisoned Mothers, Inc.

Duncan, Greg, and Jeanne Brooks-Gunn. 1997. *Consequences of Growing Up Poor.* New York: Russell Sage Foundation.

Eddy, Bruce, Melissa J. Powell, Margaret H. Szubka, Maura L. McCool, and Susan Kuntz. 2001. "Challenges in Research with Incarcerated Parents and Importance in Violence Prevention." *American Journal of Preventive Medicine* 20(1 Suppl): 56–62.

Elder, Glen H. 1998. "The Life Course and Human Development." In *Handbook of Child Psychology, vol. 1: Theoretical Models of Human Development,* 5th ed., edited by William Damon and Richard M. Lerner (939–92). New York: Wiley.

Fagan, Joseph, and Alan J. Hawkins. 2001. *Clinical and Educational Interventions with Fathers.* New York: Haworth Press.

Fishman, Susan H. 1983. "Impact of Incarceration on Children of Offenders." *Journal of Children in Contemporary Society* 15 (2): 89–99.

Forgatch, Marion, and David S. DeGarmo. 1999. "Parenting through Change: An Effective Prevention Program for Single Mothers." *Journal of Consulting and Clinical Psychology* 67 (5): 711–24.

Furstenberg, Frank F. 1995. "Fathering in the Inner-City: Paternal Participation and Public Policy." In *Fatherhood: Contemporary Theory, Research, and Social Policy,* edited by William Marsiglio (119–47). Thousand Oaks, Calif.: Sage Publications.

Furstenberg, Frank F., S. Philip Morgan, and Paul D. Allison. 1987. "Paternal Participation and Children's Well-being after Marital Dissolution." *American Sociological Review* 52 (3): 695–701.

Gabel, Katherine, and Katherine Girard. 1995. "Long Term Care Nurseries in Prison: A Descriptive Study." In *Children of Incarcerated Parents,* edited by Katherine Gabel and Denise Johnston (237–51). New York: Lexington Books.

Gadsden, Vivian L. 1999. "Black Families in Intergenerational and Cultural Perspective." In *Parenting and Child Development in "Nontraditional" Families,* edited by Michael E. Lamb (221–46). Mahwah, N.J.: Erlbaum.

Gadsden, Vivian L., and R. Karl Rethemeyer. 2001. "Linking Father Involvement and Parental Incarceration: Conceptual Issues in Research and Practice." Paper presented at the National Center for Fathers and Families Conference, Philadelphia, November 20.

Garfinkel, Irwin, Sara S. McLanahan, Daniel R. Meyer, and Judith A. Seltzer, eds. 1998. *Fathers under Fire.* New York: Russell Sage Foundation Press.

Gaudin, James M. 1984. "Social Work Roles and Tasks with Incarcerated Mothers." *Social Casework* 65 (5): 279–86.

Genty, Philip M. 1995. "Termination of Parental Rights among Prisoners." In *Children of Incarcerated Parents,* edited by Katherine Gabel and Denise Johnston (167–82). New York: Lexington Books.

———. 1998. "Permanency Planning in the Context of Parental Incarceration: Legal Issues and Recommendations." *Child Welfare* 77 (5): 543–59.

Goldstein, Lauren H., Marissa L. Diener, and Sarah C. Mangelsdorf. 1996. "Maternal Characteristics and Social Support across the Transition to Motherhood: Associations with Maternal Behavior." *Journal of Family Psychology* 10 (1): 60–71.

Grych, John H., and Frank D. Fincham, eds. 2000. *Interparental Conflict and Child Development.* New York: Cambridge University Press.

Hagan, John, and Ronit Dinovitzer. 1999. "Collateral Consequences of Imprisonment for Children, Communities and Prisoners." In *Prisons,* edited by Michael Tonry and Joan Petersilia (121–62). Chicago: University of Chicago Press.

Hairston, Creasie F. 1991. "Mothers in Jail: Parent-Child Separation and Jail Visitation." *Affilia* 6 (1): 9–27.

———. 1995. "Fathers in Prison." In *Children of Incarcerated Parents,* edited by Katherine Gabel and Denise Johnston (31–40). New York: Lexington Books.

Hairston, Creasie F., and Patricia W. Lockett. 1987. "Parents in Prison: New Direction for Social Sciences." *Social Work* 32 (3): 162–64.

Harm, Nancy J., and Patricia J. Thompson. 1997. "Evaluating the Effectiveness of Parent Education for Incarcerated Mothers." *Journal of Offender Rehabilitation* 24 (2): 135–52.

Harrison, Kim. 1997. "Parental Training for Incarcerated Fathers: Effects on Attitudes, Self-Esteem, and Children's Self-Perceptions." *Journal of Social Psychology* 137 (5): 588–93.

Hetherington, E. Mavis. 1991. "Families, Lies and Videotapes." *Journal of Adolescent Research* 1 (4): 323–48.

Hetherington, E. Mavis, and John Kelley. 2002. *For Better or For Worse.* New York: Norton.

Hetherington, E. Mavis, Margaret Bridges, and Glendessa M. Insabella. 1998. "What Matters? What Does Not? Five Perspectives on the Association between Marital Transitions and Children's Adjustment." *American Psychologist* 53 (2): 167–84.

Hoag, Matthew J., and Gary M. Burlingame. 1997. "Evaluating the Effectiveness of Child and Adolescent Group Treatment: A Meta-analytic Review." *Journal of Clinical Child Psychology* 26 (3): 234–46.

Horowitz, Sarah M., Kathleen M. B. Balestracci, and Mark D. Simms. 2001. "Foster Care Placement Improves Children's Functioning." *Archives of Pediatrics and Adolescent Medicine* 155 (11): 1255–60.

Howes, Carollee, and Claire E. Hamilton. 1993. "The Changing Experience of Child Care: Changes in Teachers and in Teacher-Child Relationships and Children's Social Competence with Peers." *Early Childhood Research Quarterly* 8 (1): 15–32.

Jaffe, Philip D., Francisco Pons, and Rey Helene Wicky. 1997. "Children Imprisoned with Their Mother: Psychological Implications." In *Advances in Psychology and Law: International Contributions,* edited by Santiago Redondo, Vicente Garrido, Jorge Perez, and Rosemary Barberret (397–461). Berlin: Walter de Gruyter.

Johnston, Denise. 1991. *Jailed Mothers.* Pasadena, Calif.: Pacific Oaks Center for Children of Incarcerated Parents.

———. 1995. "Effects of Parental Incarceration." In *Children of Incarcerated Parents,* edited by Katherine Gabel and Denise Johnston (59–88). New York: Lexington Books.

Jose-Kampfner, Christina. 1991. "Michigan Program Makes Children's Visits Meaningful." *Corrections Today* (August): 130–34.

———. 1995. "Post-traumatic Stress Reactions in Children of Imprisoned Mothers." In *Children of Incarcerated Parents,* edited by Katherine Gabel and Denise Johnston (89–100). New York: Lexington Books.

Kahn, Sharon R. 1994. "Children's Therapy Groups: Case Studies of Prevention, Reparation, and Protection through Children's Play." *Journal of Child and Adolescent Group Therapy* 4 (1): 47–60.

Kaplan, Mark S., and Jennifer E. Sasser. 1996. "Women behind Bars: Trends and Policy Issues." *Journal of Sociology and Social Welfare* 23 (1): 43–56.

Kazura, Kerry. 2001. "Family Programming for Incarcerated Parents: A Needs Assessment among Inmates." *Journal of Offender Rehabilitation* 32 (2): 67–83.

Konopka, Gisela. 1949. *Therapeutic Group Work with Children.* Minneapolis: University of Minnesota Press.

Landreth, Garry L., and Alan F. Lobaugh. 1998. "Filial Therapy with Incarcerated Fathers: Effects on Parental Acceptance of Child, Parental Stress, and Child Adjustment." *Journal of Counseling and Development* 76 (2): 157–65.

Luthar, Suniya S., Dante Cicchetti, and Bronwyn Becker. 2000. "The Construct of Resilience: A Critical Evaluation and Guidelines for Future Work." *Child Development* 71 (3): 543–62.

Maccoby, Eleanor E., and Robert Mnookin. 1993. *Dividing the Child.* Cambridge, Mass.: Harvard University Press.

Marsh, Richard L. 1983. "Services for Families: A Model Project to Provide Services for Families of Prisoners." *International Journal of Offender Therapy and Comparative Criminology* 27 (3): 156–62.

Minuchin, Patricia. 2002. "Looking toward the Horizon: Present and Future in the Study of Family Systems." In *Retrospect and Prospect in the Psychological Study of Families,* edited by James P. McHale and Wendy S. Grolnick (259–78). Mahwah, N.J.: Erlbaum.

Moffitt, Terrie E. 1993. "Adolescence-Limited and Life-Course-Persistent Antisocial Behavior: A Developmental Taxonomy." *Psychological Review* 100 (4): 674–701.

Moore, Alvin R., and Mary J. Clement. 1998. "Effects of Parenting Training for Incarcer-ated Mothers." *Journal of Offender Rehabilitation* 27 (2): 57–72.

Morris, Peter. 1965. *Prisoners and Their Families.* New York: Hart.

Mumola, Christopher J. 2000. *Incarcerated Parents and Their Children.* Bureau of Justice Statistics Special Report. Washington, D.C.: U.S. Department of Justice.

Myers, Barbara J., Tina M. Smarsh, Kristine Amlund-Hagen, and Suzanne Kennon. 1999. "Children of Incarcerated Mothers." *Journal of Child and Family Studies* 8 (1): 11–25.

Nolen-Hoeksema, Susan, and Judith Larson. 1999. *Coping with Loss.* Mahwah, N.J.: Erlbaum.

Nurse, Anne M. 2001. "The Structure of the Juvenile Prison: Constructing the Inmate Father." *Youth and Society* 32 (4): 360–94.

Parke, Ross D. 1988. "Families in Life-Span Perspective: A Multi-level Developmental Approach." In *Child Development in Life-Span Perspective,* edited by E. Mavis Hether-ington, Richard M. Lerner, and Marion Perlmutter (159–90). Hillsdale, N.J.: Erlbaum.

———. 1996. *Fatherhood.* Cambridge, Mass.: Harvard University Press.

———. 2002. "Fathers and Families." In *Handbook of Parenting,* edited by Marc H. Born-stein (27–73). Mahwah, N.J.: Erlbaum.

Parke, Ross D., and Raymond Buriel. 1998. "Socialization in the Family: Ethnic and Eco-logical Perspectives." In *Handbook of Child Psychology, vol. 3: Social, Emotional and Personality Development,* edited by William Damon and Nancy Eisenberg (463–552). New York: Wiley.

Patterson, Gerald R., Barbara DeBaryshe, and Elizabeth Ramsey. 1989. "A Developmen-tal Perspective on Antisocial Behavior." *American Psychologist* 44 (2): 329–35.

Phillips, Susan, and Barbara Bloom. 1998. "In Whose Best Interest? The Impact of Changing Public Policy on Relatives Caring for Children with Incarcerated Par-ents." *Child Welfare* 77 (5): 531–41.

Poehlmann, Julie. 2001. "Disrupted Relationships in Children of Incarcerated Mothers: Preliminary Findings." Unpublished manuscript, University of Wisconsin, Madison.

Ramey, Craig T., Sharon L. Ramey, Robin G. Lanzi, and Janice N. Cotton. 2001. "Early Educational Interventions for High-Risk Children: How Center-Based Treatment Can Augment and Improve Parenting Effectiveness." In *Parenting and the Child's World,* edited by John G. Borkowski, Sharon L. Ramey, and Marie Bristol-Power (125–40). Mahwah, N.J.: Erlbaum.

Russo, Mary F., and Deborah C. Beidel. 1994. "Comorbidity of Childhood Anxiety and Externalizing Disorders: Prevalence, Associated Characteristics, and Validation Issues." *Clinical Psychology Review* 14 (3): 199–221.

Rutter, Michael. 1987. "Psychosocial Resilience and Protective Mechanisms." *American Journal of Orthopsychiatry* 57 (3): 316–31.

Rutter, Michael, and Marjorie Rutter. 1993. *Developing Minds*. New York: Basic Books.

Rutter, Michael, and Alan L. Sroufe. 2000. "Developmental Psychopathology: Concepts and Challenges." *Developmental Psychopathology* 12 (3): 265–96.

Sack, William H. 1977. "Children of Imprisoned Fathers." *Psychiatry* 40 (2): 163–74.

Sack, William H., Jack Seidler, and Susan Thomas. 1976. "The Children of Imprisoned Parents: A Psychosocial Exploration." *American Journal of Orthopsychiatry* 46 (4): 618–28.

Sameroff, Arnold. 1994. "Developmental Systems and Family Functioning." In *Exploring Family Relationships with Other Social Contexts*, edited by Ross D. Parke and Sheppard G. Kellam (199–214). Hillsdale, N.J.: Erlbaum.

Sameroff, Arnold, Todd W. Bartko, Alfred Baldwin, Clara Baldwin, and Ronald Seifer. 1998. "Family and Social Influences on the Development of Child Competence." In *Families, Risk, and Competence*, edited by Michael Lewis and Candice Feiring (161–86). Mahwah, N.J.: Erlbaum.

Seymour, Cynthia. 1998. "Children with Parents in Prison: Child Welfare Policy, Program, and Practice Issues." *Child Welfare* 77 (5): 469–93.

Showers, Jacy. 1993. "Assessing and Remedying Parenting Knowledge among Women Inmates." *Journal of Offenders Rehabilitation* 20 (1): 34–46.

Simon, Rita J., and Jean Landis. 1991. *The Crimes Women Commit: The Punishments They Receive*. Lexington, Mass.: Lexington Books.

Snell, Tracy. 1994. *Women in Prison*. Washington, D.C.: U.S. Department of Justice, Bureau of Justice Statistics.

Snyder-Joy, Zoann K., and Teresa A. Carlo. 1998. "Parenting through Prison Walls: Incarcerated Mothers and Children's Visitation Programs." In *Crime Control and Women: Feminist Implications of Criminal Justice Policy*, edited by Susan L. Miller (130–50). Thousand Oaks, Calif.: Sage Publications.

Solomon, Zahava. 1988. "The Effect of Combat-Related Post-traumatic Stress Disorder on the Family." *Psychiatry: Journal for the Study of Interpersonal Processes* 51 (4): 323–29.

Springer, David W., Courtney Lynch, and Allen Rubin. 2000. "Effects of a Solution-Focused Mutual Aid Group for Hispanic Children of Incarcerated Parents." *Child and Adolescent Social Work Journal* 17 (4): 431–42.

Sroufe, L. Alan. 1988. "The Role of Infant-Caregiver Attachment in Development." In *Clinical Implications of Attachment*, edited by Jay Belsky and Teresa Nezworski (18–38). Hillsdale, N.J.: Erlbaum.

Stanton, Annette. 1980. *When Mothers Go to Jail*. Lexington, Mass.: D.C. Heath.

Sullivan, Michael L. 1993. "Young Fathers and Parenting in Two Inner-City Neighborhoods." In *Young Unwed Fathers: Changing Roles and Emerging Policies*, edited by Robert J. Lerman and Theodora J. Ooms (52–73). Philadelphia: Temple University Press.

Thompson, Ross A. 1995. *Preventing Child Maltreatment through Social Support: A Critical Analysis*. Newbury Park, Calif.: Sage Publications.

———. 1998. "Early Socio-emotional Development." In *Handbook of Child Psychology, vol. 3: Social, Emotional, and Personality Development*, edited by William Damon and Nancy Eisenberg (25–104). New York: Wiley.

Thompson, Ross A., Michael E. Lamb, and David Estes. 1982. "Stability of Infant-Mother Attachment and Its Relationship to Changing Life Circumstances in an Unselected Middle-Class Sample." *Child Development* 53 (1): 144–48.

Trice, Ashton D. 1997. "Risk and Protective Factors for School and Community Problems for Children of Incarcerated Women." Paper presented at the biennial meetings of the Society for Research in Child Development, Indianapolis, Ind., April 19.

U.S. Department of Justice. 1993. *Sourcebook of Criminal Justice Statistics, 1993.* Washington, D.C.: U.S. Department of Justice, Bureau of Justice Statistics.

———. 1994. *Sourcebook of Criminal Justice Statistics, 1994.* Washington, D.C.: U.S. Department of Justice, Bureau of Justice Statistics.

Vaughn, Brian, Byron Egeland, L. Alan Sroufe, and Everett Waters. 1979. "Individual Differences in Infant-Mother Attachment at Twelve and Eighteen Months: Stability and Change in Families under Stress." *Child Development* 50 (4): 971–75.

Weissman, Marsha, and Candace M. LaRue. 1998. "Earning Trust from Youths with None to Spare." *Child Welfare* 77 (5): 579–94.

Werner, Emmy E. 1993. "Risk, Resilience and Recovery: Perspectives from the Kauai Longitudinal Study." *Development and Psychopathology* 5 (4): 503–15.

Wilezck, Ginger L., and Carol A. Markstrom. 1999. "The Effects of Parent Education on Parental Locus of Control and Satisfaction in Incarcerated Fathers." *International Journal of Offender Therapy and Comparative Criminology* 43 (2): 90–102.

Wood, Peter B., and Harold G. Grasmick. 1999. "Toward the Development of Punishment Equivalencies: Male and Female Inmates Rate the Severity of Alternative Sanctions Compared to Prison." *Justice Quarterly* 10 (1): 19–50.

Young, Diane S., and Carrie J. Smith. 2000. "When Moms Are Incarcerated: The Needs of Children, Mothers, and Caregivers." *Families in Society: The Journal of Contemporary Human Services* 81 (2): 130–41.

7

The Adolescent Children of Incarcerated Parents

A Developmental Perspective

J. Mark Eddy and John B. Reid

At least half of the 1.4 million people incarcerated in state and federal prisons are parents (Mumola 2000). Collectively, these parents have an estimated 1.5 million children under age 18, accounting for 2 percent of all U.S. children. Almost 50 percent of incarcerated parents report having lived with their children prior to their incarceration. Furthermore, 80 percent of incarcerated parents report that their children currently live with the other parent or with a relative. Thus, it is highly likely that parental incarceration has at least some impact on most of the children of incarcerated parents.

Despite the statistics, the children of incarcerated parents historically have been an invisible population, most likely because the judicial and the adult corrections systems have frequently viewed inmates as neither deserving of nor desiring contact with their children (e.g., Jeffries, Menghraj, and Hairston 2001). Thus, both the numbers and issues of children and families affected by incarceration have been ignored, except in situations where this was not possible (i.e., female inmate pregnancy). In addition, though the child welfare, mental health, and juvenile justice systems regularly interact with a significant number of these children, none of these systems has the responsibility for tracking or providing services for these children at large. Finally, neither the academic disciplines associated with these various service systems (i.e., criminology, sociology, social work, psychology, and public health) nor the government agencies and foundations that fund the researchers from these disciplines have claimed the children of incarcerated parents as a population of keen interest, thus limiting the scientific knowledge generated about these children.

This chapter reviews the published research literature on the adolescent children of incarcerated parents. While an estimated 40 percent of the children of incarcerated parents are between the ages of 10 and 17 (Mumola 2000), only a few studies have been conducted with samples from this population. Most studies have utilized nonrepresentative convenience samples and have focused on the problems rather than the strengths of these youth (Phillips et al. 2002). Problems reported for some of the adolescents of incarcerated parents, for example, include conduct problems (e.g., defiance, aggression, fighting, lying, stealing), depression, academic difficulties, and substance use (e.g., Sharp and Marcus-Mendoza 2001). Unfortunately, scant information is available on the prevalence of these problems. Little information is available on the proportion of adolescents who exhibit these problems to a clinically severe degree (i.e., their day-to-day functioning is impaired). Finally, almost nothing is known about how the symptoms of these problems change over the course of a parental incarceration (see Gabel 1992). Thus, while it is commonly assumed that adolescent children of incarcerated parents exhibit these problems at a higher rate than do adolescents in the general population (U.S. Department of Health and Human Services [DHHS] 1999), insufficient data are available to draw this conclusion with a high degree of confidence.

The possible relationship between parental incarceration and adolescent conduct problems is of special significance in the context of this book because persistent conduct problems place youths at high risk both to display criminal behavior during young adulthood and to enter the adult criminal justice system (Moffitt 1993). Thus, at some point, these children, too, may be dealing with the transition from prison to home. Notably, conduct problems frequently precede or co-occur with other teenage problems (e.g., academic failure, early substance use), which in turn place youths at high risk for other serious outcomes (e.g., school dropout, substance abuse) and therefore require them to access other social service systems. A recent study of a sample of adolescents receiving "routine" mental health services (i.e., services not linked to the foster care or juvenile justice systems) clearly illustrates the relationships among parental incarceration, youth service utilization, and conduct problems (Phillips et al. 2002). Not only had a significant number of youth in this sample experienced parental incarceration (43 percent), those who had were significantly more likely than those who had not to exhibit clinically significant levels of conduct problems (40 vs. 26 percent). Attention deficit/hyperactivity disorder (ADHD) was the only other clinical problem displayed more frequently by youth who had experienced parental incarceration (23 vs. 11 percent). ADHD is a strong correlate of persistent conduct problems across childhood and some researchers view it as a key precursor to adolescent conduct problems (Lahey and Loeber 1997).

Because of the multiple potential links between parental incarceration, conduct problems, and other problems of childhood and young adulthood, this chapter will focus on the conduct problems exhibited by adolescent children of incarcerated parents. Our focus is not intended to minimize the seriousness of other potential problems, such as traumatic stress reactions and depression related to parent-child separation. Unfortunately, except for conduct problems, there is very little relevant information to report on these topics. In the only study that indexed clinically severe levels of either traumatic stress or depression, youth who had experienced parental incarceration were significantly less likely than youth who had not to be diagnosed with major depression (9 vs. 23 percent; Phillips et al. 2002). This result is clearly counter to the anecdotal literature on the children of incarcerated parents, and more research is needed.

This chapter begins with a brief overview of adolescent conduct problems and the potential links between these problems and parental incarceration. A science-based model for the development of conduct problems during childhood and adolescence follows. The chapter concludes with a discussion of preventive interventions congruent with this developmental model that have been shown in rigorous scientific studies to significantly decrease adolescent conduct problems. With some adaptations, these interventions may decrease the likelihood that the adolescent children of incarcerated parents will display conduct and related problems.

Adolescent Conduct Problems

Conduct problems include persistent and pervasive disobedience, aggression, temper tantrums, stealing, and violence (see Patterson 1982).

Generally, *persistent* is defined as lasting at least six months, and *pervasive* is defined as occurring in more than one setting (e.g., home and school; see Eddy 2001). This does not mean that each of these problems occurs on an ongoing basis in multiple settings, but rather that some of them do. Youth who exhibit conduct problems during adolescence frequently exhibit a host of other problems, including academic difficulties, depression, substance abuse, and early sexual behavior, each of which may have serious long-term consequences not only for the adolescents themselves, but also for their families and for society as a whole (Dryfoos 1990; Hawkins 1995; Howell 1995). Adolescent conduct problems are one of the strongest predictors of adult adjustment problems, including criminal behavior (Kohlberg, Ricks, and Snarey 1984). Specifically, from 40 to 75 percent of youths who exhibit severe levels of conduct problems exhibit adult criminality as indexed by police arrests and/or psychiatric diagnoses (Harrington et al. 1991; McCord 1991; Robins 1966; Zoccolillo et al. 1992).

At highest risk for adult criminality are those youth who first begin to exhibit persistent and pervasive conduct problems during their grade school years (Gendreau, Goggin, and Little 1996; Loeber, Stouthamer-Loeber, and Green 1991; Moffitt 1993; Patterson, Capaldi, and Bank 1991). These children are significantly more likely than their peers during young adulthood to have problems in the workplace, to abuse substances, and to have serious problems in marriage or parenting (Caspi, Elder, and Herbener 1990; Farrington 1991; Magnusson 1992; Quinton and Rutter 1988; Robins 1993; Roenkae and Pulkkinen 1995). Given the extent of these immediate and long-term negative outcomes, it is not surprising that youth conduct difficulties are considered one of the most costly child mental health problems in the United States (Kazdin 1994). Many researchers view early-starting conduct problems in particular as a key marker of social maladjustment (e.g., Reid, Patterson, and Snyder 2002).

Parental Incarceration, Parent Criminality, and Adolescent Conduct Problems

Though adolescents are arrested for only about 5 percent of the crimes they commit (Dunford and Elliot 1982), police arrest is one of the most commonly used indicators of conduct problems among adolescents. Incarcerated parents reported in cross-sectional surveys that 5 to 30 percent of their adolescent children were arrested at least once (Johnston 1995; Myers et al. 1999; Sharp and Marcus-Mendoza 2001). In contrast, nationally representative surveys of youth found that 10 to 12 percent of U.S. youth reported being arrested at least once by age 14 to 16 (Snyder and Sickmund 1999). Thus, the adolescent children of incarcerated parents are anywhere from one-half to three times as likely to be arrested as their peers.

Clearly, the available data on youth arrest are not very illuminating. However, numerous studies have been conducted on a related topic: the relationship between parent criminality, regardless of incarceration status, and adolescent conduct problems. In the most rigorous meta-analytic review of the longitudinal studies on this topic, Lipsey and Derzon (1998) found that having a *criminal* parent or parents (defined as a parent who was either arrested as an adult or who demonstrated antisocial tendencies in some way) was a significant but weak predictor ($r = .16$ to $.23$) of violent or serious conduct problems during adolescence and young adulthood (table 7.1).

Translated into a percentage, 15 to 20 percent of the children of the most acutely criminal parents (i.e., the top 25 percent of parents in terms

Table 7.1. *The Top 10 Middle Childhood and Early Adolescent Predictors of Violent or Serious Delinquent or Criminal Behavior at Age 15 to 25*

Age predictor measured			
Middle childhood (age 6 to 11)		*Early adolescence (age 12 to 14)*	
Child general offenses	.38	Child social ties	.39
Child substance use	.30	Peer antisocial behavior	.37
Child gender	.26	Child general offenses	.26
Family socioeconomic status	.24	Child aggression	.19
Parent antisocial behavior	**.23**	Child school attitude/performance	.19
Child aggression	.21	Child psychological condition	.19
Child ethnicity	.20	Parent-child relations	.19
Child psychological condition	.15	Child gender	.19
Parent-child relations	.15	Child physical violence	.18
Child social ties	.15	**Parent antisocial behavior**	**.16**

Source: Adapted from Lipsey and Derzon (1998).

Note: Total sample size contributing to the parent antisocial behavior mean effect size for age 6 to 11 years: $n = 1049$, and for age 12 to 14 years: $n = 442$.

of total arrests in a given sample, and presumably the most likely parents to be incarcerated at some point during adulthood) are likely to exhibit serious conduct problems themselves during adolescence and young adulthood. Assuming that the overall base rate of violent or serious delinquency in the general population is 8 percent (e.g., McGee et al. 1992; Rutter et al. 1975), the adolescent children of parents with the most involvement in the criminal justice system are three to six times more likely to exhibit violent or serious delinquency than peers with parents who have little or no criminal justice system interaction.

This level of risk parallels our findings in the Oregon Youth Study (OYS) (Capaldi and Patterson 1991); this longitudinal study of 206 males from Eugene and Springfield began in 1983 and was not included in the Lipsey and Derzon (1998) analysis. OYS participants were recruited from fourth grade classes in 12 public elementary schools. The schools were randomly selected for all schools located in neighborhoods with higher-than-average rates of delinquency for the local area. Seventy-five percent of the boys in these classes participated in the study originally, and 99 percent of the original participants are still in the study today. The typical participant grew up in a lower- to working-class family and is European American.

In the fourth grade, 2 percent of the boys had both a mother and a father who had been arrested as adults; 9 percent had a mother (biological or step) who had been arrested, and 22 percent had a father (biological or step) who had been arrested. By age 18, 80 percent of the youth from homes where only the mother had been arrested or where the mother and father had both been arrested had themselves been arrested two or more times. In contrast, among the youth from homes where only the father had been arrested, 50 percent were arrested two or more times by age 18. The lowest arrest rates were found among youth from homes where neither parent had ever been arrested as an adult; only 20 percent of these adolescents had two or more arrests. Again, the youth with the most "criminal" parents were found to be two to four times more likely to be arrested than the youth with the least criminal parents. Youth arrests in "mother-arrested" homes appear more likely, probably because women are more likely than men with criminal records (Leve and Chamberlain, in press) to exhibit numerous problems (e.g., mental health issues, histories of sexual and physical abuse) that could disrupt effective parenting and initiate or exacerbate conduct problems (see developmental model below).

In summary, youth with parents who exhibit criminal behavior during adulthood are at least two to three times more likely to exhibit conduct problems than are youth without such parents. Further, based on a very limited set of studies, the risk for conduct problems among adolescent children whose parents are incarcerated is *at most* equal to this level of risk. Thus, given the available data, incarceration does not appear to increase the risk for adolescent conduct problems over and above parent criminality. We will discuss a possible explanation for this later in the chapter.

Linking Parental Incarceration and Adolescent Conduct Problems

What accounts for the relationship between parental incarceration and adolescent conduct problems? Unfortunately, no published studies have directly examined this question. We can, however, draw conclusions from related research. The most relevant line of research concerns outcomes for youth following changes, or transitions, in parental figures. Such transitions are part of the experience of parental incarceration for youth who lived with their parent before the parent's incarceration. When a father goes to prison, the children's mother usually continues to care for his children, although stepfathers, boyfriends, and grandparents often play a parenting role as well (Mumola 2000). In contrast, when a mother goes to prison, the father cares for the children only 25 percent of the time; children most typically live with a grandmother (51 percent), although some live with another relative (20 percent), a family friend (4 percent), or in a foster home (11 percent) (Mumola 2000). Furthermore, most children of incarcerated mothers experience at least two changes in caregivers during the course of a parental incarceration (Johnston 1995).

In a variety of studies (e.g., Capaldi and Patterson 1991; Eddy, Bridges Whaley, and Stoolmiller 2002; Martinez and Forgatch 2001; Pett et al. 1999), researchers have found that parental transitions influence youth conduct problems via their direct effects on the child's social relationships, particularly the parent-child relationship. In scientific terms, parenting "mediates" the relationship between parental transitions and adolescent conduct problems (Baron and Kenny 1986). Using data from the aforementioned OYS, Eddy et al. (2002) examined the mediators of parental transitions on conduct problems from the fourth through the tenth grade. Parental transitions included any change to a potential parenting figure for any reason, including separation, divorce, re-partnering (cohabiting partners or remarriage), parental death, parental incarceration, in or out movement of a grandparent, and placement in foster care.

While parental transitions were related to child and adolescent conduct problems, neither parental transitions nor parental criminality (measured for the mother only) were related to adolescent conduct problems when in the presence of two other key variables: the extent to which the child wandered in the evening without parental supervision and the extent to which the adolescent associated with deviant peers (i.e., peers with conduct problems). In short, and not surprisingly, regardless of factors such as parental transitions or parent criminality, the more the child was under adult supervision and away from deviant peer influences, the less the adolescent exhibited conduct problems.

Results from studies such as the OYS suggest that effective parenting practices by a caregiver can dampen the effects of parent criminality, parental transitions, and other stressful circumstances that adolescents experience, which in turn can decrease their risk for negative outcomes. In terms of youth conduct problems per se, who the caregiver is (i.e., parent, stepparent, grandparent, foster parent) or what individual characteristics he or she possesses do not seem to be as important as how the caregiver actually parents the child (e.g., Eddy and Chamberlain 2000). To date, the key positive parenting behaviors that dampen the risk for conduct problems the most appear to be reinforcement (i.e., rewarding a youth for prosocial behaviors), discipline (i.e., providing a youth timely and consistent consequences for antisocial and other undesirable behavior), supervision (i.e., closely tracking what a youth does, where he does it, and with whom), and problem solving (i.e., involving a youth in proactive and constructive methods of resolving family conflict) (see Reid, Patterson, and Snyder 2002).

Thus, if parental incarceration decreases the quality of positive parenting behaviors, one outcome may be an initiation or exacerbation of adolescent conduct problems. For example, if a hard-working employed parent who has a good relationship with his children is incarcerated for manslaughter following an alcohol-related fight in a bar, the result may be extreme family hardship, a significant decrease in positive parenting, and an initiation of adolescent conduct problems. On the other hand, parental incarceration that leads to an improvement in the quality of positive parenting behaviors may prevent or decrease adolescent conduct problems. For example, if a substance-abusing parent who regularly invites other abusers into the home and who also spends a great deal of time on the streets is incarcerated for drug dealing, then the children may be moved to a safer environment, positive parenting may increase, and adolescent conduct problems may not be a significant issue. A third alternative is that parental incarceration has no impact at all on parenting because of a lack of contact between the incarcerated parent and the youth prior to the incarceration.

Of course, the influence that parental incarceration has on adolescent conduct problems will depend not only on the types of parenting behaviors exhibited and received following the incarceration, but also on the types of parenting behaviors exhibited and received prior to the incarceration. If parenting was compromised in some significant ways before the incarceration, a youth may already be well on his or her way to conduct problems, and the incarceration may serve as the "tipping point" to more serious delinquency through the further disruption of positive parenting (Gladwell 2000). While little is known about the quality of parenting by incarcerated parents and their partners prior to their sentences, several researchers have found that the upbringing that many parents with criminal and/or incarceration histories received as children was seriously compromised, and thus a significant number of incarcerated parents themselves may not be well prepared to parent effectively. For example, men with criminal histories and their partners frequently report risk-laden childhoods bereft of adequate parenting and parental role models (Capaldi et al. 2001). Compared with noninmates, male and female inmates report having received more authoritarian (i.e., harsh, controlling, punitive) parenting during childhood (Chipman et al. 2000). Female inmates report having received the highest levels of such parenting, and, not surprisingly, female inmates commonly report experiences of physical and sexual abuse (e.g., U.S. Department of Justice [DOJ] 1993). Abuse experiences during childhood are not uncommon for male inmates as well. Men and women who have been parented in maladaptive ways are at higher risk for problems in their own parenting, which, in turn, increases the likelihood that their children will exhibit behavior problems during adolescence (Reid, Patterson, and Snyder 2002).

A Developmental Model of Antisocial Behavior

If positive parenting can decrease the risk that the adolescent children of incarcerated parents will have conduct problems, yet many incarcerated parents and their partners may lack positive parenting skills, what types of interventions could bridge the gap? This question can best be answered within the context of a developmental model for conduct problems. A developmental model provides a roadmap for how a child gets from point A (e.g., noncompliance) to point B (e.g., stealing), and points to possible factors that an intervention might target at each point in development so that the child reaches a different destination. Figure 7.1 provides an overview of our "coercion theory" conceptualization of a life-course trajectory toward conduct problems and serious delinquency (Patterson 1982; Patterson, Reid, and Dishion 1992; Reid 1993; Reid and Eddy 1997; Reid, Patterson, and Snyder 2002). The main part of the figure illustrates our hypotheses on the most powerful and potentially malleable antecedents of antisocial behavior, delinquency, and substance use during childhood and adolescence. In previous studies, each youth or family factor in the model has been shown to be a predictor of later youth conduct problems.

Within coercion theory, the development of child conduct problems can gain momentum before birth and then increase in velocity and intensity through successive antecedents during childhood and adolescence. Throughout such a developmental process, parenting plays a powerful role. Longitudinal studies have provided evidence that use of clear and consistent discipline techniques, close monitoring and supervision of the child, high rates of positive reinforcement, and secure, responsive parent-child attachment relationships produce prosocial outcomes in childhood, adolescence, and adulthood (Fagot and Pears 1996; Fisher, Ellis, and Chamberlain 1999; Patterson 1982; Patterson, Reid, and Dishion 1992). However, the exact nature, topography, and functions of family factors change markedly over development.

During gestation, direct parental antecedents to later conduct problems are maternal nutrition, maternal exposure to toxins, and maternal stress. Such factors are particularly pertinent to incarcerated mothers. Johnson and O'Leary (1987) found that 77 percent of the children of currently or previously incarcerated women had been prenatally exposed to drugs and/or alcohol. Olds, Henderson, and Kitzman (1994), for example, found that heightened prenatal exposure to substances was related

Figure 7.1. *Developmental Model of Antisocial Behavior*

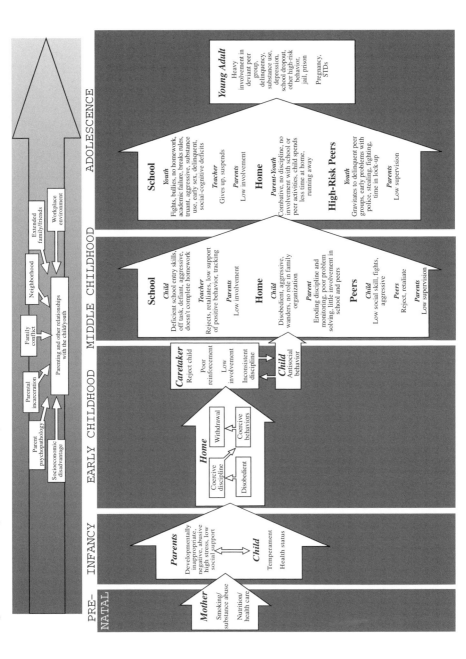

Source: Adapted from Reid and Eddy (1997).

to conduct problems 15 years later. In contrast, during infancy and toddlerhood, serious child problem behaviors are incubated in the context of parent- and sibling-child relationships when some if not all effective parenting strategies and qualities are absent (e.g., Olweus 1980; Patterson, Reid, and Dishion 1992; Robins 1978; Speltz, DeKlyen, and Greenberg 1999). This is not to imply that child temperament is not an important component in terms of parent-child interaction, but rather that, for most children, parenting behaviors can play a key role in shaping even difficult children toward a prosocial path.

Later, during elementary school and early adolescence, early failures in discipline, continued child noncompliance, insecure parent-child attachment relationships, and low levels of prosocial skills set the stage for reactions from teachers, peers, and parents that cause the child to be rejected and isolated (Fagot and Pears 1996; Patterson 1982; Reid and Eddy 1997). Such responses further compound compliance and discipline problems, severely restrict the prosocial options for a child, and increase the likelihood that a child will begin to relate more frequently with other similarly isolated and troubled children. As clearly documented in the recent U.S. Surgeon General's report on youth violence (DHHS 2001), the factors that place adolescents at highest risk for serious delinquency have to do with their peers, and particularly their association with a deviant peer group (e.g., Zimring 1981). Involvement with deviant peers further restricts a youth's options and increases the likelihood of heavy substance use, risky sexual behavior, and academic failure.

Events and enduring situations or circumstances, such as parental transitions, parental incarceration, parental criminality, parental education, and poverty, are considered "contextual factors" in our model (figure 7.1, top section). Based on research findings similar to those addressing parental transitions, we hypothesize that contextual factors are most important in the life of an adolescent to the extent that they directly impact the relationships the adolescent has with his or her parents, siblings, peers, teachers, and the other adult mentors in his or her life (Capaldi et al. 2002). Thus, contextual factors can be and often are successfully negotiated by skilled parents and other involved adults, who help children succeed despite the difficult aspects of their environmental context.

Contextual factors often cluster together. For example, low-income and low-educated parents may live in an impoverished neighborhood in which parental arrest rates are higher than average and parental incarceration rates are extreme. This clustering of factors may explain why, on average, the risk of adolescent conduct problems appears to be relatively similar for parent criminality and for parental incarceration. In other words, these two variables may be simply two sides to the same general issue—a very difficult context within which to raise a child. The equivalence of parent criminality and incarceration in terms of impact on conduct problems is based on little quality research, however. We need more scientifically rigorous studies examining the many impacts of incarceration on children and families. We suspect that if such research were done, unique effects of incarceration on adolescent conduct problems would probably be found. For example, parental incarceration may lead to youth traumatic stress reactions and depression, which may lead to increased youth inattention and irritability. This situation may, in turn, lead to increased parent-youth conflict, which may serve as a crucible for training a youth in interpersonal coercion. Increased adolescent conduct problems at home and at school would result.

Effective Interventions for the Adolescent Children of Incarcerated Parents

Based on our developmental model, interventions that target the relationships between a child and peers and a child and parental figures would be the most likely to affect the potential or existing conduct problems exhibited by the children of incarcerated parents. Unfortunately, there is no data on how these programs impact relationships within this population. Even the anecdotal literature on peer interventions for the adolescent children of incarcerated parents is almost nonexistent. Regardless, the success of individual and peer group work in decreasing the risk for conduct problems among at-risk and high-risk adolescents has yet to be demonstrated convincingly (e.g., Taylor, Eddy, and Biglan 1999), and there is some evidence that bringing at-risk adolescents together in groups for the purposes of preventing negative outcomes may actually exacerbate problems (see Dishion, McCord, and Poulin 1999). Thus, we will not consider peer interventions further here.

In contrast, while there is only a small anecdotal literature on parenting interventions that is directly relevant to the children of incarcerated parents, findings on the impact of parenting interventions with other high-risk populations are extremely promising. Parenting interventions have been tailored for and scientifically evaluated at several points along the developmental life course: nurse visitation before and after birth; skills-training programs for parents of preschool, elementary, and middle school aged children; and outpatient and residential interventions for at-risk and high-risk adolescents that include a family focus. Key to each of these interventions is helping parents develop specific positive parenting skills and providing the mentoring and support necessary to help them develop a sense of mastery and confidence. In many interventions, the work is of two sorts: didactic instruction and skills practice, often done in groups; and individual follow-up geared to help parents tailor their new skills to their specific family situations, including supervised practice with children.

Over the past few years, various task forces around the country have attempted to evaluate the growing scientific database on the outcomes of family-based interventions and to identify which interventions are "best practices" for the prevention and treatment of child problems. Two outcomes of particular interest for these task forces have been conduct problems (e.g., aggression, violence, rule breaking) and substance use. Many of these task forces have been sponsored by federally funded entities, such as the U.S. Department of Education, the Center for Substance Abuse Prevention, and the Office of Juvenile Justice and Delinquency Prevention. We recently compared the various "best practice" programs identified by these task forces (Metzler, Eddy, and Taylor 2003; Taylor, Eddy, and Metzler 2003) and found four family-based approaches that were consistently rated as a "best practice" by multiple task forces: nurse home visitation during pregnancy and infancy (Olds, Henderson, et al. 1998); parent management training (e.g., Webster-Stratton 1997); multisystemic treatment (Henggeler, Schoenwald, et al. 1998); and multidimensional treatment foster care (Chamberlain and Reid 1998). Each of these programs has been shown to significantly decrease adolescent conduct problems.

Nurse Home Visitation

David Olds and colleagues developed a comprehensive prevention strategy for economically disadvantaged mothers (Olds, Henderson, et al. 1998). Delivered by nurses in participants' homes, the intervention seeks to improve prenatal care and maternal health as well as provide other support and educational services for single mothers living in high-risk circumstances. Specifically, the intervention includes procedures designed to educate and encourage pregnant mothers to reduce or quit smoking, to reduce the use of other substances, and to increase the amount of time between subsequent pregnancies; in addition, it provides basic training and support in parenting and provides mentoring to help mothers improve their educational and job skills. The program begins in the third trimester of pregnancy and continues through the second year of a child's life.

In a randomized study of nurse home visitation, Olds, Hill, et al. (1998) demonstrated substantial preventive effects not only on several early antecedents of conduct problems (e.g., child abuse, coercive parenting, parental rejection), but also on delinquent behavior by the target children during their adolescence. The impressive and long-term success of this intervention strategy constitutes support for the notion that decreasing parental substance use, increasing the skill and support of parents, reducing physical abuse and harsh discipline, and creating a stable, predictable, and safe early environment are key ingredients to an early prevention strategy for adolescent conduct and related problems.

Parent Management Training

A variety of research teams around the country have developed and tested interventions that train parents in positive parenting skills (Reid et al. 2002). Known as parent management training (PMT) or behavioral parent training (BPT), these behavioral interventions emphasize hands-on instruction and intensive practice in positive reinforcement, discipline, monitoring, and family problem solving (Eddy 2001; Sanders and Dadds 1993). The intervention focuses mainly on parents, though children are often included at various points as well. The intervention may last from four weeks to several months, with meetings usually held once a week.

First used in outpatient mental health settings, PMT has, over the years, been adapted to inpatient, school, and community settings. In addition, PMT interventions have been designed for children across the development continuum. Within experimental or quasi-experimental designs, participants in PMT interventions have demonstrated reductions in child antisocial behavior, as rated by parents and teachers (e.g., Webster-Stratton 1998; Webster-Stratton and Hammond 1997; Webster-Stratton, Hollinsworth, and Kolpacoff 1989); problem behaviors at school (Forgatch and DeGarmo 1999); physical aggression on the play-ground (Reid et al. 1999); depression (Forgatch and DeGarmo 1999); and police contacts (Eddy, Reid, and Fetrow 2000), number of days insti-tutionalized (Chamberlain and Reid 1998), and substance use (Eddy et al. In press) during adolescence. Longitudinal evaluations of PMT interventions have uncovered enduring benefits to child adjustment at least two (Martinez and Forgatch 2002) to three years (Eddy et al. In press) after completion. Furthermore, several studies have demonstrated that the effects of this intervention on child adjustment were fully medi-ated by changes in parenting practices (Eddy and Chamberlain 2000; Forgatch and DeGarmo 1999).

Multisystemic Treatment

Developed by Scott Henggeler and colleagues, multisystemic treatment (MST) utilizes varying therapeutic techniques, including parent man-agement training, to assist parents and children in gaining the skills and the resources they need to address child and family problems (see Henggeler, Schoenwald, et al. 1998). The key to this intervention is a clinician available 24 hours a day, seven days a week, to help families find ways to support youth prosocial behaviors and to decrease youth conduct problems. Treatment sessions usually occur in the home, and may occur daily. At various times, sessions may involve many pertinent individuals, including extended family members, neighbors, teachers, and peers.

In several randomized studies, MST has positively impacted young offenders. For example, compared with youth on probation, youth who received MST were less likely to be arrested, to be locked up, and to self-report various crimes (see Henggeler, Schoenwald, et al. 1998). In another study contrasting MST to individual therapy, only 22 percent of youth in the MST group had reoffended within five years following treatment termination compared with 71 percent of those in individual therapy (Henggeler, Melton, and Smith 1992). Outcomes from a variety of other studies are described in Henggeler, Mihalic, et al. (1998).

Multidimensional Treatment Foster Care

Designed by Patricia Chamberlain and colleagues, multidimensional treat-ment foster care (MTFC) is a residential version of PMT (Chamberlain

1994). The program is designed to provide a minimally restrictive, alternative family situation for children who are removed from their homes by the courts. In addition to providing the youth with structure, supervision, and mentoring, the program works toward reunification and support of the natural family. Therapists work with the youth and the natural parents; foster parents receive training, supervision, and support (including access to a therapist 24 hours a day); and a case manager coordinates the team's efforts. The intervention attempts to decrease affiliation with deviant peers, increase prosocial behaviors, decrease youth antisocial behavior, and increase parenting skills within the natural family.

In a number of randomized studies, Chamberlain and her colleagues (Chamberlain and Reid 1998; Chamberlain, Fisher, and Moore 2002) have shown that it is both feasible and cost-effective to train and support carefully selected foster parents to provide multisystemic treatment and care for extremely delinquent boys and girls. Such treatment has significantly impacted adolescent delinquent behavior. For example, only 59 percent of serious juvenile offender boys in the MTFC group were rearrested within one year following intervention compared with 93 percent of boys in services-as-usual group homes (Chamberlain and Reid 1998).

A Science-Based Preventive Intervention Package

Modified versions of these four interventions show great potential for significantly reducing problems among adolescent children of incarcerated parents. This potential could be heightened further if such programs were delivered together and to an entire population of inmate parents and caregivers. Such a practice would be in stark contrast to the typical situation today, where the inmate family programming that exists in the typical correctional system impacts a rather small proportion of the total population of inmates and their families.

A science-based preventive intervention package targeting the children of incarcerated parents would utilize versions of each of the interventions to target the specific developmental needs of these children. For children at the beginning of life, nurses could deliver the nurse visitation program to pregnant inmates, and infants could stay with their incarcerated mothers while these mothers continue to receive parenting and life-skills advice and training. Historical precedence for such arrangements exists (Jeffries et al. 2001), and several states around the country do have residential programs for infants (e.g., New York and Washington). Since many female inmates will become pregnant when they leave prison, key content from the nurse home visitation program also could be delivered via groups to incarcerated women of child-bearing age in preparation for future pregnancies.

Parent management training targeting children from toddlerhood to adolescence and tailored for inmates and the current caregivers of their children could be the main component of a larger prevention strategy. Through corrections departments or via contractors, group-based programs provided to inmates early on in their sentences could improve their interactions with their children *during* incarceration (i.e., improve the quality of interaction via phone, letters, and in-person visits). More positive interactions between parents and children during this time could launch a cascade of positive outcomes for all. Positive interactions could be encouraged through ongoing skills-training groups for which graduates of the initial parent management training course would be eligible. "Transition home" parent management training programs could be designed for and offered to inmates in the months just before their release to prepare them for parenting on the outside.

Group-based programs that complement the inmate program could be developed for the caregivers of the children of incarcerated parents and offered in community settings. Parent management training could also be offered to individual caregivers with children who are exhibiting serious antisocial behavior. Such services would most logically be delivered by the nonprofit sector. Programs with the skill development and support characteristics of MTFC and MST could be delivered to the incarcerated parents of youth who are either in foster care or involved with the juvenile justice system. These interventions could address numerous family needs and, in coordination with other programs inside prison—like parent management training—could improve outcomes for youth. This group of interventions would clearly require more open communication between the health and human services and the criminal justice systems than exists in most states. Information would need to be shared so that families could be identified and resources appropriately targeted.

Finally, support services could be established to ease the transition home (Travis, Waul, and Solomon 2001) and help parents assume positive roles in the lives of their children when they return home from prison. These services might include education, job training, support groups, mentoring, or personal support via hotlines available for guidance and referral. Initial contacts with mentors could occur during the final months of a prison sentence. One proposal being considered in Oregon would make such a mentor available via phone 24 hours a day, 7 days a week, for a given period of time (e.g., six months) after an ex-inmate returns home. The ex-inmate could call for the mentor for parenting advice as needed and the mentor would call the ex-inmate weekly. The mentor could also conduct weekly support groups for interested ex-inmates. More intensive mentoring could be delivered to a particular family if needed through a version of MST.

Where We Go from Here

The evidence indicates that the adolescent children of incarcerated parents are at increased risk for conduct problems. The earlier such problems become a persistent part of a child's life, the more likely that child will go on to commit crimes resulting in incarceration as an adult. Findings from developmental research indicate that the best way to decrease the likelihood of adolescent conduct problems is to ensure that a youth receives positive parenting (i.e., reinforcement, discipline, supervision, and problem solving).

In our integrated prevention effort, multiple service systems coordinate their efforts to deliver comprehensive programs that teach positive parenting skills to incarcerated parents and caregivers of all types. This effort would include

- corrections departments conducting scientifically based parent education programs on a broader scale than currently exists and with both mothers and fathers;
- child welfare departments not only conducting foster care, but also providing the support and skills training that are key to success in programs like MTFC and MST;
- youth authorities providing not only residential or community services, but also infusing those services with MST and MTFC-like practices; and finally,
- community nonprofits delivering a variety of services that are also grounded in scientific evidence.

Each of these efforts could be informed by community members and groups who have the skills and expertise needed to adapt existing "proven" interventions so that they are culturally compatible with members of the minority groups that are overrepresented in the corrections population (see Hall 2001). Finally, the outcomes of each of these efforts could be studied in a systematic and ongoing way. Such data need to be collected as a standard part of service delivery, rather than simply gathered in an isolated study here and there. With information on outcomes of existing services available to policymakers, the programs that do, in fact, help the children of incarcerated parents could be retained. Ineffective programs could be changed until they do help, or discontinued.

Such an integrated system would certainly be costly, but in the long run and in concert with efforts in other sectors in the community, it could make a difference in decreasing adolescent delinquency and adult criminal behavior. In turn, this trend could help reduce the many associated social, emotional, and financial costs of crime and incarceration during adolescence and adulthood. It stands in contrast to the current and at best piecemeal and limited approach to prevention that ultimately is unlikely to make a difference.

A vision of prevention such as this is all well and good. Making it happen is another matter, however, particularly in a time of shrinking state and federal budgets. Containing today's ballooning corrections budgets in fact requires a long-term vision. In terms of scientific questions, the lack of information about the children of incarcerated parents is staggering, and federal and foundation funding is sorely needed for further research on this population. Such research must include epidemiological studies, which gather information about the lifelong development of these children. We need to know what characterizes the families that succeed in the face of incarceration versus the characteristics of those families that fail, and then use this information to improve preventive interventions. Adequately addressing the needs of the adolescent children of incarcerated parents requires a developmental approach that can only be accomplished with concerted and long-term collaborations among members of the public and private sectors, including the federal government, private foundations, state legislatures, corrections departments, child welfare agencies, youth authorities, other service providers, researchers, professional organizations, and community members. The time to begin such collaborations is now.

REFERENCES

Baron, Reuben M., and David A. Kenny. 1986. "The Moderator-Mediator Variable Distinction in Social Psychological Research: Conceptual, Strategic, and Statistical Considerations." *Journal of Personality and Social Psychology* 51 (6): 1173–82.

Capaldi, Deborah M., and Gerald R. Patterson. 1991. "Relation of Parental Transitions to Boys' Adjustment Problems: I. A Linear Hypothesis. II. Mothers at Risk for Transitions and Unskilled Parenting." *Developmental Psychology* 27 (3): 489–504.

Capaldi, Deborah M., David DeGarmo, Gerald R. Patterson, and Marion Forgatch. 2002. "Contextual Risk across the Early Life Span and Association with Antisocial Behavior." In *Antisocial Behavior in Children and Adolescents: A Development Analysis and the Oregon Model for Intervention,* edited by John B. Reid, Gerald R. Patterson, and James J. Snyder (123–46). Washington, D.C.: American Psychological Association.

Capaldi, Deborah M., Thomas J. Dishion, Mike Stoolmiller, and Karen Yoerger. 2001. "Aggression Toward Female Partners by At-Risk Young Men: The Contribution of Male Adolescent Friendships." *Developmental Psychology* 37 (1): 61–73.

Caspi, Avshalom, Glen H. Elder Jr., and Ellen S. Herbener. 1990. "Childhood Personality and the Prediction of Life-Course Patterns." In *Straight and Devious Pathways from Childhood to Adulthood,* edited by Lee N. Robins and Michael Rutter (13–35). New York: Cambridge University Press.

Chamberlain, Patricia. 1994. *Family Connections: Treatment Foster Care for Adolescents with Delinquency.* Eugene, Ore.: Castalia Publishing.

Chamberlain, Patricia, and John B. Reid. 1998. "Comparison of Two Community Alternatives to Incarceration for Chronic Juvenile Offenders." *Journal of Consulting and Clinical Psychology* 66 (4): 624–33.

Chamberlain, Patricia, Philip A. Fisher, and Kevin J. Moore. 2002. "Multidimensional Treatment Foster Care: Applications of the OSLC Intervention Model to High-Risk Youth and Their Families." In *Antisocial Behavior in Children and Adolescents: A Developmental Analysis and the Oregon Model for Intervention,* edited by John B. Reid, Gerald R. Patterson, and James J. Snyder. Washington, D.C.: American Psychological Association.

Chipman, Stacey, Susanne Olsen, Shirley Klein, Craig Hart, and Clyde Robinson. 2000. "Differences in Retrospective Perceptions of Parenting of Male and Female Inmates and Non-inmates." *Family Relations* 49 (1): 5–11.

DHHS. See U.S. Department of Health and Human Services.

Dishion, Thomas J., Joan McCord, and Francois Poulin. 1999. "When Interventions Harm: Peer Groups and Problem Behavior." *American Psychologist* 54 (9): 755–64.

DOJ. See U.S. Department of Justice.

Dryfoos, Joy G. 1990. *Adolescents at Risk: Prevalence and Prevention.* New York: Oxford University Press.

Dunford, F. W., and Delbert S. Elliot. 1982. *Identifying Career Offenders with Self-Report Data.* Washington, D.C.: National Institute of Mental Health.

Eddy, J. Mark. 2001. *Aggressive and Defiant Behavior: The Latest Assessment and Treatment Strategies for the Conduct Disorder.* Kansas City, Mo.: Compact Clinicals.

Eddy, J. Mark, and Patricia Chamberlain. 2000. "Family Management and Deviant Peer Association as Mediators of the Impact of Treatment Condition on Youth Antisocial Behavior." *Journal of Consulting and Clinical Psychology* 68 (5): 857–63.

Eddy, J. Mark, John B. Reid, and Rebecca A. Fetrow. 2000. "An Elementary School–Based Prevention Program Targeting Modifiable Antecedents of Youth Delinquency and Violence: Linking the Interests of Families and Teachers (LIFT)." *Journal of Emotional and Behavioral Disorders* 8 (3): 165–76.

Eddy, J. Mark, Rachel Bridges Whaley, and Mike Stoolmiller. 2002. *Parental Transitions: The Influence of Accumulation and Timing on Delinquency.* Manuscript submitted for publication.

Eddy, J. Mark, John B. Reid, Mike Stoolmiller, and Rebecca A. Fetrow. In press. "Outcomes during Middle School for an Elementary School–Based Preventive Intervention for Conduct Problems: Follow-up Results from a Randomized Trial." *Behavior Therapy.*

Fagot, Beverly I., and Katherine C. Pears. 1996. "Changes in Attachment During the Third Year: Consequences and Predictions." *Development and Psychopathology* 8 (2): 325–44.

Farrington, David P. 1991. "Childhood Aggression and Adult Violence: Early Precursors and Later Life Outcomes." In *The Development and Treatment of Childhood Aggression,* edited by Debra J. Pepler and Kenneth H. Rubin (5–29). Hillsdale, N.J.: Lawrence Erlbaum.

Fisher, Philip A., B. Heidi Ellis, and Patricia Chamberlain. 1999. "Early Intervention Foster Care: A Model for Preventing Risk in Young Children Who Have Been Maltreated." *Children Services: Social Policy, Research, and Practice* 2 (3): 159–82.

Forgatch, Marion S., and David S. DeGarmo. 1999. "Parenting through Change: An Effective Prevention Program for Single Mothers." *Journal of Consulting and Clinical Psychology* 67 (5): 711–24.

Gabel, Stewart. 1992. "Children of Incarcerated and Criminal Parents: Adjustment, Behavior, and Prognosis." *Bulletin of the American Academy of Psychiatry and the Law* 20 (1): 33–45.

Gendreau, Paul, Claire Goggin, and Tracy Little. 1996. "A Meta-analysis of the Predictors of Adult Offender Recidivism: What Works?" *Criminology* 34 (4): 575–607.

Gladwell, Malcolm. 2000. *The Tipping Point: How Little Things Can Make a Big Difference.* Boston: Little, Brown and Company.

Hall, Gordon C. Nagayama. 2001. "Psychotherapy Research with Ethnic Minorities: Empirical, Ethical, and Conceptual Issues." *Journal of Consulting and Clinical Psychology* 69 (3): 502–10.

Harrington, Richard, Hazel Fudge, Michael Rutter, Andrew Pickles, and Jonathan Hill. 1991. "Adult Outcome of Childhood and Adolescent Depression: I. Links with Antisocial Disorder." *Journal of the American Academy of Child and Adolescent Psychiatry* 30: 434–39.

Hawkins, J. David. 1995. "Controlling Crime Before It Happens: Risk-Focused Prevention." *National Institute of Justice Journal* 229 (August): 10–18.

Henggeler, Scott W., Gary B. Melton, and Linda A. Smith. 1992. "Family Preservation Using Multisystemic Therapy: An Effective Alternative to Incarcerating Serious Juvenile Offenders." *Journal of Consulting and Clinical Psychology* 60 (6): 953–61.

Henggeler, Scott W., Sharon F. Mihalic, Lee Rone, Christopher Thomas, and Jane Timmons-Mitchell, eds. 1998. *Blueprints for Violence Prevention, Book Six: Multisystemic Therapy.* Boulder, Colo.: Center for the Study and Prevention of Violence.

Henggeler, Scott W., Sonja K. Schoenwald, Charles M. Borduin, Melisa D. Rowland, and Phillippe B. Cunningham. 1998. *Multisystemic Treatment of Antisocial Behavior in Children and Adolescents.* New York: Guilford Press.

Howell, James C. 1995. *Guide for Implementing the Comprehensive Strategy for Serious, Violent, and Chronic Juvenile Offenders.* Washington, D.C.: U.S. Department of Justice, Office of Juvenile Justice and Delinquency Prevention.

Jeffries, John M., Suzanne Menghraj, and Creasie Finney Hairston. 2001. *Serving Incarcerated and Ex-offender Fathers and Their Families: A Review of the Field.* New York: Vera Institute of Justice.

Johnson, Patti L., and K. Daniel O'Leary. 1987. "Parental Behavior Patterns and Conduct Disorders in Girls." *Journal of Abnormal Child Psychology* 15 (4): 573–81.

Johnston, Denise. 1995. "Effects of Parental Incarceration." In *Children of Incarcerated Parents,* edited by Katherine Gabel and Denise Johnston (59–88). New York: Lexington Books.

Kazdin, Alan E. 1994. "Interventions for Aggressive and Antisocial Children." In *Reason to Hope: A Psychosocial Perspective on Violence and Youth,* edited by Leonard D. Eron, Jacquelyn H. Gentry, and Peggy Schlegel. Washington, D.C.: American Psychological Association.

Kohlberg, Lawrence, David Ricks, and John Snarey. 1984. "Childhood Development as a Predictor of Adaptation in Adulthood." *Genetic Psychology Monographs* 110 (1): 91–172.

Lahey, Benjamin B., and Rolf Loeber. 1997. "Attention-Deficit/Hyperactivity Disorder, Oppositional Defiant Disorder, Conduct Disorder, and Adult Antisocial Behavior: A Life Span Perspective." In *Handbook of Antisocial Behavior,* edited by David M. Stoff, James Breiling, and Jack D. Maser (51–59). New York: John Wiley & Sons, Inc.

Leve, Leslie D., and Patricia Chamberlain. In press. "Girls in the Juvenile Justice System: Risk Factors and Clinical Implications." In *The Development and Treatment of Girlhood Aggression,* edited by Debra J. Pepler, Kirsten C. Madsen, Christopher D. Webster, and Kathryn S. Levene. Hillsdale, N.J.: Lawrence Erlbaum.

Lipsey, Mark W., and James H. Derzon. 1998. "Predictors of Violent or Serious Delinquency in Adolescence and Early Adulthood: A Synthesis of Longitudinal Research." In *Serious and Violent Juvenile Offenders: Risk Factors and Successful Interventions,* edited by Rolf Loeber and David P. Farrington (86–105). Thousand Oaks, Calif.: Sage Publications, Inc.

Loeber, Rolf, Magda Stouthamer-Loeber, and Stephanie M. Green. 1991. "Age of Onset of Problem Behavior in Boys, and Later Disruptive and Delinquent Behavior." *Criminal Behaviour and Mental Health* 1 (3): 229–46.

Magnusson, David. 1992. "Individual Development: A Longitudinal Perspective." *European Journal of Personality* 6 (2): 119–38.

Martinez, Charles R., Jr., and Marion S. Forgatch. 2001. "Preventing Problems with Boys' Noncompliance: Effects of a Parent Training Intervention for Divorcing Mothers." *Journal of Consulting and Clinical Psychology* 69 (3): 416–28.

———. 2002. "Adjusting to Change: Linking Family Structure Transitions with Parenting and Boys' Adjustment." *Journal of Family Psychology* 16 (2): 107–17.

McCord, Joan. 1991. "Questioning the Value of Punishment." *Social Problems* 38 (2): 167–79.

McGee, Rob, Michael Feehan, Sheila Williams, and Jessie Anderson. 1992. "DSM-III Disorders from Age 11 to Age 15 Years." *Journal of the American Academy of Child and Adolescent Psychiatry* 31 (1): 50–59.

Metzler, Carol, J. Mark Eddy, and Ted Taylor. 2003. *Finding Common Ground in the "Best Practices" Literature, Part 1: For Researchers.* Manuscript in preparation.

Moffitt, Terrie E. 1993. "Adolescence-Limited and Life-Course-Persistent Antisocial Behavior: A Developmental Taxonomy." *Psychological Review* 100 (4): 674–701.

Mumola, Christopher J. 2000. *Incarcerated Parents and Their Children.* Washington, D.C.: U.S. Department of Justice, Bureau of Justice Statistics.

Myers, Barbara J., Tina M. Smarsh, Kristine Amlund-Hagen, and Suzanne Kennon. 1999. "Children of Incarcerated Mothers." *Journal of Child and Family Studies* 8 (1): 11–25.

Olds, David L., Charles R. Henderson Jr., and Harriet Kitzman. 1994. "Does Prenatal and Infancy Nurse Home Visitation Have Enduring Effects on Qualities of Prenatal Caregiving and Child Health at 25 to 50 Months of Life?" *Pediatrics* 93 (1): 89–98.

Olds, David, Peter Hill, Sharon Mihalic, and R. O'Brien, eds. 1998. *Blueprints for Violence Prevention, Book Seven: Prenatal and Infancy Home Visitation by Nurses.* Boulder, Colo.: Center for the Study and Prevention of Violence.

Olds, David, Charles R. Henderson Jr., Robert Cole, John Eckenrode, Harriet Kitzman, Dennis Luckey, Lisa Pettitt, Kimberly Sidora, Pamela Morris, and Jane Powers. 1998. "Long-Term Effects of Nurse Home Visitation on Children's Criminal and Antisocial Behavior: 15-Year Follow-up of a Randomized Controlled Trial." *Journal of the American Medical Association* 280 (14): 1238–44.

Olweus, Dan. 1980. "Familial and Temperamental Determinants of Aggressive Behavior in Adolescent Boys: A Causal Analysis." *Developmental Psychology* 16: 644–60.

Patterson, Gerald R. 1982. *Coercive Family Process.* Eugene, Ore.: Castalia.

Patterson, Gerald R., Deborah Capaldi, and Lew Bank. 1991. "An Early Starter Model for Predicting Delinquency." In *The Development and Treatment of Childhood Aggression,* edited by Debra J. Pepler and Kenneth H. Rubin (139–68). Hillsdale, N.J.: Lawrence Erlbaum.

Patterson, Gerald R., John B. Reid, and Thomas J. Dishion. 1992. *A Social Learning Approach: Vol. IV. Antisocial Boys.* Eugene, Ore.: Castalia.

Pett, Marjorie A., Bruce E. Wampold, Charles W. Turner, and Beth Vaughan-Cole. 1999. "Paths of Influence of Divorce on Preschool Children's Psychosocial Adjustment." *Journal of Family Psychology* 13 (2): 145–64.

Phillips, Susan D., Barbara J. Burns, H. Ryan Wagner, Teresa L. Kramer, and James M. Robbins. 2002. "Parental Incarceration among Adolescents Receiving Mental Health Services." *Journal of Child and Family Studies* 11 (4): 385–99.

Quinton, David, and Michael Rutter. 1988. *Parenting Breakdown: The Making and Breaking of Inter-generational Links.* Aldershot, England: Avebury.

Reid, John B. 1993. "Prevention of Conduct Disorder Before and After School Entry: Relating Interventions to Developmental Findings." *Development and Psychopathology* 5: 243–62.

Reid, John B., and J. Mark Eddy. 1997. "The Prevention of Antisocial Behavior: Some Considerations in the Search for Effective Interventions." In *Handbook of Antisocial Behavior,* edited by David M. Stoff, James Breiling, and Jack D. Maser (343–56). New York: John Wiley & Sons, Inc.

Reid, John B., Gerald R. Patterson, and James J. Snyder, eds. 2002. *Antisocial Behavior in Children and Adolescents: A Developmental Analysis and the Oregon Model for Intervention.* Washington D.C.: American Psychological Association.

Reid, John B., J. Mark Eddy, Rebecca Ann Fetrow, and Mike Stoolmiller. 1999. "Description and Immediate Impacts of a Preventive Intervention for Conduct Problems." *American Journal of Community Psychology* 27 (4): 483–517.

Robins, Lee N. 1966. *Deviant Children Grown Up: A Sociological and Psychiatric Study of Sociopathic Personality.* Baltimore, Md.: Williams & Wilkins.

———. 1978. "Sturdy Childhood Predictors of Adult Antisocial Behavior: Replications from Longitudinal Studies." *Psychological Medicine* 8: 611–22.

———. 1993. "Childhood Conduct Problems, Adult Psychopathology, and Crime." In *Mental Disorder and Crime,* edited by Sheilagh Hodgins. Newbury Park, Calif.: Sage Publications.

Roenkae, Anna, and Lea Pulkkinen. 1995. "Accumulation of Problems in Social Functioning in Young Adulthood: A Developmental Approach." *Journal of Personality and Social Psychology* 69 (2): 381–91.

Rutter, Michael, Antony Cox, Celia Tupling, Michael Berger, and William Yule. 1975. "Attainment and Adjustment in Two Geographical Areas: I. The Prevalence of Psychiatric Disorder." *British Journal of Psychiatry* 126: 493–509.

Sanders, Matthew R., and Mark R. Dadds. 1993. *Behavioral Family Intervention.* Needham Heights, Mass.: Allyn & Bacon.

Sharp, Susan F., and Susan T. Marcus-Mendoza. 2001. "It's a Family Affair: Incarcerated Women and Their Families." *Women & Criminal Justice* 12 (4): 21–50.

Snyder, Howard N., and Melissa Sickmund. 1999. *Juvenile Offenders and Victims: A National Report.* Washington, D.C.: Office of Juvenile Justice and Delinquency Prevention, U.S. Department of Justice.

Speltz, Matthew L., Michelle DeKlyen, and Mark T. Greenberg. 1999. "Attachment in Boys with Early Onset Conduct Problems." *Development and Psychopathology* 11 (2): 269–85.

Taylor, Ted K., J. Mark Eddy, and Anthony Biglan. 1999. "Interpersonal Skills Training to Reduce Aggressive and Delinquent Behavior: Limited Evidence and the Need for an Evidence-Based System of Care." *Clinical Child and Family Psychology Review* 2 (3): 169–82.

Taylor, Ted, J. Mark Eddy, and Carol Metzler. 2003. *Finding Common Ground in the "Best Practices" Literature, Part I: For Practitioners.* Manuscript in preparation.

Travis, Jeremy, Michelle Waul, and Amy Solomon. 2001. *From Prison to Home: The Dimensions and Consequences of Prisoner Reentry.* Washington, D.C.: The Urban Institute.

U.S. Department of Health and Human Services. 1999. "HHS Reports New Child Abuse and Neglect Statistics." http://www.acf.dhhs.gov/news/abuse.htm. (Accessed August 5, 1999.)

———. 2001. "Youth Violence: A Report of the Surgeon General." http://www.mental health.org/youthviolence/surgeongeneral/SG_Site/toc.asp. (Accessed July 2, 2003.)

U.S. Department of Justice. 1993. *Survey of State Prison Inmates.* Washington, D.C.: Bureau of Justice Statistics.

Webster-Stratton, Carolyn. 1997. *The Incredible Years: A Trouble-Shooting Guide for Parents of Children Aged 3–8.* Toronto, Ont.: Umbrella Press.

————. 1998. "Preventing Conduct Problems in Head Start Children: Strengthening Parenting Competencies." *Journal of Consulting and Clinical Psychology* 66 (5): 715–30.

Webster-Stratton, Carolyn, and Mary Hammond. 1997. "Treating Children with Early-onset Conduct Problems: A Comparison of Child and Parent Training Interventions." *Journal of Consulting and Clinical Psychology* 65 (1): 93–109.

Webster-Stratton, Carolyn, Terri Hollinsworth, and Mary Kolpacoff. 1989. "The Long-Term Effectiveness and Clinical Significance of Three Cost-effective Training Programs for Families with Conduct-problem Children." *Journal of Consulting and Clinical Psychology* 57 (4): 550–53.

Zimring, Franklin E. 1981. "Kids, Groups, and Crime: Some Implications of a Well-Known Secret." *Journal of Criminal Law and Criminology* 72 (3): 867–85.

Zoccolillo, Mark, Andrew Pickles, David Quinton, and Michael Rutter. 1992. "The Outcome of Childhood Conduct Disorder: Implications for Defining Antisocial Personality Disorder and Conduct Disorder." *Psychological Medicine* 22: 971–86.

8

Prisoners and Their Families

Parenting Issues during Incarceration

Creasie Finney Hairston

The preservation and strengthening of families has a long-standing history as a public policy priority and as a major objective of governmental agencies and not-for-profit service organizations in the United States. The nation's political leaders recognize social welfare policies and programs that help families protect, nurture, and care for their children and adult family members as a social investment and direct many formal and informal efforts toward that end. Notwithstanding the millions of families affected by incarceration on any given day, the well-being of prisoners' families and children has not been an important part of this social policy agenda. Similarly, the strategic plans of social services agencies and corrections departments have seldom included services and activities that assist prisoners in carrying out family roles and responsibilities.

Several recent developments are challenging the historical treatment of prisoners' families in public policy discourse and decisionmaking. Among the many factors influencing this shift in thinking are a large and growing correctional population currently numbering over two million, unprecedented increases in the number of women prisoners, disproportionate numbers of imprisoned African-American males, high recidivism rates, and the annual return of hundreds of thousands of prisoners to communities. In addition, the tremendous cost involved with maintaining large numbers of children in foster care placements and providing welfare assistance to poor women and children is demanding attention. These pressing issues have led politicians and social scientists alike to examine more closely the consequences of the nation's war on drugs and, in so doing, to discover that incarceration's impact extends far beyond imprisoned men and women. Consequently, experts and concerned citizens are asking about the impact of imprisonment on children and families and the extent to which prisoners' families might be resources and assets, rather than liabilities, in promoting safe, resourceful communities. Recognition that the majority of women and men in prison are parents of dependent children and concerns about intergenerational crime and children at risk have placed parenting issues at the center of these discussions.

This chapter provides an overview of family matters during incarceration as one means of informing public debate and actions in this emerging area of social policy and practice. It begins by describing the problems that families face when a parent is incarcerated and the strategies they use to manage those problems. Subsequent sections discuss the relevance and importance of maintaining prisoners' family and parental relationships as a means of facilitating certain societal and family goals. The chapter concludes by examining the ways in which social policies and administrative practices hinder or support families' efforts to stay connected during incarceration.

The Importance of Family

Social scientists and program providers define the significance of families and family ties to prisoners and to the achievement of social goals in numerous ways. Incarceration's impact on families has been conceptualized as a form of family crises (Fishman 1990), loss and demoralization (Schneller 1976), and victimization of children (Bloom and Steinhart 1993). More recent work has focused on social capital—that is, the impact of social disinvestment in prisoners' families and communities (Hagan and Coleman 2001)—and on the unintended and intended consequences of social policy (Hairston 1998, 2002).

Studies using theoretical perspectives, which focus on the positive roles and functions that families serve as opposed to the problems that they experience, indicate that families are important to prisoners and to the achievement of major social goals, including the prevention of recidivism and delinquency. In most of these studies, "success" was defined in terms of lower rates of recidivism and fewer parole violations. Hairston's (1988, 1991a) review of research on prisoners' family relationships yielded two consistent findings: Male prisoners who maintain strong family ties during imprisonment have higher rates of postrelease success than those who do not maintain such ties, and men who assume responsible husband and parenting roles upon release have higher rates of success than those who do not assume such roles. Dowden and Andrews' (1999) analysis of research on female offenders identified family process variables, concepts like affection and supervision, as the strongest predictors of female offenders' success. Slaght (1999) found family relationships to have a significant influence on relapse prevention among parolees. Social scientists and practitioners have used these findings to surmise that programs that include family members in prisoners' treatment during incarceration and after their release can produce positive results for prisoners, families, institutions, and communities (Jeffries, Menghraj, and Hairston 2001; Wright and Wright 1992).

Practitioners providing or advocating for parenting programs in prison offer the perspective that incarcerated parents' involvement with and attachment to their children can prevent intergenerational crime and that such programs can help prisoners become better parents. Parenting programs also enjoy support from groups concerned not only about how some incarcerated parents have negatively affected their children, but also about preventing child abuse and neglect among parents returning to community living.

Though the effectiveness of parenting programs in achieving these objectives has not been soundly demonstrated, the rationale behind these programs has a strong research and theoretical base. The importance of positive family relationships and parenting practices in child development and the prevention of delinquency is a recurring finding in delinquency studies (Tolan, Guerra, and Kendall 1995). Furthermore, maintaining family ties is important for juvenile as well as adult prisoners (Borgman 1985). The more nurturing aspects of parenting, or absence thereof (e.g., parental involvement, attachment and rejection) have also consistently shown a strong association with delinquency. Moreover, research indicates that the effects of parental criminality on delinquency are indirect and mediated by parental attachment and discipline style (Larzelere and Patterson 1990).

While family connections are important to prisoners and their families and children, some family members care little that a relative is in prison and others feel relieved that the prisoner is no longer a part of their daily lives. Sometimes wives who had poor relationships with their husbands prior to the husbands' confinement and the caregivers of children who suffered parental abuse voice such feelings. The prisoner's preprison lifestyle and/or lack of respect and concern for his or her children and other family members may have permanently damaged these relationships. In these situations, families may feel that the social and psychological costs of prisoner-family connections far outweigh any conceivable benefits and choose to use the incarceration period to sever, rather than strengthen, family ties.

Family Definitions

Most research on prisoners' families defines families as (1) married couples with children (and study the wives of incarcerated husbands and their children) (Bakker, Morris, and Janus 1978; Carlson and Cervera 1991; Daniel and Barrett 1981; Fishman 1990; Schneller 1976; Swan 1981) or as (2) single mothers with children (and study incarcerated mothers and their children) (Baunach 1985; Bloom and Steinhart 1993; Hairston 1991b; Hungerford 1993). Incarcerated fathers and their children (Hairston 1989, 1995; Lanier 1991, 1993; Martin 2001) and the caregivers of children of incarcerated mothers (Bloom and Steinhart 1993; Poe 1992) have also been studied, but these are far less popular topics in prisoner family studies.

Surveys of prisoners indicate that prisoners' family networks are far more complex than these subgroups suggest. Mumola's (2000) analysis of the 1997 survey of state and federal prisoners indicates that the majority of parents in prison are not married. While many mothers (46 percent) and some fathers (15 percent) lived in single-parent households at the time of their arrest, most parents who were living with their children shared caregiving responsibilities with relatives and other household members. Other studies indicate that parental roles and responsibilities differ not only among families but also among children within the same family.

Hairston's (1995) study of men in two southeastern prisons found that most fathers (69 percent) had more than one child. Most had never been married to the mother of one or more of their children. Half of the men with more than one child indicated that their children had different mothers. Fathers' provider and nurturing roles varied for their different children: Some children lived with their fathers at the time of arrest, other children were regularly seen and supported financially, and still others were neither seen nor supported by these fathers. Only 50 percent of fathers indicated that they were living in the same household as their youngest child at the time of arrest; two-thirds of the fathers, however, stated that they were contributing to the financial support of at least one of their children.

Fathers in prison consider their biological children to be family, but do not generally regard the mothers of their children as such if they are not in a committed relationship (Jeffries et al. 2001; Nurse 2001). These mothers are not insignificant in family life, however, as they control fathers' access to their children before, during, and after imprisonment and generally play a significant role in shaping children's development. Incarcerated men, on the other hand, may consider the children of women with whom they lived prior to incarceration and/or with whom they have a romantic attachment to be family though they are not the biological fathers of those children. In these situations, they may have parental obligations and commitments that are similar to those of other responsible parents.

Most incarcerated mothers do not function in the single-parent roles presented in the popular media. Mumola (2000) notes that only 31 percent of mothers incarcerated in state facilities lived in single-parent households alone with their children in the month prior to their arrest. Twelve percent lived in two-parent households and 15 percent lived in single-parent households with other related and nonrelated adults. Forty-two percent of the mothers had relinquished responsibility for the daily physical care and protection of their children to others.

Surveys of women in prisons and jails conducted by Bloom and Steinhart (1993) and Hairston (1991b) indicate that similar to fathers, mothers with more than one child have varying roles and relationships with their different children. Forty-seven percent of the mothers in the Hairston study who had more than one child had all of their children living with them at the time of arrest; 32 percent had some of their children living with them; and 21 percent had none of their children living with them. About one-half of the mothers who had only one child lived in the same household as that child at the time of arrest. Many mothers who did not have responsibility for the daily care of their children still saw them regularly prior to their incarceration, while others reported not seeing their children at all. Lack of communication between parents and children was common in situations where children were under the custody of the child welfare department and/or mothers' parental rights had been terminated.

Prisoners' mothers are the central family figure in prisoners' lives, an expected finding given the high percentage of African-American prisoners in most studies and the central role mothers play in sociological descriptions of African-American families (see, for example, Martin and Martin 1995). Mothers are male and female prisoners' most important sources of support and their most frequent visitors (Hairston 1992, 1995) and, in the case of incarcerated mothers, caregivers for their children (Bloom and Steinhart 1993; Hairston 1992, 1995). Yet, the incarceration's impact on these mothers and their influence on their grandchildren and incarcerated children have seldom been studied. Similarly, studies have examined extended kinship networks only superficially, though the social and behavioral sciences literature on African-American families identifies these networks as crucial in understanding African-American family structure, adaptability, and functioning.

Financial Difficulties

Most families experience financial losses and/or incur additional financial expenses as a result of parental incarceration. Financial problems are greatest for those families that try to maintain the convicted individual as a family member and for families where the imprisoned family member functioned in responsible parenting roles prior to imprisonment. Families face the loss of the imprisoned parent's income; legal fees associated with criminal defense and appeals; and the costs of maintaining the household, maintaining contact during imprisonment, and providing personal items for the prisoner.

Since just over half of prisoners indicate that they were employed before incarceration and most report a history of drug problems (Mumola 2000), we can reasonably assume that they were drains on family income rather than contributors and that their imprisonment places their families in a better, rather than worse, financial position. This is no doubt the case in some situations. Furthermore, parental incarceration likely has no, or very limited, financial impact on children and family members who were not a part of prisoners' lives prior to their incarceration. The reestablishment of parent-child connections during imprisonment could lead, however, to new financial obligations and commitments for family members as well as imprisoned parents.

Although there are no published research reports specifically documenting the financial impact of incarceration on families, several indicators demonstrate that many families are affected negatively. Surveys of wives whose husbands are in prison have consistently identified financial problems and the loss of spousal income as a major problem (Daniel and Barrett 1981; Fishman 1990; King 1993; Schneller 1976). Likewise, we can reasonably assume that mothers who were not married to their children's father before his incarceration, but were receiving financial or other support (such as child care), also experience financial losses resulting from the incarceration.

Grandparents and other relatives who care for the children of incarcerated mothers certainly incur additional financial expenses. Incarcerated mothers are not able to provide financial support for their children, and if they were receiving welfare benefits before their incarceration, those monies are not automatically awarded to the grandparents. Grandparents eligible for welfare benefits still suffer a financial deficit because these benefits do not cover the full cost of providing care. Some caregivers must discontinue their paid employment in order to assume child care responsibilities, thereby suffering additional income losses. Studies of grandparents raising grandchildren affirm that financial problems represent one of their main difficulties (Altshuler 1999; Bloom and Steinhart 1993; Petras 1999; Poe 1992).

Relatives caring for prisoners' children incur additional financial expense if they promote parent-child relationships. Allowing children to converse with their incarcerated parents by phone is a very expensive endeavor. Depending on the prison, a 30-minute collect telephone call from a prisoner once a week could put a $125 or higher dent in the family's monthly budget. (The monthly cost for similar calls placed from a residential telephone would be $15 or less.) Nor are prison visits cost free; monies must be budgeted to cover transportation—usually to geographically remote locations—meals and vending machine snacks during visits, and, sometimes, overnight lodging.

Relatives find that providing money and other items for their imprisoned relatives is a byproduct of maintaining family contact. Correctional institutions do not furnish many basic items that prisoners need or want, and wages for prison work—usually less than a dollar a day—

are generally too meager to allow for such purchases. Families either voluntarily or by request send money to the prisoner for toiletries, reading materials, stamps, extra food, and clothing items not furnished by the institution.

Prisoners' funds come primarily from family members and friends who deposit money into the prisoners' institutional accounts. Families also end up paying involuntarily for a variety of in-prison fees, such as health care charges, institutional fines, and child support payments, when corrections departments collect money for those services and items by placing a levy on all monies that are deposited into prisoners' financial accounts. The federal prison system and 90 percent of state prison systems, for example, require prisoners to pay a fee/copayment for health services ("Congress Gives Final Approval" 2000; Inmate Health Care 1999). In 1999, medical copayments ranged from $.50 to $5.00, with an average cost of $2.00 for medications.

Parent-Child Relationships and Children's Care

The protection, care, and nurturance of prisoners' children are principal concerns of prisoners and their families. When parents go to prison, most children go to or continue to live with relatives (Bloom and Steinhart 1993; Mumola 2000). These child care arrangements provide love, connections to kin, and a sense of belonging for children; however, they are not ideal. The physical absence of men and father figures in the daily lives of prisoners' children is obvious as women carry the primary and often sole caregiving responsibility for the children of both imprisoned men and women (Bloom and Steinhart 1993; Hairston 1991a, 1995; Mumola 2000). In addition to their limited financial resources, many grandparent caregivers have age-related issues and health problems and previously had no plans to take on new child care responsibilities (Bloom and Steinhart 1993; Petras 1999).

Generally, custodial caregivers and imprisoned parents are not adequately prepared to address children's needs arising from parental incarceration. Children's parents and caregivers are ambivalent about children's visits with their incarcerated parents and about what to tell children about their parents' incarceration. Some children do not know that their father or mother is in jail because relatives have told them the parent is away for other reasons, such as the army, school, or work. If the child did not live with the parent before the incarceration and their time together was sporadic, the child may not be told anything about the parent's absence (Hairston 1991b).

Some incarcerated parents do not want their children to visit them in prison and/or make no effort to contact their children. They do not believe that their children's custodial caregivers will welcome such contact, do not know where their children are, or believe such visits will be too emotionally painful for themselves and their children. Some parents in jail reason that they will be away only a short time and that visits from children are unnecessary (Hairston 1991b). Other parents mistakenly believe that there is little that they can do for their children from prison and that they can compensate for their absence once they are released. Mothers and fathers in prison report that their children's "other" parents also limit or refuse to allow communication with the children. Incarcerated parents frequently cite conflict with the other parent and/or other family members and limited financial resources as major factors influencing the level of ongoing contact with children (Hairston 1991b, 1995; Nurse 2001). The perspective necessary in order to gain a more complete understanding of how families cope with incarceration is missing: Research providing the perspectives of children's other parents, namely the women to whom incarcerated fathers are not married, is absent from the current knowledge base.

Children's custodial parents and other caregivers are not the only parties opposed to children's communication with their incarcerated parents. Corrections and social services professionals alike raise questions about the wisdom of children's visits to prison. Some reason that the prison environment is too oppressive for children. Others believe that such visits will lead to children's acceptance of incarceration as normal. Others have questioned whether contact between prisoners and their children should be encouraged for prisoners in general (given assumptions about their criminality, dangerousness, etc.) or for certain groups of criminals, namely fathers who have been violent with children's mothers. Those concerned about family histories of domestic violence point to the negative effects of children's exposure to family violence, reasoning that an incarcerated father's contacts with his children place the mother and children at risk of harm.

No body of theory or research supports prohibiting prisoners' communication with their children as a matter of social policy and practice. On the contrary, scientific studies point to the positive aspects of children's ongoing involvement with and attachment to adults who care about them and to the negative effects of paternal absence and family disruption (Gary 1996; Larzelere and Patterson 1990; McLanahan and Sandefur 1994; Morehouse Research Institute and Institute for American Values 1999). There are, however, individual situations where communication between an incarcerated parent and his or her children would not be in the child or family's best interest. In such cases, there are well-established practice principles to guide professional decisionmaking and protect children from harmful situations. State child welfare departments have, for example, policies and practice guidelines to cover family-child visitation for the children under their care. The Alliance for Children and Families' guidelines for clinical practice (Bernt 2001) address family relationship problems, domestic violence, child abuse and neglect, and other child and family issues. These general principles are also relevant to families separated by incarceration.

Although most mothers and a substantial number of fathers plan to reunify with their children upon their release, they worry that their children will be taken from them or that someone else will take their place in their children's lives (Hairston 1991b, 1995; Koban 1983; Lanier 1991). Incarcerated mothers and fathers report a common fear that their children will be taken by the state or that their parent-child bonds will be legally severed while they are in prison (Baunach 1985; Hairston, Wills, and Wall 1997).

Prisoners' personal experiences and child welfare policies and practices indicate that these fears are not unfounded. Although visiting increases the reunification prospects for separated families, most parents in prison never see their children. Fifty-seven percent of fathers and 54 percent of mothers in a national survey of incarcerated parents indicated that they had not visited with any of their children since admission to prison (Mumola 2000). In addition, each parental prison term reduces the likelihood that children will reside with their mothers upon release (Hairston 1991b). At this point, there is no research establishing that a similar situation also exists for fathers. Most incarcerated fathers, however, lack a legal or emotional bond with their children's mothers sufficient to support household reunification (Hairston 1995; Mumola 2000; Nurse 2001). In addition, communication between these mates or former partners is more often contentious than cordial (Hairston 1995; Jeffries et al. 2001; Nurse 2001).

Though one might expect that being married would protect or support prisoners' relationships with their children, many marital relationships are strained and end during imprisonment (Lynch and Sabol 2001). In a study of long-term prisoners, Hairston (1989) found that three-fourths of the men who were married at the time of their arrest were divorced at the time of the study. Sharp and Marcus-Mendoza (1998) reported that 50 percent of the married men in their study of men incarcerated on drug charges had discussed divorce with their wives. In most cases, someone had filed a divorce petition.

Incarcerated parents whose children are in state custody definitely have reasons to be concerned about the legal and permanent severance of parent-child bonds. Parental rights can be terminated in some states solely on the basis of a parent's criminal activity and incarceration (Genty 2001). Termination can also occur if parents fail to communicate regularly with their children or fail to adhere to prescribed treatment program plans.

The Adoption and Safe Families Act of 1997 (ASFA), enacted with the intent of achieving permanency for children, can potentially lead to less, rather than more, stability in the lives of prisoners' children. We still know very little about the outcomes associated with this policy: There is neither published research as to the law's impact on the lives of incarcerated parents and their children nor documentation of the approaches states are using to apply the law to incarcerated parents. Johnston (2001) reports, however, that her preliminary analysis of data obtained in a study of prisoners' children in long-term foster care shows an increase in parental rights terminations following ASFA's enactment.

Theoretically, few prisoners are able to meet the law's requirements. As Genty (2001) points out, ASFA requires that termination proceedings be filed whenever a child has been in foster care for 15 of the previous 22 months, a period that is significantly shorter than the 1997 expected average prison stay of seven years. Even parents serving much shorter prison or jail terms find it very difficult to comply with child welfare mandates. Prisoners have little or no control over their contact with their children or over their ability to participate in treatment programs. In addition, correctional institutions and child welfare departments have neither a history of collaboration nor, for the most part, systems in place to address effective in-prison parenting—a particularly difficult situation for incarcerated parents when children are under state custody (Child Welfare League of America 1998; Wall 1997).

Parental incarceration may lead not only to the termination of a parent's rights, but also to the severance of other family relationships. Many state child welfare agencies will not allow children under their custody to be placed in homes where a convicted felon will also be residing. In these situations, a former prisoner returning to the home of a grandparent kinship caregiver would place the children in jeopardy of being removed from the home. A grandparent seeking custody of her incarcerated son's infant shared confidentially with this author correspondence suggesting that a relative's ongoing contacts with an incarcerated parent can also be used as a basis for denying that relative's request to become the child's foster or adoptive parent. The letter from the state child welfare agency to the grandparent specified the grandparent's ongoing relationship with her incarcerated son as the reason for custody denial.

Though concerns about parental rights are serious, the social issue surrounding children's futures is perhaps even more pressing. Fundamental questions remain: What will happen to these children once their parents' rights are terminated? If large numbers of parents will no longer be legally responsible for their children, then who will be the children's parents? Will prisoners' children become permanent wards of the state who then move from one foster care placement to another? Who and where are the families waiting in line to adopt prisoners' children, especially given the pervasive "like father, like son" public attitude and scholars' declarations that children of prisoners are five or six times more likely to become criminals themselves (Reed and Reed 1997)? Is ASFA predicated on the assumption that no parent is better than a parent who is a convicted criminal? Or have the implications of this law for prisoners' children simply been overlooked in the political debates?

Emotional and Social Issues

Prisoners and their families experience a tremendous sense of loss when incarceration occurs and that loss is compounded when children are involved. Couples are usually denied sexual intimacy and are unable to engage in the day-to-day interactions, experiences, and sharing that sustain marital and other intimate, adult relationships. Loneliness and a host of other feelings about the separation, justice system, criminal activity, and each partner's honesty and faithfulness are common. Some prisoners' families also experience guilt and a sense of relief that a troublesome relative has finally been sent away. Difficulties in adjusting to separation and loss have led to depression and other mental health problems among prisoners and their families (Daniel and Barrett 1981; King 1993; Lanier 1993).

Social and emotional difficulties are not confined to just adults, but also extend to children. When asked about their children, incarcerated parents and children's custodial caregivers frequently list a number of social and emotional problems—school difficulties, withdrawal, acting out behavior, excessive crying—that they believe to be related to parental absence and incarceration (Bates 2001). Practitioners who provide services to prisoners' children also note that many children miss their parents, yearn for them to come home, and worry about how their parents are doing.

Incarcerated mothers cite separation from their children as one of the most difficult aspects of imprisonment (Baunach 1985; Hairston 1991b), and incarcerated fathers and mothers worry about what is happening to their children during their absence. Fathers and mothers express concern, and often remorse, about the disruption that they are causing in their children's lives and about the lost opportunities for parental involvement—attending the high school graduation, seeing the baby's first steps, etc.—that cannot be recaptured. Parents believe that their children are in safe living situations and are not being abused or neglected; nevertheless, they worry about their children's well-being and about their guidance and supervision (Hairston 1992, 1995). Some worries may result from incarcerated parents' limited contact with their children and necessary reliance on relatives and friends for information about their children (Hairston 1991a, b, 1995; Lanier 1993; Martin 2001).

Prisoners' children and families must also deal with feelings of shame and social stigma. Many family members do not tell even their closest friends about a relative's incarceration and go to great lengths to protect the prisoner's children from the consequences of revealing this family secret. Depending on the crime and the prevalence of imprisonment in the neighborhood in which they live, family members may not experience social stigma or hostility in that neighborhood (Schneller 1976). Nevertheless, families are stigmatized by other elements of society. Prisoners' wives report that revealing to others that their husband is in prison exposes them and their children to ostracism and discrimination (Fishman 1990; Koenig 1985). As a result of this type of exposure, prisoners' children sometimes become the victims of cruel jokes, and at times their families are excluded from social events or refused apartment rentals.

Information Needs

Inadequate understanding of and access to information about the criminal justice process present additional challenges to normal family functioning. Close relatives' knowledge of the prisoner's crime and sentence often amounts to little more than "she's doing time for drugs." Unless family members regularly visit a correctional institution and/or have a lot of savvy about how to navigate bureaucratic systems and are connected with prison family support groups, they most likely also have limited knowledge of correctional system policies and procedures.

Information about prison operations is obtained primarily from other families and through frustrating experiences. As a standard practice, correctional institutions do not disseminate formal policies and regulations to prisoners' families. If rules governing family communication are posted at prison facilities, they are often outdated and families may have to use a considerable amount of visiting time reading and digesting these rules. In addition, family members are generally not able to speak with anyone in authority who is either able or willing to provide information about the prisoner's status or to explain the rationale for certain rules, their varying interpretations, or the most recent changes in policy implementation. The person in charge of whatever the family member is concerned about is rarely accessible for in-person or telephone inquiries, and officials' responses, if any, to family members' letters are typically perfunctory rather than explanatory.

With few exceptions, useful information is not available to families via handbooks or public web sites either. The absence of accessible information for families is not a question of capacity because many corrections departments use their public web sites to provide registries, pictures, and criminal histories of current and former prisoners, and all corrections departments regularly promulgate numerous rules and regulations. The limited use of these same web sites and other means of providing useful information to families may reflect a lack of awareness about the importance of such information to families, a general disregard for families, or simply benign neglect because no correctional administrator is responsible for addressing family matters.

Uncertainty about a particular prisoner's situation and questions about the corrections department's rules and policies that coincide with that uncertainty are among the greatest concerns of prisoners' families (Ferraro et al. 1983; Fishman 1990). Families seeking benefits and services for children cite similar confusion and frustration in their quest to understand not only child welfare rules and regulations, but also the eligibility requirements and operating procedures of other human service systems (Petras 1999; Poe 1992). The uncertainty and confusion surrounding correctional and social services policies and operations produce far-ranging consequences for children and families. For example, families may be denied a prison visit because a family member's attire is considered improper or because the adult escorting a child does not have the child's birth certificate—simple but painful penalties. Furthermore, family relationships may be permanently severed because a grandparent caregiver failed to adhere to a rule or regulation that she did not know about or understand. Often, children's caregivers do not understand the implications of child welfare policies and practices related to criminal background checks and foster home approval. A grandmother may not understand, for example, that if she allows her son to live with her when he is released from prison, then the grandchild for whom she provides relative foster care could be removed from her home and placed with nonrelatives.

Prisoner-Family Communication

Communication between prisoners and their families provides the most concrete and visible strategy for managing separation and maintaining connections. Families personally visit their imprisoned relatives, talk with them by phone, and exchange cards and letters as a means of staying connected. These contacts allow adults, parents, and children to share family experiences and participate in family rituals (birthday celebrations, religious observances, etc.) and help them to remain emotionally attached. Communication assures incarcerated parents that their children have not forgotten them and reminds children that their parents love and care about them. Such contacts allow prisoners to see themselves and to function in socially acceptable roles rather than as prison numbers and institutionalized dependents.

Corrections departments permit these types of communication between prisoners and their kin and encourage the maintenance of family ties, in theory, as desirable correctional practices. In actuality, support for such relationships varies considerably from one jurisdiction to another and, within jurisdictions, from one facility to another. As a rule, prisons allow families and children to visit, though prisoners in administrative segregation or super maximum prisons may be restricted to televideo and other types of no-contact visits. Some jails allow only no-contact visits and/or prohibit children from visiting. Six states permit prisoners to have private family visits with their spouses and children on prison grounds; a few allow nonviolent female prisoners with infants to reside in alternative community residences. Most prisons for women, and a few for men, provide parent education courses and a few offer other parenting supports, including counseling, parent support groups, and special visiting areas and programs for parents and their children. (See Bates [2001] and Jeffries et al. [2001] for descriptions of parenting programs.)

The correctional policies and practices that govern contact between prisoners and their families often impede, rather than support, the maintenance of family ties. Many correctional policies are driven by the security and safety rationale that dominates the prison environment. Other policies, such as those governing the rate structure for the telephone systems for prisoner use, seem to be intended primarily to subsidize prison budgets and generate profits and/or to exert social control, not only over prisoners, but also over their families as well. Rules often bear little relevance to correctional goals and are insensitive to prisoners' family structures, cultural differences, and children's needs. Many rules appear to be arbitrary; others are inconsistently interpreted and applied by different staff members and with different visitors (Fishman 1990; Jeffries et al. 2001). Correctional institutions commonly require children's custodial parents to escort them on visits, require child visitors to produce birth certificates listing the prisoner as the biological parent, and house prisoners in locations hundreds or thousands of miles from their homes—all policies that create obstacles for healthy parent-child relationships.

For many families and friends of prisoners, the visit to a prison is a highly charged and anxiety-producing exercise in humility, intimidation, and frustration (Fishman 1990; Girshick 1996). It is not unusual for visitors, the majority of whom are women and children, to endure many indignities. Among the problems noted in the Florida legislature's report of prison visiting were long waits, sometimes in facilities without seating, toilets, and water; the lack of nutritious food in visiting room vending machines; and the absence of activities for children (Taylor 1999). Body frisks and intrusive searches, rude treatment by staff, and hot, dirty, and crowded visiting rooms are the norm in many prisons.

Visitors may be denied entry to the prison for diverse reasons, including noncompliance with constantly changing dress codes, lack of identification for children, and alleged possession of illegal drugs (as ion drug scanners may inaccurately signal that a visitor is carrying drugs).

Pitching In and Helping Out

Family members rely primarily on each other, rather than on formal organizations, to maintain family connections and address children's and adult family members' problems related to parental incarceration. When the protection of children and the maintenance of parent-child relationships are involved, many incarcerated parents and their relatives distrust formal organizations, avoid them when they can, and find them to be less than helpful (Bates 2001; Beckerman 1994; Hairston et al. 1997).

Families engage in a process of role change and adaptability simply known as pitching in and helping out. Some relatives pitch in by taking full or major responsibility for something the prisoner used to do. The grandmothers, sisters, and aunts who take on child-rearing responsibilities for dependent children of single mothers and fathers in prison are examples. The spouses of men and women in prison may take on new roles in decisionmaking and financially supporting their children. Some relatives help out with new responsibilities that families acquire as a result of incarceration, such as negotiating with the prison system, accepting collect phone calls from the prisoner, serving as an emissary between the prisoner and his/her children and other relatives, and arranging for and paying the costs of prison visits.

Prisoners who maintain family connections also adapt to new family roles. Incarcerated parents are not in a position to make significant financial contributions to their family, regardless of whether they are mandated to do so, nor are they able to physically take care of or protect their children. Family role expectations of prisoners, therefore, center on demonstrations of caring and concern for children or other family members or participation in decisionmaking about select family issues. Prisoners participate in family life by sending cards to acknowledge birthdays and other events of family relevance, calling home or the place where other family members have gathered on holidays, writing letters inquiring about and encouraging children's school progress, and giving advice on how to handle different problems.

The "pitching in and helping out" way of managing, like so many aspects of incarceration, is not without problems. Pitching in can raise feelings and family tensions among relative helpers who are concerned about "having to help out again" or bearing an unfair share of the burden. This responsibility can also be taxing and burdensome, especially when prisoners make selfish demands or when relatives feel the incarcerated individual had already "burned his/her bridges" before incarceration. Many prisoners also experience difficulties adjusting to new roles and expectations. Prisoners accustomed to independence and their role as family provider, for example, express strong feelings about occupying a less central and more dependent role in the family pecking order (Fishman 1990).

Some families do seek assistance—Medicaid, relative foster care payments, or public assistance welfare benefits, such as Temporary Assistance for Needy Families (TANF)—from human services organizations as an alternative or supplement to family help. These families do so at great emotional and social costs, however, because seeking help from organizations exposes the family to external scrutiny, raises the risk of children being removed from the homes of relatives or friends and placed in foster care, and exposes families to the shame and stigma that accompanies incarceration. When seeking help, these families may, therefore, choose not to reveal that parental incarceration is the precipitating factor. On the other hand, some needy families do not seek help because they are unaware of their eligibility for benefits and lack information that would help them access those resources (Bloom and Steinhart 1993). Others see little reason to engage in organizational efforts that will be of little benefit to them and could exacerbate the prisoner's situation. It is hardly worth the effort to seek child support if the money will go to the state's coffers, the prisoner is not making any money, or the prisoner's trust account is primarily funded by poor family members. Furthermore, most communities lack services to help families address needs specific to incarceration (Bates 2001; Jeffries et al. 2001).

Policy Directions and Strategies

The preservation and strengthening of prisoners' family ties and parent-child relationships will require vision and direction from the highest levels of public policy decisionmaking and a fundamental shift in the prevailing system responses to prisoners' children and families. Placing the responsibility for the creation of family-oriented prison environments and systemwide change on individual prison administrators and directors of corrections departments is unreasonable. In the face of escalating prison budgets and priorities focused on safety and security, few prison administrators will make family matters and postrelease success their major goals or priorities. In fact, the administrators who have maintained comprehensive parenting programs at New York's Sing Sing and Bedford Hills correctional institutions for several years are the exceptions rather than the rule.

Congressional bodies and state legislatures must take ownership of family-related incarceration issues as a matter of national interest and make prisoners' family matters an integral part of the discussion on criminal justice and family policy. Sentencing policies, alternatives to corrections, prison locations, and funding for family programs and services are legislative issues. It is equally important for legislators to oversee correctional policies and practices and to use the power of the law to institute policies that could improve the well-being of prisoners' children and families. The correctional environment and prison programming are not internal matters to be left solely to the discretion of prison administrators. They are instead public concerns with relevance to broad social welfare goals and of importance to different community constituencies.

Leaders in child welfare, corrections, and professional associations must develop principles and national standards covering parents in prison and their children and adopt these standards as a part of the accreditation process for child welfare agencies and correctional institutions. When parents are in prison and their children are under the custody of the state, families and children experience unique problems, and corrections and child welfare staff are faced with unique challenges. Most states do not have child welfare policies or procedures to address parenting issues during incarceration, and child welfare staff are left, more or less, to their own problem-solving initiative and ingenuity. Child welfare–corrections system collaboration models, family-oriented policy directives, and agency protocols are necessary components of serious efforts to meet the best interests of the child. (See McCarthy, Meyers, and Jackson [n.d.] and Women's Prison Association [n.d.] for examples of collaboration models and protocols.)

New York State has devoted resources to address criminal justice–child welfare collaborations and the Illinois Department of Children and

Family Services provides a staff liaison to handle situations involving children whose mothers are in prison. Development, replication, and evaluation of approaches such as these, and dissemination of products and program reports will help agencies avoid "reinventing the wheel" and enhance their ability to meet children's needs.

Research on prisoners' family roles and relationships and family matters in the criminal justice system must be conducted and the findings incorporated in policy and program development and implementation. To date, no federal agency or foundation has provided funding for a comprehensive program of research on families and the correctional system or identified this topic as a research priority. Most research studies have been one-time efforts with few ongoing programs of research covering any aspect of prisoner family functioning. Consequently, many unanswered questions and untested assumptions remain about such issues as the impact of parental criminality on children and the impact of parental attachments and responsibilities on adult recidivism, among others. Our knowledge about how major human services and corrections policies (such as the Adoption and Safe Families Act), community reentry legislation, and welfare reform affect prisoners' families is also limited, and the true outcomes of policy directives and reforms for families and children must be inferred.

Information about and understanding of program processes and outcomes must also be among the objectives of a knowledge development agenda. It is important to assess the current state of the field. These types of assessments enable program designers and practitioners to build on pioneering research and existing program efforts and on day-to-day work and experiences of program providers, families, and children. The Vera Institute of Justice review of programs serving fathers in prison and the community (Jeffries et al. 2001) and the University of Illinois study of programs serving children and families of prisoners (Bates 2001) provide examples of these types of reviews.

Moving Forward

Prisoners' families face very difficult circumstances and receive limited community support. Nevertheless, they display many strengths and demonstrate a keen sense of kinship and caring that includes their publicly sanctioned family member. They keep trying, often against all odds, to maintain their families and nurture their children. Their commitments and the nation's general interest in protecting children and strengthening families provide sound reasons for policymakers to adopt policies and establish programs that will help prisoners maintain family ties and help families carry out their family obligations and parenting responsibilities. A social investment in prisoners' families and children will require the adoption of more positive views of prisoners' families and family relationships, better understanding of family needs and societal responses, and dedicated attention to changing the prevailing system responses.

REFERENCES

Altshuler, Saundra J. 1999. "The Well-being of Children in Kinship Foster Care." In *Kinship Care: Improving Practice through Research,* edited by James P. Gleeson and Creasie Finney Hairston (117–43). Washington, D.C.: CWLA Press.

Bakker, Laura J., Barbara A. Morris, and Laura M. Janus. 1978. "Hidden Victims of Crime." *Social Work* 23 (2): 143–48.

Bates, Robin. 2001. *Improving Outcomes for Children and Families of Incarcerated Parents.* Chicago: University of Illinois at Chicago, Jane Addams College of Social Work, Jane Addams Center for Social Policy and Research.

Baunach, Phyllis. 1985. *Mothers in Prison.* New Brunswick, N.J.: Transaction Books.

Beckerman, Adele. 1994. "Mothers in Prison: Meeting the Prerequisite Conditions for Permanency Planning." *Social Work* 39 (1): 9–14.

Bernt, Harold, ed. 2001. *Clinical Practice Guidelines.* Milwaukee, Wisc.: Alliance for Children and Families.

Bloom, Barbara, and David Steinhart. 1993. *Why Punish the Children? A Reappraisal of the Children of Incarcerated Mothers in America.* San Francisco: National Council on Crime and Delinquency.

Borgman, Robert. 1985. "The Influence of Family Visiting upon Boys' Behavior in a Juvenile Correctional Institution." *Child Welfare* 64 (6): 629–38.

Carlson, Bonnie E., and Neil Cervera. 1991. "Inmates and Their Families: Conjugal Visits, Family Contact, and Family Functioning." *Criminal Justice and Behavior* 18 (3): 318–31.

Child Welfare League of America. 1998. "State Agency Survey on Children with Incarcerated Parents." Washington, D.C.: Child Welfare League of America.

"Congress Gives Final Approval to Inmate Health Care 'Co-Pay.'" 2000. *Criminal Justice Newsletter* 31 (4): 1.

Daniel, Sally W., and Carol J. Barrett. 1981. "The Needs of Prisoners' Wives: A Challenge for the Mental Health Professions." *Community Mental Health Journal* 17 (4): 310–22.

Dowden, Craig, and Donald A. Andrews. 1999. "What Works for Female Offenders: A Meta-analytic Review." *Crime and Delinquency* 45 (4): 438–52.

Ferraro, Kathleen J., John M. Johnson, Stephen R. Jorgensen, and F. G. Bolton Jr. 1983. "Problems of Prisoners' Families: The Hidden Costs of Imprisonment." *Journal of Family Issues* 4 (4): 575–91.

Fishman, Laura T. 1990. *Women at the Wall: A Study of Prisoners' Wives Doing Time on the Outside.* Albany: State University of New York Press.

Gary, Lawrence. 1996. "African American Male Teenagers: Values and Ideal Traits for Success." Jane Addams College of Social Work, University of Illinois at Chicago, Chicago, Illinois.

Genty, Philip. 2001. "Incarcerated Parents and the Adoption and Safe Families Act ("ASFA"): A Challenge for Correctional Service Providers." *The ICCA Journal on Community Corrections* (November): 42–47.

Girshick, Lori. 1996. *Soledad Women.* New York: Praeger Publishing.

Hagan, John, and Jurleigh P. Coleman. 2001. "Returning Captives of the American War on Drugs: Issues of Community and Family Reentry." *Crime and Delinquency* 47 (3): 352–67.

Hairston, Creasie Finney. 1988. "Family Ties during Imprisonment: Do They Influence Future Criminal Activity?" *Federal Probation* 52 (1): 48–52.

———. 1989. "Men in Prison: Family Characteristics and Parenting Views." *Journal of Offender Counseling, Services and Rehabilitation* 14: 3–30.

———. 1991a. "Family Ties during Imprisonment: Important to Whom and for What?" *Journal of Sociology and Social Welfare* 18 (1): 87–104.

———. 1991b. "Mothers in Jail: Parent-Child Separation and Jail Visitation." *Affilia* 6 (2): 9–27.

———. 1992. "Women in Jail: Family Needs and Family Supports." In *The State of Corrections: Proceedings ACA Annual Conference* (179–84). Laurel, Md.: American Correctional Association.

———. 1995. "Fathers in Prison." In *Children of Incarcerated Parents,* edited by Denise Johnston and Katherine Gabel (31–40). Lexington, Mass.: Lexington Books.

———. 1998. "The Forgotten Parent: Understanding the Forces That Influence Incarcerated Fathers' Relationships with Their Children." *Child Welfare* 77 (5): 617–38.

———. 2002. "Fathers in Prison: Responsible Fatherhood and Responsible Public Policies." *Marriage and Family Review* 32 (3/4): 111–35.

Hairston, Creasie Finney, Shonda Wills, and Nancy Wall. 1997. *Children, Families, and Correctional Supervision: Current Policies and New Directions.* Jane Addams College of Social Work, University of Illinois at Chicago, Chicago, Illinois.

Hungerford, G. P. 1993. "The Children of Inmate Mothers: An Exploratory Study of Children, Caregivers and Inmate Mothers in Ohio." Ph.D. diss., Ohio State University, Columbus.

"Inmate Health Care." 1999. *Corrections Compendium* 24 (10): 8–15.

Jeffries, John, Suzanne Menghraj, and Creasie F. Hairston. 2001. *Serving Incarcerated and Ex-offender Fathers and Their Families.* New York: Vera Institute of Justice.

Johnston, Denise. 2001. "Incarceration of Women and Effects on Parenting." Paper presented at the Conference on the Effects of Incarceration on Children and Families, Northwestern University, Evanston, Ill., May 5.

King, Anthony. 1993. "The Impact of Incarceration on African American Families: Implications for Practice." *Journal of Contemporary Human Services* 74 (3): 145–53.

Koban, Linda A. 1983. "Parents in Prison: A Comparative Analysis of the Effects of Incarceration on the Families of Men and Women." *Research in Law, Deviance and Social Control* 5: 171–83.

Koenig, Chelene. 1985. *Life on the Outside: A Report on the Experiences of the Families of Offenders from the Perspective of the Wives of Offenders.* Canada, Pacific Region: Chilliwack Community Services and Correctional Service of Canada.

Lanier, Charles S., Jr. 1991. "Dimensions of Father-Child Interaction in a New York State Prison Population." *Journal of Offender Rehabilitation* 16 (3/4): 27–42.

———. 1993. "Affective States of Fathers in Prison." *Justice Quarterly* 10: 49–65.

Larzelere, Robert E., and Gerald R. Patterson. 1990. "Parental Management: Mediator of the Effect of Socioeconomic Status on Early Delinquency." *Criminology* 28 (2): 301–24.

Lynch, James P., and William J. Sabol. 2001. *Prisoner Reentry in Perspective.* Crime Policy Report No. 3. Washington, D.C.: The Urban Institute.

Martin, Elmer, and Joanne Martin. 1995. *Social Work and the Black Experience.* Washington, D.C.: NASW Press.

Martin, Jamie S. 2001. *Inside Looking Out: Jailed Fathers' Perceptions about Separation from Their Children.* New York: LFB Scholarly Publishing LLC.

McCarthy, Jan, Judith Meyers, and Vivian Jackson. n.d. "The Adoption and Safe Families Act: Exploring the Opportunity for Collaboration between Child Mental Health and Child Welfare Service Systems." Washington, D.C.: National Technical Assistance Center for Children's Mental Health and National Resource Network for Child and Family Mental Health Services.

McLanahan, Sara, and Gary Sandefur. 1994. *Growing Up with a Single Parent: What Hurts, What Helps.* Cambridge, Mass.: Harvard University Press.

Morehouse Research Institute and Institute for American Values. 1999. *Turning the Corner on Father Absence in Black America.* Atlanta, Ga.: Author.

Mumola, Christopher J. 2000. *Incarcerated Parents and Their Children.* Bureau of Justice Statistics Special Report. Washington, D.C.: U.S. Department of Justice.

Nurse, Anne. 2001. "Coming Home to Strangers: Newly Paroled Juvenile Fathers and Their Children." Paper presented at the Conference on the Effects of Incarceration on Children and Families, Northwestern University, Evanston, Ill., May 5.

Petras, Donna. 1999. "The Effect of Caregiver Preparation and Sense of Control on Adaptation of Kinship Caregivers." In *Kinship Care: Improving Practice through Research,* edited by James P. Gleeson and Creasie Finney Hairston (233–55). Washington, D.C.: CWLA Press.

Poe, Lenore M. 1992. *Black Grandparents as Parents.* Berkeley, Calif.: Author.

Reed, Diane F., and Edward L. Reed. 1997. "Children of Incarcerated Parents." *Social Justice* 24 (3): 152–69.

Schneller, Donald P. 1976. *The Prisoner's Family: A Study of the Effects of Imprisonment on the Families of Prisoners.* San Francisco: R and E Research Associates.

Sharp, Susan, and Susan Marcus-Mendoza. 1998. "Gender Differences in the Impact of Incarceration on Children and Spouses of Drug Offenders." Paper presented at the annual meeting of the Academy of Criminal Justice Sciences, Albuquerque, N.M.

Slaght, Evelyn. 1999. "Family and Offender Treatment Focusing on the Family in the Treatment of Substance Abusing Criminal Offenders." *Journal of Drug Education* 19 (1): 53–62.

Swan, L. Alex. 1981. *Families of Black Prisoners: Survival and Progress.* Boston, Mass.: G.K. Hall.

Taylor, Vincent. 1999. "Florida Law Requires Prisons to Improve Visiting Conditions." *Corrections Journal* 3 (21): 3–4.

Tolan, Patrick H., Nancy G. Guerra, and Philip C. Kendall. 1995. "A Developmental-Ecological Perspective on Antisocial Behavior in Children and Adolescents: Toward a Unified Risk and Intervention Framework." *Journal of Consulting and Clinical Psychology* 63 (4): 579–84.

Wall, Nancy. 1997. "Policies Affecting Children Whose Parents Are Incarcerated." *Dialogues on Child Welfare Issues Report.* Chicago: University of Illinois at Chicago.

Women's Prison Association. n.d. *Partnerships between Corrections and Child Welfare.* New York: Author.

Wright, Kevin N., and Karen E. Wright. 1992. "Does Getting Married Reduce the Likelihood of Criminality? A Review of the Literature." *Federal Probation* 56 (3): 50–56.

PART III
The Impact of Incarceration and Reentry on Communities

9

Criminal Justice and Health and Human Services

An Exploration of Overlapping Needs, Resources, and Interests in Brooklyn Neighborhoods

Eric Cadora, with Charles Swartz and Mannix Gordon

A s unprecedented numbers of people return home from prison, state officials, government agencies, community-based programs, and neighborhood residents all face a new set of challenges in maximizing these prisoners' successful reentry into the freeworld. Most incarcerated people come from and return to a small set of inner-city neighborhoods. This situation makes the challenges associated with the reentry phenomenon qualitatively different from considerations restricted exclusively to individuals—it affects entire communities. Traditionally, criminal justice analysis has not taken account of this important community dimension. However, a new analytical tool is making that research possible as never before. Geographical Information Systems (GIS) analysis, otherwise known as computer mapping, has become key to understanding how the removal and return of so many people from a given neighborhood influences health, housing, employment, and social networks in that community and others like it. Even more important, adding information about the residential patterns of other populations participating in government needs-based programs makes the overlap between criminal justice populations and these other groups starkly apparent.

The maps in this chapter represent a step toward better understanding the substantial overlapping needs, resources, and interests of neighborhood residents being served by needs-based programs and the criminal justice system. Developing a neighborhood-level account of demographic and social characteristics, criminal justice populations and resources, and needs-based program populations makes it increasingly apparent that reentry constitutes a critical backdrop to a range of other government services and activities. More important, neighborhood-level analysis suggests opportunities for cross-sector government collaborations and pooled investments that can achieve substantial economies of scale. The maps in this chapter illustrate these overlaps and opportunities using Brooklyn, New York, as an example. In Brooklyn, like most other cities, the challenges of reentry are highly concentrated in a few specific neighborhoods, which turn out to be the same neighborhoods where most people receiving needs-based program services also reside.

Administrative Boundaries

Traditionally, criminal justice and other public policy analyses take place on either a case-by-case basis or at the broad jurisdictional level. However, both these analytical ends of the spectrum miss the cumulative impact that individual decisions have on neighborhoods. To register that important dimension, data must be mapped at the census tract or block-group level. Figure 9.1 provides a bird's-eye view of Brooklyn, New York, showing the administrative boundaries for police precincts and census tracts. Data in the remaining maps will be aggregated to the census tract level so that they register the real contours of resident characteristics, needs-based program services, and criminal justice activity otherwise masked by data analyzed only on the larger jurisdictional level.

Population Profile

It is difficult to understand the impact of needs-based programs or criminal justice services without taking account of important demographic concentrations, such as a community's racial makeup and the percentage of single-parent households and young people living in the community. Figures 9.2 through 9.5 provide a demographic profile of people living in Brooklyn. It is important to note in figures 9.2 and 9.3 the stark difference in residential concentration between the black and white populations (which continues to pervade most urban areas), because criminal justice activity disproportionately affects low-income communities of color. In Brooklyn, communities of color are highly concentrated in the central and eastern sections of the borough.

Figure 9.4 illustrates the high percentage of single-parent households in the census tracts that make up central, east central, and west central Brooklyn, areas that represent populations with fewer familial resources at hand. Figure 9.5 shows the high percentage of youth in these tracts as well as in those tracts in south central and north Brooklyn, demonstrating where child support resources are most needed. Figures 9.4 and 9.5 set the stage for information about the concentrated provision of government needs-based program services—such as Temporary Assistance to Needy Families (TANF) and public assistance for children—found in figures 9.6 and 9.7.

Needs-Based Program Populations

Figures 9.6 through 9.8 identify those census tracts in Brooklyn that are home to the highest percentages of government needs-based program recipients (e.g., those individuals receiving TANF, public assistance to children, and Medicaid). Recipients of needs-based program services are typically concentrated in particular neighborhoods. Figure 9.6 illustrates how TANF recipients tend to cluster in the same places as single-parent households (see figure 9.4), and figure 9.7 shows how children receiving public assistance tend to be located in areas with high concentrations of youth (see figure 9.5).

Although not evenly distributed across neighborhoods, Medicaid recipients (figure 9.8) are much more widely disbursed than are recipients of TANF and public assistance for children. Medicaid is accessed by a broader spectrum of residents, including other white ethnic populations that, although they constitute low-income residents, do not otherwise coincide with patterns of single-parent households or households with high proportions of children.

Criminal Justice Populations

It is vitally important to understand incarceration, reintegration, and community supervision as a backdrop to the provision of needs-based program services. Figures 9.9 through 9.13 illustrate the concentration of criminal justice populations, resources, and activity across Brooklyn neighborhoods. Figure 9.9 shows the number of residents who are admitted to jail and prison in a single year, and identifies those few neighborhoods in which these residents are most concentrated. In Brooklyn, neighborhoods exhibiting the highest incarceration rate experience nine times as many admissions to jail and prison each year as those areas exhibiting the lowest rate. Moreover, incarceration and reentry takes place over a relatively short period of time—66 percent of incarcerated residents return home in fewer than three years—producing a potentially destabilizing migration pattern in these neighborhoods.

Neighborhood incarceration rates differ from the more traditionally mapped crime rates. In addition, crime patterns differ according to type of crime. Figures 9.10a and 9.10b identify police precincts with the highest crime rates according to type of crime. For example, figure 9.10a illustrates how property crime tends to concentrate in neighborhoods that are better off and do not experience high incarceration rates (e.g., downtown Brooklyn's 84th precinct is a high property-crime precinct, but not a high-incarceration neighborhood). Figure 9.10b indicates that violent crime is more common in high-incarceration neighborhoods (e.g., the 73rd precinct is a high violent-crime precinct and a high-incarceration neighborhood). Moreover, overall crime rates are more evenly distributed across neighborhoods than are incarceration rates. In Brooklyn, the crime rate for the precinct with the most crime is only about three times higher than the rate for the precinct with the lowest crime rate.

Another way to understand criminal justice policy as a backdrop to the provision of needs-based program services is to specify the deployment of resources geographically. For example, case-by-case decisions sending large numbers of residents from a few particular neighborhoods to and returning them from incarceration adds up financially. Figure 9.11 tallies the dollars spent on jail and prison for each census tract during a single year. Some neighborhoods are home to "million dollar blocks" in which more than a million dollars per year are spent to incarcerate and return residents. Cumulatively, nearly $50 million dollars are spent each year to remove residents from and return them to each of the Brooklyn neighborhoods with the highest incarceration rates. Accounting for resource deployment in any particular geographical location is important because the cumulative social impact may be broader than intended by any individual decision. Furthermore, when considered in retrospect as a pool of resources, more strategic options for investing these monies to affect positive changes in the neighborhood as a whole may become apparent.

Concentrations of residents under the supervision of probation and parole authorities mirror those of incarcerated residents (see figure 9.9). Figure 9.12 shows that, in a single neighborhood, thousands of residents are under the supervision of two separate criminal justice agencies—the New York City Department of Probation and the New York State Division of Parole. From a community perspective, therefore, these overlaps present opportunities for collaborations among these agencies.

As with incarceration expenditures, the deployment of probation and parole supervision resources is important to understand geographically. For example, figure 9.13a shows the distribution of one probation officer's caseload in Brooklyn. That officer supervises 76 "high-risk" probationers. The police precinct (75th) highlighted in figure 9.13b maps 218 high-risk probationers. Notably, these probationers fall into the caseloads of 43 different officers despite the fact that 218 probationers constitute numbers equal to only about three caseloads.

The obvious opportunity made evident by this geographical caseload analysis is that all the high-risk probationers in this precinct could theoretically be assigned to three officers. Moreover, if these officers worked in the precinct instead of the downtown office, they would have a substantially greater understanding of the neighborhood in which their caseloads were located.

Criminal Justice and Needs-Based Program Populations

Comparing the rates of incarcerated residents and residents receiving TANF in Brooklyn (figures 9.14a and 9.14b, expressed in terms of standard deviations from the mean) shows substantial overlap in the highest concentration neighborhoods. This geographical overlap suggests coincident populations. Furthermore, such overlap implies that considerable resources are being invested in the same place by different government agencies without coordination, indicating policy interventions that, at worst, are working against one another other and, at best, do not maximize opportunities to blend resources in more effective service combinations.

Figures 9.15a and 9.15b show that when we further specify populations, such as incarcerated parents and children receiving public assistance, the overlap in neighborhood concentrations is even more acute. Such overlapping suggests not only that government policies may be in conflict with one another, but also that opportunities exist for economy-of-scale collaborations between criminal justice and health and human service agencies.

Incarcerated Residents and TANF Recipients in Nine Blocks in the 79th Precinct

Figure 9.16 provides a close-up view of nine specific blocks in the 79th precinct. Figure 9.16a shows the number of incarcerated residents from those blocks, and figure 9.16b shows the number of TANF recipients in those same nine blocks. The substantial overlap in such a small area is more evidence of the coincident populations being served by each of these government agencies and further suggests that involvement in the criminal justice system provides an undeniable backdrop to the provision of needs-based government services.

Conclusion

As the coincidence between criminal justice populations and populations served by other government programs becomes increasingly apparent, opportunities for collaboration also emerge. Although the reentry phenomenon is currently understood as a criminal justice issue, solutions to the challenges that are posed by so many people returning to their neighborhoods from prison cannot be found within the justice system alone. Instead, such problem solving requires a coordinated effort among actors ranging from state officials to neighborhood associations. The most prominent opportunities for community-level collaboration already exist between the health and human services and the criminal justice systems. And by penetrating the community level, mapping can help foster these collaborations, particularly now as the criminal justice system is more open to partnership than ever before.

NOTE

This chapter has been adapted from a mapping presentation developed for the "From Prisons to Home" National Policy Conference sponsored by the U.S. Department of Health and Human Services on January 30–31, 2002. The author would like to thank Charles Swartz, Geographic Research Solutions, and Mannix Gordon, Pratt Institute Center for Community and Environmental Development, for their assistance in producing the maps for this project. The author would also like to thank the New York State Division of Criminal Justice Services, the New York State Division of Parole, the New York City Department of Corrections, the New York City Department of Probation, and the New York City Human Resources Administration for their cooperation in providing and analyzing the data.

Figure 9.1. *Administrative Boundaries for Brooklyn, New York, 2000*

Data source: New York City Department of City Planning.

Figure 9.2. *White Population of Brooklyn, New York, 2000 (Percentage)*

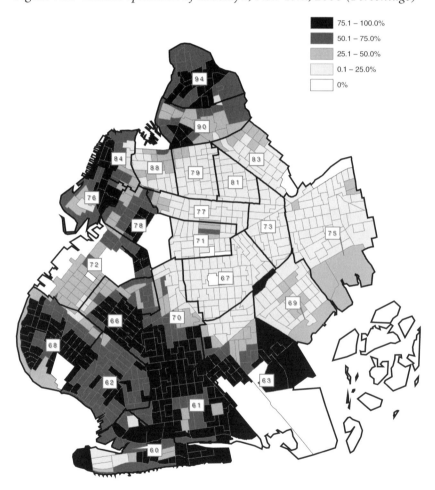

Data source: U.S. Census 2000.

Figure 9.3. *Black Population of Brooklyn, New York, 2000 (Percentage)*

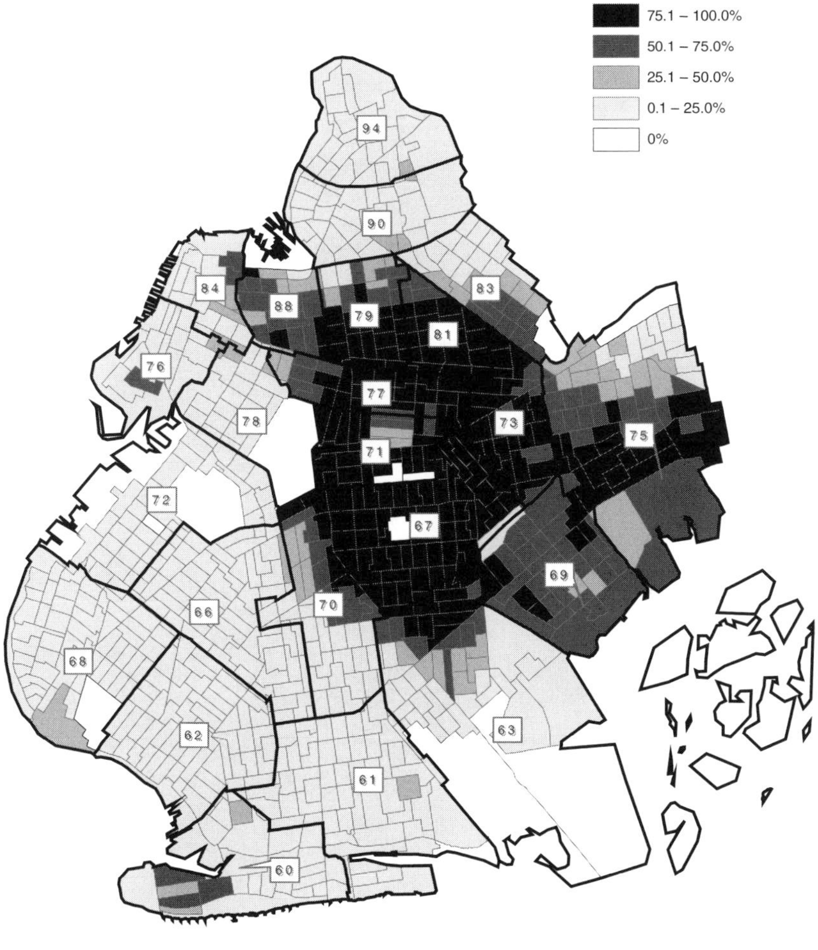

Data source: U.S. Census 2000.

Figure 9.4. *Single-Parent Households in Brooklyn, New York, 2000 (Percentage)*

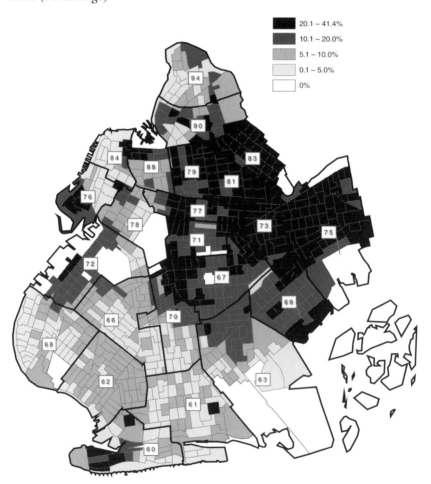

Data source: U.S. Census 2000.

Figure 9.5. *Children under Age 18 in Brooklyn, New York, 2000 (Percentage)*

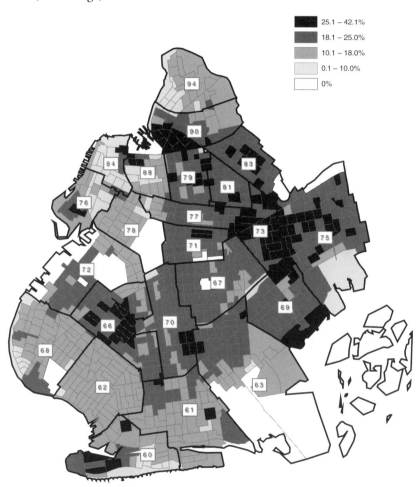

25.1 – 42.1%
18.1 – 25.0%
10.1 – 18.0%
0.1 – 10.0%
0%

Data source: U.S. Census 2000.

Figure 9.6. *Residents Receiving TANF in Brooklyn, New York, 2000 (Percentage)*

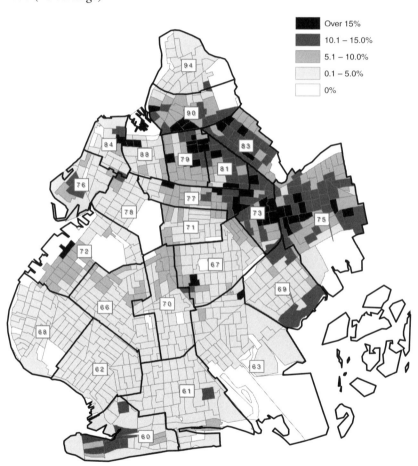

Data source: New York City Human Resources Administration.

Figure 9.7. *Children Receiving Public Assistance in Brooklyn, New York, 2000 (Percentage)*

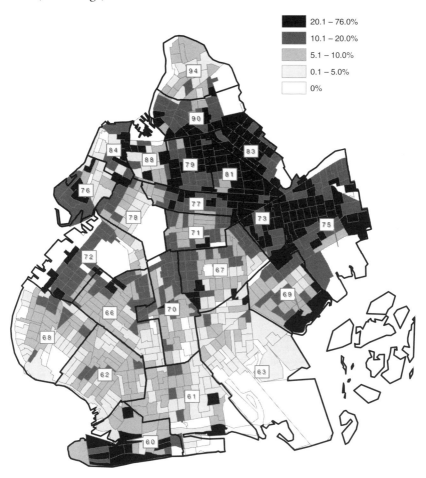

20.1 – 76.0%
10.1 – 20.0%
5.1 – 10.0%
0.1 – 5.0%
0%

Data source: New York City Human Resources Administration.

Figure 9.8. *Population on Medicaid in Brooklyn, New York, 2000 (Percentage)*

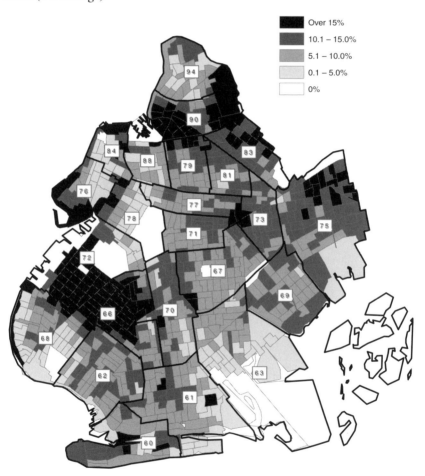

Data source: New York City Human Resources Administration.

Figure 9.9. *Jail and Prison Admissions in Brooklyn, New York, 1998*

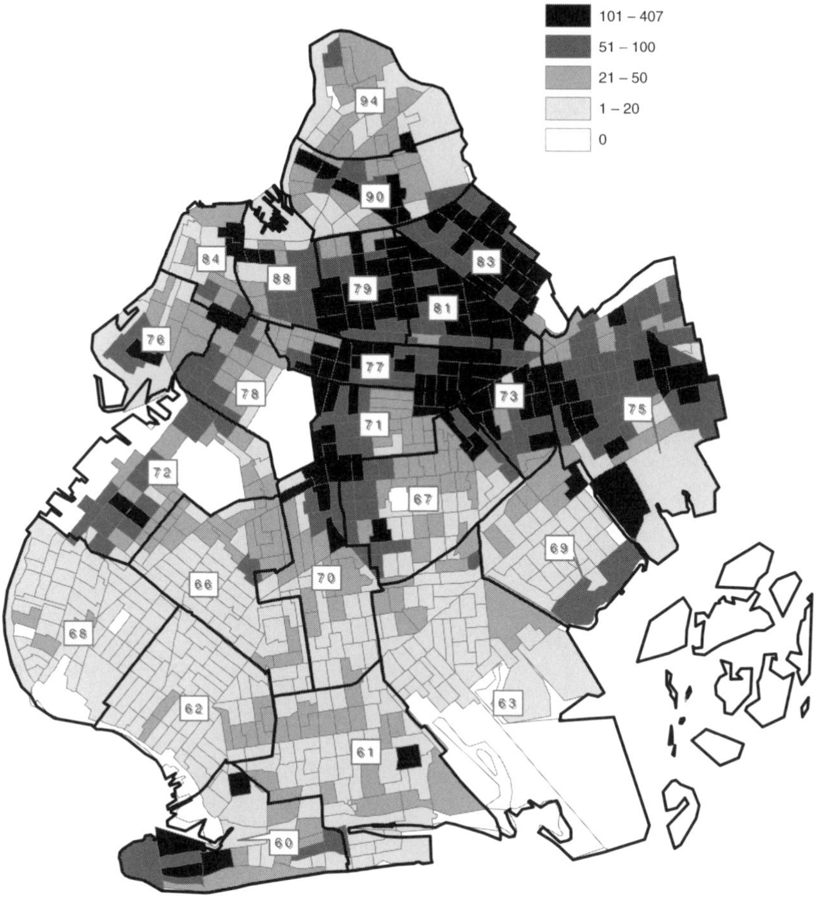

Data sources: New York City Department of Corrections and the New York State Division of Criminal Justice Services.

Figure 9.10a. *Property Crime per 1,000 Residents in Brooklyn, New York, 2000*

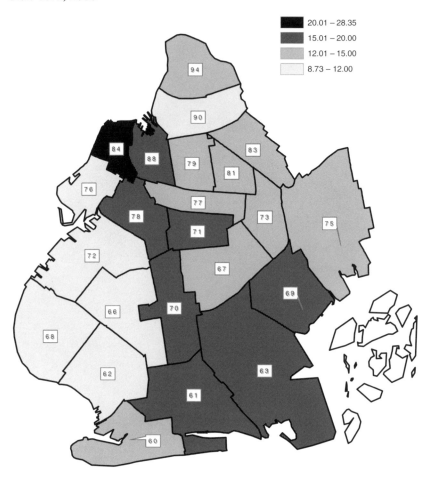

Data source: New York City Police Department.

Figure 9.10b. *Violent Crime per 1,000 Residents in Brooklyn, New York, 2000*

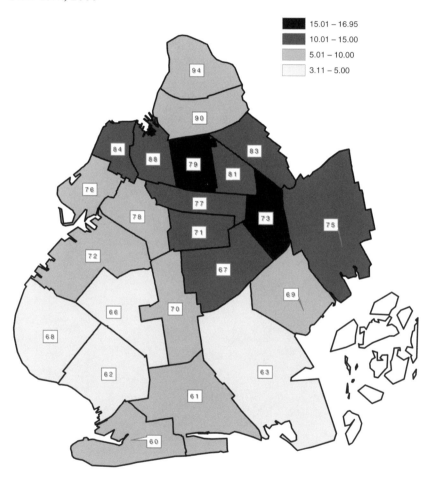

Data source: New York City Police Department.

Figure 9.11. *Jail and Prison Expenditures in Brooklyn, New York, 1998*

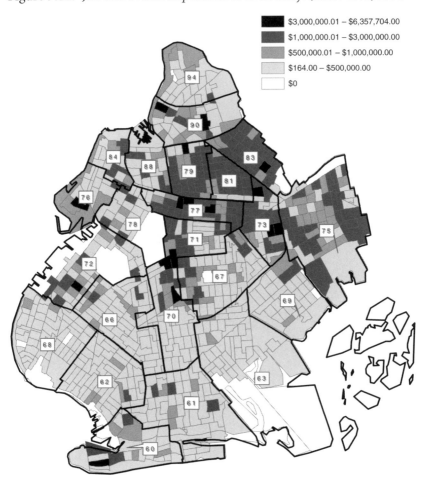

Data sources: New York City Department of Corrections and the New York State Division of Criminal Justice Services.

Figure 9.12. *Residents on Probation and Parole in Brooklyn, New York, 1999–2000*

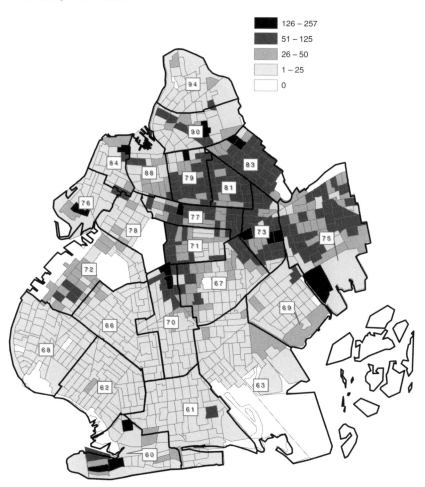

Data sources: New York City Department of Probation and the New York State Division of Parole.

Figure 9.13a. *Caseload of Probation Officer A ("High-Risk" Supervision Level Three) in Brooklyn, New York, 1999*

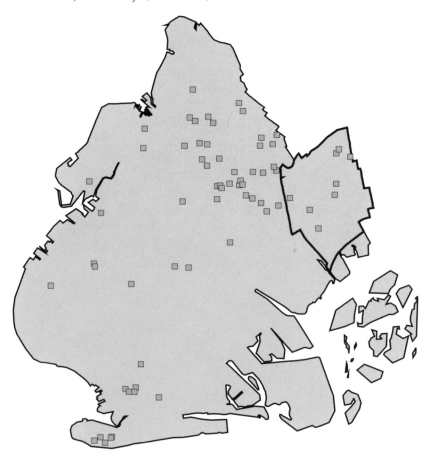

Data source: New York City Department of Probation.

Figure 9.13b. *Number and Residence of All "High-Risk" Supervision Probationers in the 75th Precinct Showing Ideal Caseload Assignments, 1999*

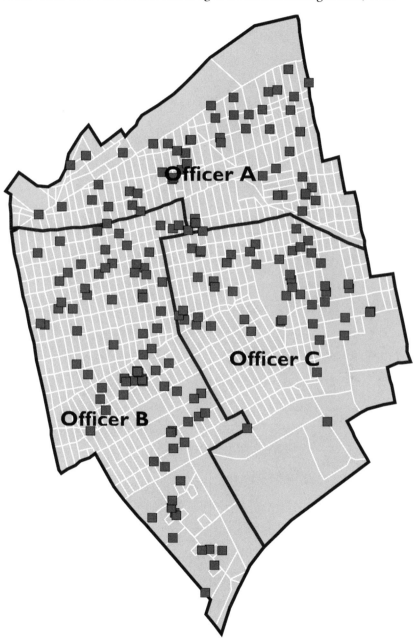

Data source: New York City Department of Probation.

Figure 9.14a. *Rate of Incarcerated Residents in Brooklyn, New York, 1998*

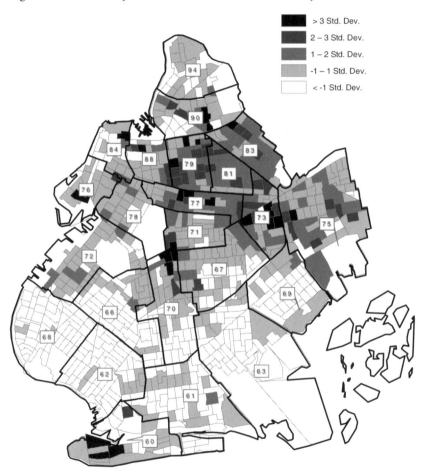

Data sources: New York City Department of Corrections and the New York State Division of Criminal Justice Services.

Figure 9.14b. *Rate of TANF Recipients in Brooklyn, New York, 2000*

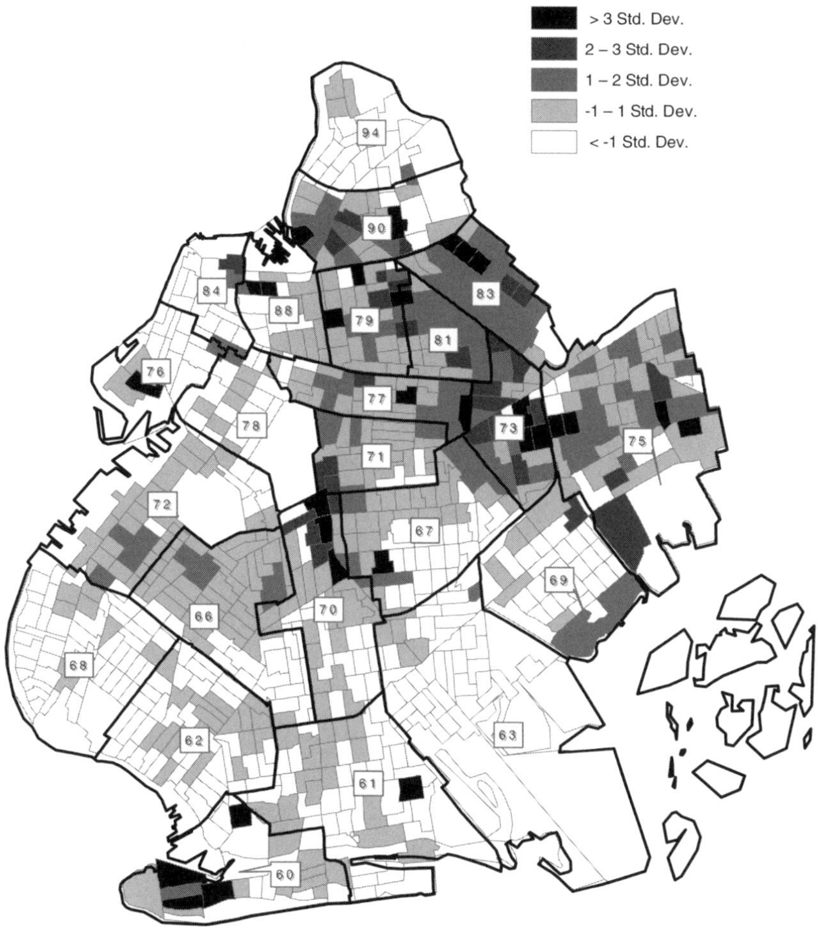

> 3 Std. Dev.
2 – 3 Std. Dev.
1 – 2 Std. Dev.
-1 – 1 Std. Dev.
< -1 Std. Dev.
94
90
83
84
88
79
81
76
77
78
73
75
71
72
67
69
66
70
68
62
63
61
60

Data source: New York City Human Resources Administration.

Figure 9.15a. *Rate of Incarcerated Parents in Brooklyn, New York, 1998*

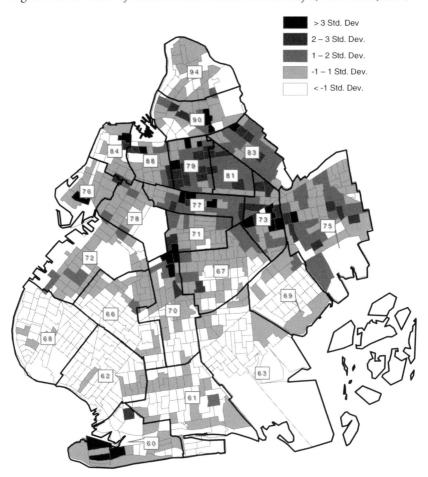

Data sources: New York City Department of Corrections and the New York State Division of Criminal Justice Services.

Figure 9.15b. *Rate of Children Receiving Public Assistance in Brooklyn, New York, 2000*

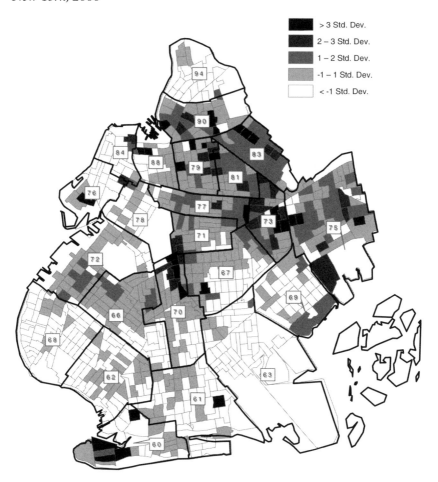

Data source: New York City Human Resources Administration.

Figure 9.16a. *Incarcerated Residents, Nine Blocks in Brooklyn, New York, 1998*

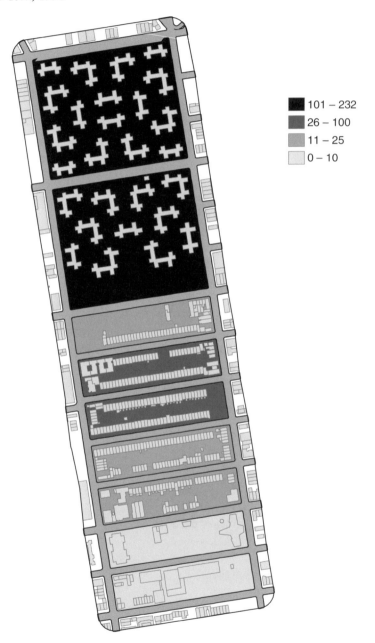

101 – 232
26 – 100
11 – 25
0 – 10

Data sources: New York City Department of Corrections and the New York State Division of Criminal Justice Services.

Figure 9.16b. *TANF Recipients, Nine Blocks in Brooklyn, New York, 2000*

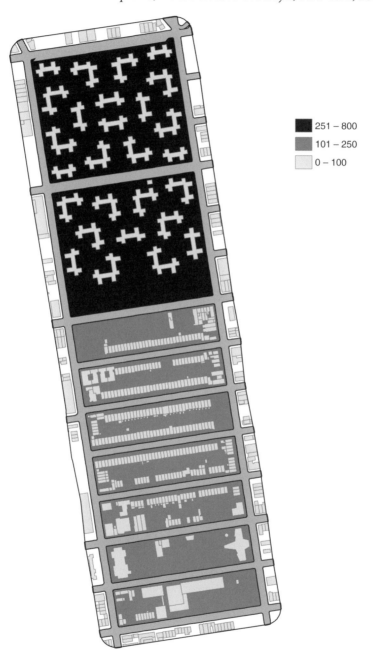

251 – 800
101 – 250
0 – 100

Data source: New York City Human Resources Administration.

10

Incarceration, Reentry, and Social Capital

Social Networks in the Balance

Dina R. Rose and Todd R. Clear

Recent reports indicate that 606,226 individuals were released from state and federal prisons in 2000 (Beck, Karlberg, and Harrison 2002) and even more have been released each year since then. Obviously, policymakers and citizens alike are concerned about preventing recidivism among these offenders as they make the transition from prison to the community. Equally important, however, is the process of reuniting released prisoners with their families and, since many prisoners are parents, with their children. Not much is known about the reentry process, especially within communities that experience high concentrations of incarceration. This chapter explores how reentry is likely to affect social networks and the implications of these effects for residents, particularly children, living in these areas.

Most prisoners have children. A 1999 study by the Bureau of Justice Statistics indicates that 55 percent of state prisoners and 63 percent of federal prisoners reported having a child under the age of 18. Further, 46 percent of these inmate parents lived with their children prior to incarceration. As a result, in 1999, incarceration affected more than 300,000 households with minor children (Mumola 2000). While some children benefit from the incarceration of a parent, research shows most children also experience some degree of harm (Hagan and Dinovitzer 1999). Whether or not the time of release is an opportunity for ex-prisoners to reestablish or create positive parent-child relationships is unclear, because not much is known about the reentry process and the impact of prisoners' release on their children.

The current focus on ex-prisoners' propensity toward recidivism also overlooks the cumulative impact of incarceration and reentry when it is concentrated in a handful of communities. Due to the spatial concentration of incarceration, certain neighborhoods are affected more than others by offenders' removal and return. In these areas, therefore, children experience the effects of incarceration not only in their own homes, but also in the community at large. Even those residents whose immediate family members have not been incarcerated are subject to its influence because it shapes the quality of life in those communities. As Case and Katz (1991) note, in some neighborhoods, children "are more likely to know someone involved in the criminal justice system than to know someone who is employed in a profession such as law or medicine" (cited in Hagan and Dinovitzer 1999). At the same time, certain unintended consequences of incarceration—elevated stigma, financial stress, fractured identities, and low self-esteem—affect all the residents living in these areas (Clear, Rose, and Ryder 2001; Rose, Clear, and Ryder 2000). While these results are problematic on their own, they are additionally troublesome because they lead to other detrimental outcomes. For instance, one way people manage the impact of stigma is to withdraw from community life. When this occurs on a large scale, the vitality and well-being of local businesses, churches, and other elements of community life are diminished.

This chapter considers how incarceration, concentrated in certain places, can damage the capacity of those places to meet the needs of residents, especially children. We begin by reviewing studies of "coercive mobility," the process of removing and returning community residents through incarceration and release from prison. We then consider the implications of coercive mobility for a community's ability to exercise informal social control—the capacity to enforce local norms and values. Social capital and collective efficacy—the capability of groups to achieve desired outcomes, particularly related to safety—are direct byproducts of the vitality of local social linkages and networks. Thus, we examine how coercive mobility affects informal social control by studying its influence on local social networks and their subsequent impact on levels of social capital and collective efficacy, the building blocks of healthy communities.

This study provides a theoretical framework for understanding coercive mobility as a potential threat to communities and shows how children in particular can be at risk from high levels of incarceration in the neighborhoods where they live. Having built this theoretical framework, we examine the practical implications of the reentry process for a community's social capital. Using the results of qualitative research in two high-incarceration neighborhoods, we show how reentry can be thought of as an opportunity to build the kind of stronger social networks that can serve as a framework for enhanced social capital. We show, in particular, how a comprehensive reentry program operating at the neighborhood level might improve the social capital of that area.

Coercive Mobility and Neighborhoods

Recently, Rose and Clear (1998a) theorized that incarceration and reentry destabilize neighborhoods by increasing levels of disorganization. Social disorganization is the inability of communities to regulate their residents' behavior because of deleterious environmental conditions. These conditions lead to a disrupted neighborhood organizational structure that subsequently attenuates residents' ties to each other and to the community. As a result, some residents no longer submit to normative social controls. Therefore, some communities are unable to realize the common values of their residents and solve commonly experienced problems (Kornhauser 1978). Disorganized communities cannot establish or maintain consensus concerning values, norms, roles, or hierarchical arrangements among its members (Kornhauser 1978; Shaw and McKay 1942).

The original theorists Shaw and McKay (1942) identified three characteristics associated with variation in crime rates across different neighborhoods: economic status, degree of residential mobility, and the extent of ethnic heterogeneity. Since then, researchers have identified other factors associated with social disorganization and crime, such as the percentage of unemployed workers and single parents in the population and the structural density of housing units. Working from the social disorganization framework, we argued (Rose and Clear 1998a) that coercive mobility (the dual processes of incarceration and reentry) is harmful in high concentrations because it can disrupt local social networks. In high-incarceration neighborhoods, the process of incarceration and reentry creates an environment where many residents are constantly in flux. In some neighborhoods, as many as 15 percent of parent-aged, male residents are incarcerated every year (CASES 2000). Upon release, ex-prisoners continue their pattern of residential instability, frequently relying upon local shelters for lodging (Fleisher and Decker 2001). Consequently, combining the number of people admitted to prison with the number released annually shows how coercive mobility would decrease residential stability.

Coercive mobility also contributes to residential mobility because it increases the likelihood that family members and other residents will also move. Family members often move because of financial hardship resulting from a loved one's incarceration. Studies show that children, especially those whose mothers are imprisoned, frequently move to live with a new caregiver because of the incarceration of one of their parents (O'Brien 2001; Sharp and Marcus-Mendoza 2001). Siblings sometimes are separated from each other (Sharp and Marcus-Mendoza 2001) and sent to new homes to live. Furthermore, families sometimes try to help relatives returning from prison by moving to new areas without the old "bad" influences. At the same time, residents without incarcerated family members sometimes seek to escape a neighborhood they view as either deteriorating or limited in its ability to provide appropriate opportunities for families and children (Rose et al. 2000). Thus, in high-incarceration neighborhoods, incarceration and reentry produce significant rates of residential mobility, a condition associated with disrupted social networks and diminished community stability.

Communities that experience turnover are considered less stable in many ways, and a large body of literature examines the relationship between residential mobility, social disorganization, and crime. Experts believe that high rates of residential mobility impact communities by creating an environment where residents are isolated from one other. This condition reduces collective sentiment and action (Sampson 1991). In these environments, low levels of integration and high levels of anonymity impede social cohesion (Crutchfield 1989; Crutchfield, Geerken, and Gove 1982). Mobility is also thought to reduce residents' commitment to their community, thereby reducing their stake in collective action. In this sense, mobility contributes to an atmosphere of anonymity that impedes informal social control (Warner and Pierce 1993).

As a form of residential mobility, incarceration disrupts social networks in a variety of ways. Some results are straightforward—incarceration removes people from their familial and friendship relationships. Some results are more complex—relationships are strained when residents withdraw from community life to cope with financial problems or the stigma of having a family member in prison. Reentry, however, does not automatically remediate these problems; sometimes it might exacerbate them. Fractured families may reunite and repair relationships with one another with the return of a loved one. On the other hand, they may disintegrate further under the strain of trying to reabsorb a formerly absent family member. Neighbors may welcome back old friends or they may withdraw further out of fear. Other effects are more indirect. For instance, residents may stop socializing when groups of people are targeted for increased police surveillance in neighborhoods known to house ex-prisoners. In this way, networks among nonincarcerated individuals may also be disrupted (Rose et al. 2000).

To the extent that excessive coercive mobility can damage local social networks, it can also increase the level of disadvantage in the community overall. According to a growing body of empirical evidence, high levels of coercive mobility can result in increased crime. Two recent studies find that, just as crime increases incarceration, concentrated incarceration increases crime at the neighborhood level (Clear et al. 2003; Lynch et al. 2001). Clear et al. (2003) also find that reentry increases crime. Thus, incarceration can contribute to the very problem it is intended to solve. Furthermore, while some empirical evidence provides inconclusive information on incarceration's effects on family structure (Myers 2000), other work is beginning to show that the connection between incarceration, reentry, and crime is the disruption of social networks, including weakened families and other institutions in the community (Rose et al. 2000; Lynch et al. 2001). Indeed, Lynch et al. (2001) find that incarceration decreases participation in voluntary associations and feelings of community solidarity. They also find that incarceration marginally increases participation in informal social control (e.g., the willingness to intervene in neighborhood burglaries and rowdy teen behavior), but incarceration's positive effects are much smaller than its negative effects. Lynch et al. interpret their findings to mean that incarceration weakens the community's organizational life at the same time that it "taints" the area for those who remain. Thus, "coercion may solve one problem in the short term but create others in the longer term" (Lynch et al. 2001, 30).

These studies have begun to clarify how incarceration impacts the community, but we still know very little about this process. At the same time, reentry's implications are also unclear. Will these communities be disadvantaged further by receiving high numbers of ex-prisoners, some of whom are bound to recidivate? Will an increase in residential mobility associated with ex-prisoners returning home diminish already low levels of social capital? Or, will these areas benefit from the opportunity to strengthen social networks made possible by returning people to their homes, their families, and their communities? For children living in these communities, the answers are crucial.

To address these questions, we explore the aggregate impact of offender reentry on community levels of social capital and its effect on children living in these areas. We consider the relationship between reentry and social capital by drawing upon recent research from a series of focus group and individual interviews in two high-incarceration neighborhoods in Florida (Rose et al. 2000). Then we discuss the unique ways in which reentry is expected to impact children living in these types of areas.

Neighborhoods, Social Capital, and Collective Efficacy

Individualistic public policies that focus solely on offenders overlook the importance of neighborhoods. Local areas must be considered when we think about the impact of incarceration and reentry because they provide the environments that contextualize the lives of offenders and nonoffenders alike. Local areas afford opportunities and constraints for both normative and nonnormative behavior.

For children, the neighborhood context is especially important. Children's lives are centered more on the neighborhood than are the lives of adults because children's families, friends, schools, and so on are in one area. Many aspects of children's development are influenced by neighborhood environment (see Furstenberg and Hughes 1997 for review). It is not hard to see how family, school, community organizations, and peer groups are important social spheres for children and that these tend to be geographically centered (Stanton-Salazar 1997). While this is true for some adults, particularly those living in disadvantaged neighborhoods, many adults are influenced by multiple contexts because they live in one environment, work in a second, and socialize in yet a third. Furthermore, because children are in the process of acquiring all their skills and resources, deficits in one area (i.e., educational attainment) are likely to contribute to deficits in another area (i.e., social development). This is true particularly for children with weaker family structures because they depend more on institutional forms of support (Stanton-Salazar 1997).

Although research on incarceration's impact has not focused much on community, the neighborhood as a unit of analysis is nothing new to researchers interested in the spatial concentration of crime. For instance, the "broken windows" thesis (Wilson and Kelling 1982) attributes crime to resident apathy and low levels of social control evidenced by signs of disorder, such as graffiti, vacant lots, and boarded-up houses. Similarly, social disorganization theory (Shaw and McKay 1942) centers on the idea that some communities experience more crime than others because aggregate poverty, joblessness, single-parent families, and other factors reduce the capacity for informal social control (the ability to informally regulate residents' behavior).

Connecting these neighborhood-level theories of crime is the idea that community structure can increase or decrease levels of informal social control and, subsequently, residents' ability to combat crime. Since informal social control is partly a byproduct of networks within the family, within the community, and between the community and the broader society (Bursik and Grasmick 1993), factors that influence networks affect informal social control as well. Therefore, understanding how incarceration and reentry impact social networks at the community level is crucial.

Community-level research now recognizes the importance of networks for community well-being. In particular, networks are necessary for building and maintaining social capital—the ability of groups to obtain resources (such as better jobs, schools, and roads) through connections they have to one another (Paxton 1999). Thus, communities successful at getting what they need often do it through whom they know. Social capital is important because people who have it also have access to people with greater amounts of economic and cultural capital who may serve as important resources (Wall, Ferrazzi, and Schryer 1998). In this way, social capital is important for neighborhoods because it helps residents realize their collective goals: reduced crime, increased supervision of children, accumulation of new resources, and so on. Neighborhoods with disrupted social networks suffer from diminished social capital and, as a result, are less capable of securing goods and services for their residents. Consequently, activists and policymakers need to evaluate social policies based upon the ways in which they alter social networks.

Although there seems to be consensus that social capital contributes to neighborhood quality of life, researchers have had a difficult time defining it. For instance, Coleman first defined social capital as a form of social organization that "makes possible the achievement of certain ends" (Coleman 1990, 302). Subsequently, Portes (1998) defined social capital more in terms of the benefits secured by membership in social networks, and Putnam defined it as the "features of social organization, such as networks, norms and trust, that facilitate coordination and cooperation for mutual benefit" (Putnam 1993a, 36). Social capital, then, is *a byproduct of social relationships that provides the capacity for collective understanding and action.*

Most people think of social capital as a resource that groups use to obtain positive goals, but this need not be the case. The presence of ample supplies of social capital in a neighborhood does not guarantee that residents will benefit. In fact, Sampson, Morenoff, and Earls (1999) point out that social capital can be used for negative as well as positive outcomes. The "networks, norms, and trust" at the heart of Putnam's (1993a) definition of social capital, for instance, can either foster or inhibit criminal activity. To the extent that returning ex-prisoners maintain ties with former "colleagues," pockets of social capital may be enhanced or maintained, but in ways that do not benefit the community. Indeed, Fleisher and Decker (2001) comment that it is unrealistic to expect ex-prisoners to sever ties to gangs because forgoing social capital investments increases their social isolation and reduces the amount of social support available to them. In these cases, individuals indeed associate with groups characterized by high levels of social capital, but not the kind of social capital ex-prisoners attempting to navigate successful reentry can utilize.

Despite attempts to sharpen our understanding of social capital, it has been difficult to move beyond these vague definitions. In fact, refining the definition of social capital is outside the scope of this chapter. Instead, we work with the concept of social capital by recognizing that most definitions include statements about social relations, norms, trust, and obligations. They also infer that social capital is a resource derived from relationships among group members in which groups (and the people within them) obtain things they need. In other words, social capital is only good for what it gets you.

Children and Social Capital

Social capital is important for children because it shapes their life chances. For example, communities with high levels of social capital have lower levels of homicide (Rosenfeld, Messner, and Baumer 2001) and violent crime associated with firearms (Kennedy et al. 1998). Social capital also is related to school performance (Coleman 1988; Israel, Beaulieu, and Hartless 2001; Parcel and Dufur 2001a) because communities with ample social capital provide an environment in which academic achievement is supported on many levels. For instance, areas with low levels of social capital also exhibit low trust levels, a situation that makes developing ties between youth and school personnel difficult, particularly for minority students. In these cases, therefore, diminished social capital translates into poorer school experiences for children needing this type of support the most. It also translates into attenuated networks and a reduction in the production of new social capital (Stanton-Salazar 1997).

Social capital also has been shown to increase child well-being. One study (Runyan et al. 1998) found that children with social capital were 66 percent more likely than children without such capital to obtain developmental and behavioral scores within normal limits. Another shows social capital impacts child anxiety, bullying, tendency to withdraw, and difficulty relating to peers (Parcel and Dufur 2001b).

Since one way social capital is transmitted to children is through their parents, family social capital (the byproduct of relationships between adults and children) is important to consider as well. Family capital reduces delinquency and increases prosocial adult development (Wright, Cullen, and Miller 2001). On the other hand, marital discord reduces family capital by diminishing parent-child relationships. This result, in turn, is associated with higher levels of child aggression (Harrist and Ainslie 1998). Consequently, policies that disrupt intrafamily relations can be as damaging as those that disrupt interfamily relations. Additionally, because these two forms of capital are related—each producing more of the other—policies that impact one form of capital will naturally impact the other.

Collective Efficacy

To distinguish between social capital in general and social capital geared toward public safety, researchers have begun to explore "collective efficacy" and its relationship to community levels of crime. Work on collective efficacy is still in its infancy, and definitions have alternately focused on distinguishing between social control and other outcomes of social capital and between the presence of a potential resource (social capital) and the activation of the resource (collective efficacy) (see Sampson, Raudenbush, and Earls 1997; Sampson et al. 1999). Despite these definitional problems, the concept of collective efficacy is useful because it focuses on social capital utilized specifically for social control purposes. Furthermore, research shows that local organizations, voluntary associations, and social ties *do* promote collective efficacy (Morenoff, Sampson, and Raudenbush 2001) and that collective efficacy has been shown to reduce crime (Morenoff et al. 2001; Sampson et al. 1997; Sampson and Raudenbush 1999).[1] For the purpose of understanding the reentry's impact on community structure, distinguishing between social capital and collective efficacy is less important than recognizing that community social control is a byproduct of social networks that can be affected by incarceration and reentry. In fact, Sampson et al.'s (1999) recent call for a renewed focus on the role of residential stability in contributing to collective efficacy mirrors Rose and Clear's (1998a) argument that coercive mobility is a destabilizing process because of its impact on social capital. Both views recognize that the volume and pattern of residents moving in and out of a neighborhood influence the networks that, in part, determine the neighborhood's quality of life.

Social Capital and Reentry

The utility of social capital as a concept for both policy analysis and implementation is impeded by the abstract definitions of social capital. Given the lack of specificity in defining this concept, it is not surprising that different researchers have operationalized or measured social capital differently. Putnam (1993b), for instance, measures social capital as the density of voluntary organizations. Paxton (1999) identifies trust and associations as the key components of social capital. Rosenfeld et al. (2001) measure it as social trust and civic engagement. Taking a slightly different approach, Forrest and Kearns (2001) recently identified eight domains of social capital with the goal of developing measures that could be influenced directly by social policy. Social capital, they argue, is composed of the following factors:

- Empowerment (residents feel they have a voice, are involved in processes that affect them, and can take action to initiate change)
- Participation (in social and community activities so local events are well attended)
- Associational activity and common purposes (cooperation resulting in the formation of formal and informal groups to further collective interests)
- Supporting networks and reciprocity (individual and organizational cooperation to support mutual and one-sided gain and an expectation that help is available if needed)
- Collective norms and values
- Trust (both between co-residents and between residents and local organizations)
- Safety (resulting in no restrictions of public space because of fear)
- Belonging (residents feel connected to each other and their home area and feel they belong to the place and its people)

While only one of the eight components specifically relates to networks in the community, it is clear that each component is a byproduct of the strength and quality of social relations in the neighborhood. The benefit of Forrest and Kearns's approach to understanding social capital is that it provides a strategy for assessing the impact of public policy on communities. Thus, to the extent a policy enhances one or more of these domains it can be said to positively affect community life, and to the extent a policy diminishes a dimension of social capital it can be said to negatively impact community life.

In a recent report (Rose et al. 2000), we identified some of the ways residents living in areas characterized by high concentrations of coercive mobility thought they, their families, and their communities were affected by the processes of incarceration and reentry. Through thematic content analysis from a series of focus group and individual interviews with residents in two high-incarceration neighborhoods, we identified four main issues stemming from incarceration and reentry and affecting residents living in high-concentration communities: finances, stigma, identity, and relationships. Here we summarize some of the ways reentry influences these factors and then look at how these factors, in turn, might impact social capital using Forrest and Kearns's (2001) components of social capital as a framework.[2] Figures 10.1 through 10.4 provide an overview of these effects.

Reentry Problem: Finances

By far the most important effect of coercive mobility on individuals and communities is financial. Our respondents report that ex-prisoners return to the community with limited financial resources but many financial needs. Not only do they need the fundamental means for survival (food and shelter), but they also regularly need money for new clothes, transportation, and, frequently, criminal justice expenses such as fines, restitution, and court fees. At the same time, many ex-prisoners also have to pay back child support, outstanding credit card debts, and other consumer bills. Upon their return to the community, these individuals have three financial choices: find a job, remain unemployed, or return to crime.

Jobs available to ex-prisoners tend to be low paying and highly unstable. Ex-prisoners we interviewed who had found jobs were offered too few hours, which meant they did not qualify for benefits and therefore had to hold more than one job. Most, however, unable to find employment, opted for unemployment. Unemployed individuals typically relied upon their families for financial support. As a result, families experienced additional financial strains. As figure 10.1 shows, at the community level, financial hardship among returning prisoners and their families reduces their level of civic participation and also may undermine their ability for successful association activity and common purpose. Our respondents spoke of having less time and energy to participate in any events outside of job and family. At the same time, they found that financial hardship reduced residents' ability to provide assistance to their neighbors, thus reducing the community's overall capacity for supporting networks and reciprocity.

One byproduct of large-scale unemployment experienced by these two high-incarceration neighborhoods was the increase in men congregating on street corners, oftentimes near or in front of local stores. This situation produced two effects. First, shop owners reported they had fewer legitimate customers willing to shop. Second, the appearance of disorder meant customers from outside the neighborhood were reluc-

Figure 10.1. *Social Capital and the Financial Effects of Reentry*

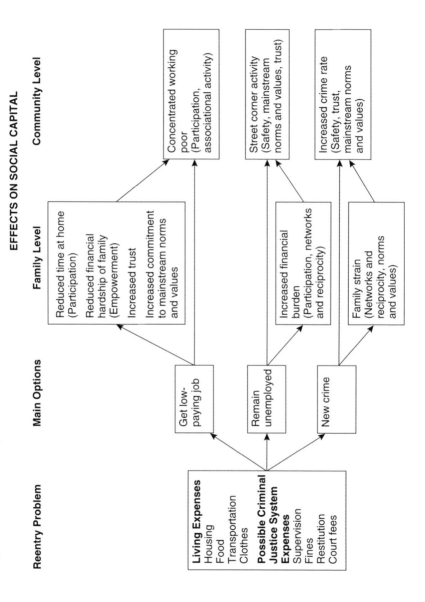

tant to frequent stores within the neighborhood, and outside investors did not see these neighborhoods as desirable places to establish businesses. Fewer employers meant fewer jobs for ex-prisoners and residents alike. Duneier (1999) shows the importance of work for building self-esteem and for keeping individuals tied to mainstream norms and values. Thus, at the community level, aggregate unemployment may impede the development of collective norms and values.

Finally, ex-prisoners may return to crime to resolve their financial needs—many of our respondents reported they had considered this alternative and knew of others who had chosen it. In the aggregate, this alternative reduces community safety. To the extent it makes residents fearful, it also reduces community-level trust.

Reentry Problem: Stigma

Offenders in transition report a sense of being stigmatized by their communities and fellow residents, and their families report similar feelings. They sense that they are labeled as "bad" or otherwise flawed by those living near them. Those individuals who feel stigmatized may deal with it in one of four ways: They may (1) actively try to change the others' opinions, (2) go on about their business, disregarding these opinions, (3) isolate themselves from others who judge them, or (4) move to a new community and start over.

Effectively changing the opinions of others has positive implications for social capital (figure 10.2). When neighbors form an improved opinion, as our respondents reported they were ready to do if the person's behavior warranted this change, this change promotes a renewed sense of connectedness within the family and between the family and the community. Such a change enhances both the belonging and the empowerment domains of social capital, as both residents and ex-prisoners learn they can influence one another's beliefs and mutually share a sense of connection. It also enhances a sense of trust among members of the community.

The other ways of dealing with stigma have less positive implications for social capital. Either ignoring one's neighbors in daily business or becoming isolated from them promotes a sense of alienation. Our respondents reported that those who are stigmatized avoid contact with others, stop participating in social functions such as church services, and look upon their neighbors with distrust and foreboding. This response undermines any sense of belonging both for ex-prisoners and for resi-

Figure 10.2. *Social Capital and the Stigma Effects of Reentry*

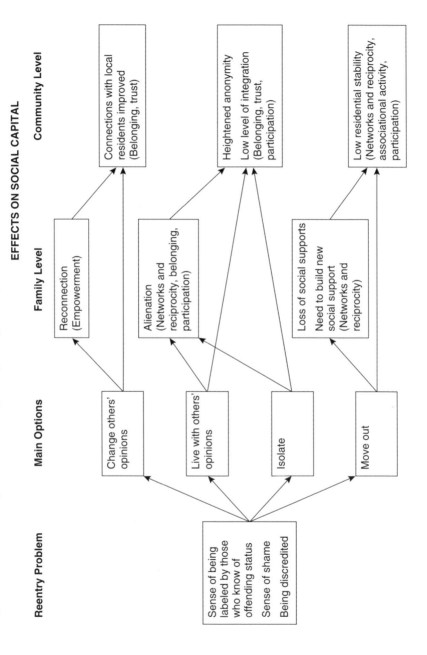

dents, all of whom are trying to cope by withdrawing from community life. Sometimes this means withdrawing completely, other times this means limiting associations. The byproduct of this phenomenon is the development of insular groups within a community. Even if some of those groups have ample social capital, the community as a whole does not benefit unless bridges or a common purpose tie the groups together (Paxton 1999). Additionally, as residents withdraw further from each other, participation in community activities diminishes (Skogan 1990), crime increases, and trust erodes.

Finally, ex-prisoners have the option of moving to a new neighborhood entirely. Indeed, while some ex-prisoners reported their success was due to the help they received from family members when they moved back to the old neighborhood, some attributed their success to their decision to move to a new environment altogether. Family members discussed moving as a strategy they sometimes employed as a way of enhancing the likelihood of their loved one's successful reentry. Moving has its downside, however. It can be expensive and takes people farther away from social supports. Consequently, moving negatively affects supporting networks and reciprocity. New residents also diminish, at least temporarily, communities' abilities to establish associational activity and common purpose because these require time and established networks to develop.

Reentry Problem: Identity

At one level, incarceration impacts how offenders and their families feel about themselves. At another level, it affects how residents in high-incarceration neighborhoods perceive themselves and the communities in which they live. Neighborhoods are important for developing self-esteem and a social identity (Forrest and Kearns 2001). These, in turn, help shape the life chances of individuals living in these areas.

Our respondents reported that incarceration could lead ex-prisoners to make a positive change in their self-perceptions. Sometimes, residents believed, these changes could not have happened without the individual serving a prison sentence. Maruna (2001) also shows that when ex-prisoners try to reform their lives, they begin by developing a new "personal narrative" and adopting a revised version of their life story, one which reinterprets life events and personal priorities in potentially prosocial ways. Ex-prisoners who want to "make good" are thus a considerably positive potential resource for communities.

Positive changes in offenders can improve social capital in a few ways (figure 10.3). Reentering prisoners can serve as positive role models, enthusiastic social participants (if newly so), and advocates for conventional values in a setting where such a voice may not typically be heard. Likewise, men and women who reenter their communities are untapped potential resources for voluntary participation in civic organizations, economic participation in local priorities, and other types of social network supports. Our study shows that residents concur: Ex-prisoners can make a positive contribution to the neighborhood if they have changed and can communicate that change to others (particularly children). Moreover, the presence of a larger number of prosocial adults increases collective norms and values.

Alternatively, incarceration can lead to reduced feelings of empowerment. For example, studies of disenfranchisement show that prisoners in most states are denied voting rights and that at least 14 states revoke the voting rights of prisoners and ex-prisoners for life (Austin et al. 2001). Other studies have found that upwards of 2 million African-American males cannot participate in electoral politics as a consequence of felony convictions (Human Rights Watch and The Sentencing Project 1998). This is perilous to the sense of empowerment in certain neighborhoods where, perhaps, a significant number of males cannot vote.

High levels of coercive mobility also impact the identities of residents of the community at large because they identify themselves, as do others outside the community, as coming from a "bad" neighborhood. Our respondents reported that this perception translated into residents withdrawing from mainstream society, believing their options were limited and life chances diminished. For children, this situation reduced their stake in conforming to collective norms and values.

The knowledge that others thought less of them because of where they lived also meant residents were inclined to believe government officials did not care about them or their neighborhoods and that persistent racism was the true cause of neighborhood conditions. In addition, residents in high-incarceration neighborhoods reported that as their neighborhoods developed a reputation as a place for returning offenders to reside, other "undesirable" people (such as the homeless) migrated there as well. As a consequence, residents experienced diminished feelings of safety in the

Figure 10.3. *Social Capital and the Identity Effects of Reentry*

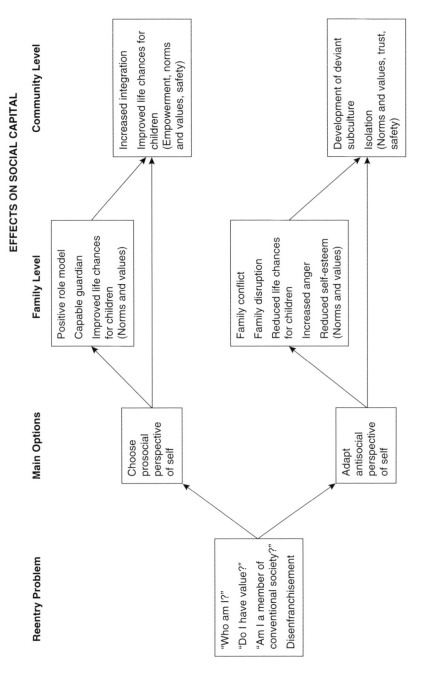

neighborhood. While many residents took pride in their neighborhood, others expressed a desire to leave, indicating a low sense of belonging.

Inhabitants of high-incarceration neighborhoods frequently call for more crime control in their communities. However, they also demonstrate mixed feelings about the relationship between residents and the police and the criminal justice system in general. Reentry exacerbates these feelings as ex-prisoners are returned to communities where residents have little say in the process. Our respondents reported high levels of dissatisfaction with the criminal justice system and a strong belief that the system was racist and biased against poor people. Other research (Rose and Clear 1998b) demonstrates that when people know someone who has been to prison and hold a low opinion of formal social control (actions taken by the police and other aspects of the criminal justice system to produce safety), they also are likely to hold a dim view of informal social control (actions taken by residents to produce safety). Combined, these studies show us that people in neighborhoods with high levels of incarceration are likely to have a negative view of formal social control. They are also highly likely to know someone who has been to prison and therefore are more likely to have a low assessment of informal social control. Thus, reentry can diminish safety by directly reducing informal social control.

Reentry Problem: Relationships

By removing people from their neighborhoods, incarceration interferes with social networks in that it disrupts marriages, families, and friendships (figure 10.4). For instance, female prisoners are often incarcerated too far away from their communities to permit frequent visits by their children. Furthermore, some women report not wanting to feel close to their children because they fear being relocated to a facility even farther away (O'Brien 2001). Reentry also can impact supporting networks and reciprocity. Once they return home, ex-prisoners must face the task of piecing together their lives. While this process often entails finding shelter, employment, and other necessities, individuals also need to repair relationships with family members. O'Brien (2001) finds this is particularly important for mothers whose own mothers may have served as caregivers during the incarceration period. Such reconciliation can prove difficult, especially for individuals who may have victimized family and friends (Rose et al. 2000). Sometimes, reentering prisoners may find their families have moved or are unprepared to welcome them

Figure 10.4. *Social Capital and the Relationship Effects of Reentry*

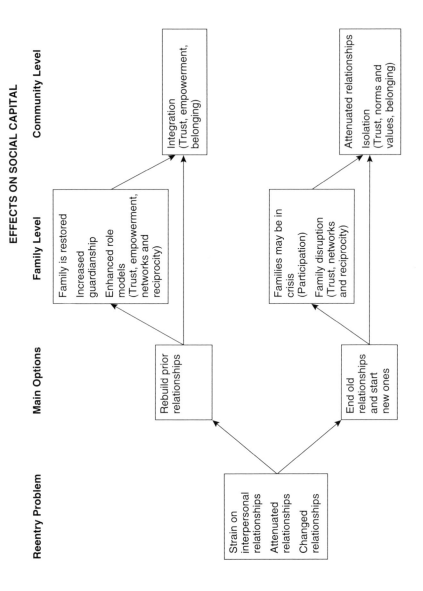

home (Fleisher and Decker 2001). For example, women who have become independent in their husbands' absence may not want to return to their former role in the household (Fishman 1983).

Our research shows that, while family and friends may welcome a reunion with a released family member, social networks still suffer strain from trying to reincorporate formerly absent individuals. Many respondents reported difficulty in reincorporating ex-prisoners into their lives—individuals who themselves are relearning their roles as husbands and fathers. Some prisoners may spend time in prison thinking about their role in family and community life, and upon release, may be overeager to assume a role in a family accustomed to living without someone in that position. A male ex-prisoner's desire to be a "father" does not in fact guarantee that the children's mother is ready to accept him in that role. This is particularly true when a spouse has moved on to another relationship.

At the micro level, severed ties make it difficult for individual ex-prisoners to reenter community life. Without social networks in place, ex-prisoners have little social support to draw upon during the transition process. Often, however, ties to former friends and gang networks are easily reestablished, enabling ex-prisoners to reoffend and relapse (Fleisher and Decker 2001). At the macro level, communities characterized by multiple severed ties produce lower levels of collective efficacy because of lowered levels of reciprocated exchange. People less likely to know and interact with others are less likely to expect exchange. Reciprocated exchange is built upon the expectation: "If I do for others, others will do for me." This simply is not true where people do not know and trust people in their community. While many residents reported they would offer assistance to fellow church members who might be experiencing the incarceration of a loved one (a supportive action), many also said that ex-prisoners would have to prove their worthiness before assistance (and interaction) would be offered.

Reentry poses ex-prisoners and their families with a challenge—whether or not to rebuild the relationship. Rebuilding the relationship means interaction can be restored, resulting in enhanced levels of trust and empowerment, both within the family and within the community at large. Choosing not to rebuild, however, impacts levels of trust, norms and values, and an overall sense of belonging. While this choice may reflect a healthy alternative within the family when the returning prisoner has not "mended his/her ways," it perpetuates an environment of distrust between people in the community. Ex-prisoners stay isolated and their families remain wary.

Reentry and Children

Since many people assume that children benefit from the removal of a criminal (perhaps violent) parent from the home (Hagan and Dinovitzer 1999; Sharp and Marcus-Mendoza 2001), it may follow that these children do not benefit from the parent's return. Yet, it is clear that children feel the loss of their parent and typically want that person home (Fishman 1983). While we know that more contact with families during incarceration is associated with lower recidivism (Johnson, Selber, and Lauderdale 2001), we know very little about how the reunion impacts the family.

The preceding discussion highlights some of the ways reentry affects the components of social capital, and these processes, of course, translate into effects upon children. For instance, the sense of empowerment felt by children who live in a particular place is influenced by the way they perceive adults dealing with their sense of power. Likewise, individuals' feelings of belonging are influenced by the degree to which they perceive local institutions are open to participation and involvement and to the extent these individuals see others as being actively involved. Adults who disdain participation, as those who are disenfranchised or feel stigmatized might be expected to, do not model civic participation or feelings of membership in the community. The manner in which ex-prisoners return to their communities is also important. Those who fail to reconnect prosocially with their social networks (especially their families) represent a missed opportunity for adult supervision of children and adolescents. In abandoning this chance to strengthen family units, ex-prisoners weaken these units as sources of social capital for the children who live within them.

Sampson et al. (1999) examined the impact of collective efficacy on the three aspects of neighborhood social organization they believe impact the lives of children: intergenerational closure (the extent to which adults and children are connected to each other), reciprocal exchange (the extent to which information with respect to child rearing is shared by adults in the neighborhood), and expectations for the informal social control and mutual support of children. All three components are related to social control in the community, resting on the assumption that residents are connected to one another and that a core set of values exists among neighbors.

A body of evidence now exists showing that removing offenders from communities in order to impose prison sentences affects intergenerational closure and reciprocal exchange. In communities where lots of parents are incarcerated, many children are raised by stand-in relatives or the remaining parent. In addition, these are places where many adults withdraw from community life (Rose et al. 2000), which increases the likelihood of intergenerational impairment and limited reciprocal exchange.

The big question is, What happens when the incarcerated adult returns home? Much of the answer depends upon the person who returns to this family unit. There are functions this person is positioned to perform—parental, economic, and interpersonal—that are critical to the effective functioning of the family unit. Ex-prisoners who fail to fulfill these new challenges not only place their children back into their disadvantaged position, but also usually exacerbate the family's difficulties by becoming an additional demand upon its already diminished resources. Thus, other adults in the household will find their contribution to child social control and reciprocal exchange diluted by the needs of the returning ex-prisoner. For instance, a mother serving as the sole source of support for her household may need to support not just her children, but also an unemployed ex-prisoner. Reestablishing this relationship will require time, and this time will inevitably have to be stolen from that available to the children.

Here, again, reentry is an opportunity—it can bring not only increased demands, but also increased resources. A returning adult can fill a gap in a family's generational relationships and take on responsibilities of reciprocal exchange with regard to children in the neighborhood. Much depends on how the reentry proceeds because, just as there is no reason to suggest reentry will damage these important collective capacities, there is equally no reason to say these capacities will be augmented. Moreover, there is plenty of reason to suspect that negative consequences will occur more easily than positive ones, if only because of inertia. Change is difficult to accomplish and the situation is set up for negative, not positive, outcomes.

Recommendations and Conclusions

Apparently, reentry has a predominantly negative impact on the quality of life in communities hardest hit by incarceration. This is particularly true in light of the fact that these same neighborhoods are overwhelmingly disadvantaged in other ways as well. Prisoner reentry into the community creates an environment where people become increasingly isolated from each other and from the broader society and where social relationships are increasingly taxed.

This need not always be the case, however. Reentry is a time, if managed correctly, when networks can be enhanced, collective capacities augmented, and reentering residents assisted in improving rather than depleting their family resources. Currently, few programs for former prisoners and their families focus exclusively on easing the transition from prison to home. Some programs, for instance, offer discharge planning to prisoners about to be released. Most of these, however, concentrate on the individual's immediate needs rather than on combining discharge planning with family needs. Some in-prison programs recognize the importance of family ties for promoting parent-child relationships. These programs are important as the initial venue for offsetting problems associated with reentry because ties built, maintained, or strengthened during incarceration are networks that need less remedial work upon reentry. However, such programs are not positioned to bridge the gap between returning inmates and the homes set to receive them.

Noting this program deficiency, Fleisher and Decker (2001) call for a comprehensive approach to reintegrating ex-prisoners into the community—an approach that operates at both the individual and the community levels. They suggest programs to establish help for inmates in planning for difficult reunions with family members, long-term drug and alcohol treatment and other social services in a community-based setting, community-based parole officers, and efforts to develop ties between the community and larger society that integrate people into the dominant society. Bursik and Grasmick (1993) also call for strategies to improve the relationship between the community and larger society. These strategies mirror the local policies Forrest and Kearns (2001) suggest to increase the level of neighborhood social capital.

Rose, Clear, and Ryder (2001) recently proposed a comprehensive, community-level program for supporting reentry as a way of addressing the community-level impact of incarceration; it contains several components that target aspects of the community's social capital and collective efficacy. For example, a community center that would provide mentoring for children and their returning adult role model could help orient these returning adults to greater associational activity and strengthened social norms. Helping ex-prisoners obtain the right to vote and supporting their efforts to become full participants in their communities (by, for example, obtaining loans and buying homes) would increase their sense of empowerment and promote a greater sense of belonging. Systemic family counseling designed to facilitate more effective social units inevitably would increase social capital by strengthening social networks.

The key to this type of approach is to think of locations rather than individuals as the recipient of such services because this enables us to address the multifaceted ripple effects of incarceration and reentry. Caseworkers familiar with a given area would not only be able to identify any particular needs unique to that area, but also could determine which individuals needed assistance and the type of service that would benefit these individuals the most. Because there are only a handful of areas hardest hit by coercive mobility in any given jurisdiction, a neighborhood center in these locations is a targeted way to provide services tailored to these areas. Thus, services are improved and costs are minimized.

A comprehensive approach to reentry that fosters social capital and collective efficacy involves recognizing that reentry is not just about individuals coming home; it is also about the homes and communities to which ex-prisoners return. This fact is more important for children than for any other group because neighborhood is the place where people are socialized into the wider society (Forrest and Kearns 2001). If nothing else, the residential mobility associated with incarceration and reentry disrupts relationships and impairs children's educational attainment (see Coleman 1988; Israel, Beaulieu, and Hartless 2001). Yet, children growing up in high-incarceration neighborhoods characterized by diminished social capital also grow up in an environment that fosters low levels of civic participation, trust, safety, and belonging. In addition, because children are exposed to environments with attenuated networks, they lose such benefits as employment connections. The cycle continues—diminished social capital and collective efficacy produce high levels of incarceration and reentry, which in turn result in even less of these important community resources.

Attention to social capital, then, is the key to overcoming this cycle. Community-level research now recognizes the importance of networks for community well-being. It is time for criminal justice policy to recognize this as well. Programs designed to develop social capital are the only way to ultimately enhance the quality of life in neighborhoods. Empirical research, in fact, shows that community organizations and programs can affect local levels of social capital (Gittell, Ortega-Bustamante, and Steffy 2000; Smidt 1999). Furthermore, when we recognize that communities are not islands unto themselves and that social capital and collective efficacy in one area affect adjacent neighborhoods simply by proximity (Sampson et al. 1999), the need to develop social capital becomes even more significant. Finally, once cultivated, social capital produces other types of capital as well (Wood 1997). Consequently, social policies need to be evaluated in terms of their effect on social capital. Otherwise, policies intended to enhance an area's quality of life may actually reduce it instead.

NOTES

1. For a complete description of the research on collective efficacy, see Sampson (2001).
2. See Rose et al. (2000) for a review of the data and methods and for an extended discussion of the findings.

REFERENCES

Austin, James, Marino A. Bruce, Leo Carroll, Patricia L. McCall, and Stephen C. Richards. 2001. "The Use of Incarceration in the United States." *Critical Criminology* 10 (1): 1–25.

Beck, Allen J., Jennifer C. Karlberg, and Paige M. Harrison. 2002. *Prison and Jail Inmates at Midyear 2001*. Bureau of Justice Statistics Bulletin. Washington, D.C.: U.S. Department of Justice. Office of Justice Programs.

Bursik, Robert J., Jr., and Harold Grasmick. 1993. *Neighborhoods and Crime: The Dimensions of Effective Community Control*. New York: Lexington.

Case, Anne C., and Lawrence F. Katz. 1991. *The Company You Keep: The Effects of Family and Neighborhood on Disadvantaged Youths*. Cambridge, Mass.: National Bureau of Economic Research.

CASES. See Center for Alternative Sentencing and Employment Services.

Center for Alternative Sentencing and Employment Services. 2000. *The Community Justice Project: Report to the Open Society Institute*. New York: Center for Alternative Sentencing and Employment Services.

Clear, Todd R., Dina R. Rose, and Judith A. Ryder. 2001. "Incarceration and Community: The Problem of Removing and Returning Offenders." *Crime and Delinquency* 47 (3): 335–51.

Clear, Todd R., Dina R. Rose, Elin Waring, and Kristen Scully. 2003. "Coercive Mobility and Crime: A Preliminary Examination of Concentrated Incarceration and Social Disorganization." *Justice Quarterly* 20 (1): 33–64.

Coleman, James S. 1988. "Social Capital in the Creation of Human Capital." *American Journal of Sociology* 94 (Suppl.): 95–120.

———. 1990. *Foundations of Social Theory.* Cambridge, Mass.: Harvard University Press.

Crutchfield, Robert D. 1989. "Labor Stratification and Violent Crime." *Social Forces* 68 (2): 489–512.

Crutchfield, Robert D., Michael R. Geerken, and Walter R. Gove. 1982. "Crime Rate and Social Integration: The Impact of Metropolitan Mobility." *Criminology* 20 (3–4): 467–78.

Duneier, Mitchell. 1999. *Sidewalk.* New York: Farrar, Straus and Giroux.

Fishman, Susan Hoffman. 1983. "The Impact of Incarceration on Children of Offenders." In *Children of Exceptional Parents,* edited by Mary Frank (85–99). Journal of Children in Contemporary Society Series, vol. 15, no. 1. New York: The Haworth Press, Inc.

Fleisher, Mark S., and Scott H. Decker. 2001. "Going Home, Staying Home: Integrating Prison Gang Members into the Community." *Corrections Management Quarterly* 5 (1): 65–77.

Forrest, Ray, and Ade Kearns. 2001. "Social Cohesion, Social Capital and the Neighborhood." *Urban Studies* 38 (12): 2125–43.

Furstenberg, Frank F., Jr., and Mary Elizabeth Hughes. 1997. "The Influence of Neighborhoods on Children's Development: A Theoretical Perspective and a Research Agenda." In *Neighborhood Poverty Volume II: Policy Implication in Studying Neighborhoods,* edited by Jeanne Brooks-Gunn, Greg J. Duncan, and J. Lawrence Alber (23–47). New York: Russell Sage Foundation.

Gittell, Marilyn, Isolda Ortega-Bustamante, and Tracy Steffy. 2000. "Social Capital and Social Change: Women's Community Activism." *Urban Affairs Review* 36 (2): 123–47.

Hagan, John, and Ronit Dinovitzer. 1999. "Collateral Consequences of Imprisonment for Children, Communities, and Prisoners." In *Prisons,* edited by Michael Tonry and Joan Petersilia (121–62). Chicago: University of Chicago Press.

Harrist, Amanda W., and Ricardo C. Ainslie. 1998. "Marital Discord and Child Behavior Problems: Parent-Child Relationship Quality and Child Interpersonal Awareness as Mediators." *Journal of Family Issues* 19 (2): 140–63.

Human Rights Watch and The Sentencing Project. 1998. *Losing the Vote: The Impact of Felony Disenfranchisement Laws in the United States.* Washington, D.C.: The Sentencing Project.

Israel, Glenn D., Lionel J. Beaulieu, and Glen Hartless. 2001. "The Influence of Family and Community Social Capital on Educational Achievement." *Rural Sociology* 66 (1): 43–68.

Johnson, Toni, Katherine Selber, and Michael Lauderdale. 2001. "Developing Quality Services for Offenders and Families: An Innovative Partnership." In *Children with Parents in Prison: Child Welfare Policy, Program, and Practice Issues,* edited by Cynthia Seymour and Creasie Finney Hairston (595–615). New Brunswick, N.J.: Transaction Publishers.

Kennedy, Bruce P., Ichiro Kawachi, Deborah Prothrow-Stith, Kimberly Lochner, and Vanita Gupta. 1998. "Social Capital, Income Inequality and Firearm Violent Crime." *Social Science and Medicine* 47 (1): 7–17.

Kornhauser, Ruth Rosner. 1978. *Social Sources of Delinquency: An Appraisal of Analytic Models.* Chicago: University of Chicago Press.

Lynch, James P., William J. Sabol, Michael Planty, and Mary Shelley. 2001. *Crime, Coercion, and Community: The Effects of Arrest and Incarceration Policies on Informal Social Control in Neighborhoods.* Report to the National Institute of Justice. Washington, D.C.: The Urban Institute.

Maruna, Shadd. 2001. *Making Good: How Ex-convicts Reform and Rebuild Their Lives.* Washington, D.C.: American Psychological Association.

Morenoff, Jeffrey D., Robert J. Sampson, and Stephen W. Raudenbush. 2001. "Neighborhood Inequality, Collective Efficacy, and the Spatial Dynamics of Urban Violence." *Criminology* 39 (3): 517–61.

Mumola, Christopher J. 2000. *Incarcerated Parents and Their Children.* Bureau of Justice Statistics Special Report. Washington, D.C.: U.S. Department of Justice, Office of Justice Programs.

Myers, Samuel L., Jr. 2000. "The Unintended Impacts of Sentencing Guidelines on Family Structure." Paper presented at the annual meeting of the American Sociological Association, Washington, D.C., Aug. 12–16.

O'Brien, Patricia. 2001. " 'Just Like Baking a Cake': Women Describe the Necessary Ingredients for Successful Reentry after Incarceration." *Families in Society: The Journal of Contemporary Human Services* 82 (3): 287–95.

Parcel, Toby L., and Mikaela J. Dufur. 2001a. "Capital at Home and School: Effects on School Achievement." *Social Forces* 79 (3): 881–912.

———. 2001b. "Capital at Home and at School: Effects on Child Social Adjustment." *Journal of Marriage and Family* 63 (1): 32–47.

Paxton, Pamela. 1999. "Is Social Capital Declining in the United States? A Multiple Indicator Assessment." *American Journal of Sociology* 105 (1): 88–127.

Portes, Alejandro. 1998. "Social Capital: Its Origins and Applications in Modern Sociology." *Annual Review of Sociology* 24: 1–24.

Putnam, Robert. 1993a. "The Prosperous Community: Social Capital and Community Life." *The American Prospect* 4 (13): 35–42.

———. 1993b. *Making Democracy Work: Civic Traditions in Modern Italy.* Princeton, N.J.: Princeton University Press.

Rose, Dina R., and Todd R. Clear. 1998a. "Incarceration, Social Capital and Crime: Implications for Social Disorganization Theory." *Criminology* 36 (3): 441–79.

———. 1998b. "Who Doesn't Know Someone in Jail? The Impact of Exposure to Prison on Attitudes of Public and Informal Control." Paper presented at the annual meeting of the Southern Sociological Society, Atlanta, Apr. 2–4.

Rose, Dina R., Todd R. Clear, and Judith A. Ryder. 2000. *Drugs, Incarceration and Neighborhood Life: The Impact of Reintegrating Offenders into the Community.* Final Report to the National Institute of Justice. New York: John Jay College of Criminal Justice.

———. 2001. "Addressing the Unintended Consequences of Incarceration through Community-Oriented Services." *Corrections Management Quarterly* 5 (3): 69–78.

Rosenfeld, Richard, Steven Messner, Eric P. Baumer. 2001. "Social Capital and Homicide." *Social Forces* 80 (1): 283–309.

Runyan, Desmond K., Wanda M. Hunter, Rebecca R. S. Socolar, Lisa Amaya-Jackson, Diana English, John Landsverk, Howard Dubowitz, Dorothy H. Browne, Shrikant

I. Bangdiwala, and Ravi M. Mathew. 1998. "Children Who Prosper in Unfavorable Environments: The Relationship to Social Capital." *Pediatrics* 101 (1): 12–18.

Sampson, Robert J. 1991. "Linking the Micro- and Macrolevel Dimensions of Community Social Organization." *Social Forces* 70: 43–64.

———. 2001. Edwin H. Sutherland Address. Annual meeting of the American Society of Criminology, Atlanta, Nov. 9.

Sampson, Robert J., and Stephen W. Raudenbush. 1999. "Systemic Social Observation of Public Spaces: A New Look at Disorder in Urban Neighborhoods." *American Journal of Sociology* 105 (3): 603–51.

Sampson, Robert J., Jeffrey D. Morenoff, and Felton Earls. 1999. "Beyond Social Capital: Spatial Dynamics of Collective Efficacy for Children." *American Sociological Review* 64 (5): 633–60.

Sampson, Robert J., Stephen Raudenbush, and Felton Earls. 1997. "Neighborhoods and Violent Crime: A Multilevel Study of Collective Efficacy." *Science* 277: 918–24.

Sharp, Susan F., and Susan T. Marcus-Mendoza. 2001. "It's a Family Affair: Incarcerated Women and Their Families." *Women and Criminal Justice* 12 (4): 21–49.

Shaw, Clifford R., and Henry D. McKay. 1942. *Juvenile Delinquency and Urban Areas.* Chicago: University of Chicago Press.

Skogan, Wesley G. 1990. *Disorder and Decline: The Spiral of Decay in American Neighborhoods.* New York: Free Press.

Smidt, Corwin. 1999. "Religion and Civic Engagement: A Comparative Analysis." *Annals of the American Academy of Political and Social Science* 565 (September): 176–92.

Stanton-Salazar, Ricardo D. 1997. "A Social Capital Framework for Understanding the Socialization of Racial Minority Children and Youths." *Harvard Educational Review* 67 (1): 1–40.

Wall, Ellen, Gabriele Ferrazzi, and Frans Schryer. 1998. "Getting the Goods on Social Capital." *Rural Sociology* 63 (2): 300–22.

Warner, Barbara D., and Glenn L. Pierce. 1993. "Reexamining Social Disorganization Theory Using Calls to the Police as a Measure of Crime." *Criminology* 31 (4): 493–517.

Wilson, James Q., and George Kelling. 1982. "The Police and Neighborhood Safety: Broken Windows." *Atlantic Monthly* 249 (3): 29–38.

Wood, Richard L. 1997. "Social Capital and Political Culture: Good Meets Politics in the Inner City." *American Behavioral Scientist* 40 (5): 595–605.

Wright, John Paul, Francis T. Cullen, and Jeremy T. Miller. 2001. "Family Social Capital and Delinquent Involvement." *Journal of Criminal Justice* 29 (1): 1–9.

11

Building Partnerships to Strengthen Offenders, Families, and Communities

Shelli Balter Rossman

Offenders often experience multiple problems, such as physical and mental illness, substance abuse, family collapse, and unemployment or low income, that make it difficult for them to access and maintain the services they require to meet their basic needs. Recent research underscores the importance of prerelease preparation and initial postrelease support, not only to meet such needs, but also to reduce offender recidivism (Nelson and Trone 2000). However, neither correctional facilities nor community-based providers are likely on their own to have the necessary resources or skills to resolve the diverse, and often deeply entrenched, problems confronting returning prisoners and their families. Further, informal support networks that have been properly prepared to respond effectively may meet some needs more efficiently.

Cross-institutional and interagency partnerships have attracted considerable interest as vehicles for providing more comprehensive service while redressing fragmentation in health and human service systems. As Hammett, Harmon, and Maruschak (1999) suggest, an integrated continuum of care[1] with provider continuity offers a strong approach for addressing the complex needs of offenders as they transition from correctional facilities and resettle in their home communities. Ideally, such a continuum would link public health agencies and community-based providers to correctional facilities, serving as a conduit to ease offenders' transition from prison to home. In addition, an integrated service network would connect community organizations to one another, facilitating improved interaction among providers and encouraging more holistic responses that suit clients' individual needs. However, while such system and services integration are likely to benefit offenders, more expansive partnerships may be needed to (1) offer returning inmates meaningful informal supports that can improve their chances of successful community reintegration and (2) extend both formal and informal service provision to family members who may be instrumental in facilitating (or conversely, undermining) offenders' reentry.

Community justice partnerships should be examined as potential solutions to meet the needs of recently released prisoners and their families. At minimum, such partnerships involve a participatory problem-solving process that engages diverse stakeholders (e.g., offenders and their supporters, victims, government agencies, service providers, civic leaders, and other community members/groups) in sustained interactions, supported by the commitment of partner resources, focused on improving community safety and healing harms associated with crime (see Gouvis Roman et al. 2002, for an expanded discussion).

Correctional authorities and community leaders should consider as critically important the formation and strengthening of cross-jurisdictional, multiagency, and community justice partnerships that target offenders and families for the following reasons:

- Failure to address offenders' needs for supportive services may hamper individuals' abilities to reconnect with family members or otherwise impede successful negotiation of life in the community, increasing the likelihood of recidivism. Recidivism is not only a hardship for offenders and their families, but also entails harm to local property and people, and engenders huge social costs resulting from the crimes committed, convictions, and incarceration. Thus, communities and the justice system can benefit greatly by investing in treatment and supportive services for ex-offenders (and their families) that demonstrably reduce recidivism (Jacksonville Community Council Inc. 2001).
- The unresolved problems of returning offenders not only compromise their lives and those of their families, but also may heavily impact the well-being of the entire community. For example, some health conditions (e.g., asthma, diabetes, heart disease, and high blood pressure) primarily affect the life quality of the offenders and

their families or households; the impact on the community is largely limited to strains potentially introduced by the increased need for health services or funding to treat the uninsured. However, other illnesses—such as human immunodeficiency virus/ autoimmunodeficiency virus (HIV/AIDS), Hepatitis B and C (HBV and HCV, respectively), sexually transmitted diseases (STDs, such as syphilis, gonorrhea, and chlamydia), tuberculosis (TB), severe psychiatric disorders, and substance abuse—not only disproportionately affect offenders (Hammett et al. 1999), but also potentially threaten the well-being of family members and the public as inmates return to the community.

- Community-based agencies are unlikely to have the human and fiscal resources, or the jurisdiction, to fully address the diverse needs of offenders and their families unless procedures are implemented to span organizational boundaries (e.g., local service cabinets that meet to identify and address delivery problems or gaps in service; co-location of providers from different agencies in neighborhood centers that are accessible to would-be clients, or possibly the diversification of some single-service organizations into "multiservice, one-stop shopping" agencies). Integrating local service networks places community-based providers in a better position to offer more comprehensive and coordinated support to offenders and their families, and to monitor the results of these efforts. Furthermore, improving community-based service delivery for returning offenders also benefits other segments of society who depend on the same service networks.

- Service networks that are unconnected to various justice system entities leave communities and local providers—not to mention offenders and their families—vulnerable in several ways. For example, absent the link to the correctional system, communities are unable to realistically project the flow of returning offenders and the resulting demand for local resources. Consequently, communities may be ill prepared to meet the needs of former inmates, potentially undermining successful prisoner reentry and possibly risking public health and safety. Similarly, lack of meaningful contact with criminal justice agents may circumscribe service providers' willingness and ability to effectively support clients who are former prisoners. Providers may feel skittish and ill equipped to deal with offenders; they may be unable to locate the information needed to help reentering prisoners qualify for available services; or they may be unable to access sufficiently detailed treatment and service histories, hampering their efforts to respond with appropriate types and levels of service, and ensure consistent and uninterrupted support (i.e., continuity of care) from prison to home.

- Linking local service providers to correctional facilities can benefit communities and penal institutions. For example, service providers may have earlier access to future clients, which may translate into more effective interventions and better planning, thereby ensuring relevant services are available in the community. At the same time, inviting community-based providers into prison facilities may offer a vehicle for augmenting existing prison programs and services with new approaches or activities that reflect the expertise and interests of the local agency staff.
- Partnerships comprised of criminal justice and service-providing agencies and other community leaders provide a framework and infrastructure for accurately assessing offender needs; determining the potential impact of these needs on community resources; undertaking strategic planning to properly deploy existing resources while proactively developing approaches to fill existing gaps; and improving accountability and transparency in examining the success of reintegration efforts. In addition to properly focusing discussions of returning offenders' impact on specific communities, such collaborations can facilitate improved communication among policymakers and decisionmakers, organizations that directly serve offenders and their families, and the public, offsetting inflammatory rhetoric that encourages public opinion opposing any assistance, even health or social services, for offenders. Thus, crosscutting collaborations can become extremely useful advocates for offenders and other underserved populations.

This chapter focuses on issues related to improving services for incarcerated offenders or those recently released from prisons; for the most part, the discussion excludes the characteristics and needs of those in, or returning from, jails. Some of the more compelling service needs of offenders and their families are highlighted, and key principles of integrating services, promising models of specific programs or approaches that integrate services, and challenges confronting organizations and communities interested in proceeding along these lines are identified. Lastly, suggestions are made regarding the building of community justice partnerships and other actions (e.g., improved needs assessments and discharge planning, mapping of community resources, planning for gap-filling services, and involvement of informal community support networks) that may enhance outcomes for offenders, their families, and the community at large.

Service Needs of Institutionalized and Newly Released Offenders

Offenders are a diverse population, but many display certain common characteristics—low income, limited education, disrupted home and family life, inadequate job skills and employment experience, and alcohol or drug addiction. Aside from medical, mental health, and substance abuse treatment, key service requirements for those returning to the local community are related to immediate basic needs (food, shelter, clothing), ongoing personal support, housing, education, employment, and legal assistance. Furthermore, inmates who have been imprisoned for long terms (e.g., a decade or more) may experience a kind of culture shock associated with dramatic changes that may have occurred within their interpersonal networks or communities during their absence.

Basic Survival, Family Dynamics, and Other Psychosocial Issues

Correctional facilities offer limited programs that assist offenders with meeting some of their short- and longer-term basic needs. For example, in 1997,

- 38 percent of state prison inmates participated in education classes.
- 31 percent participated in vocational training programs, including in-class training or on-the-job training (not including institutional job assignments).
- 3 percent worked in income-producing prison industry jobs, though 60 percent had some work assignment (such as food service, laundry, grounds maintenance).
- 8 percent participated in prerelease programs covering such topics as budgeting, stress reduction, and job interviewing skills (GAO 2001).

These programs are necessary but generally insufficient to provide the level of assistance offenders require.

Offenders returning to the community are in need of safe, affordable housing and stable employment. Some can return to the households they occupied prior to incarceration, or can find suitable accommodations with family or friends. However, many returning offenders face homelessness—a fact they may try to conceal to prevent a release delay. Some may need immediate emergency shelter once released; others may require transitional housing while gaining life, educational, and employment skills. Transitional housing services have an added benefit; they often help offenders to establish residency credentials that facilitate access to other needed services.

While some fortunate individuals are able to return to the jobs they held before their incarceration and others can independently find employment using their own resources or networks, many newly released offenders need help in securing gainful employment (Rossman et al. 1999). Often, individuals have educational or vocational deficiencies that limit their preparedness for employment, and they may require support to enroll in and complete a GED course or to obtain technical training. Some individuals are psychosocially ill prepared to maintain stable employment; they require guidance on work ethics and appropriate workplace behavior (e.g., the need for consistent punctuality, the importance of understanding and abiding by workplace rules, and the value of negotiating satisfactory relationships with supervisors and coworkers). Logistical limitations (e.g., the lack of a driver's license, reliable transportation, or appropriate clothing) can also hamper individuals' abilities to seek, accept, or retain a position. In addition to job referral and placement services, ex-prisoners may require basic job search skills training, largely focused on how to develop a resume, fill out applications, identify job openings, and conduct job interviews.

Families generally are expected to be the primary source of ongoing personal support for their members; however, incarceration conditions may undermine families' abilities to fulfill this role. Since correctional agents are mostly concerned with managing offenders—exclusive of family considerations—and protecting public safety, families receive few services that would keep them informed and prepare them for the return of incarcerated relatives. In fact, family advocates often point to various prison policies or practices that adversely affect families (e.g., movement of offenders to facilities far away from their home communities, entrance procedures that intimidate visitors, and inhospitable visitor waiting areas).

In addition, based on past experiences, families of offenders sometimes are ambivalent about relatives returning to the community (Denckla and Berman 2001; Jacksonville Community Council Inc. 2001; Nelson and Trone 2000). Often, the period of incarceration, the facility's location or regulations, or the offender's own behavior have created physical or psychological distance. There may be unresolved issues related to harm the offender inflicted on family members before incarceration. Newly released offenders may be unable to respond appropriately. Under stress, those with histories of violent behavior may lash out physically or emotionally. Parents who have been incarcerated may have added problems of reconnecting emotionally with their children, reestablishing custody rights or gaining visitation privileges, and providing financial support. Families may need such services as family therapy or counseling, anger management, parenting classes, family bridge building, and child reunification.

Offenders also need to acquire basic life skills, such as time management, financial management, communication, problem solving, anger management and conflict resolution, and decisionmaking abilities (Nelson and Trone 2000; Rossman et al. 1999). Many people who end up in prison suffer from impaired judgment; they need to learn to wait before acting, consider several alternatives, and choose wisely among different courses of action. Cognitive behavior therapy, which has become increasingly common in correctional environments, can help offenders acquire better skills. Nelson and Trone (2000) suggest that exposure to this type of intervention can help at any time, but is especially useful close to release.

Legal advice and assistance available during incarceration, or immediately thereafter, could help offenders anticipate and deal with legal issues before they spiral out of control (Jacksonville Community Council Inc. 2001). For example, changes in family situations may warrant legal action. Offenders may want or need a divorce, or they may have to deal with property transfers. During their incarceration, parents may not have paid child support, thus triggering legal actions; these parents may need to ask the court to alter payment requirements. In addition, incarcerated parents may have lost custody of their children and may need to seek court action to reestablish custody.

Additionally, offenders may lose certain civil rights and need legal assistance to understand eligibility requirements and to petition the court to have their rights reestablished. For example, Florida is one of 13 states that permanently disenfranchise ex-felons unless they are specifically granted clemency (only those with just one felony conviction are eligible for clemency) (Jacksonville Community Council Inc. 2001). Only 24.5 percent of those eligible were granted clemency during 1998–99. Applicants were denied reinstatement of civil rights if they still owed sentence-imposed fines or had other outstanding debts that could cast doubt on their "readiness" for full citizenship. Some have questioned the constitutionality of this practice; nonetheless, this restriction on ex-felons diminishes their ability to establish themselves as stable productive citizens in the fullest sense and also undermines the civic life of communities impacted by high felony rates.

Health Issues

Inmates have more health and psychosocial problems than the general populace. Factors that contribute to diseases among offenders include high-risk lifestyles, such as

- heavy use of tobacco, alcohol, and drugs
- injection drug use or tattooing
- multiple sex partners
- unprotected sex, in or out of prison
- transience, particularly if it involves homelessness
- financial instability
- poor or delayed access to health care and treatment
- emotional circumstances characterized by the lack of supportive relationships
- overcrowded conditions and movement among prisons that spreads contagion (Field 1998; McVey 2001; Nicodemus and Paris 2001)

Although some offenders first experience health, mental health, and psychosocial problems in prison, most enter the criminal justice system with problems that span multiple domains. Prior to incarceration, most offenders have been seriously underserved in terms of medical care, drug treatment, and psychosocial needs in the community (e.g., many have not received primary medical or dental care for years) (Hammett et al. 1999). The criminal justice system often represents offenders' primary source of health and human services. Poor health due to long-term neglect may be addressed for the first time during long incarcerations.

The 1997 Survey of Inmates found that nearly 31 percent of males and 34 percent of females reported a physical impairment or mental condition; specifically, 10 percent had physical problems, 10 percent reported emotional or mental conditions, 10 percent reported learning disabilities (e.g., dyslexia or attention deficit disorders), 4 percent had speech disabilities, 6 percent had difficulty hearing normal conversations even with hearing aids, and 8 percent could not see ordinary newsprint while wearing glasses. Taken together, 25 percent reported either that they had multiple impairments or that the nature of their impediment limited the kind or amount of work they could do (Maruschak and Beck 2001).

Individuals who have chronic health conditions requiring medication or other treatment, and those who have or are at risk for communicable diseases, need to be assessed and given satisfactory care while imprisoned. However, health services offered to incarcerated individuals vary significantly.[2] Thus, some individuals will return to the community in better condition than when they entered prison. Others, however, will continue to struggle with unresolved preexisting conditions, experience deterioration in health exacerbated by prison circumstances, or contract new diseases while incarcerated (see, for example, Nicodemus and Paris 2001). Overall, McVey (2001) estimates that 25 to 40 percent of inmates have significant health care conditions that require continued care upon release to the community.

Generally speaking, returning offenders should be linked with community-based providers who can continue to support and adjust reentering prisoners' health regimens, as necessary, after they leave prison. Typically, employment, which provides benefits or an income sufficient to cover medical fees, is a prerequisite for accessing community-based health care. Therefore, to avoid disruptions in health care access, most inmates (who do not have jobs awaiting them when they return home) should receive assistance in obtaining needed identification and in completing and submitting applications for Medicaid before leaving their facility. Applications for community-based assistance (e.g., Medicaid and SSI) should be initiated well in advance of release dates (states differ in processing time, but several months should probably be expected). In order to avoid care interruption, memoranda of agreement should be established between corrections departments and the state agencies administering entitlement programs, such as Medicaid. Transition planning personnel, for example, should try to obtain Medicaid approval for a reentering prisoner within two days of release to ensure continuity of medication renewal and health monitoring/treatment.

Other transition planning should include arrangements to ensure that:

- Medical records can be transferred from the correctional facility to community-based providers.
- Offenders will be supplied with reasonable amounts of prescribed medications to "tide them over" during their early days in the community.

Those returning prisoners with compromised mental health, substance abuse histories, HIV/AIDs, or communicable diseases may have additional specialized needs, as described below.

MENTAL HEALTH

Estimates of the prevalence of mental illness among state prisoners vary widely, with some suggesting that more than one-third of the population has some degree of mental health impairment. The recent National Commission on Correctional Health Care (NCCHC) report suggests returning prisoners have rates of mental illness two to four times higher than the general population (NCCHC 2002). Existing mental illnesses may be exacerbated by incarceration, and conditions of incarceration may precipitate mental illness; prolonged idleness, the constant threat of violence, and feelings of guilt, hopelessness, or helplessness may all contribute to psychological disorders.

Based on inmates who reported either a mental or emotional condition or an overnight stay in a mental hospital or program, Ditton (1999) estimates that 16 percent of the individuals incarcerated in state prisons are mentally ill. Of these,

- 53 percent were incarcerated for violent offenses,
- 69 percent were under the influence of alcohol or drugs at the time they committed the current offense, and
- 20 percent had been homeless in the year preceding their most recent arrest.

In addition, more than 30 percent of mentally ill male offenders and 78 percent of females reported prior physical or sexual abuse (Ditton 1999; Ortiz 2000).

Roughly 12 percent of all state prisoners received mental health therapy or counseling in 2000, and 10 percent received psychotropic drugs, including antidepressants, stimulants, sedatives, tranquilizers, or other anti-psychotic drugs (Beck and Maruschak 2001; Fabelo 2000). Such estimates likely underestimate the need for mental health intervention because some individuals may refuse to participate or be ineligible to receive services. For example, only 61 percent of mentally ill inmates reported receiving counseling, medication, or other mental health services in prison (Ditton 1999; Fabelo 2000).

Between 15 and 20 percent of inmates who experience mental health difficulties, particularly those requiring psychotropic medications, have sufficiently serious disorders to require continuity of care as they move from institutional to community settings. Older offenders, and those released after long periods of incarceration, may experience depression, isolation, or loneliness, all of which can contribute to difficult community reintegration (McVey 2001). Often, offenders returning to the community confront multiple challenges, including homelessness, unemployment, substance abuse, and impaired physical health (Conly 1999).

Without adequate continuing care that coordinates treatment in prison with community-based services, released offenders are likely to deteriorate and run the risk of returning to prison. Depending on the services they received while in prison, offenders released to the community may need periodic reassessment, continuing or new medication, or connections to therapeutic and support groups.

Many mentally ill offenders are poorly equipped to advocate for their own welfare. Those who are fortunate can turn to family and friends for assistance in this regard, although such informal support networks may require significant preparation before they can effectively assume advocacy roles. Furthermore, mental illnesses often place severe strains on personal relationships. Thus, some offenders are estranged from family and friends, a situation sometimes directly related to unstable or anti-social behavior stemming from the offenders' mental or emotional state. In such cases, offenders may require assistance managing not only their mental health needs, but also their efforts to rebuild viable family and friendship networks.

SUBSTANCE ABUSE

While various studies capture offender self-report of substance use, few studies systemically address the prevalence of drug abuse and drug dependency/addiction disorders in correctional facilities, as defined by

the American Psychological Association's *Diagnostic Statistical Manual,*
Fourth Edition (DSM-IV) (Mears et al. 2001). Nevertheless, substance
abuse disorders are perceived to disproportionately affect incarcerated
individuals: A recent study suggests that although only 21 percent of
state inmates had drug convictions as their most current offense, 83 percent had some history of illegal drug use, and 70 percent reported having used drugs regularly (i.e., at least once weekly for a period of at least
one month) before incarceration (GAO 2001). Furthermore, this population is significantly undertreated:

- With the exception of detoxification, most offenders have not
  received treatment in the community (Field 1998).
- Only about 24 percent of offenders in state prisons participated in
  drug treatment programs while incarcerated (GAO 2001).
- A Substance Abuse and Mental Health Services Administration
  (SAMHSA) study suggests that nearly half of state prisons offer no
  treatment, and even where treatment is provided, the programs are
  minimal and generally not provided in the segregated settings that
  have been found to be most effective. Thus, substance-abusing
  offenders returning to the community are at high risk of relapse
  and possibly recidivism (GAO 2001).

Periods of incarceration provide opportunities for treatment; however, treatment that stops with release from prison may not be effective.
Those who are coerced into treatment and remain substance free while
in prison still are at great risk of relapse and recidivism when released
(Field 1998). Such individuals require a variety of services to support
continued sobriety, and, at a minimum, their family or informal support
networks need to understand how to avoid enabling substance abuse.

HIV/AIDS
Prison rates of HIV positive and confirmed AIDS cases are five times
the rates in the U.S. general population, and increases in incarceration
coupled with high rates of HIV infection present a public health challenge (Maruschak 2001; NCCHC 2002). At the end of 1999, 3.4 percent
of females and 2.1 percent of males (i.e., 24,607 inmates, or 2.3 percent
of the total population) in state prisons were HIV positive. However,
there was considerable variation across states: 50 percent of HIV positive
inmates were concentrated in New York, Florida, and Texas. Thus, the

7,000 inmates known to be HIV positive in New York accounted for more than 25 percent of the nationwide total and 9.7 percent of the state's custody population. In three states, more than 20 percent of female inmates were HIV positive: Nevada (30.6 percent), the District of Columbia (22.4 percent), and New York (21.5 percent) (Maruschak 2001).

As Hammett et al. (1999) note, (1) policies for HIV counseling and testing have assumed increasing importance given the promising results of early intervention with antiretroviral therapy and (2) though some gaps remain, HIV and STD educational programs have become more widespread in correctional facilities. For example:

- HIV antibody testing policies vary across correctional facilities, but virtually all systems offer HIV testing on request or if clinical indication warrants follow-up. However, only 17 states mandate such testing at either intake or release. Approximately 86 percent of facilities offer pre– and post–HIV test counseling. Such counseling provides basic information on disease and the meaning of test results; however, topics pertinent to behavioral risk reduction—safer sex practices, negotiating safer sex, safer injection practices, and triggers for behavioral relapse—are less commonly covered.
- 71 percent of state/federal systems mandate HIV/STD education for incoming inmates, 20 percent mandate such training at release, and 51 percent report that participation is voluntary at release. However, few offer comprehensive or intensive HIV prevention programs: The 1997 NIJ/CDC survey of HIV/AIDS, STDs, and TB in correctional settings revealed that 39 percent of state and federal facilities were not providing instructor-led HIV/AIDS sessions. In addition, 87 percent were not offering peer-led programs (Hammett 1998).[3]

However, some individuals who are truly at risk of HIV/AIDS are in denial and will not seek testing. Others may avoid testing and counseling due to confidentiality concerns.[4] Either way, infected individuals who are unaware of their own health status or of how to effectively manage their condition compromise their own health and potentially expose others to health risk.

Offenders who are HIV positive or living with AIDS need considerable health care and social support. Many such individuals learn of their health status while incarcerated. Under such circumstances, release from prison marks the first time these individuals will have to manage the physical and emotional challenges of living in the community with a chronic or terminal illness (Conly 1998). Like other offenders returning from incarceration, they may lack an established health care network and an adequate social support system. Many return with inadequate information about treatment sources and transmission prevention, information that will protect their lives and the lives of others with whom they interact.

OTHER COMMUNICABLE DISEASES

Recent outbreaks of communicable diseases in correctional settings (e.g., TB in Alabama in 1999 and in South Carolina in 2000, and HBV in Georgia in 2001) underscore the importance of identifying communicable diseases, educating inmates and staff, and ensuring provision of appropriate treatment (Nicodemus and Paris 2001). Nevertheless, very little information is available about the transmission of communicable diseases in prison or the spread of prison-incubated diseases to the outside community.

Less is known about STDs, HBV, HCV, and TB than is known about HIV/AIDS in prison populations, reflecting the relative rarity of screening for these infections. For example, testing for STDs as a whole appears to be less widespread than testing for HIV/AIDS. While approximately 88 percent of state and federal correctional systems have instituted mandatory or routine testing for syphilis at intake, only 16 percent carry out mandatory testing for gonorrhea and only 8 percent conduct mandatory screening for chlamydia (Hammett et al. 1999).

Behavioral profiles and anecdotal reports consistently suggest that inmates make up a high-risk group disproportionately infected with STDs; however, correctional systems provide markedly little documentation corroborating this fact. Although most state correctional systems call for mandatory or routine inmate syphilis screening, 64 percent of state and federal systems did not report rates for this infection on the 1997 NIJ/CDC survey of HIV/AIDS, STDs, and TB in correctional facilities. Systems that provided information reported syphilis positivity rates of less than 5 percent. Correctional systems apparently make even less attempt to routinely screen for gonorrhea or chlamydia (73 percent of state and federal systems have no mandatory or routine gonorrhea screening, while 80 percent conduct no mandatory or routine screening for chlamydia). However, those systems that do screen for gonorrhea and chlamydia reported positivity rates of less than 5 percent for incoming inmates (Hammett et al. 1999).

The recent congressionally mandated health profile of inmates approaching release reports HCV infection rates five times higher than those of the general population (NCCHC 2002). In fact, various studies report 22 to 41 percent of inmates tested positive for HCV. HCV antibody positive rates are particularly high among injection-drug users and HIV-positive inmates; for example, 70 percent of female injection-drug users in a study of the Connecticut prison system were HCV positive, as were 36 percent of their sexual partners (Hammett et al. 1999).

The incidence of TB increased in the 1980s and early 1990s, spurring concerns not only because of the disease's resurgence, but also because some cases—including a 1991 outbreak among New York inmates—were multidrug resistant. More recently, the incidence of TB has declined in both the general population and the inmate population. However, the incidence remains higher among inmates; improvements are needed in the use of directly observed therapy as well as in the support systems that monitor postrelease adherence to TB disease treatment (Hammett et al. 1999).

Services Integration

Services integration refers to organizational-level responses to ensure continuity of care. Such integration involves both (1) the development of collaborations across institutional boundaries and among public and private organizations and (2) the coordination of policies and procedures to achieve a multiorganizational infrastructure designed to ensure that individuals do not "fall through the cracks" formed by the boundaries of various institutional domains and service providers. While fragmented service delivery exists for various reasons (e.g., tightly constrained organizational missions or reliance on categorical funding), agency officials demonstrate continuing interest in collaboration across institutional lines because of its potential benefits not only in addressing the multifaceted needs of clients who require health and human services, but also in making more efficient use of limited agency resources (Morley et al. 1998). Such efforts aim to:

- **Reduce service fragmentation** and **provide more holistic services** that meet the comprehensive needs of individuals and families and ensure continuity of care as clients move from one institutional domain to another or from one provider to another.

- **Identify gaps in service delivery,** set priorities for redressing the problems, and assign organizational responsibility for implementing needed services.
- **Mitigate barriers to obtaining services** (e.g., streamline application procedures, reduce the physical distance between provider and client, decrease unacceptably long waiting periods before treatment commences).
- **Conserve institutional resources** by sharing some efforts across systems or by reducing unnecessary duplication of efforts.

Integration efforts range from those that seek to unify different agencies and programs under a single umbrella or system to those that recognize the autonomy of participating organizational units while coordinating their activities. Various mechanisms, such as memoranda of agreement setting forth the roles and responsibilities of key actors; service cabinets comprised of representatives from different sectors and organizations; case management; centralized intake, assessment, or referral; increased information sharing, possibly using transparent or linked management information systems; cross-disciplinary training and case staffing; joint fundraising or resource sharing; and staff co-location may be implemented to achieve such results (Baker 1995; Morley et al. 1998; Rossman et al. 1999).

Collaborations among the Criminal Justice System and Health and Human Service Systems

Historically, corrections systems have focused their efforts only on offenders during the period of their incarceration, concentrating on such key concerns as security and classification as well as such basic services as limited education and vocational training, essential health care, and some counseling (McVey 2001). For the most part, state corrections systems have not forged seamless connections to community-based criminal justice entities, much less to health and human service systems. For example, in evaluating the community-based, case management "Opportunity to Succeed" model implemented to serve substance-abusing felons returning to targeted communities, Rossman et al. (1999) found that correctional facilities often did not even inform probation officers (POs) in advance of inmates' impending or actual release. Instead, prison administrators relied on offenders to report to their POs within stipulated time frames (e.g., 72 hours after return to the community). Although most complied, some did not. At minimum, this situation resulted in unnecessary delays in linking individuals to needed services. However, because returning offenders are probably most vulnerable during their earliest days of community reentry, the consequences were more extreme in certain cases. The absence of supportive services coupled with new uncertainties caused some individuals to revert to their preprison lifestyles—reestablishing ties with peers who undermined their commitment to prosocial activities, relapsing to substance use, or actively engaging in new criminal activities. Relatively little attention has been paid to developing substantial partnerships between correctional facilities and health and human service providers or to linking inmates with community-based services. For those prisoners discharged without further supervision requirements, there is a strong possibility that no entity will assume responsibility for assessing their individual needs across different service sectors or for ensuring that needed services are forthcoming.

Individuals released with community supervision requirements, on the other hand, become the responsibility of the probation/parole system. Although probation and parole departments have varied across time and place, they typically have provided some direct or subcontracted services to returning offenders in addition to fulfilling their monitoring and oversight functions. Some offenders—such as sex offenders and others assigned to specialty caseloads—may receive more varied as well as more intensive services. However, such involvement usually is not predicated on services integration across institutional lines, nor has it reached the level of comprehensive case management. In general, POs have huge caseloads and are focused on the primary mission of public safety, rendering them unlikely to provide the intensive, individualized assistance needed by many offenders.

In addition to parole and probation agencies, departments of health, alcoholism and substance abuse, labor, and social services have a stake in improving what happens to inmates after release, since returned offenders make up much of these organizations' client base. However, agency staff members generally have little or no access to inmates prior to their release. As Nelson and Trone (2000) suggest, involving such agencies in the custody side of programming could improve outcomes by creating a more transparent system of continuous care. In addition, correctional systems could benefit from both the expertise available from other substantive domains and the additional resources that may translate into stronger prison programs and services.

Increasingly, correctional systems are exhibiting interest in developing partnerships with other institutional stakeholders (e.g., state health departments, community-based service providers) to conduct health screening, deliver health education, or incorporate transition mechanisms such as release planning or postrelease day reporting. Several promising models exist (as indicated below); however, most communities do not currently have such approaches in place for many reasons.

Barriers to Coordinating Prison and Community-Based Services

Typically, prison and parole systems' functional boundaries are not adequately integrated with one another and not sufficiently integrated with health and human service systems to achieve seamless transition (McVey 2001). Various factors can impede service coordination from prison to the community, or services integration within the community. Correctional institutions often are highly independent and resistant to change; correctional officials have to be willing to open their facilities to outside organizations (Hammett 1998; Holmes et al. n.d.). Also, because prisons are frequently located a distance from the community to which offenders are returning, state agencies and community-based organizations sometimes adopt an "out of sight, out of mind" perspective: they do not serve the inmates in prison and do not come to regard them as potential clients (McVey 2001).

DIFFERENT GOALS AND PRIORITIES
In the quest for collaboration, different organizational missions and "corporate cultures" have to be negotiated. Correctional facilities and community-based service agencies (e.g., public welfare, probation and parole, health and mental health, and other social service providers) have individually mandated responsibilities, which the agencies are accustomed to completing independently. Agency staff members may lack information that facilitates collaboration, or they may be operating on questionable information that undermines interest in collaborating. For example:

- As part of their legal mandate to make reasonable efforts to reunify families, child welfare caseworkers are obligated to facilitate relationships between parents and children, even when parents are incarcerated. Thus, for example, caseworkers need to prepare and support kinship and foster families in dealing with (1) children's psychosocial needs related to parental dysfunction; (2) challenges to parent-child contact during parental incarceration; and (3) preparation and planning for family reunification, or if that is not possible, permanent placements. In addition, caseworkers are expected to help parents access services that will assist them in properly parenting their children while they are incarcerated and after their release. As Seymour (1998) notes, caseworkers may recognize parents' service needs, but have little knowledge of services available within prisons, or have difficulty linking parents to these services. In addition, geographic distance, prison security requirements, and high caseloads may impede caseworker–parent communication.

- Denckla and Berman (2001) suggest that the behavioral health treatment community (e.g., state and county agencies of mental health, mental retardation, substance abuse, and the programs they fund, including psychiatric hospitals and community-based service providers) historically has shied away from addressing the issue of people with mental illness who have repeated contacts with the criminal justice system. Community-based providers often find mentally ill offenders challenging to serve because of their coexisting conditions, noncompliance, unkempt appearance, and their clinically difficult and challenging presentation (Conly 1999). Furthermore, providers often have no experience in treating "forensic" clients. Providers able to select their own clients frequently avoid offenders, who are associated with disruptive or violent behavior. As a result, people coming directly from the criminal justice system may be underserved because staff members fear for their own safety and that of other clients, perceive forensic clients as burdened with a host of very severe problems that are difficult to treat effectively, recognize that the more challenging cases are likely to require more expensive resources (e.g., hospitalization), and worry that treatment failure may jeopardize performance-based funding (Denckla and Berman 2001).

Institutional staff also may be put off by "cultural clashes." Hammett (1998, 9), for example, notes that there are "real differences between the philosophies, perspectives, and priorities of public health and correctional agencies that can make collaboration difficult if they are not sensitively handled":

- Correctional staff's primary mission is security protecting inmates, staff, and visitors from violence. Care providers are concerned with individuals' health status and quality of life. The social work view of client self-determination may not be valid or safe and may well conflict with criminal justices policies. For example, community-based health educators often try to improve clients' independent decisionmaking and self-efficacy skills; however, prison staff may be concerned that empowering inmates in this way will undermine discipline and order in their facility.
- Similarly, community-based providers addressing issues such as HIV/AIDS or STDs may adopt harm-reduction rather than abstinence-based models. Therefore, they are prepared to educate individuals on when and how to use condoms during sexual encounters or on how to reduce risks associated with injection drug use. Such information is antithetical to criminal justice policies; for example, only two state/federal systems make condoms available (Hammett et al. 1999). Furthermore, the harm-reduction stance may be particularly troubling to some correctional officials because sexual and needle-using activities (e.g., drug use and tattooing) are expressly prohibited in prison, and administrators may not want to acknowledge that such problems exist on their premises.

LIMITED RESOURCES

Resources are always a concern. Inflexible or inadequate funding represents a major impediment to coordination of services within and across institutional systems. In addition, limitations on physical plants and manpower may undermine both correctional institution and service system capacities to offer enhanced services (e.g., there may be no infrastructure or available space). In-prison programs designed to assess and treat inmates and aid in the preparation of transition plans require adequate resources. In addition, resources must be found to support community-based service delivery for those offenders unable to cover "fees for services." Often, inadequate understanding of postrelease assistance entitlement hampers resourcing. For example, Medicaid and Supplemental Security Income (SSI) may be viable funding sources for offenders with long-term health and mental health care issues. However, associated paperwork is cumbersome and unfamiliar, and it can take months to process applications, during which time needy people may not receive medical services, housing, and so on. Other logistical issues impede coordination; for example, uncertain release dates complicate transition planning (McVey 2001; Rossman et al. 1999).

INADEQUATE INFORMATION

Information sharing across systems is notoriously troublesome—data-sharing agreements across systems are typically nonexistent (Morley et al. 1998; Rossman et al. 1999). Record keeping is often scanty or erroneous. For example, Jacksonville Community Council Inc., a nonprofit, non-partisan civic organization that seeks to improve quality of life based on informed citizen participation, undertook a local study to strategically plan for improved community responses to the needs of returning offenders. Organization officials reported considerable difficulty in obtaining information from the county and state corrections systems that would allow them to be proactive (Jacksonville Community Council Inc. 2001):

- The state system was unable to provide data on offender needs at release with respect to emergency spending money, clothes, or personal identification; the state system was able to indicate only what correctional facilities provide offenders upon release: $100, clothes (if needed, with the costs deducted from the $100), and a corrections department photo identification card.
- The Florida Department of Corrections could not provide information on the proportion of inmates who have a home to return to, are financially capable of paying rent or a mortgage, or are ready after the incarceration period to assume rental or homeownership responsibilities.
- The state system reported that about 58 percent of inmates tested at less than fifth grade reading level; it could not provide data on degree of literacy or advancement in education classes during incarceration, nor was information available on the marketable skills of those prisoners returning to the community.
- Information was not available on the percentage of inmates who had jobs to return to upon their release or the number who had physical disabilities, mental illness, or other conditions that limited

their ability to work competitively. Upon release, the state provides a bus ticket to the offender's destination of choice within the state; no information was available on those returning prisoners who had access to cars or could not use public transport due to location or limitations.

- The state was aware of the incidence of certain health conditions because treating them was important to maintaining health and order within the correctional facility; however, the state apparently was unaware of those prisoners lacking health insurance or the ability to pay for care when released.
- Data were not available on the percentage of offenders who had families to return to; the degree to which those families were functional and supportive; the percentage of offenders who had minor children, were required to pay child support, or had officially lost custody of children; or the status and location of those children.

Inmates and offenders returning to the community tend to be fairly mobile (e.g., prisoners are often transferred from one facility to another, while those in the community experience unstable housing situations). Personal information should go with them as they move within correctional facilities and throughout the community; however, in many cases, vital medical records (including test results and medication status) and other information relevant to service coordination are never sent to new health and human service providers, or are seriously delayed. Information may be manually recorded, making it difficult to share widely across different organizations and staff. Or data may be automated but entered only after long delays, rendering the information obsolete by the time it is accessible.

FAMILY MATTERS

Adding families to the mix represents a new approach for some agencies, challenging them to find effective ways to work with and engage family members. Staff may need to rethink the assumptions that service systems have made about families: Who should be included in family? Who should determine what is right for family members? Should involvement be coerced or voluntary? Service providers across different domains hold different perspectives and may be challenged to achieve consensus. In addition, efforts to involve family members may encounter significant resistance from affected individuals. The behavior of some offenders may sometimes alienate them from their families, and one-sided or mutual antipathy or ambivalence may need to be overcome.

Barriers to Local Service Delivery

Barriers to local services integration occur for a variety of reasons (Jacksonville Community Council Inc. 2001; Morley et al. 1998; Rossman et al. 1999). Significant gaps exist between offender needs and locally available resources. Communities may face deficiencies in the spectrum of services; insufficient resources to address the full need; a changing landscape of local service providers and high staff turnover in the service sector, which undermine stable cross-agency interaction; and an ineffective network of information sharing that ideally should help offenders learn about and take advantage of available services.

The recent Jacksonville study identifies many of the same difficulties local Opportunity to Succeed (OPTS) programs[5] encountered as they attempted to implement case management and services integration (Jacksonville Community Council Inc. 2001; Morley et al. 1998; Rossman et al. 1999). For example:

- Services to meet offender needs are not comprehensively available, and those that do exist may be insufficient to meet the demand. Additionally, the effectiveness of formal services may be limited by the degree of fragmentation among service providers and by lack of coordination among providers. An informal word-of-mouth, information-sharing network may exist among offenders, but not all are connected to it. Returning offenders need assistance in understanding, contacting, and obtaining services.
- Data to plan for services are insufficiently available (see earlier discussion).
- The recent political climate has favored punitive rather than rehabilitative responses; "get tough on crime" attitudes have prevailed. Consequently, citizens and members of some service-providing organizations lack an accurate understanding of the needs of and services for ex-offenders and the political will to respond appropriately.
- Certain legal restrictions society feels justified in imposing effectively impede offenders' efforts to obtain needed services and build stable, productive lives. For example, emergency housing is in big demand, but beds are limited (Jacksonville Community Council

Inc. 2001). Offenders convicted of certain kinds of crime are legally excluded from some publicly funded housing; in addition, housing applications for apartment rental request information about prior convictions, permitting rental agents to informally discriminate and limiting ex-prisoners' housing choices. Some reentering prisoners also face informal discrimination from lenders when they seek to establish credit for mortgage approval or apartment rental. In addition, laws requiring notification of sex offender residence may trigger some discriminatory reactions.

Promising Models

SAFER FOUNDATION (ILLINOIS)

Despite barriers to collaboration and services coordination, a number of promising approaches have been implemented in various communities to meet the needs of returning prisoners. For example, the Safer Foundation has forged a long-standing and viable partnership with the Illinois Department of Correction[6] (Finn 1998). In addition to operating the Crossroads Community Correctional Center (the state's largest work release center), Safer offers a "one-stop" community-based operation that emphasizes not only employment services (e.g., preemployment training, job referral, and follow-up), but also offers intake and assessment, HIV-prevention education, and support services (e.g., referrals to substance abuse or mental health rehabilitation programs). Key program components include (1) a six-week basic skills course using professional facilitators and a peer learning model; (2) employment specialists who assist returning offenders in completing job applications and preparing for interviews and who actively monitor client progress during the first 30 days of job placement; and (3) case managers (called "lifeguards") who continue to follow and support participants for one year, providing assistance as needed with job-related difficulties, personal problems (e.g., substance abuse or other counseling needs), and family concerns (e.g., child care). In addition to its professional staff, the organization relies heavily on volunteers to offer expertise as they serve on its various policy and advisory boards as well as direct services to clients (e.g., literacy tutoring and prevention education).

MARYLAND COMMUNITY CRIMINAL JUSTICE TREATMENT PROGRAM

The Maryland Community Criminal Justice Treatment Program (MCCJTP) targets mentally ill offenders. MCCJTP brings treatment and criminal justice professionals together to screen mentally ill individuals while they are confined in local jails, prepare treatment and aftercare plans, and provide postrelease community follow-up. The program targets those individuals age 18 or older who have serious mental illness (i.e., schizophrenia, major affective disorder, organic mental disorder, other psychotic disorders) with or without co-occurring substance abuse. Although the program focuses on jail populations, parolees from state prison may be referred to an MCCJTP case manager by prison or parole officials, or may self-refer following release.

In most jurisdictions, county health departments receive funding to hire full-time MCCJTP case managers who are experienced mental health professionals with advanced counseling degrees. Each manager's caseload includes approximately 35 individuals. The general protocol includes screening and needs assessment (including determination of need for and provision of medication if indicated); counseling and discharge planning (covering such considerations as mental health and substance abuse counseling, recreational activities, educational services, employment training, and housing placement); criminal justice system liaison; and referral and monitoring in the community (Conly 1999).

Empowerment Through HIV Information, Community and Services (New York)

The Fortune Society's Empowerment Through HIV Information, Community and Services Coordinated Health Care (ETHICS 3/CHC) program supports HIV-positive offenders. This program provides these offenders with transitional services from prison to community using a family-focused approach, intensive case management (including crisis intervention, counseling, and service referral), partnerships with networked medical care facilities, and formal and informal social and recreational group interaction (such interaction provides peer support and opportunities for staff to encourage the development of social skills, which in turn facilitate smoother reintegration into the community).

All clients are assessed upon release (and every two months thereafter) and provided with an initial medical referral; medical services are available through an agreement with the Institute of Urban Family Health, although clients often choose other health providers. Depending on individual needs, additional referrals may help offenders obtain financial benefits, housing, substance abuse counseling, psychotherapy, food resources, educational and vocational services, and day treatment programs. Staff or peer counselors/educators escort clients to referred services, and case managers confirm acceptance and monitor ongoing participation.

For offenders to participate in the ETHICS 3 program, their families must be willing to participate in and access health services through the program. Project staff members conduct home visits to engage and assist family members, in addition to hosting family-oriented events (e.g., picnics, parties, and completion ceremonies). Nevertheless, families have been less engaged than expected, primarily because (1) offenders' relationships with family members have deteriorated beyond repair; (2) family members are engaged in other programs or receive services from other providers with whom they evidently have developed more satisfactory relationships; (3) family members are willing to offer support, but at a distance; and (4) clients have not disclosed their health status to family members.

WOMEN'S PRISON ASSOCIATION (NEW YORK)
Similarly, recognizing that the service needs of women offenders are different from those of their male counterparts, the Women's Prison Association (WPA) directly offers or brokers institutional and community-based services to women offenders through several interrelated programs. WPA case managers develop individualized service plans and provide individual counseling to help clients organize and prioritize their service needs and learn how to advocate for themselves. Case managers also work with clients on recovery, relapse, and reunification issues, and facilitate peer support through group workshops, support groups, and household assignments. WPA also coordinates other services in the community, having negotiated formal agreements with 44 service providers who assist women offenders.

Emergency funds are available from WPA and earmarked for overdue rent payments, security deposits, utilities, food, and clothing. In addition, WPA also conducts outreach to the local business community to identify employment opportunities; employment testing; job placement assistance (which addresses how to find and keep a job, develop a resume, complete job applications, handle such sensitive issues as criminal history during interviews, and manage job conflicts); job training when appropriate; and employment counseling. The agency supports enhanced independent-living skills by helping clients develop decisionmaking and problem-solving abilities focused on time management, household budgeting, checking account maintenance, and community services access. In addition, the organization offers a 10-week parenting-skills course, peer mentoring, relapse prevention services, and various other support groups.

Working with correctional supervisors in both a maximum-security facility (that also serves as a diagnostic/classification center for all women sentenced to prison for more than one year) and a medium-security prison, WPA staff provide a full range of HIV services, including prevention education, pre- and post-test counseling for those inmates who voluntarily request HIV testing, correctional staff and peer educator training, and facilitation of peer support through inmate volunteers who assume active roles in shaping the programs. In addition, discharge planning is offered to women who have six or fewer months remaining on their sentences. During this process, counselors and inmates review available community services, discuss parole regulations, collect all paperwork needed for a smooth transition (e.g., birth certificates, medical release summaries resulting in access to the documentation necessary for Medicaid and other financial assistance), establish appointments for community-based medical care, and consider housing options (upon release, former inmates will be connected to WPA's housing experts). Once in the community, women can receive transitional case management for up to three months. At that point, they are likely to have qualified to participate in the agency's Community Follow-Up Program (CFP), a fee-for-service component that supports case management to nonincarcerated offenders for as long as they are eligible to receive Medicaid.

In addition, the agency offers numerous services designed to meet the needs of homeless women. For example, a transitional residence provides housing for homeless female offenders, including those with HIV/AIDS, who seek to reunite with their children. Over time, women can have supervised visits with their children, and later, children can visit overnight. After six to nine months in transitional housing, clients and their children can move into their own apartments within a facility operated by the organization and receive assistance in locating suitable permanent housing. The facility includes a children's center for infants and preschoolers, which is set up as a classroom with age-appropriate educational supplies and a structured curriculum; mothers are expected to volunteer at the center for an hour each week. In addition, WPA has developed a comprehensive program to support families that include school-aged children. The client, her children, and her caseworker meet

with key criminal justice system or service agency staff (e.g., parole officers, drug treatment staff, child welfare workers) to discuss the family's
goals and familiarize all service providers with the program. After-school
and weekend activities include counseling and recreational therapy,
homework assistance and tutoring, and on- and off-site cultural and
recreational activities.

The organization also conducts housing readiness workshops and
provides individual counseling to assist clients in learning how to inspect
apartments, negotiate leases, obtain furniture, and establish a household.
For up to one year after the transition to permanent housing, aftercare
workers help women maintain housing and negotiate with landlords for
repairs or access other services.

La Bodega de la Familia (New York)

La Bodega de la Familia and the Montgomery County Pre-Release Center (see below) emphasize family-oriented approaches. Service delivery
is consistent with the realization that offenders' families need to be prepared for the invasiveness of supervision (e.g., home visits at odd hours)
and also need to understand supervision requirements so they do not
unwittingly enable or encourage behavior that is inappropriate or illegal
for those under supervision (Nelson and Trone 2000).

While the La Bodega de la Familia model could be applied to a
broader range of circumstances, the program currently assists families
whose newly released relatives are in drug treatment. New York parole
officers must inspect offenders' anticipated housing before their release.
Bodega staff members, therefore, accompany certain POs on home
inspections to inform families of available services, including intensive
family counseling and 24-hour emergency support. Staff members work
with families and keep POs informed as to families' progress, helping
offenders whose questionable behavior endangers their continued ability to remain in the community (Nelson and Trone 2000).

Montgomery County Pre-Release Center (Maryland)

Similarly, the Montgomery County Pre-Release Center believes families
need to prepare before the inmate returns home. The center requires
every inmate to have a sponsor—parent, grandparent, spouse or partner,
or even a child—who agrees to attend six weekly educational sessions. It
also provides family therapy for inmates and their sponsors who want
counseling (Nelson and Trone 2000). For those with substance abuse

issues, the center runs a two-week relapse prevention course that provides techniques for living clean in a drug-filled world. The course teaches inmates how to locate and receive optimal benefit from outpatient treatment programs and provides basic exposure to principles of addiction and recovery for those who have not received treatment while incarcerated.

Building Partnerships to Improve Services Integration, Quality of Care, and Outcomes for Individuals, Families, and Communities

Offenders returning home after periods of incarceration (and, by extension, their families) have a range of needs that require varying types and amounts of informal and formal supports. How can communities prepare to effectively respond to such needs?

Organizing to Support Internal and External Collaboration

The National GAINS Center for People with Co-Occurring Disorders in the Justice System has developed the APIC model for transition planning,[7] which identifies four key components to the successful reintegration of returning offenders (Osher, Steadman, and Barr 2002):

- **A**ssessment of offenders' clinical and social needs and the risks they pose to public health and safety.
- **P**lanning for the treatment and services required to address these needs.
- **I**dentifying required correctional and community programs responsible for postrelease services.
- **C**oordinating the transition plan to ensure appropriate service delivery and mitigate gaps in care.

These principles provide a useful backdrop against which to begin considering appropriate partnership-building responses to returning prisoners. APIC intrinsically requires collaboration among correctional authorities with prerelease custody of offenders and community-based systems that must be responsive to offenders after release (and, conceivably, to their families during and after the offenders' incarceration).

The cohesive and comprehensive ability to meet the needs of returning offenders and their families clearly requires the joint support of three levels of organizations (see Gouvis Roman et al. 2002, 23–24):

- State correctional facilities, which have custody and oversight of offenders before their release and return to local communities. In addition, state and regional—and possibly national (level three)—organizations can directly affect systems change by introducing new policies and practices as well as by focusing greater resources on this problem and raising practitioner and public understanding of relevant issues. Offenders' quality of life and access to services, for example, may be influenced not only by correctional policies, but also by health care financing or other social program coverage/entitlement practices.
- Local government agencies (i.e., level two organizations that traditionally hold power), such as probation/parole offices and police departments, may be called on to supervise or otherwise monitor the activities of individuals who have returned from prison.
- Frontline organizations (level one), such as service providers, faith-based organizations, local business employers, and neighborhood or community associations that provide informal services (e.g., social clubs, recreational departments, and tutoring or literacy services), are already serving offenders' families and are well situated to extend their services to implement the postrelease transition plans of returning offenders.

Hence, communities need to reach out to state correctional and possibly health and social service agencies, and to organize local government agencies and frontline organizations for a coordinated effort.

Developing a coordinated system of services is an evolutionary process. At minimum, the process requires direct contact among potential partners to build firsthand familiarity and trust. In addition, partners must jointly explore the parameters of the problem within the local area and reach consensus on priorities and strategies for implementing reforms that are expected to produce better outcomes for offenders, their families, and the community at large. Communities and organizations that have pursued service coordination or partnerships frequently recommend that early steps include the formation of a policy board (including agency/organizational decisionmakers) and the development of a service cabinet of line staff and community volunteers. As Gouvis Roman et al. (2002) note, human resources, such as leadership and continued commitment to core tasks, are key components for the vitality of partnerships. Recognizing the criticality of leadership and committed human resources, some communities house partnerships in independent organizations or in a community-based organization that is widely respected as a nonpartisan team player. Additionally, community partnerships often create dedicated positions, such as organizers or administrators, to oversee day-to-day operations, ensuring that strategic activities are addressed in a timely manner.

Convening Cross-Jurisdictional and Multiorganizational Meetings and Training

Cross-jurisdictional meetings between the local policy board and state or regional leadership permit the community policy board to identify the strengths and weaknesses of the current external system(s) and any planned changes that are likely to affect local activities in the near term. Such collaboration might support the community's ability to gather baseline data helpful in forecasting the expected flow of offenders to the home community and the likely services that the community should be prepared to offer. Together, local and state leaders could explore ways to strengthen current policies and practices, thereby reducing offenders' risk of recidivism and enhancing community safety. For example, if state correctional facilities are not a great distance from the local community (or alternatively, despite the inconvenience, if a large number of local offenders are incarcerated in a distant institution), state and community leaders might consider empowering a local provider outreach team. This team could periodically visit the prison to make in-person contact with offenders (whose release and return home is imminent) to motivate them to seek out and participate in services suggested by their in-prison assessment. The same team also could visit family members to inform them of the transition plan and to enlist their support in encouraging offender compliance.

Cross-jurisdictional meetings permit clarification of roles and responsibilities among state/regional agencies and local community-based entities or among the network of potential local partners. Once consensual agreements have been reached, these can be formalized in memoranda of understanding/agreement (MOUs/MOAs). MOUs/MOAs not only institutionalize partnership formation, but also provide a foundation for other seminal activities, including joint fundraising and relevant and timely sharing of information.

Locally, the mere act of bringing together actors from different domains can yield immediate benefits. Local practitioners often are unfamiliar with agencies other than their own and those with whom they have frequent contact. The local service landscape may be in constant flux, or providers may be so burdened with their own cases that they have little time to become acquainted with the workings of other organizations. It is not unusual for local service providers to have misconceptions about other agencies' missions or activities.

Service cabinets offer an efficient mechanism for practitioners (who often are serving the same populations) to learn about resources previously unknown to them or to discover new ways to access services for clients with particular needs or characteristics. In addition, such cross-organizational dialogue can uncover service gaps that, as new market niches, provider entities could fill.

In addition to convening working meetings where participants identify shared visions, develop conjoint strategies, and formulate collaborative roles and responsibilities, state organizations and community-based agencies should try to hold cross-training, particularly for systematically assessing individual needs, matching needs to relevant services/interventions, and determining individuals' eligibility for various kinds of services.

Information Sharing—Crucial for Effective Decisionmaking and Service Provision

Improving community-based services for returning inmates requires two types of information: (1) specific services needed by returning individuals and (2) up-to-date data on available services and service gaps. Developing mechanisms for transferring or sharing information in ways that facilitate enhanced client access to and receipt of needed supports is also critical.

Aggregated data, representing individual needs assessment, in order to forecast likely demands on the local system of services. Increasingly, departments of correction are recognizing the value of transition planning that includes systematic assessment of the psychosocial needs of prisoners pending release. While care must be taken to preserve the rights of individuals and families, particularly when exchanging sensitive information, opportunities exist to use such information for various applications. Certainly, such information can be used for its intended purpose—to identify and plan for the specific service needs of return-ing individuals. Such planning should involve local parole offices and community-based service providers so they are reasonably prepared to carry out the plan. In addition, such information can be used to help inmates and their families appreciate the challenges they are likely to encounter in the period immediately following release, and to motivate them to seek and be more receptive to available services and other social supports.[8] Importantly, such information also can and should be aggre-gated by locale and shared with community leaders to permit forecasts of service demands, particularly in communities anticipating a large influx of returning prisoners.

A detailed inventory of community-based resources. Community-based providers often operate in their own substantive domain, and have only limited contact and familiarity with the actual services provided by other organizations. In addition, many communities encounter consid-erable turnover in practitioner staff or provider organizations, or confront dramatic changes in funding or eligibility that affect service delivery, par-ticularly for harder-to-serve populations. Information about existing services and how to access them is not readily available. Professionals and would-be clients alike have little knowledge about where and how to gain quick access to emergency services. Typically, communities lack a single, easily accessible and authoritative source of information. For these reasons, it is important to map existing services (including the nature of each service, real estimates of actual number of clients who can be served at any given time, eligibility requirements, and funding or other limitations, such as defined catchment boundaries or client groups the provider will not serve) and establish a local procedure for updating such information to reflect the current environment. Ideally, more com-prehensive resource guides would include informal services offered by community organizations, such as faith-based mentoring or tutoring activities, or other services that are provided by volunteers.

Information of this type has several applications. Transition planners certainly could use such information when devising individualized plans for returning offenders and determining which organizations might assume local responsibility for various types of service provision. How-ever, such information has more widespread utility as the potential back-bone of a centralized information and referral operation that permits both practitioners and the general public, including offenders, to locate suitable services to meet individual or family needs.[9] In addition, the information is critical to assessing service gaps and possibly in guiding the consideration of which existing community organizations might be well positioned to expand their activities to help introduce more of the missing services. Gouvis Roman et al. (2002), for example, point out that communities with the ability to assess assets and deficits are more likely to obtain support from a more diverse pool of community stakeholders.

Thinking Creatively about Resources

Organizations and collaborative partnerships must optimize their efforts not only by making the most effective use of their discrete resources, but also by leveraging resources from each other and from other entities not directly involved in the partnership (Gouvis Roman et al. 2002). Continuing federal and foundation interest in community-based partnership initiatives may present unanticipated funding opportunities that community partnerships can pursue.

Community residents, as well as volunteer and advocacy organizations, represent other potential resources that reentry partnerships could tap as mechanisms for offering supportive services to returning offenders who do not require more structured, formal interventions. Volunteer resources appear to be underutilized with this population and could be beneficial to different stakeholders in a number of ways. For example, peer mentoring could be developed using former inmates who have successfully established stable lifestyles. Such guidance could be a highly efficient way to model more productive, law-abiding lifestyles to inmates anticipating release and inmates newly returned to the community. What's more, such an approach could offer peer mentors the opportunity to achieve recognition for their volunteer activities, in effect providing a reverse right of passage—from offender to contributing member of society.

NOTES

1. At the individual level, *continuity of care* has two dimensions: (1) *cross-sectional,* such that, at any given time, services provided to an individual are comprehensive and coordinated, and (2) *longitudinal,* ensuring that, over time, services are matched to the changing needs of the individual. It requires "maintaining a chain of professional responsibility as a [client] moves from one program to another to receive needed services" (Baker 1995, ix).

2. Facilities within the federal prison system are accredited and routinely surveyed by the Joint Commission on Accreditation in Health Care Organizations (JCAHO); however, national uniform standards are not applied across all state correctional facili-

ties. Accreditation of facilities within individual states may be mandated by their respective governing bodies, but there is no single entity to which all facilities are accountable.

3. Peer-based services and prevention education programs can be cost-effective: peers often have more inherent credibility with offenders than do correctional staff or health practitioners (Hammett et al. 1999). In addition, peers can offer formal and informal services, such as introductory workshops (e.g., AIDS 101), individual and group risk-reduction counseling, and support groups for persons with AIDS (PWAs) in need of psychosocial assistance or substantive information. In addition, peer leadership skills may help offenders find employment in service organizations that perform advocacy or prevention education functions.

4. Inmates' concerns for confidentiality may be more heightened than those of the general populace, precisely because they are incarcerated and unable to choose service providers they trust. In either case, such individuals may well continue to engage in high-risk behaviors while incarcerated, and they are likely to do so without the opportunity to access condoms or other prevention protocols that are available to the outside community. A related and serious concern for children and families exists with regard to female inmates. Given that AZT treatment significantly reduces perinatal HIV transmission, 1995 Public Health Service guidelines recommend routine counseling and voluntary testing of pregnant women as early as possible. Nevertheless, fewer than half of state correctional systems routinely test all incoming women for pregnancy, although 84 percent test on request, and all test if there are clinical indications. Overall, state systems typically exercise the same policy for HIV testing of pregnant women as they do for all inmates; only seven states perform mandatory or routine HIV testing for pregnant women, and voluntary or on-request testing for other new inmates (Hammett et al. 1999). Thus, review of HIV and pregnancy testing policies may be desirable given current standards for treating HIV/AIDS.

5. Hillsborough County, Florida; St. Louis and Kansas City, Missouri; Oakland, California; and New York, New York.

6. At various times, parole officers have been outstationed at Safer offices to facilitate referral of offenders to services, and Safer staff have been outstationed in correctional centers in the Chicago area to conduct health awareness and prevention sessions. In addition, the partnership has included cross training (e.g., Safer staff have been invited to training sessions for Department of Correction personnel).

7. The American Association of Community Psychiatrists recommends using the term *transition planning* instead of *discharge* or *reentry planning* because it implies bi-directional responsibilities and collaboration among providers (Osher et al. 2002).

8. This is an important and probably underused application for assessment information, which is often furnished only to practitioners and service providers. A number of reentry studies (LaVigne and Lawrence 2002; Rossman et al. 1999) have documented that returning offenders often underestimate their own needs for service, are overly optimistic about their chances of success, and therefore may be unnecessarily resistant to accepting assistance that could improve their outcomes.

9. Some communities develop annual directories of services in hard copy or automated versions. More recently, 211 telephone exchanges have been introduced in a number of states to expedite calls about health and social services and also to log information about individuals who want to volunteer or make other contributions to community efforts.

REFERENCES

Baker, Frank. 1995. *Coordination of Alcohol, Drug Abuse, and Mental Health Services.* Technical Assistance Series 4, DHHS 95-3069. Washington, D.C.: U.S. Department of Health and Human Services.

Beck, Alan, and Laura Maruschak. 2001. *Mental Health Treatment in State Prisons, 2000.* Bureau of Justice Statistics Special Report. Washington, D.C.: U.S. Department of Justice.

Conly, Catherine. 1998. *The Women's Prison Association: Supporting Women Offenders and Their Families.* NCJ 172858. Washington, D.C.: U.S. Department of Justice, National Institute of Justice.

———. 1999. *Coordinating Community Services for Mentally Ill Offenders: Maryland's Community Criminal Justice Treatment Program.* NCJ 175046. Washington, D.C.: U.S. Department of Justice, National Institute of Justice.

Denckla, Derek, and Greg Berman. 2001. *Rethinking the Revolving Door: A Look at Mental Illness in the Courts.* New York: Center for Court Innovation.

Ditton, Paula M. 1999. *Mental Health and Treatment of Inmates and Probationers.* Bureau of Justice Statistics Special Report. Washington, D.C.: U.S. Department of Justice.

Fabelo, Tony. 2000. "Intervention for Mentally Ill Offenders: Planning and Policy Issues to Consider." Presentation to House County Affairs Committee, Criminal Justice Policy Council, August 22. http://www.cjpc.state.tx.us. (Accessed July 21, 2003.)

Field, Gary. 1998. *Continuity of Offender Treatment for Substance Use Disorders from Institution to Community.* Treatment Improvement Protocol (TIP) Series No. 30. Washington, D.C.: U.S. Department of Health and Human Services, Substance Abuse and Mental Health Services Administration, Center for Substance Abuse Treatment.

Finn, Peter. 1998. "Chicago's Safer Foundation: A Road Back for Ex-offenders." NCJ 167575. Washington, D.C.: National Institute of Justice, National Institute of Corrections, and Office of Correctional Education.

GAO. See U.S. General Accounting Office.

Gouvis Roman, Caterina, Gretchen E. Moore, Susan Jenkins, and Kevonne M. Small. 2002. *Understanding Community Justice Partnerships.* Washington, D.C.: The Urban Institute.

Hammett, Theodore M. 1998. *Public Health/Corrections Collaborations: Prevention and Treatment of HIV/AIDS, STDs, and TB.* Research in Brief, NCJ 169590. Washington, D.C.: U.S. Department of Justice, National Institute of Justice.

Hammett, Theodore M., Patricia Harmon, and Laura M. Maruschak. 1999. *1996–1997 Update: HIV/AIDS, STDs, and TB in Correctional Facilities.* NCJ 176344. Washington, D.C.: U.S. Department of Justice, National Institute of Justice.

Holmes, Leah, Deborah Davis, Randy Sell, Len Mitnick, and Robert Sember. n.d. "Linking HIV-Positive Inmates to Services After Release." http://www.hawaii.edu/hivandaids/links_prisonshiv.htm. (Accessed July 21, 2003.)

Jacksonville Community Council Inc. 2001. *Services for Ex-offenders: A Report to the Citizens of Jacksonville.* http://www.jcci.org. (Accessed December 6, 2001.)

LaVigne, Nancy G., and Sarah Lawrence. 2002. *Process Evaluation of the Pennsylvania Community Orientation and Reintegration (COR) Program: Final Report.* Washington, D.C.: The Urban Institute.

Maruschak, Laura M. 2001. *HIV in Prisons and Jails, 1999.* Bureau of Justice Statistics Bulletin. Washington, D.C.: U.S. Department of Justice.

Maruschak, Laura M., and Alan J. Beck. 2001. *Medical Problems of Inmates, 1997.* Bureau of Justice Statistics Special Report. Washington, D.C.: U.S. Department of Justice.

McVey, Catherine C. 2001. "Coordinating Effective Health and Mental Health Continuity of Care." *Corrections Today* 63 (5): 58–62.

Mears, Daniel P., Laura Winterfield, John Hunsaker, Gretchen E. Moore, and Ruth M. White. 2001. *Strong Science for Strong Practice: Linking Research to Drug Treatment in the Criminal Justice System (Executive Summary).* Washington, D.C.: The Urban Institute.

Morley, Elaine, Shelli Rossman, Janeen Buck, and Caterina Gouvis. 1998. *Linking Supervision and Services: The Role of Collaboration in the OPTS Program.* Washington, D.C.: The Urban Institute.

National Commission on Correctional Health Care. 2002. *The Health Status of Soon-to-Be-Released Inmates.* A Report to Congress. Chicago: Author.

NCCHC. See National Commission on Correctional Health Care.

Nelson, Marta, and J. Trone. 2000. *Why Planning for Release Matters.* New York: Vera Institute of Justice. http://www.vera.org. (Accessed October 30, 2001.)

Nicodemus, Marthali, and Joseph Paris. 2001. "Bridging the Communicable Disease Gap: Identifying, Treating and Counseling High-Risk Inmates." *HEPP Report* 4 (8/9): 1–4. http://www.hivcorrections.org. (Accessed October 30, 2001.)

Ortiz, Madeline M. 2000. "Managing Special Populations." *Corrections Today* 62 (7): 64–67.

Osher, Fred, Henry J. Steadman, and Heather Barr. 2002. "A Best Practice Approach to Community Re-entry from Jails for Inmates with Co-occurring Disorders: The APIC Model." http://www.gainsctr.com/pdfs/apic.pdf.

Rossman, Shelli, Caterina Gouvis, Janeen Buck, and Elaine Morley. 1999. *Confronting Relapse and Recidivism: Case Management and Aftercare Services in the OPTS Programs.* Washington, D.C.: The Urban Institute.

Seymour, Cynthia. 1998. "Children with Parents in Prison: Child Welfare Policy, Program and Practice Issues." *Child Welfare Journal of Policy, Practice and Program,* Special Issue: Children with Parents in Prison. http://www.cwla.org/programs/incarcerated/so98journalintro.htm. (Accessed December 7, 2001.)

U.S. General Accounting Office. 2001. *Prisoner Releases: Trends and Information on Reintegration Programs.* Washington, D.C.: U.S. General Accounting Office.

About the Editors

Jeremy Travis is a senior fellow at the Urban Institute, developing research and policy agendas on crime in community context, new concepts of the agencies of justice, sentencing and prisoner reentry, and international crime. He is cochair of the Reentry Roundtable, a group of nationally prominent researchers and policymakers devoted to exploring the dimensions of prisoner reentry. Before joining the Urban Institute, Mr. Travis was the director of the National Institute of Justice (NIJ), and was particularly instrumental in developing and directing the Institute's research agenda on sentencing and corrections issues. He has also been a key figure in the development of new approaches to prisoner reentry. He developed the concept of the reentry court, designed the Department of Justice's reentry partnership initiative, and created the federal reentry program in President Clinton's FY2000 budget. In 2001, Mr. Travis won the American Society of Criminology's August Vollmer Award for excellence and outstanding contributions in the field of criminal justice. In addition, he has taught courses on criminal justice, public policy, history, and law at Yale College, New York University's Wagner Graduate School of Public Service, New York University School of Law, and George Washington University. Mr. Travis has written and published extensively on constitutional law, criminal law, and criminal justice policy, including "But They All Come Back: Rethinking Prisoner Reentry" (National Institute of Justice, 2000).

Michelle Waul is the director of special projects at the National Center for Victims of Crime. She is managing the development of several policy and practice initiatives, including a multiyear demonstration project in three cities, focused on providing better and more comprehensive services for victims of crime. Before joining the National Center, she was a research associate with the Urban Institute working to link the research activities of the Justice Policy Center to policy and practice arenas in the field. Ms. Waul managed the national policy conference on the impact of incarceration and reentry on children and families, funded by the U.S. Department of Health and Human Services, which led to this publication. She also served as project manager for the Reentry Roundtable and coauthored a policy monograph on prisoner reentry titled "From Prison to Home: The Dimensions and Consequences of Prisoner Reentry (Urban Institute, 2001). Ms. Waul also served as the project manager for the Victims of Crime Act program for the state of Illinois.

About the Contributors

Donald Braman is currently studying law at Yale University. Previously, he spent three years in Washington, D.C., studying the effects of incarceration on family life and is currently completing a book on the subject. Dr. Braman has published on a variety of subjects, including the role of race in constitutional law and the role of culture in political conflict.

Eric Cadora is a program officer for The After Prison Initiative, part of the Open Society Institute's (OSI's) Criminal Justice Initiative, and serves as a community justice advocate and consultant. Before joining OSI, he worked for 14 years at the Center for Alternative Sentencing and Employment Services (CASES), during which time he oversaw the Center's court communications, information systems, research, and policy units, as well as its day center program, and launched the Community Justice Project, which advocates for a reinvestment of justice resources in communities suffering high rates of incarceration and provides technical assistance to corrections and communities to implement community justice programs. In 1996, Mr. Cadora was the recipient of an Edna McConnell Clarke justice grant to help the North Carolina Division of Adult Probation/Parole—with whom he worked for the following five years as a criminal justice consultant—implement alternative-to-incarceration programs under the state's new structured sentencing guidelines. Using geographical analyses of criminal justice activity at the neighborhood level, he has spoken in national forums about the impact of high rates of incarceration on communities of color and promoted the use of financial reinvestment strategies to interrupt the existing cycle of impoverishment and criminalization.

K. Alison Clarke-Stewart is a developmental psychologist whose work focuses on child development, specifically on the effects of social environments on children's cognitive and emotional development. She has investigated the effects of day care, divorce and custody, and mothers' and fathers' behavior on children's development. Dr. Clarke-Stewart is a professor in the Department of Psychology and Social Behavior and associate dean for research in the School of Social Ecology at the University of California, Irvine. She is also a fellow of the American Psychological Association and the American Psychological Society and a member of the Society for Research in Child Development. Her new publications include *Childcare: A Continuing Concern* (Harvard University Press, in press) and *Divorce* (Yale University Press, in press).

Todd R. Clear is Distinguished Professor at the John Jay College of Criminal Justice, City University of New York (CUNY), and executive officer of the Program of Doctoral Studies in Criminal Justice, CUNY Graduate Center. He is currently involved in studies of religion and crime, the criminological implications of "place," and the concept of "community justice." Dr. Clear is also the editor of *Criminology and Public Policy*, published by the American Society of Criminology. A programming and policy consultant to public agencies in over 40 states and five nations, his work has been recognized through several awards, including those of the Rockefeller School of Public Policy, the American Probation and Parole Association, the American Correctional Association, and the International Community Corrections Association. Dr. Clear has served on the faculties of Ball State University, Rutgers University, and Florida State University, and previous publications cover the topics of correctional classification, prediction methods in correctional programming, community-based correctional methods, intermediate sanctions, and sentencing policy. His recent books include *Community Justice, The Offender in the Community,* and *American Corrections* (all by Wadsworth, 2003); *What Is Community Justice?* (Sage, 2002); *The Community Justice Ideal* (Westview, 2000); and *Harm in American Penology* (State University of New York Press, 1995).

Stephanie S. Covington is the codirector of the Center for Gender and Justice in La Jolla, California. With more than 24 years of experience in the design and implementation of treatment services for women, she is recognized for her work in both the public and private sectors. For the past 15 years, Dr. Covington has worked to help institutions and programs in the criminal justice system develop effective gender-responsive services. She has provided training, technical assistance, and consulting services to the National Institute of Corrections, the Center for Substance Abuse Treatment, Correctional Services of Canada, the Federal Bureau of Prisons, and many state and local jurisdictions. Dr. Covington has published extensively, including three gender-responsive curricula: *Helping Women Recover: A Program for Treating Substance Abuse; Beyond Trauma: A Healing Journey for Women;* and *Voices: A Program of Empowerment and Self-Discovery for Girls.* She also coauthored *Gender-Responsive Strategies: Research, Practice, and Guiding Principles for Women Offenders* (with Barbara Bloom and Barbara Owen, National Institute of Corrections, 2003).

J. Mark Eddy is an associate director and a research scientist at the nonprofit Oregon Social Learning Center in Eugene. He is an investigator on several long-term follow-up studies of preventive and clinical interventions conducted within the juvenile justice and the school systems. For the past three years, Dr. Eddy has been working closely with the Oregon Department of Corrections on the development of a research-based parenting program for incarcerated mothers and fathers. He is also a licensed psychologist in the state of Oregon.

Gerald G. Gaes is a visiting scientist at the National Institute of Justice since retiring as director of the Office of Research, Federal Bureau of Prisons, in July 2002. His research interests include prison privatization, evaluation methodology, inmate gangs, inmate classification, simulating criminal justice processes, prison crowding, prison violence, the effectiveness of prison program interventions on postrelease outcomes, prisoner reentry, and cost-benefit analysis. In July 2000, he received the Attorney General's Distinguished Service Award, U.S. Department of Justice, for his work in correctional research. Dr. Gaes's articles have appeared in such publications as the *Journal of Substance Abuse Treatment, The Prison Journal,* and *Criminology and Public Policy.* His recent book chapters appear in *Securing Our Children's Future: New Approaches to Juvenile Justice and Youth Violence* (edited by Gary Katzmann, Brookings, 2002), *Privatization in Criminal Justice* (edited by David Shichor and Michael Gilbert, Anderson, 2001), and *Prisons: Crime and Justice* (edited by Michael Tonry and Joan Petersilia, University of Chicago Press, 1999). He also coauthored a forthcoming book entitled *Prison Performance: Laying the Groundwork to Compare Public and Private Prisons* (with Scott Camp, Julianne Nelson, and William Saylor). Dr. Gaes's paper, "Using Inmate Survey Data in Assessing Prison Performance: A Case Study Comparing Private and Public Prisons" (with Scott Camp, Jody Klein-Saffran, Dawn Daggett, and William G. Saylor, *Criminal Justice Review,* 2002), was nominated for the Joseph Wholey Distinguished Scholarship Award, American Society of Public Administration.

Creasie Finney Hairston is professor of social work and dean of the Jane Addams College of Social Work at the University of Illinois at Chicago. She has also served on the faculties of the University of Tennessee, the State University of New York, West Virginia University, and Indiana University. Dr. Hairston provides program consultation on parenting programs in correctional settings and conducts research on issues affecting families involved in the criminal justice and child welfare systems. She has reviewed and documented programs serving families of prisoners, conducted program evaluations of parenting programs in prisons and jails, and studied the impact of incarceration on families and communities. Dr. Hairston's recent articles on parents in prison and their children appear in publications for general audiences and in leading academic journals, including the *Marriage and Family Review, Michigan Family Impact Seminar Briefing Report Series, Child Welfare,* and the *International Community Corrections Association Journal.*

Craig Haney is professor of psychology at the University of California, Santa Cruz. One of the principal researchers on the highly publicized "Stanford Prison Experiment" in 1971, he has spent his career studying the psychological effects of living and working in actual prison environments. His work has taken him to dozens of maximum-security prisons across the United States and in several different countries, where he has evaluated conditions of confinement and interviewed prisoners about the mental health consequences of incarceration. Dr. Haney has also served as a consultant to various governmental agencies, including the U.S. Department of Justice, the California legislature, and various courts. His scholarly writing and empirical research have addressed a wide range of crime- and punishment-related topics and his articles have appeared in a variety of scholarly journals, including the *American Psychologist* and *Psychology, Public Policy, and Law.*

Newton E. Kendig is the medical director for the Bureau of Prisons and an infectious disease physician with Johns Hopkins University. He is a member of the American College of Physicians and the Infectious Disease Society of America. Dr. Kendig has served on advisory panels for the Centers for Disease Control and Prevention, the U.S. Department of Justice, and the Office of the Surgeon General. His involvement in correctional health care dates back to 1991, when he was appointed medical director for the Maryland Division of Corrections.

Ross D. Parke is distinguished professor of psychology and director of the Center for Family Studies at the University of California, Riverside. He is past president of the Society for Research in Child Development and will complete his term as editor of the *Journal of Family Psychology* in 2003. Dr. Parke is also past president of the American Psychological Association's Division of Developmental Psychology, the 1995 recipient of this division's G. Stanley Hall Award, and past editor of *Developmental Psychology*. His research interests include fathers' roles in the family, family-peer linkages, and ethnic variations in families. Dr. Parke is the author of numerous books, including *Fatherhood* (Harvard University Press, 1996), and the coauthor of *Throwaway Dads* (with Armin Brott, Houghton Mifflin, 1999).

John B. Reid is a research scientist and a founder of the nonprofit Oregon Social Learning Center in Eugene. A licensed psychologist, he also directs the National Institute of Mental Health–funded Oregon Prevention Research Center. Dr. Reid's research focuses primarily on assessment methodology and the treatment of child abusive families and conduct disorder. He works closely with collaborators throughout the country on the study of the impact of preventive and clinical interventions delivered within the public school and the child welfare systems.

Dina R. Rose is director of research at the Women's Prison Association. She has also served on the faculties at John Jay College of Criminal Justice, the City University of New York, Florida State University, and the University at Buffalo, State University of New York. Dr. Rose has written articles for such publications as *Crime and Delinquency* and the *Corrections Management Quarterly*, and has coauthored (with Todd Clear) a chapter in *Crime Control and Social Justice: The Delicate Balance* (edited by Darnell Hawkins, Samuel Myers, and Randolph Stone, Greenwood Press, 2003). She recently completed a National Institute of Justice grant, *Drugs, Incarceration and Neighborhood Life: The Impact of Reintegrating Offenders into the Community,* which examines the impact of high levels of prison admissions and releases on community life and the problems of reintegrating offenders into two neighborhoods in Tallahassee, Florida.

Shelli Balter Rossman is a senior research associate in the Urban Institute's Justice Policy Center, focusing on community-based services related to public health and safety issues. Over the past decade, she has directed several research projects that emphasize integrated services for juvenile and adult offenders as well as other high-risk populations. She was the principal investigator for the Opportunity to Succeed (OPTS) project, funded in California, Florida, Missouri, and New York by the National Institute of Justice and the Robert Wood Johnson Foundation. OPTS provided case-managed aftercare—including substance abuse treatment, employment services, medical and mental health care, and family strengthening and emergency support—to substance-abusing felons returning to targeted communities from incarceration treatment programs. Ms. Rossman is currently the principal investigator for the multiyear National Evaluation of Drug Courts (2003–2008) and also served as co–principal investigator for the National Evaluation of Juvenile Drug Courts Project (both funded by the National Institute of Justice).

Jenifer L. Wood is managing director of the National Center for Child Traumatic Stress, a national coordinating center jointly operated by the University of California, Los Angeles, and Duke University. The Center provides leadership and support to a national network of university- and community-based sites focused on expanding access and raising the standard of care for traumatized children and their families. Dr. Wood has worked as an advocate, researcher, and clinician, focusing on children and families exposed to violence and trauma as well as those who have been drawn into the criminal and juvenile justice systems. Before her arrival at the Center, Dr. Wood served at the National Mental Health Association and the National Institute of Justice and she worked as a consultant to UNICEF in Bosnia and Herzegovina.

Index